LANGUAGE IN THE NEGOTIATION OF JUSTICE

Applying the expertise and tools of corpus linguistics, discourse analysis, and sociolinguistics, the authors of this interesting melange of essays analyse and discuss a number of legal spheres in a wide variety of countries, including both civil and common law jurisdictions. The volume is a useful and often engaging addition to the growing literature on the intersection between language and the law.

Peter Tiersma, Loyola Law School, USA

Looking at law through the lens of language shows that all legal action has an aspect of argumentation and negotiation of meaning. This volume gives a broad overview of relevant contexts and approaches and is a valuable consolidation of these issues in legal linguistics.

Jan Engberg, Aarhus University, Denmark

Law, Language and Communication

Series Editors
Anne Wagner, Lille University – Nord de France, Centre for Legal Research and Perspectives of Law, René Demogue Group, France and
Vijay Kumar Bhatia, City University of Hong Kong

This series encourages innovative and integrated perspectives within and across the boundaries of law, language and communication, with particular emphasis on issues of communication in specialized socio-legal and professional contexts. It seeks to bring together a range of diverse yet cumulative research traditions related to these fields in order to identify and encourage interdisciplinary research.

The series welcomes proposals – both edited collections as well as single-authored monographs – emphasizing critical approaches to law, language and communication, identifying and discussing issues, proposing solutions to problems, offering analyses in areas such as legal construction, interpretation, translation and de-codification.

Language in the Negotiation of Justice

Contexts, Issues and Applications

Edited by

CHRISTOPHER WILLIAMS
University of Foggia, Italy

GIROLAMO TESSUTO
Second University of Naples, Italy

Routledge
Taylor & Francis Group
LONDON AND NEW YORK

First published 2013 by Ashgate Publishing

2 Park Square, Milton Park, Abingdon, Oxon OX14 4RN
711 Third Avenue, New York, NY 10017, USA

Routledge is an imprint of the Taylor & Francis Group, an informa business

First issued in paperback 2016

British Library Cataloguing in Publication Data
A catalogue record for this book is available from the British Library

The Library of Congress has cataloged the printed edition as follows:
Language in the negotiation of justice: contexts, issues and applications / edited by Christopher Williams and Girolamo Tessuto.
pages cm
Includes bibliographical references and index.
ISBN 978-1-4094-3839-7 (hardback)
1. Law—Language. I. Williams, Christopher, (professor), editor of compilation.
II. Tessuto, Girolamo, editor of compilation.

K213.L37 2013
340'.14—dc23

2013007770

ISBN 978-1-4094-3839-7 (hbk)
ISBN 978-1-138-25085-7 (pbk)

Contents

List of figures

List of tables

Notes on contributors

Lucia Abbamonte is an Adjunct Professor of ESP at the Department of Psychology of the Second University of Naples where she has taken part in several interdisciplinary research projects and PRINs (Research Projects of National Relevance). She is now responsible for the Teaching of English for Science Communication to Adult Learners in the PhD Course 'Sciences of the Mind'. Her present research interests lie in the fields of Multimodal Critical Discourse Analysis – in particular language in professional practice and mediation (Restorative Justice) – ESP for Cognitive Sciences, and the translation of scientific texts and of measurement scales (in Psychology and Psychiatry). She has authored three books and several articles and essays.

Vijay K. Bhatia, Emeritus Professor (Department of English and Communication, City University of Hong Kong), is President of the Asia-Pacific LSP and Professional Communication Association. His research interests cover genre analysis of academic and professional discourses in legal, business, newspaper and advertising contexts. He has published extensively in these areas with research articles, books chapters, edited volumes and monographs. His major books are *Analyzing Genre: Language Use in Professional Settings* and *Worlds of Written Discourse: A Genre-Based View*. Recent research projects have been directed towards 'Analyzing Genre-Bending in Corporate Disclosure Documents' and 'International Arbitration Practice: A Discourse Analytical Study,' in which he leads research teams worldwide.

Hugo Bowles (PhD, Cambridge, UK) is an Associate Professor of English Language at the Department of Economics and Law at the University of Rome 'Tor Vergata'. His research interests include genre, discourse, conversation and narrative analysis and their applications to specialized discourse, and he has published widely in many areas of applied linguistics, particularly ESP, legal and health communication and stylistics. His recent book *Storytelling and Drama* (John Benjamins 2010) won the ESSE Book Award for Linguistics 2012 and he is currently editing a collection on teaching English as a lingua franca in international contexts for Palgrave Macmillan.

William Bromwich is a Researcher in English Linguistics at the Marco Biagi Faculty of Economics at the University of Modena and Reggio Emilia, and is a member of the Doctoral Research School Council at the Marco Biagi Foundation in Modena. His research interests include legal English, courtroom discourse, the linguistic construction of social reality, language and disability, and metaphor in economic and financial discourse. An expert witness at the Tribunal of Bologna, he is also English language editor of the *International Journal of Comparative Labour Law and Industrial Relations* and *Ratio Juris: An International Journal of Jurisprudence and Philosophy of Law.*

Flavia Cavaliere works as Adjunct Professor of English Language at the University of Naples 'Federico II', Department of Humanities. She has taught Translation in many post-degree courses, and is currently teaching ESP on an international PhD course. Her research interests focus on Translation Studies – mainly in the field of Audio-Visual Translation – Cross-cultural Communication, Language in Professional Practice and Mediation, English for Specific Purposes, and the use of CALL and Internet for English Teaching. Her research interests have culminated in a variety of publications and participation in various interdisciplinary research projects.

Ross Charnock is *Maître de Conférences* in the University of Paris 'Dauphine', specializing in the language of the law. After studying at Exeter University, UK, he took his doctorate in linguistic pragmatics in Paris during the early 1980s under Oswald Ducrot. His research articles concentrate mainly on the rhetorical and semantic analysis of common law judgments. He also has research interests in pragmatics and argumentation as applied to language testing. He continues to publish regularly on classical music for strings.

Isabel Corona (PhD) is a Lecturer in English Philology at the University of Zaragoza. Her main research interests are genre analysis, intercultural analysis of professional communication and multimodality. She has participated in the international project 'International Commercial Arbitration Practices: A Discourse Analytical Study'. Her most recent publications include 'Arbitration Recontextualized' (*World Englishes* 30(1) 2011); 'Confidentiality at Risk: The Interdiscursive Construction of International Commercial Arbitration' (*Discourse & Communication* 5(4) 2011); 'Confidentiality vs Publicity: The Impact of International Arbitration in the Media' in V.K. Bhatia/C.N. Candlin/M. Gotti (eds) *Discourse and Practice in International Commercial Arbitration: Issues, Challenges and Prospects* (Ashgate 2012). Her current research focuses on professional media discourse and spoken academic genres. She is a member of the research group InterLAE (www.interlae.com).

Olga Denti is a Researcher and Lecturer of English Language and Translation at the University of Cagliari, Department of Philology, Literature and Linguistics. Her research interests include applied linguistics, ESP, corpus analysis, teaching methodology, discourse and genre analysis for academic and professional purposes, especially in the economic/financial, legal and tourism fields. Her most recent publications investigate Sardinia's tourist communication, *Mediation and Online Dispute Resolution*, and EU Financial Stability Reviews and Analyst Reports.

Michela Giordano (MA in Linguistics, California State University, Long Beach) is a Researcher and Lecturer of English Language and Translation in the Department of Philology, Literature and Linguistics at the University of Cagliari. Her research activity focuses on psycholinguistics, applied linguistics, ESP, discourse and genre analysis applied to the academic, political and legal fields. She has recently published *18 Million Cracks in the Glass Ceiling. Language, Gender and Power in Hillary R. Clinton's Political Rhetoric* (2012) and *Public Administration in the UK. English for Administrative Science* with Cheryl M. Wolley (2012).

Christopher Goddard is based at the Riga Graduate School of Law. His background is interdisciplinary, with a master's degree in education in addition to a legal and linguistic background. As a legal linguist, he translates legal texts into English from German, Russian and French; proofreads and edits legal texts; and trains NNS lawyers and translators. He has been a consultant at the International Criminal Court in The Hague, with the State Prosecutor's office in Tbilisi and for a European Commission-funded legal linguistics project in Kosovo. This paper is one of a series towards the requirements of a doctoral programme in legal linguistics at the University of Lapland.

Bronwen Hughes has a PhD in Linguistics and Modern and Comparative Literature (European School for Advanced Studies). She has extensively worked as a mother-tongue language teacher at the University of Naples 'L'Orientale'. Currently, she also works as a contracted professor at the University of Suor Orsola Benincasa in Naples, where she teaches English for Tourism and National Heritage, as well as the University of Sannio, Benevento, where she teaches English for Legal Studies. Her research interests lie in the fields of translation as a tool for second language acquisition, cross-cultural media studies, and forensic linguistics. In addition to a recently published research monograph, *Investigating Format: A Conversation Analytical Study of the Interview Room Scenes in* The Bill *and* La Squadra (Seam 2010), she has also published research articles which have appeared in collected volumes.

Ersilia Incelli is an English language lecturer in the Faculty of Economics, University of Rome 'La Sapienza'. Her research interests currently lie in discourse analysis, sociolinguistics and corpus linguistics, with particular reference to the specialized fields of law and economics, professional identities and workplace discourse.

Meizhen Liao obtained his PhD in linguistics from the Chinese Academy of Social Sciences. He is currently Professor of Linguistics and Dean of the School of Foreign Languages, Central China Normal University. His academic interests include forensic linguistics, discourse pragmatics and discourse metaphor. His representative publications include 'Metaphor as a Textual Strategy in English', *Text* 19(2), 1999; 'A Study of Interruption in Chinese Criminal Courtroom Discourse', *Text & Talk* 29(2), 2009; *A Study of Courtroom Questions, Responses and their Interaction*, Law Press, Beijing, 2003, and 'The Principle of Goal and Communication', *Journal of Foreign Languages*, 2009(4 and 6).

Valeria Moretti graduated from the Faculty of Humanities, University of Rome 'Tor Vergata', with a specialist thesis on interactional narrative in literary texts. She is an applied linguist combining specialist teaching of English and Italian L2 with research on conversation analysis applied to computer-mediated communication; in this area, she has worked as a language consultant on the European Psychonaut web-mapping project.

Antonella Napolitano is an Adjunct Professor of English Language and Translation at the University of Sannio, Benevento, where she teaches undergraduate courses of English for legal and business communication. She has carried out research in ESP teaching methodology and published ESP teaching materials: *A Practical Approach to ESP. Teaching Legal English in a University Setting* (2005). Her research interests focus on legal and institutional discourse, media discourse and gender. She has also published on the language of the European Union institutions. She is currently involved in a research project on 'Diversity, identity and translation'.

Natale Rampazzo graduated from the Law Faculty of the University of Naples 'Federico II'. Since then he has collaborated with the chairs of History of Roman Law. In 2001, he obtained a Master of Law at Munich. From 2001 to the present, he has been engaged as a Researcher at the Institute for International Legal Studies (ISGI) of the National Research Council (CNR). In 2003, he obtained a PhD in the History of Administrative Law from the University of Salerno. From 2007 to date, he has worked as Adjunct Professor for Roman Law and Roman History at the Law Faculty of the Second University of Naples. His current interests include procedural law and contract law.

Tarja Salmi-Tolonen was awarded the degrees of Doctor of Law (LL.D.) and Licentiate of Philosophy (Phil.Lic.). She has held the chair of legal linguistics at the University of Lapland and research and teaching posts at numerous Finnish universities, currently at the University of Turku. She has worked as a visiting scholar at the University of Cambridge, UK, and has been invited to speak on legal language at universities in the US and Europe. She has published on legal language and proactive law and contracting. By invitation of the Ministry of Justice, she has trained practising judges on legal language and acted as the principal national examiner of English legal translators, and is a consultant for the language division of the Finnish Prime Minister's Office.

Girolamo Tessuto is Associate Professor of English Language and Linguistics in the Department of Law, Second University of Naples. His main research interests are in genre analysis of academic and professional discourses in legal contexts. In addition to several publications appearing as research papers, book chapters and co-edited work, he has recently published a research monograph *Investigating English Legal Genres in Academic and Professional Contexts* (2012). He is Editorial Board member of international linguistic journals and chief editor of the *Explorations in Language and Law* publication series.

Judith Turnbull is a foreign-language assistant at the Faculty of Economics of the University of Rome 'La Sapienza'. Her research interests include discourse analysis applied to the fields of economics and law and cross-cultural business communication, with a particular focus on websites. Her recent publications include 'How "Glocal" is Corporate Discourse? A Case Study of a Multinational's Website' in *Intercultural Interactions in Business and Management* (Peter Lang 2011), and 'The Language of EU Judges' (*Rassegna Italiana di Linguistica Applicata* 2011).

Christopher Williams is full Professor of English Language and Linguistics in the Department of Law at Foggia University in southern Italy. He has published extensively in the field of legal English. Besides his monographic work *Tradition and Change in Legal English: Verbal Constructions in Prescriptive Texts* (2005), he has co-edited with Maurizio Gotti the volume *Legal Discourse across Languages and Cultures* (2010). He has also co-edited with Ilse Depraetere a volume on future time reference which appeared in a special issue of *English Language and Linguistics* in 2010. He is chief editor of the journal *ESP Across Cultures*.

Introduction

Christopher Williams and Girolamo Tessuto

The interface between law and language provides a continuous source of analytical insights, not only for researchers in applied linguistics but also for legal scholars and practitioners, thus offering an opportunity to refine, update and broaden current understanding of the way language is used by the professional legal community for the communication of its main business, i.e. the negotiation of justice.

With this in mind, the 14 chapters included in this volume represent the outcome of a selection and, in many cases, a subsequent re-elaboration of some of the presentations offered at the 1st International Conference on *The Language of Law: pulling together different strands and disciplines* held between 17 and 19 June 2010 at the Law Faculty of the Seconda Università degli Studi di Napoli (Second University of Naples), Italy. The selection was based not only on the quality of the chapters, but also bearing in mind that we intended the focus of research in this volume to be on linguistic issues relating to the various ways in which justice is negotiated in today's globalized world. In this sense, the contributions constituting this volume are much more than a disparate collection of papers from conference proceedings. By providing a balance of both theoretical as well as applied perspectives on some of the linguistic issues relating to this theme area in academic, professional and institutional contexts, and given the variety of backgrounds and fields of expertise of the contributors, the volume is an attempt to delineate the 'state of the art' on the subject of language in the negotiation of justice in the second decade of the 21st century.

The selected chapters address three main aspects of language use in the negotiation of justice, namely the legal contexts in which negotiation of justice is situated, primarily litigation, arbitration and mediation, the main issues identified in such contexts, and the applications of such research seen from an interdisciplinary perspective. In particular, the following thematic areas are addressed:

- analyses of legal discourse and genres in specific contexts
- issues of power and ideology in the use of legal language
- cross-cultural legal communication
- issues of recontextualization, accessibility and plain language
- disciplinary identity and pedagogy of legal language.

Naturally, several of the chapters in this volume cut across a variety of topic areas. To give just two examples, Isabel Corona's chapter, which we have included in the section on arbitration, also examines the topic of recontextualization, a theme that is central to the chapters presented by Ross Charnock and by Antonella Napolitano and Bronwen Hughes; and the chapter on online dispute resolution by Olga Denti and Michela Giordano clearly contains elements that link it to the theme of arbitration.

Given the three main aspects addressed in the negotiation of justice, the theme areas have therefore been broadly grouped under the headings of **Contexts** on the one hand, and **Issues** and **Applications** on the other.

The first three chapters are thematically linked insofar as they are all concerned with litigation and/or argumentation in the courtroom. However, the setting of each chapter is completely different, as we move from a Scottish High Court to Chinese criminal courts, notably in Beijing and Wuhan, and then to the European Court of Justice. The first two chapters in particular focus on the question of power relationships in the courtroom, the former highlighting the power of the advocates, the latter the power of the presiding judges.

In '"Mrs Buckley, you're telling a pack of lies": Cross-examination in the High Court of Justiciary in Edinburgh', William Bromwich begins by outlining the specificity of Scotland's judicial system in his investigation of legal discourse through the examination and cross-examination of witnesses in Edinburgh's High Court of Justiciary. The author points to the severe constraints within which such communication takes place, and he demonstrates that the exchanges often reflect asymmetrical power relations where those in power can dictate the course the narrative will take. Through carefully prepared routines, the protagonists not only establish a sequence of events on which the participants can agree, they also seek to undermine the integrity of key witnesses. The author observes that by mixing extremely formal language with more conversational tones, a rapport is established with the 'nonspeaking overhearers', i.e. the jury, as well as with the judge and the other actors in the court, at the expense of the primary addressee, the witness. Bromwich argues that the discursive rights of the jury and witnesses are severely constrained both during and after the proceedings. The courtroom exchanges can be interpreted as skilfully staged *coups de théâtre* which are met with countermoves by actors fighting to recover their credibility in a context of thinly veiled confrontation. The author affirms that the proceedings are characterized by genre mixing, since features of theatrical discourse are deployed to undermine the standing of the witness.

Meizhen Liao also looks into the relation between discourse and power in 'Power in interruption in Chinese criminal courtroom discourse', observing that courtroom discourse is notoriously known as 'power talk'. Liao notes that both discourse analysis and pragmatics have focused in recent years on the relationship between courtroom discourse and power in relation to questioning, whereas the phenomenon of interruption in the courtroom has been largely overlooked by the literature to date. The author wishes to redress this state of affairs by approaching power and discourse, and more specifically power imbalance in criminal courtroom discourse, through a detailed assessment of interruption in terms of interruption patterns, interruption positions, meta-interruptive speech acts and interruption functions. The author's study is based on a corpus of transcripts of four criminal trials heard in both lower and intermediate courts in Beijing and Wuhan (the provincial capital of Hubei). Liao shows how power is wielded by creating an imbalance in or through discourse. The author hypothesizes that this imbalance exists in six different ways, which he then goes on to illustrate. He concludes that "the exercise of power involves a latent conflict and clash of interests which may be obscured because of a society's ideologies" and that interruption in the courtroom "is highly strategic and goal-oriented, or more exactly interest-motivated." The author proposes devising a new model for discourse analysis which "not only addresses communicative action or cooperative interaction, but also strategic action or non-cooperative interaction." He also hopes that the findings may contribute to solving questions of social injustice suffered by the underprivileged.

In her chapter, Judith Turnbull explores the differences in style and approach adopted in writing judgments in common law and in civil law systems. As is well known, in the former judges interpret and may even create the law, whereas in the latter they act as 'the mouth of the law'. Thus, common law judgments may often be rhetorical and conversational in tone whereas civil law judgments tend to be fixed and impersonal. Since the European Court of Justice has judges and Advocates-Generals who are nominated by all Member States, they inevitably come from diverse legal systems and cultures. The author analyzes, with specific reference to the style and structure of the judges' argumentation, to what extent and how European Court judges have carried the conventions of their legal cultures into the new multicultural context. The author's study is based on a corpus of opinions by British and Italian Advocates-General at the European Court. Advocates-Generals assist the court and deliver independent opinions of the case written in their native language, and the author hypothesizes that it is likely that they will reflect the style of their national legal culture. Turnbull shows how Italian judgments tend to display a dialectic approach where the aim is to provide a rational explanation of the decision to prove its validity, especially on points of law. This contrasts markedly with the rhetoric of English judgments that trace the logical thought processes of the judge's reasoning, which is based on facts as much as on points of law. The author also makes a comparative analysis from an essentially linguistic perspective of how the Advocates-Generals' argumentation is presented and organized.

The next three chapters offer perspectives and insights into the subject of arbitration. The first two are to some extent interrelated and are both concerned with attempting to identify the current changes taking place in international commercial arbitration and the effects these changes are having on the type of language used. The third chapter in this trilogy takes us back to the very origin of the idea of arbitration as it was conceived in ancient Rome.

International commercial arbitration (ICA) is a theme that Vijay Bhatia has already analyzed elsewhere, most recently in Bhatia, Candlin and Gotti (2012). In his contribution in this volume, he adds a further dimension to his research by investigating exactly how ICA can be seen as a protected practice. Firstly, he asserts, this is because ICA is colonized by litigation experts, and secondly because it tends to be beyond the reach of a wider community of legal experts – in particular of junior and non-initiated practitioners – as it is in the hands of a restricted number of established legal experts. After providing a brief introduction to the institution and practice of ICA to resolve cross-border disputes, the author focuses in particular on the second kind of protectionism where he illustrates how the institution of arbitration is not encouraged to open the practice to less experienced members of the arbitration community, be they legal experts or non-legal experts. While conceding that 'privacy and confidentiality, in some cases, help firms to protect trade secrets and financial dealings from competitors', Bhatia concludes by arguing for 'greater transparency in the processes and procedures used in arbitration practices. At the moment there seems to be no independent means of conducting a critical inquiry into the good practices of arbitrators' since arbitration practice is 'closely guarded by the invocation of an absolute duty of confidentiality, which is often viewed as "given" rather than negotiable.'

'From confidential "dispute resolution technique" to public "legal war": The resemiotization of international commercial arbitration in the media' is the title of ISABEL CORONA's contribution, which complements Bhatia's chapter by shedding new light on the phenomenon of ICA as an extra-judicial way of resolving commercial disputes. Corona observes that ICA was born out of the need to provide an alternative to litigation as originally proposed by the UN and subsequently adopted by all UN members. She points out that ICA differs from litigation insofar as arbitration in the former is mainly based on party autonomy, freedom to customize the process and privacy and confidentiality of the proceedings. However, the author argues that 'the preference for the choice of legal experts as arbitrators, as Bhatia et al. (2008) have demonstrated, accounts for a growing tendency to choose litigation procedures to conduct arbitration and are believed to be compromising the spirit of arbitration as a non-legal practice.' The result is often a mixture of discourses, while the growing accessibility of ICA procedures has led to greater disclosure and publicity of major arbitration cases in the media. Hence arbitration is perceived as undergoing a process of resemiotization and recontextualization by adopting more reader-friendly semiotic resources characteristic of journalistic professional practices. Moreover, the author observes how a novel construct of arbitration in the public sphere is being created by the media, where significant elements of arbitration are transformed into new discourses, based on culturally shaped beliefs and attitudes. Drawing on Bhatia's (2004) notion of interdiscursivity, Corona examines specific cases to explain the occurrence of multiple and overlapping interdiscursivities.

In his chapter '*Arbiter*→Arbitration. Genesis of a functional word' NATALE RAMPAZZO takes us back 2000 years to where the roots of the concept of arbitration began in Roman law. Focusing on the origin and development of dispute resolution in ancient law, particularly the relationship between public and private justice, the author attempts to delineate the political and social tensions revolving around this type of agreement, which was inspired by the principle of *bona fides*. The data examined by the author provide an indication of the way arbitration worked in ancient Rome. In the author's analysis, the entire proceeding is taken into consideration, starting from the *compromissum*, the arbitration agreement, the appointment of the *arbiter*, and the type of language adopted in hearings. The author also evaluates the efficacy of the award, which was reinforced by introducing penalties in case of breach and was overseen by the authorities. This particular type of approach attempts to underline the way the meaning of certain terms has changed since the times of ancient Rome, by comparing the structure and function of arbitration against the background of the role of the State, with reference to contemporary practices and standpoints in the field of arbitration. Rampazzo identifies two major differences: the first concerns agreements to arbitrate future disputes, as the Romans permitted only a *compromissum* of existing disputes; the second is that 'during Roman times, parties who reached a settlement on their own were not allowed to insert it in the award.'

The third subtheme in the overall heading of **Contexts** is that of mediation. The two chapters in this section analyze mediation in the negotiation of justice from very different standpoints: the first in terms of so-called restorative justice (RJ), the second in the sphere of online dispute resolution (ODR).

In 'Restorative Justice, discursive practices and dialogistic exchange', Lucia Abbamonte and Flavia Cavaliere begin by observing that Italian criminal justice authorities are developing programs for cooperating with mediation services in order to reach victims and offenders more effectively. This includes providing suitable communication skills and techniques vis-à-vis victims, offenders and others involved in the mediation process as well as being aware of how victims and offenders may react to the way restorative justice is applied. The EU 2007 guidelines underscore how lack of awareness in many EU Member States about RJ needs to be overcome by disseminating information at all levels. In Italy, the practice is still used in a fairly restricted way. RJ began as a means of finding an alternative to criminal prosecution and conventional punishment, especially in relation to aboriginal populations, e.g. in New Zealand and Australia, though it is also spreading in Canada, the US and the UK. In RJ, stress is put on the victims' needs, while offenders are the focus in ordinary criminal justice. The authors single out discourse and dialogistic exchange as the chief medium of such negotiations, mainly based on encounters between victims and offenders. The authors then go on to analyze qualitative samples of such exchanges from American contexts and compare them with samples from similar practices in Italy, so as to assess the negotiation of challenging social relationships from a cross-cultural stance, and from the standpoint of interactive frames and knowledge schemas theories. The authors adopt a Critical Discourse Analysis (CDA) approach along with the Appraisal Framework for assessing Attitude.

In 'Participants' relationship in Online Dispute Resolution: Legal discourse as social practice', Olga Denti and Michela Giordano examine ODR procedures, i.e. where parties, instead of meeting in courtrooms or before arbitrators and mediators, attempt to resolve their disputes by reaching an agreement online, or by presenting the case to an online arbitral tribunal or a cybercourt. The authors stress the centrality of communication in ODR, especially in terms of delivery and the devices used to facilitate communication between the disputants and a third party. Denti and Giordano point out that if the public readership dimension is often absent from legislation insofar as ordinary citizens have little direct interest in legal minutiae, the parties to private transactions tend to feel directly involved in trying to find a solution on which both parties can agree. Hence discoursal resources and the relationship between participants are of crucial importance. The authors assert that analyzing discourse as social practice involves highlighting contextual features such as the participants' identities, the social structures, as well as the professional relationships that are likely to be preserved or transformed by a particular genre. The authors investigate the dialogic relationship of the ODR provider and the reader/user in the texts, created and fortified by adopting specific linguistic strategies including the rhetorical use of pronominal expressions for direct address, the pragmatic adoption of modality and of spoken or colloquial features, avoiding where possible archaic expressions, passives, nominalization and redundant expressions or phraseology, but also through the use of multimodal tools supplied by modern digital communication.

The second half of this volume looks into some of the specific **Issues** and **Applications** involved in the negotiation of justice. The first chapter in this section, 'Negotiating legal identity online: Narratives of drug use', co-authored by HUGO BOWLES and VALERIA MORETTI, is concerned with the way legal identities are created in an online drug user forum. To ensure legal immunity from prosecution, the house rules of drug user forums often suggest adopting particular linguistic forms when participants refer to themselves in narratives about drug consumption, e.g. the use of the acronym SWIM ('someone who isn't me') and third person pronouns in subject position. The authors illustrate the diverse consequences of this type of self-positioning in online interaction by applying Goffman's (1981) categories for responsibility for talk to the discourse of the forum. Since adopting a pseudonym in the online context already ensures anonymity, the results demonstrate that additional pseudonyms such as SWIM produce a twice-removed level of discourse, creating a storyworld within a storyworld. Secondly, the posters' self-conscious use of linguistic devices to distance themselves from personal and legal liability for narrated activities implies that they are aware of the illicit nature of the narrated activities. The authors suggest that such an awareness enhances the affiliation achieved by co-narration, binding the discourse community closer together. Finally, it is noted that the posters' strict adherence to the rules of the forum strengthens its hierarchical structure, which contrasts with the nonconformist nature of the narrated activities themselves.

The common feature of the next two chapters is that of recontextualization, even if the topics analyzed are quite different. 'Ethical particularism and contextualist interpretation of criminal attempts' is the title of ROSS CHARNOCK's contribution, where he argues that 'Dancy's theory of unprincipled ethics has been largely ignored in jurisprudence, partly because of the apparent contradiction inherent in the concept of a law without rules.' But Charnock observes that this model corresponds closely to legal practice in cases where the law is unclear or where there are no directly applicable rules to follow, and he shows how legal adjudication raises theoretical problems both in ethics and in philosophy of language. By illustrating cases regarding criminal attempts, Charnock highlights the contradictory nature of the results not only in cases where an attempt happens to be either legally or physically impossible, but also where the attempt was in fact carried out but did not amount to a crime. The author affirms that for many years, there were no clear legal rules regulating impossible attempts. He hypothesizes that since even recent efforts to clarify the applicable law have failed, this strengthens the idea that the particularist approach may be more generally applicable, and may be relevant in all cases where there is room for disagreement. Charnock also stresses the importance of story-telling since the way the case is formulated will lead the judge to interpret the rules more or less favourably where possible, and he concludes that the development of the law on failed attempts shows that the narrative can also affect the legal rules themselves, in cases where the new rule appears to be in direct contradiction to previous understanding.

Context is also key in 'From primary legislation to public presence: The language of gay rights from legislation to lobbying' by ANTONELLA NAPOLITANO and BRONWEN HUGHES, who show how discrimination based on sexual orientation has been a major issue in terms of public interest and debate throughout the EU, particularly after the wave of hate-crimes in both Italy and the UK. They explore the way discrimination is dealt with and subsequently fought against in three different contexts: legislative, institutional and public. The authors focus on the situation in the United Kingdom over the last ten years where the legislative framework has been substantially shaped by Parliamentary Acts to safeguard the rights of homosexuals. The authors stress that such protection has also come about thanks to the action of pressure groups such as *Stonewall* and *Outrage*. Even if homosexual rights and entitlements in the UK are now well established, the authors claim that the language used in the Acts is frequently vague and ambiguous, illustrating their case by providing examples. The authors also examine the performativity and immediacy of the language of public campaigns in terms of the empowering function and political potential of both legal texts and public campaigns. They illustrate the way language changes according to the context, observing that 'there is also a process of reciprocal endorsement whereby the progressive simplification which occurs in the move from the legislative to the institutional and on to the lobbying comes full circle and will, in turn, have an influence on subsequent primary legislation.'

Metaphor in legal language is the subject of ERSILIA INCELLI's chapter 'Formulating legal policy: Metaphors in the law in a case study on immigration policy: A corpus-assisted approach'. Using a corpus of 400,000 words relating to texts drafted between 1999 and 2009, made up of two sub-corpora, namely EU and UK legislation, the author shows how metaphors can be identified by adopting corpus linguistic techniques and how they can inform a descriptive analysis of legislative language. Through the concordance analyses of keywords, collocations, *n*-grams and specific terms, the author analyzes representative lexical items from target domains and the metaphorical expressions associated with them. The author notes how the UK is depicted as a 'container', an area to be protected from 'outside' danger, while in the EU we have the analogous metaphor of 'Fortress Europe'. Incelli points out that metaphors related to 'uncontrollable' fluids, e.g. *flows*, *influx*, *curb*, are frequently used in immigration laws. She argues that the lexico-semantic and grammatical patterns produced reveal an underlying discourse related to metaphorical concepts which imply controlling immigration by maintaining border security. These metaphorical concepts are also construed by means of specialized terminology, e.g. *entry stamp*, *entry clearance*, *liable to deportation*. Adopting a theoretical and methodological approach which combines discourse analysis and corpus linguistic techniques, Incelli focuses in particular on conceptual metaphor theory, analyzing the interaction between metaphor and lexical semantics. In her investigation, she also applies the related notions of semantic prosody, semantic preference and discourse prosody, e.g. by examining cultural keywords and collocates such as *alien.*

The last two chapters in this volume are complementary as they both deal with the phenomenon known as 'legal linguistics'. It is no coincidence that both authors have been academically involved with the person who is considered to be one of the founding fathers of legal linguistics as a scientific discipline, namely Heikki Mattila, with his seminal work *Comparative Legal Linguistics* (2006).

In 'Legal linguistics as a line of study and an academic discipline', Tarja Salmi-Tolonen presents the idea that legal linguistics constitutes much more than just teaching foreign languages to law students or studying multilingual legal terminology. The author claims that until recently, legal science has investigated language 'either through jurisprudence, legal theories, or legal philosophy or scrutinized jurisprudence, legal theories, or legal philosophy with the help of the language philosophical framework', and that 'no legal methodology introduces any kind of linguistic approach or linguistic method for studying or interpreting law.' She claims that language has tended to be considered by legal practitioners and scientists as instrumental, 'a necessary tool for the legislator and the legal professionals for carrying out their duties.' But she argues that this reductionist view of language as nothing more than a tool or instrument is rejected by linguists for whom language is intrinsically linked to human cognitive processes. Today, these issues are combined in questions of linguistic knowledge and legal knowledge and how they are intertwined in legal discourse. The author argues that whoever studies law, be it for applying or translating or in search of information, is first of all confronted with language. It should therefore be acknowledged that because of the way in which language and law are intertwined, the study of legal language and its methods should be more evident in the legal sciences. If this were the case, the author concludes, it would constitute legal linguistics.

In 'Learning to fly: The prospects for legal linguistics in the academic curriculum' CHRISTOPHER GODDARD observes that in cross-cultural legal communication, legal linguistics offers knowledge and skills that are essential to lawyers and legal translators who work with two or more legal languages, particularly in view of the context of the globalization and internationalization of law where English has achieved the rank of global legal language. However, Goddard asserts that the present position of legal linguistics is still not well established in academia. In his chapter, he attempts to redress this balance by trying to establish core and peripheral legal linguistic skills with a view to completing both the spectrum and content of course and programme components. To balance the academic aspect, the chapter also explores practical applications of legal linguistics. References to the literature complemented by focus group survey data form the basis of his analysis and discussion. The author's aim is 'to affirm the relevance of legal linguistics in the curriculum for future law professionals, to consider ways to strengthen its position, and to strengthen its status: in short, to examine "how to nurture the fledgling discipline until it takes wing and soars as an established component of the academic curriculum."'

We are particularly indebted to Vijay Bhatia for his invaluable guidance and advice during the initial stages of this project. Our thanks also go to Stephen J. Spedding (Department of Law, Second University of Naples) for his tireless work 'behind the scenes' in uniforming all of the formatting and in checking through the entire volume during its various stages of development. As editors we assume full responsibility for any remaining errors or imperfections that there may be.

References

Bhatia, V.K. 2004. *Worlds of Written Discourse: A Genre-Based View*. London: Continuum.

Bhatia, V.K., Candlin, C.N. and Gotti, M. (eds) 2012. *Discourse and Practice in International Commercial Arbitration: Issues, Challenges and Prospects*. Farnham, UK: Ashgate Publishing Company.

Goffman, E. 1981. *Forms of Talk*. Philadelphia: University of Pennsylvania Press.

Mattila, H.E.S. 2006. *Comparative Legal Linguistics*. Aldershot, UK: Ashgate Publishing Company.

PART I
Contexts

Litigation

Chapter 1

'Mrs Buckley, you're telling a pack of lies': Cross-examination in the High Court of Justiciary in Edinburgh

William Bromwich*

> Who is speaking? Who, among the totality of speaking individuals, is accorded the right to use this sort of language? Who is qualified to do so? Who derives from it his own special quality, his prestige, and from whom, in return, does he receive if not the assurance, at least the presumption that what he says is true? What is the status of the individuals who – alone – have the right, sanctioned by law and tradition, juridically defined or spontaneously accepted, to proffer such a discourse?
>
> (Foucault 1972: 50-51)

1. Introduction

This chapter analyzes discourse strategies in the examination and cross-examination of witnesses in the High Court of Justiciary in Edinburgh, highlighting the rigid institutional constraints within which the verbal interaction takes place. The analysis aims to show that many of the exchanges reflect an asymmetrical power relation, in which certain actors lay claim to more extensive rights to frame the discourse and to lead the narrative in a certain direction. In particular, carefully rehearsed routines are deployed, enabling the protagonists not simply to establish a sequence of events on which the participants can agree, but crucially to undermine the credibility of key witnesses. The sense of drama is heightened by means of a careful juxtaposition of highly formalized ritual language with more colloquial tones for establishing a rapport with the secondary addressee, the jury, who from a conversation analysis (CA) perspective are 'nonspeaking overhearers' (Drew 1992: 475), and the tertiary addressee, the judge and the other actors in the court, at the expense of the primary addressee, the witness. It is argued that not only are the discursive rights of the members of the jury during and after the proceedings severely constrained, as outlined in Section 3 below, but also those of the witnesses. An account is given of courtroom exchanges in which artfully

* The author wishes to thank the Marco Biagi Foundation for financial support, the organizers and the participants at the Conference on Language and the Law, Second University of Naples, held in Caserta, Italy, 17-19 June 2010, and the editors of this volume for their insights and suggestions.

staged *coups de théâtre* are met with countermoves by actors fighting to salvage their credibility in a confrontational encounter, providing evidence for the view that crucial moments in the cross-examination of witnesses display a degree of genre mixing between legal proceedings and theatrical performances.

2. The institutional framework: The Scottish legal system

Before examining the data from the courtroom exchanges, a brief overview of the institutional framework is provided. For historical reasons, dating back to well before the Act of Union 1707, the Scottish legal system has a structure of its own distinct from that of England and Wales. Not only in the United Kingdom but also in global terms, Scots law may be said to be unique. Related to Roman law, it developed over the centuries in the civil law tradition but also has common law elements, including the particularly significant feature of adversarial procedures and trial by jury. It may therefore be seen as a mixed system, and an analogy may be drawn with the legal system of South Africa (influenced by the laws brought to the Cape by early Dutch settlers and later by British administrators).[1] The Act of Union makes reference to the Court of Justiciary and its privileges, and established that:

> the Court of Justiciary do also after the union and notwithstanding thereof remain in all time coming within Scotland as it is now constituted by the laws of that kingdom, and with the same authority and privileges as before the union.[2]

As a result of this historical tradition, the terminology for the courts and the legal profession is in many cases specific to Scotland (Butterworths/The Law Society of Scotland 1992), including terms not used in England, e.g. *outwith* in the sense of outside or beyond, *desert the diet*, in the sense of abandoning a criminal charge, and the co-existence of the terms *arbiter* and *arbitrator* (Dossena 2003). In addition, terms that bear a *prima facie* resemblance to terms in the English legal system may have a completely different meaning, e.g. in Scots law *libel* is the formal statement of a criminal charge, not a kind of tort.[3]

In order to contextualize the cross-examination under analysis, a further important point is that the Scottish High Court of Justiciary, unlike the High Court in England and Wales, which deals primarily though not exclusively with civil

1 The legal systems of Quebec and Louisiana may also be considered to be pluralistic, due to historical links to French law. For a comparative overview, see Galgano and Ferrari (1993).

2 Act of Union, 1707, Article XIX in Browning, A. 1953. *English Historical Documents*, 1660-1714. London: Eyre and Spottiswoode, 680-695.

3 See http://www.britannia.org/scotland/scotsdictionary/l.shtml [accessed: 30 September 2011].

cases,[4] is part of the *criminal* jurisdiction, with trial by jury: the corresponding level of jurisdiction in the English system would be the Crown Court, or in London the Central Criminal Court, the Old Bailey. The Scottish courts differ from those of England and Wales: in ascending order, Scotland has District Courts, Sheriff Courts, the High Court of Justiciary, and at the highest level, the High Court of Justiciary sitting as the Court of Criminal Appeal, with powers equivalent to those of the House of Lords (since 2009, the Supreme Court) in the English system.

A brief note on the terminology for the legal profession may also be useful before examining the data. In the English courts, pleading in jury cases is generally carried out by barristers, but in Scotland this term is not used: those who plead in the higher courts are *advocates*, and the prosecuting counsel is the *Advocate Depute*. In England and Wales, barristers are members of the General Council of the Bar, whereas in Scotland advocates belong to the *Faculty of Advocates*. In England and Wales, solicitors, who are members of the Law Society, submit cases to barristers for pleading in the higher courts, whereas solicitors in Scotland, who are members of the Law Society of Scotland, submit cases for the higher courts to *advocates*.

A further significant difference is that the jury in criminal cases in Scotland consists not of 12 but of 15 men and women, and unanimity is not required, but a simple majority is sufficient for a conviction. The function of the jury, as in England and Wales, is to return the verdict, but whereas in the English system there are two possible verdicts – guilty or not guilty – in Scotland, the jury has the option of a third verdict, *not proven*, in which case the accused is treated as if not guilty. In Scotland, serious charges are tried by *solemn procedure*, instituted with an indictment and leading to trial by jury, whereas lesser charges are dealt with by *summary procedure* without a jury. The fundamental importance of the jury in trials for serious offences under Scots law was highlighted by the lack of a jury in the Lockerbie trial in 2002 due to the exceptional circumstances.[5]

Arguably, the jury in serious criminal cases in both England and Scotland could be seen as the primary or at least the secondary addressee, as they and they alone return the verdict, and as a result the evidence presented by the prosecution and the defence in the form of oral testimony by their witnesses is intended primarily to influence the jury rather than the judge. The strictly regulated institutional confines of this testimony limit the discourse strategies that witnesses are able to adopt when they are called to the witness box, and some of the institutional constraints will now be outlined.

---

4 As Sir Otto Kahn-Freund, the founder of comparative labour law, warned: 'Beware of homonyms'.

5 See http://www.scotcourts.gov.uk/library/lockerbie/index.asp [accessed: 30 June 2011].

3. Procedure and evidence in the Scottish High Court of Justiciary

It is self-evident that, 'an adequate account of legal discourse, and of legal linguistic practice more generally, requires a recognition of the complexity and diversity of legal institutional practice' (Goodrich 1987: 169). This means that in addition to examining textual features, discursive practices must be seen in their institutional framework, with a view to describing how 'specialized genres are constructed, interpreted, used and exploited in the achievement of specific goals in highly specialized academic, professional and institutional as well as other workplace contexts' (Bhatia and Gotti 2006: 9).

In this particular professional context, in order to appreciate the tight constraints within which witnesses give evidence, it may be useful to provide an overview of procedure in the Scottish High Court, which is formal, highly structured and subject to strict rules about the order of who may speak and when. However, pre-trial preparation is also an essential phase, since speaking rights are determined *prior* to the proceedings. In fact, 'when a Scottish indictment is served, there is appended to it a list of prosecution witnesses [...] this is the first official notification to the defence of the identities of the witnesses that the Crown propose to call during the trial' (Black 2000: 31). In addition, to allow the prosecution to prepare the case, 'the defence must serve lists of defence witnesses [...] on the prosecution not later than ten clear days before the start of the trial [...] The purpose of this disclosure is to enable the other side's solicitors to *precognesce* these witnesses in order to find out what evidence they are likely to be able to give at the trial' (Black 2000: 31).

In the pre-trial preparatory phase, the use of the technical term *precognesce* is particularly significant: *precognition* enables each side to prepare the case and select those who will be granted speaking rights during the trial in court.

Precognition is significant also because it highlights the distinction between the speaking rights of solicitors, who play a major role in preparing the case 'behind the scenes', and advocates, who have the right to plead in court, 'on stage':

> The Scottish legal profession is divided into solicitors who are responsible for the pre-trial preparation of the case and advocates (or counsel) who are responsible for the actual conduct of the case in court. Potential witnesses are precognesced by the solicitors, who prepare a written precognition embodying the information elicited from the witness for use by counsel. (Black 2000: footnote iv)

However, speaking rights are defined even in the pre-trial phase: in order to safeguard the integrity of witness testimony, advocates are denied the right to interview witnesses before the trial:

> It is professionally improper for an advocate to meet or to discuss the case with witnesses (other than his own client and any expert witnesses to be led for his client) before or during the trial. Counsel meets the witness for the first time when

> the latter enters the witness box, and must accordingly base his examination of the witness on the information contained in the precognition supplied to him by his instructing solicitor. (Black 2000: footnote iv)

After this outline of some of the discourse processes that may take place in the pre-trial phase (and of those that may not), it is now appropriate to look at how speaking and participation rights are distributed in court. The following schematic version of trial procedure is not intended to be exhaustive. For example, it does not include those phases in which the jury is excluded from the courtroom while the judge and counsel examine whether a certain body of evidence is admissible or not, but it may serve as an initial step to cast light on some of Foucault's questions about speaking rights in institutional settings, and it provides a framework for the courtroom exchanges to be examined later.

Stage 1. A jury of 15 men and women is appointed: the Advocate Depute (for the prosecution) and the advocate for the defence may object to up to three jurors.

Stage 2. The clerk of the court reads the indictment.

Stage 3. The accused (through his/her counsel) pleads 'guilty' or 'not guilty'.

Stage 4. The judge disposes of the case if the plea is 'guilty'.

Stage 5. If the accused pleads 'not guilty', the judge swears in the first prosecution witness.

Stage 6. The Advocate Depute examines the first prosecution witness, during the examination-in-chief, to provide evidence in support of the prosecution case.

Stage 7. The advocate for the defence cross-examines the witness, with a view to undermining the evidence or discrediting the witness in the eyes of the jury.

(Stages 5, 6 and 7, the swearing-in, examination-in-chief and cross-examination, are repeated for each of the subsequent prosecution witnesses.)

Stage 8. The judge swears in the first defence witness, who takes an oath or makes a solemn affirmation.[6]

Stage 9. The advocate for the defence examines the witness.[7]

Stage 10. The Advocate Depute cross-examines the witness, with a view to undermining the evidence or discrediting the witness in the eyes of the jury.

(Stages 8, 9 and 10, the swearing-in, examination-in-chief and cross-examination, are repeated for each of the subsequent defence witnesses.)

Stage 11. The judge swears in the accused (unless he/she opts not to give evidence).

---

6 'I swear by Almighty God that I will tell the truth, the whole truth and nothing but the truth', or 'I solemnly, sincerely and truly declare and affirm that I will tell the truth, the whole truth and nothing but the truth' (Black 2000: footnote x). See also Austin (1962), Searle (1969).

7 Ordinary witnesses who have not yet given evidence are not permitted to enter the courtroom while other witnesses are in the witness box: they have neither hearing nor speaking rights prior to their testimony (Black 2000: 32).

Stage 12. The advocate for the defence examines the accused.

Stage 13. The Advocate Depute cross-examines the accused, with a view to undermining the evidence or discrediting the accused in the eyes of the jury.

Stage 14. The Advocate Depute is entitled to address the court on the evidence and related legal issues.

Stage 15. The advocate for the defence is entitled to address the court on the evidence and related legal issues.

Stage 16. The judge gives instructions to the jury, explaining the procedure to be followed, indicating any evidence that needs to be set aside, where appropriate stating the difference between different verdicts relating to the same facts (e.g. in a murder case, the judge may allow the jury to consider an alternative verdict of culpable homicide, which is a lesser charge). In English courts, this is known as the judge's *summing up*, in Scottish courts, the judge's *charge*.

Stage 17. The jury retire to the jury room. Only the 15 members of the jury may take part in the deliberations: the judge does not enter the jury room, and the argumentation that takes place may not be reported in open court or in the press after the verdict.

Stage 18. The jury enters the courtroom and return their verdict: *guilty*, *not guilty* or *not proven*.

Stage 19. In the event of a 'not guilty' or 'not proven' verdict, the judge releases the accused; in the event of a 'guilty' verdict, the judge passes sentence. The verdict and the sentence are therefore two separate acts performed by different actors.

Stage 20. Subsequently the Advocate Depute may appeal on a point of law but an acquittal stands; the accused may appeal against conviction, or sentence, or both.

In terms of Foucault's speaking rights, one striking feature is the almost complete silence of the jury who, in spite of their absolutely central role in the proceedings, are not required to speak until Stage 17, and then only in the jury room, not the main courtroom, where just one member of the jury is called on to speak only at Stage 18, when they return their verdict. It has been noted that there is a tendency for juries, perhaps intimidated by the courtroom setting, to follow the entire proceedings in almost total silence: 'Jury members have a legal right – of which they generally seem unaware, and which they almost never exercise – to ask questions during a witness's examination, for example to clarify a point' (Drew 1992: 517).

Whereas silence on the part of the jury is the norm and does not necessarily result in any loss of 'face' (as conceptualized by Brown and Levinson 1987, but for a less Anglo-centric view and for politeness in cross-cultural settings, see Scollon and Scollon 1983, Eelen 2001, Hickey and Stewart 2005), a decision on the part of the accused (or defendant, in Scotland the *defender*) not to give evidence (Stages 12-13) is a factor that may result in a significant loss of face with the jury. Though the line of reasoning taken by jurors in a particular case is not on record – there are no transcripts and jurors may not divulge information about jury-room argumentation even after they have returned the verdict – the tendency on the part of jurors to form an unfavourable impression of defendants who choose (or are advised) not to give evidence in their own defence may be implied from judicial comment, as in the trial of Lord Archer, who stood trial at the Central Criminal Court in London in July 2001 on charges of perverting the course of justice and perjury:

> Mr Justice Potts, speaking of Archer's decision not to give evidence, told the jury that although it has been his right not to give evidence, they might draw the conclusion that he had remained silent because he had 'no answer to the prosecution's case'. Mr Justice Potts said: 'You must not assume that he is guilty because he has not given evidence, but two matters arise from his silence. In the first place you try the case on the evidence, and you will appreciate that a defendant who has not given evidence has said nothing in the trial to undermine, contradict or explain the evidence put before you by the prosecution. A defendant's silence at his trial may count against him. This is because you may draw the conclusion that he is not giving evidence because he has no answer to the prosecution's case, or none that would bear examination. If you draw that conclusion you must not convict Lord Archer wholly or mainly on the strength of it [...] you may draw such a conclusion against him only if you think it is a fair and proper conclusion and you are satisfied about two things. First that the prosecution case is so strong that it clearly calls for an answer by him, and second that the only sensible explanation for his silence is that he has no answer, or none that would bear examination.'[8]

In short, it may be said that the defendant has the right to speak but also the right to remain silent, though remaining silent is fraught with dangers, perhaps even more so when the defendant is a successful author.

4. Discourse strategies in the High Court of Justiciary

The data to be examined below are taken from the transcript of a trial held at the High Court of Justiciary in Edinburgh in 1994, as part of a television series filmed on an experimental basis by BBC 2 called *The Trial*, with the approval of the Lord President, Lord Hope.[9] *The Trial* provides a data set of considerable interest for examining communicative processes taking place in a highly structured

8 Clough, S. 'Silence may damage Archer, says trial judge', *The Daily Telegraph*, 12 July 2001.

9 The most senior judge in Scotland bears the title of Lord President in connection with his/her civil function, whereas in his/her criminal justice functions s/he is known as the Lord Justice-General; the second most senior judge in Scotland is the Lord Justice-

institutional setting: whereas in the United States court proceedings are frequently televised, in the United Kingdom this is an exceedingly rare event, as filming and even press photography is prohibited in courts and courtroom precincts under the Criminal Justice Act 1925.[10]

Although the Scottish legal system was described above as mixed, with elements of the civil law and common law traditions, Scottish courtroom proceedings are adversarial:

> The conduct of criminal cases in the Anglo-American judicial system is conventionally depicted as 'adversarial', involving a contest between the two sides as to which can produce the more convincing story about whether and how some incident happened [...] The standard for deciding which side's story is the more convincing is, of course, the verdict of the jury. The crucial role in the adversarial system of testing one side's story against the other's, in some respects in contrast to many European 'inquisitorial' legal systems, lies behind the condition that the only evidence that is admissible is that which can be orally attested in court. (Drew 1992: 472)

The fact that all evidence needs to be orally tested in court means that the examination and cross-examination of witnesses is of major importance in the proceedings (Bülow-Møller 2007), at times resulting in a high level of tension. So hostile is the cross-examination of witnesses by counsel in certain cases that those following the proceedings from the public gallery have mistakenly taken the prosecution witness to be the defendant.[11] The hostility of cross-examination is goal-oriented, and often encounters resistance on the part of the witnesses:

> In the adversarial Anglo-American criminal-judicial system, cross-examination is essentially hostile. Attorneys test the veracity or credibility of the evidence being given by witnesses with questions which are designed to discredit the other side's version of events, and instead to support his or her own side's case. When being cross-examined, witnesses are, of course, conscious of this purposefulness behind the questions they are asked. They are alive to the possibility that a question or a series of questions may be intended to expose errors or inconsistencies in their evidence, and hence to challenge and undermine it. This awareness on the part of witnesses is manifest in the guarded and defensive ways in which they answer certain questions. (Drew 1992: 470)

Clerk. Mention should also be made of the Lord Advocate, the senior law officer with responsibility for public prosecutions, assisted in each case by an Advocate Depute.

10 Gibb, F. 'Viewers become jury on TV trial', *The Times*, 17 November 1994.

11 In the Archer trial, the key prosecution witness was cross-examined for several days by the defence counsel, leading some observers in the public gallery to express the belief that she was guilty and deserved to go to prison (personal communication).

In addition to the emphasis in adversarial trials on the verbal production of evidence, another key characteristic is that except in the case of *expert witnesses*, such as pathologists, evidence is presented on behalf of one of the two parties, the prosecution or the defence. The *credit* or credibility of the witness is essential and should not be impaired, as Drew points out:

> Witnesses are regarded as being members of one or the other side's team: hence they are treated as giving evidence in support of their side's case, a view which is rather dramatically encapsulated in the legal rule that an attorney 'may not impeach the credit of his own witness' (Cross and Wilkins 1980: 93-94, quoted in Drew 1992: 473).

Cross-examination is not a generic term to be used for questioning of any kind, but refers specifically to the questioning of a witness by counsel for the opposing party, as shown in Figure 1.1, referring to the Scottish system:

	Advocate Depute for the prosecution	Advocate for the defence
prosecution witness	examination-in-chief	cross-examination
defence witness	cross-examination	examination-in-chief

Figure 1.1 Questioning in adversarial trials in Scotland

Another key distinction between examination-in-chief and cross-examination is that the rules of evidence are different in the two phases, as *leading questions*[12] are not permitted in examination-in-chief, whereas in the subsequent cross-examination, the narrative has been set out for the jury and is now held up for scrutiny, and leading questions are permitted:

> During a witness's evidence-in-chief no leading questions may be asked, except on formal or uncontroversial matters [...] In cross-examination the defence may seek to undermine any evidence favourable to the prosecution which the witness

12 A leading question is one that states the information that the examining party intends to elicit, in the form of a yes/no question, rather than as an open-ended *Wh-* question.

> had given and may also seek to elicit from him or her any evidence favourable to the defence, whether or not on issues already explored by the prosecution [...] Leading questions are permissible in cross-examination. (Black 2000: 35)

The transcript of the trial under examination, a trial for attempted murder, contains discourse by all the courtroom protagonists. On a scale of formality (Danet 1980: 471, quoted in Gotti 1991: 5) with a choice of four Styles (Frozen, Formal, Consultative, Casual) and three Modes (Written, Spoken-composed, Spoken-spontaneous), lay witness testimony is Consultative and Spoken-spontaneous, and therefore the least formal of the discourse types in the courtroom.

The transcript begins at Stage 5 of the proceedings, the swearing-in of the first prosecution witness, and continues with Stage 6, when the Advocate Depute (AD) examines the first prosecution witness (W):

AD: I wanted to ask you, Mr Nevey, about certain events
which may have taken place a year ago on a Sunday
afternoon, the second of February. Can you
remember something happening then?

In this initial move, the AD uses an epistemic modality marker, 'may have taken place', introducing an element of doubt that the witness is expected to resolve. This is an open-ended style of examination, enabling the witness to construct a narrative on the basis of his own recollection of events. The AD then continues questioning in the same way, generally avoiding the use of leading questions except in the case of uncontroversial matters such as the identification of the defendant:

AD: Can you see Mr Robertson here?
W: Yes, the gentleman over there.
AD: Sitting between the two policemen?
W: Yes. Mr Robertson and his brothers were all
standing outside the gate.

The witness has no need to adopt any defensive strategies as the questioning is non-face threatening:

AD: What were they doing?
W: Gesturing for us to go out and fight.
AD: Were they holding anything?
W: They had several weapons, sticks and poles.
AD: And what happened then?

The cross-examination of the same witness by the advocate for the defence (A) begins with a non-face-threatening statement that is not even worded as a question, as if intending to allow the witness to construct his own version of events:

A: According to you, Mr Nevey, this ill-feeling, this
grudge on Mr Robertson's part towards you
stemmed from an incident months previously when
you had done something to a gate. He wanted you to
repair a gate.

However, the apparently innocuous incident with the gate is raised as a way of discrediting the witness, as becomes immediately clear from the ensuing exchange, in which W (Mr Nevey, the witness) resorts to defensive strategies starting with an overt correction marker (line 10), then claiming to have no recollection of the incident:

W: Yes, I accidentally bumped into it with the rear of
my car.
A: The rear of your car? Now did anything happen to
you as a result of driving your car that day?
W: No.
A: Did the police come to see you?
W: No, I can't remember.

In his analysis of courtroom exchanges, Drew sees the refusal to offer confirmation (line 12) as follows: 'the witness might be anticipating that what she is being asked to confirm will turn out to be prejudicial to her story [...] Though she may not be able to project precisely how some point is going to work against her story, her suspicion that it might do so may make her reluctant to agree to the point' (Drew 1992: 481).

A: You can't remember whether they came to see you?
Is that because the police have been to see you so
many times, Mr Nevey, that you can't remember
what they were up to see you about on one incident
compared to another?
W: That's not true, no.

The overt correction marker used by W (line 18) fails to prevent A from continuing with her confrontational discourse, with the use of a leading question which, as noted above, is permitted in cross-examination:

A: And you know very well that the reason why there is
ill-feeling between you and Mr Robertson is that you
believe Mr Robertson 'shopped' you to the police at
the time you ran into his garden gate and the police
claimed that you were driving with no insurance at
the time. Is that right?

W: No, it's not right.
A: So nothing like that happened at all?
W: I was prosecuted possibly about a week or two later, I believe.

The response in lines 27-28, worded tentatively with the hedging markers 'possibly' and 'I believe', will have done little to salvage the credibility of W in the eyes of the jury, who would clearly not be impressed by a witness claiming to have only a vague recollection of being prosecuted. His vagueness and refusal to provide confirmation also work against him later in the cross-examination:

A: And what about spitting at his wife?
W: I believe I was accused of that.
A: The police were called again about that, isn't that right?
W: This is not true.

The cross-examination continues until the *coup de grâce* is delivered, seriously undermining the credibility of the witness:

A: Mr Nevey, that, like the rest of your evidence, is just *a pack of lies*.
W: It's not true.

It is significant that neither the judge nor the Advocate Depute intervene to object to this line of cross-examination, and this suggests that it complies with the Rules of Evidence. In her adroitly planned assault on the credibility of the witness, the advocate for the defence adopts a strategy in which she raises the stakes one step at a time: in Move 1, she begins with a general question not directly related to events on the day of the alleged crime and adopts a non-confrontational, almost sympathetic tone; in Move 2, midway through, she comes closer to the matter at hand and places the witness on the defensive, chipping away at his credibility as he repeatedly refuses to confirm, claims not to remember, and contradicts himself. Finally, in Move 3, she moves to open confrontation, with her devastating claim about 'a pack of lies', which clearly goes far beyond anything that Brown and Levinson in their analysis of politeness strategies would consider a face-threatening act.

Space does not permit a close reading of all the cross-examination of this witness, but the three Moves outlined above may be identified also in the following exchanges between the advocate for the defence and the next prosecution witness, Mrs Buckley. The first step is Move 1, the open-ended question, the sympathetic tone. Again, it is not even worded as a question but as a statement:

A: So that the ladies and gentlemen can understand clearly what's been happening to you, you've been troubled not just by Mr Robertson as a neighbour but you've had trouble from other neighbours in the area.

The witness fails to notice that she is on a slippery slope and gives an answer that is likely to cast her in an extremely poor light in the eyes of the jury:

W: Just accusations of shouting at deaf and dumb people and it caused a lot of stress to me and I ended up on medication from the doctor through it.

The ostensibly sympathetic tone in Move 1 of the cross-examination continues:

A: That's obviously distressed you. What other neighbours have you had trouble from?
W: None, as far as I can think, apart from Mrs Johnson, but she happens to be an alcoholic [...]

After attempting to save face by marking the distance between herself and her troublesome neighbour, W then lowers her guard, with a resulting loss of face before the court:

A: What about Mr and Mrs Fife? Have you had any trouble with them before?
W: That was the day one of her children who was 10 years old hit my daughter who was three at the time and I went round to her house. She called me an 'English cow' and slammed the door in my face.

The cross-examination then shifts up a level in terms of confrontation, to Move 2, where W is placed on the defensive:

A: Now when all of this trouble erupted outside your house on the second of February last year, who was doing all the shouting that afternoon?
W: The Robertsons. I don't even know what they were shouting about.

This attempt to deflect the question prepares the ground for A to progress to Move 3, her onslaught on witness credibility:

A: Mrs Buckley, you're telling *a pack of lies* about what happened.

However, in this case, finding herself in a corner, W attempts to fight back and salvage her credibility:

W: I'm sorry, I've got no reason to lie. Besides, I've just sworn an oath and I wouldn't lie under it.

The assault on W's version of events continues implacably, with one statement after another attacking her testimony: the term *truth* serves to provide lexical cohesion by means of anaphora referring back to *lies*, contrasting the two terms:

A: And the truth about what happened [...] there were no weapons of any kind in his hand or in his friends' hands at that time.
W: You're calling *me* a liar. There were plenty of weapons. How would I have been hit over the head if the man hadn't had a weapon? Did I just punch myself and pretend? No.
A: That brings me to my next suggestion, Mrs Buckley, that you were not hit on the head at all.
W: I beg your pardon but I *was*.

Mrs Buckley's vigorous *riposte* contrasts with the fairly bland response of Mr Nevey earlier in the hearing, recalling Drew's observation that 'the witness's attempts to counter the attorney's descriptive strategies, and hence herself control the information which is available to the jury, should not be overlooked' (Drew 1992: 517). However, Mrs Buckley's resistance to the cross-examination with an increasingly intense assault on witness credibility appears to be fairly unconvincing, and it is not only this particular witness who loses face: as Levinson has noted, 'in the courtroom a cross-examination is more like a zero-sum game, where one party's losses are the other party's gains' (Levinson 1992: 91).

The three-move structure intended to undermine Mrs Buckley is also salient in the cross-examination of the next prosecution witness, Mr Coull, the victim of the near-fatal stabbing. It was the contention of the advocate for the defence that the accused was not the aggressor at all, but that during the brawl in which the stabbing took place, Coull was accidentally stabbed by one of his own friends, who later tried to shift the blame onto the accused. The following excerpts highlight the three-move strategy:

Move 1: Sympathetic tone

A: On the night of 27 March you've told us that you were a 'wee bit tipsy', a few pints, a few Southern Comforts. What about your pals: what sort of state were they in?

Move 2: More confrontational approach

A: If you look at the photographs, Crown production number one, and you turn to the first photograph, did you do all that damage to him?

W: No, I only punched him a couple of times.

Move 3: Direct assault on witness credibility

A: [...] and what you say as to his involvement on that particular day is just *a pack of lies*. Isn't that right?

W: It's not true.

5. Concluding remarks

For reasons of space, it is not intended to examine the final speeches of AD and A in the transcript, nor the judge's charge to the jury. However, it is important to mention that the accused was acquitted of the charges laid against him, in spite of evidence from 24 prosecution witnesses and a written admission of guilt signed in a state of confusion in police custody after the assault.

The devastating assault on witness credibility launched by the advocate for the defence, in which she made highly effective use of a three-move strategy, starting from statements with a low level of confrontational force and working up to a direct attack on the veracity of the statements made and indeed on the character of the witnesses, was deployed to full effect and evidently made a powerful impression on the members of the jury, the silent overhearers in an almost theatrical performance. The use of the powerful accusation that the witnesses' testimony was 'a pack of lies' clearly goes beyond the confines of politeness delineated by Brown and Levinson, yet it appears to comply with the institutional constraints for the conduct of cross-examination.

From the analysis, there appear to be considerable similarities in discourse terms between the cross-examination analyzed by Drew in a US courtroom and the three-move structure identified here in a Scottish context. In characterizing the discourse as a goal-oriented process, 'with *constraints* on participants, settings, and so on, but above all on the kinds of allowable contributions' (Levinson 1992: 69, emphasis in the original), the various terminological differences (such as *advocate* in the Scottish courts compared to *attorney* in the US) appear to be of secondary importance since in both instances the discourse takes place within an adversarial framework. In such a framework, the jury plays a central but largely silent role, giving rise to the methodological problem that the reasoning and evaluation carried out by the members of the jury can be assessed only indirectly, in so far as it can be inferred from the discourse of the other institutional actors.

Although Foucault points to a highly skewed distribution of speaking rights, in adversarial cases such a distribution is not necessarily indicative of a lack of power, as the jury's verdict is paramount, to the extent that it can even prevail over evidence such as a written admission of guilt on the part of the defendant, as in the trial examined.

The confrontational strategy and the cross-examination moves described above would clearly be out of place in cultures in which loss of face is avoided at all costs, but in the adversarial system in Scotland, they were deployed to devastating effect. The absence at least in this data set of any objection by the actors in the courtroom to this increasingly confrontational approach is indicative of it being accepted as a norm, and as part of what in Wittgenstein's terms could be seen as a 'language game', though paradoxically a game that in the High Court of Justiciary in Edinburgh is part of 'solemn procedure'.

References

Austin, J.L. 1962. *How to Do Things with Words*. Oxford: Clarendon.

Bhatia, V.K. and Gotti, M. 2006. *Explorations in Specialized Genres*. Bern: Peter Lang.

Black, R. 2000. The Lockerbie criminal trial: the Scottish rules of evidence. *International Legal Perspectives*, 11(1), 31-40.

Brown, P. and Levinson, S. 1978. Universals of language usage: politeness phenomena, in *Questions and Politeness Strategies in Social Interaction*, edited by E. Goody. Cambridge: Cambridge University Press.

Brown, P. and Levinson, S. 1987. *Politeness: Some Universals in Language Usage Usage.* Cambridge: Cambridge University Press.

Bülow-Møller, A.-M. 2007. Trial evidence: overt and covert communication in court. *International Journal of Applied Linguistics,* 1(1), 38-60.

Butterworths/The Law Society of Scotland. 1992. *Glossary. Scottish Legal Terms, Latin Maxims and European Community Legal Terms*. Edinburgh: Butterworths.

Cross, R. and Wilkins, N. 1980. *An Outline of the Law of Evidence*. 5th Edition. London: Butterworths.

Danet, B. 1980. Language in the legal process. *Law and Society Review*, XIV(3) 445-564.

Dossena, M. 2003. Arbitration in Scotland: local specificity and international homogeneity, in *Legal Discourse in Multilingual and Multicultural Contexts: Arbitration Texts in Europe*, edited by V.K. Bhatia, C. Candlin and M. Gotti. Bern: Peter Lang, 87-109.

Drew, P. 1992. Contested evidence in courtroom cross-examination: the case of a trial for rape, in *Talk at Work. Interaction in Institutional Settings*, edited by P. Drew and J. Heritage. Cambridge: Cambridge University Press, 470-520.

Eelen, G. 2001. *A Critique of Politeness Theories*. Manchester: St. Jerome.

Foucault, M. 1972. *The Archeology of Knowledge*. London: Tavistock.

Galgano, F. and Ferrari, F. 1993. *Atlante di Diritto Privato Comparato*. 2nd Edition. Bologna: Zanichelli.

Goodrich, P. 1987. *Legal Discourse. Studies in Linguistics, Rhetoric and Legal Analysis*. Basingstoke: Macmillan.

Gotti, M. 1991. *I Linguaggi Specialistici*. Firenze: La Nuova Italia.

Hickey, L. and Stewart, M. 2005. *Politeness in Europe*. Clevedon: Multilingual Matters.

Levinson, S. 1992. Activity types and language, in *Talk at Work. Interaction in Institutional Settings*, edited by P. Drew and J. Heritage. Cambridge: Cambridge University Press, 66-100.

Scollon, R. and Scollon, S. 1983. Face in inter-ethnic communication, in *Language and Communication*, edited by I.C. Richards and R.W. Schmidt. London: Longman, 156-188.

Searle, J. 1969. *Speech Acts*. Cambridge: Cambridge University Press.

Chapter 2
Power in interruption in Chinese criminal courtroom discourse*

Meizhen Liao**

Based on the transcripts of tape-recordings of seven criminal courtroom trials, this chapter analyzes power and discourse, specifically power imbalance in criminal courtroom discourse, by a detailed examination of interruption in terms of number, position, pattern, meta-interruptive speech act and function. The author focuses on the linguistic mechanism behind the imbalance. It is hoped that the findings will be revealing for legal professionals and also instrumental in the solution of the possible injustice done to the socially underprivileged.

1. Introduction

1.1 A brief review of studies on power and discourse and interruption

Power and discourse has been a topic of great interest in the fields of sociolinguistics, discourse analysis, especially critical discourse analysis, as well as legal linguistics, ever since researchers began to take social factors into account. The past few decades have witnessed an impressive amount of academic attention to the study of

---

* This work is part of the author's China state-funded project 'A Study of Chinese Courtroom Discourse: A Multidisciplinary Perspective' (China national philosophy and social science foundation grant, 06BYY051) and a series of papers have been published or are forthcoming.

** I would like to thank the following people and organizations for their kind help with this chapter: Professor Lawrence Solan, associate dean of Brooklyn Law School, who kindly read the chapter and gave me invaluable suggestions and whose hospitality and help during my visit in Brooklyn Law School as a Fulbright scholar (2006-2007) greatly facilitated my work on this chapter; Professor John Gibbons, who kindly read the chapter and gave me his insightful comments and whose suggestion that I break the original into two made this article possible; Professor Peter Tiersma and Professor Mary Bucholtz, who invited me to present the paper at the Loyola Law School of Los Angeles and at the center of language, interaction and social organization of the University of California at Santa Barbara so that I had a chance to have the unique observations on this paper by Professor Sandra Thomson, Professor John Gumpertz, Professor Gene Lerner and their colleagues; and, last but not the least, the Fulbright Foundation, whose grant made this project possible.

discourse and power (Fowler, Hodge, Kress and Trew 1979, Foucault 1982, Kedar 1987, Fairclough 1989, van Dijk 1989, 1996, 2009, Wodak 1989, Tannen 1994, 2003, Froman 1996, Lakoff 1990, Wartenberg 1990, Watts 1991, Bourdieu 1991, Ng and Bradac 1993, Adler and Longhurst 1994, Berger 1994, Gal 1995, Chimombo and Roseberry 1998, Weigand and Dascal 2001, Locher 2004, Mayr 2008).

Law and the practice of law is one of the best sites for observing the interplay between power and discourse. Courtroom discourse is notoriously known as power talk. However, most studies in courtroom discourse are devoted to investigating power through questioning, as the trial process is basically a process of questions and answers, and legal professionals use different types of questions to control their interactants (Danet and Kermish 1978, Danet 1980a, 1980b, Harris 1995, Conley and O'Barr 1998, Ehrlich 2001, Cotterill 2002, Gibbons 2003, Liao 2003a/b, 2004, 2005a/b/c). Literature on power in courtroom discourse in terms of ways other than questioning, such as interruption, is sparse and the few authors I have found so far are Bogoch and Danet (1984), who made a study on interruption in courtroom discourse with their focus exclusively on interaction between the lawyer and the client, and the present author, who made a preliminary study in Chinese courtroom discourse correlating interruption patterns with the Chinese legal system and culture, as well as making a brief comparison of the phenomenon in Chinese and American criminal courtroom discourse (Liao 2009). On the other hand, interruption, both as a conversational phenomenon and as an important indicator of power, has also drawn the attention of scholars of sociolinguistics, discourse analysis and pragmatics. So far, the main scholarly concerns are: (1) interruption and gender (Zimmerman and West 1975, Ferguson 1977), (2) interruption and dominance (Zimmerman and West 1975, Ferguson 1977, Beattie 1981, Kollock, Blumstein and Schwarts 1985, Dindia 1987, Bilous and Krauss 1988, Hawkins 1991, Holmes 1991, Marche and Peterson 1993), and (3) conceptualization and measurement of interruption (Okamota, Rashotte and Smith-Lovin 2002, Li, Krysko, Desroches and Deagle 2004).

The most important conclusions are: (1) men interrupt more than women and women are interrupted more than men; (2) interruptions are symmetrically distributed in same-sex dyads and asymmetrically distributed in opposite-sex dyads with males interrupting females more than females interrupting males; (3) women have less assertive behaviour interrupted, interrupt less assertively, and respond less assertively to interruptions than men; (4) interruption is not necessarily derisive: it is often a sign of intimacy. However, nearly all the conclusions were based on everyday conversation, experimental interaction or interviews where interruptions are obviously less significant in terms of goals or interests concerned.

1.2 The aim and methodology of the study

The question I try to address in this chapter is: how does interruption serve as an index of power and power patterns in criminal courtroom discourse as a typical institutional and strongly goal-oriented discourse? Consequently, this study is devoted exclusively to interruption and power, specifically the linguistic mechanism behind the power imbalance as shown in Chinese criminal courtroom discourse, as well as through interruption in terms of (1) number and distribution, (2) pattern, (3) position, (4) meta-interruptive speech acts and (5) function. This study is essentially qualitative and supported with some quantitative analysis.

1.3 Approaches to power and interruption

Power has been defined variously by people in different fields of study and from different perspectives. In this study, power is seen as domination and interruption as an instantiation of this domination, be it cooperative or intrusive, disconfirming or confirming, disruptive or supportive, as I believe that power is never metaphysical and exists in the details of linguistic practice (Conley 1998). As for interruption, Zimmerman and West's (1975) syntactic definition is adopted, and interruption is defined as intrusion by one participant in a social interaction into the turn of the current speaker in an attempt to obtain the floor or achieve some other purposes. Interruption is divided into 'simple interruption' and 'overlap interruption' (Zimmerman and West 1975) with the only difference being that in the former there is no or almost no discernible overlap of the utterances by the interrupter and interruptee. However, those feedbacks were excluded.

1.4 The data

This study is data-based. Transcripts of seven criminal courtroom trials, tape-recorded with the permission of the court, were used as data. The trials took place in Beijing, Wuhan and Shanghai, three representative cities in the north, east and south of China, and in both lower and intermediate courts, with the trial participants diversified in terms of gender, age, education and attitude toward the accusation. The first trial involved a charge of fraud. Five defendants were charged with defrauding some senior citizens of their money or jewellery by purporting to predict their future. Four of the defendants were farmers and the fifth was an unemployed woman. Three of the defendants had received some primary-school education, one had received middle-school education, and one was illiterate. All the defendants pleaded guilty. The second trial involved a charge of malfeasance. The former deputy general manager of a large Beijing-based corporation was charged with dereliction of duty which resulted in huge losses to the company. The trial took place in a lower court in Beijing. The defendant was well educated and did not plead guilty. The third trial involved a charge of swindling. The defendant, a well-educated woman, who served as the general manager of a large corporation, was charged with illegally obtaining foreign currency from banks through the use of forged documentary letters of credit. She, too, pleaded not guilty. The case was heard in an intermediate court in Wuhan. The fourth trial involved a charge of manslaughter. Five defendants were charged with beating a man to death for trivial reasons. The trial took place in an intermediate court in Wuhan. The fifth trial involved a charge of destruction of private property. The defendant, a farmer in one of the districts of Beijing, was accused of blowing up the new car of his business partner out of revenge for the partner's not sharing the contracted dues to the production team. The trial took place in a lower court in Beijing. The sixth trial involved a charge of homicide. The defendant was accused of killing a fellow gambler with a knife in a fight caused by unfair distribution of the gambling money. The trial took place in Wuhan. The seventh trial involved a charge of kidnapping. Three defendants, all of them farmers, were accused of kidnapping and robbing a man from Xinjiang. The trial took place in Shanghai. For the sake of those who do not speak Chinese, all data examples were translated into English and the translation is literal so as to keep the Chinese syntax intact, especially concerning the interruptions.

2. Interruption and power imbalance

2.1 Interruption: the number and distribution

Distribution of interruptions is seriously imbalanced in that the judge or the prosecutor interrupts most and the defendant is the most interrupted, as is shown in the following tables.

Table 2.1 Judge interrupting others

Interrupter			**Judge**		
Interruptee	Defendant	Lawyer	Prosecutor	Others	Total
Number	115	20	7	1	143
Percentage	80.3	14	5	0.7	100

Table 2.2 Prosecutor interrupting others

Interrupter			**Prosecutor**		
Interruptee	Defendant	Lawyer	Judge	Others	Total
Number	267	0	2	0	269
Percentage	99.3	0	0.7	0	100

Table 2.3 Defence lawyer interrupting others

Interrupter			**Defence lawyer**		
Interruptee	Defendant	Judge	Prosecutor	Others	Total
Numbers	23	12	1	0	36
Percentage	63.9	33.3	2.8	0	100

Table 2.4 Defendant interrupting others

Interrupter			**Defendant**		
Interruptee	Judge	Lawyer	Prosecutor	Others	Total
Numbers	36	15	96	0	147
Percentage	24.5	10.2	65.3	0	100

Table 2.5 Total number of interruptions and their distribution among the interrupters

Interrupter	**Number of interruptions**	**Percentage**
Judge	143	24
Prosecutor	269	45
Defendant	147	25
Lawyer	36	6
Total	596	100

2.2 Interruption: the pattern

The ways in which the judge or the prosecutor interrupts the defendant are different from the ways the defendant interrupts the judge or the prosecutor (or the defence lawyer).

2.2.1 Successive interruption: A B, A B ...

The judge or public prosecutor can and often does interrupt the defendant several times successively, but the reverse is never true, as in:

Example 1

D: The whole thing started in the beginning of 1995. ------ This is the first point. The second is, as for the second contract, I am really not clear about it. But later, after I resigned from my position in 1997, Wang Zhaoli of the new leadership of the company told me in 1998 that the second contract▲

J: ▼*The defendant, please keep to the facts of the case, the facts of the case, understand? The prosecutor asked you to talk about the facts of the case*▲

D: ▼I just finished the first contract and as for the second one▲

J: ▼*You are required to keep to the facts of the case.*

D: I was just talking about the second loan contract▲

J: ▼*Did you hear me, the defendant?*

D: Yes. I did.

2.2.2 Alternative interruption A-B-A, B-A-B ...

If the judge or public prosecutor and the defendant interrupt each other alternately, it usually ends with the former interrupting the latter. That is, it is usually the case that the judge initiates interruption of the defendant, gets interrupted by the defendant and then interrupts the defendant again, as in:

Example 2

J: How much money?

D: At first, we said that it would be eight million. If it wasn't sufficient, we would get some more money through a loan from the bank. The loan was two, two, eh, we originally fixed it at 40 million, our company▲

J: ▼At that time how much money did you agree on? How much money were you prepared to provide? I don't care what kind of money it was, whether it was a loan from banks, or funds from other sources your company managed to get▲

D: ▼Plus the loan from the bank, it would be▲

J: ▼*How much money were you going to provide?*

2.2.3 A-B-C pattern

This is the case where in the middle of the examination of the defendant by the prosecutor, the judge suddenly cuts in, interrupting the defendant as in the following:

Example 3

P: As regards this case, the charged facts, I want you to talk about the process, the causes of the facts, talk about them, how you got to know those people, how you got those businesses and how you began talking about them in the first place?

D: According to the indictment?

P: Yes.

D: This, the business, according to the indictment, but there are some incorrect points in it, can I point them out first and then I tell you the process?

P: Well, you can correct them if there are. What I mean is you talk about the cause, how the whole thing got started, and the process.

D: The whole thing started in the beginning of 1995. ------ This is the first point. The second is, as for the second contract, I am really not clear about it. But later, after I resigned from my position in 1997, Wang Zhaoli of the new leadership of the company told me in 1998 that the second contract▲

J: ▼*The defendant, please keep to the facts of the case, the facts of the case, understand? The prosecutor asked you to talk about the facts of the case*▲

D: ▼I just finished the first contract and as for the second one▲

J: ▼*You are required to keep to the facts of the case.*

D: I was just talking about the second loan contract▲

J: ▼*Did you hear me, the defendant?*

D: Yes. I did.

2.3 Interruption: the position

The position where interruption takes place is another indicator of power imbalance as different parts of an utterance or a turn vary in semantic or discourse importance. As we know, the beginning of an utterance can often be the most important, and consequently interruption in the beginning will cause greater damage to both the syntactic and semantic completeness.

2.3.1 The judge or the prosecutor interrupting the defendant

The place where the judge or the public prosecutor interrupts the defendant is often the beginning or the middle of an utterance or a turn. Therefore, the defendant's utterances or turns are often not complete in terms of syntax and meaning as can be seen from the following:

Example 4

J: The first eight million, the second eight million, did you get it back after you lent it?
D: After we lent▲
J: ▼*Did it come back on schedule?*
D: The interest came back on time.

2.3.2 The defendant interrupting the prosecutor or the judge

Most of the time, when the defendant interrupts the judge or the prosecutor, s/he does so near to the transition relevance place (TRP), showing consideration for the syntactic or semantic completeness of the utterance of the judge or the prosecutor as shown in the following:

Example 5

P: Well, then the old lady would go back to get money?
D: Yeah.
P: To get gold or silver things?
D: Yeah.
P: Then who of you followed her when she went back to get money?
D: That one of us who had been following us, listening to our conversation.
P: The one following you listening?
D: Yeah.
P: What happened when the old lady came back to you with the money‖To whom did she give the money?
D: When the lady came back with the money, we just took the money and told her to come back to us in three days.

Obviously, the defendant interrupted the prosecutor as soon as the latter had finished the first question, assuming that would be the end of the prosecutor's utterance or turn.

2.4 Interruption: Meta-interruptive speech acts

'Meta-interruptive speech acts' are those that are used to indicate that you want to interrupt the current speaker or you are interrupting the current speaker. Interruptions can be performed with or without meta-interruptive acts. There are three kinds of such acts: (1) meta-interruptive speech acts using the word *interrupt*, (2) meta-interruptive speech acts using words like *stop*, *say no more*, or *none of this stuff (nonsense)*, and (3) meta-interruptive speech acts telling the reason for interrupting. Interruption is disruptive and (normally) rude, and the degree of the disruption and rudeness can be reduced or enhanced by the use of different meta-interruptive speech acts. The least disruptive or rude is the use of meta-interruptive speech acts with the word *interrupt*. The most disruptive is to use *stop*, *say no more* or *none of this stuff*, especially when used with a harsh tone or derogatory words. In between are interruptions using meta-interruptive speech acts indicating the reason for interruption and those without any meta-interruptive speech acts. I have found that when the judge has to interrupt the prosecutor, s/he tends to use speech acts with the word *interrupt*; that is, the least disruptive or rude, and never or very rarely does so with the defence lawyer or the defendant, as in:

Example 6

J: The prosecutor may continue to read or present the evidence please.

P: Now I'd like to read the fourth item in the table of contents of the evidence, the auditor's report, which shows the payments, debts and capital flow of the eight letters of credit opened by Tiancheng Company as well as no importation of any real goods. Then we will show the relevant documentary evidence. Wuhan Changcheng Accounting Company Ltd, the 156th▲

J: ▼*I'd like to interrupt you. I'd like to interrupt you. Could you just read the conclusions?*

P: Yes.

But when the judge interrupts the defence lawyer, s/he will switch to a less respectful meta-interruptive speech act, as in:

Example 7

L: ------ I think the defendant should be Hanpeng Company because it not only violated the commercial ethics, broke the law, but also infringed the rules of games of the Company Law. What is worse, they cheated the leaders concerned of Wuhan Municipal Government and caused serious damage to the image of the Municipal Government as well as to the soft environment for the development of Wuhan both at home and abroad. I do ask the court to make a thorough investigation of this. I would also like to remind the people present today in the gallery, especially those comrades who work in the disciplinary committee of the

Communist Party, as I once also worked in the disciplinary committee. I want to also draw the attention of my occupation to this issue▲

J: ▼*Defence lawyer, none of the nonsense unrelated with this case.*

And when it comes to interrupting the defendant, the situation is worse:

Example 8

D: My family and I are expecting justice with tears in our eyes. For four years, I have been confined to a room of 20 square meters in a detention house. ------ I have spent the four years in this way. I am now on the brink of a mental breakdown. What I am most longing for now is not freedom, but a good night's sleep in a dark quiet night. I am also thinking of a famous case involving the two innocent defendants Yang Naiwu and Xiao Baicai in the Qing Dynasty, when there was an official in the Board of Punishments, who ventured to report the case to the throne▲

J: ▼*None of this, none of this nonsense and we've got no time for this nonsense.* In this court▲

D: ▼Why did he report it to the throne? Because some of the officials in charge of the case simply wanted to stall and wait until one of the defendants died in jail. ------ Now I want to ask the court (---), I ask the court to keep up with the times, get freed from those untimely ideas and unfettered from the dogmatic and erroneous understanding of Marxism, subjectivism and metaphysics. I was brought up with Communist Party's education and I have always wanted to do something for our society. I did not purposely ignore the court or the law. In this case, I simply tried to collect funds from Hong Kong and Beijing and used them in Wuhan. Since there is no specific law forbidding this, why couldn't I make some contribution to the development of Wuhan by this means? Here and now I have no demands on the court. I thank the judge for your guidance and instruction. I am only expecting justice done to me. I am expecting justice from you judges and you prosecutors who wear the national emblem on their hats and have power in their hands. I thank the court.

Here, the judge repeats the meta-interruptive speech act (*none of this*------) three times to show his annoyance and impatience at what the defendant was saying.

2.5 Interruption: the function

The judge or the prosecutor uses interruption mainly to: (1) control the defendant by stopping him or her from saying more than is necessary or saying anything irrelevant, (2) press the defendant for more information if what is said is less than necessary, or (3) scold, condemn or criticize him/her. The defendant uses interruption mostly to: (1) insist on his/her floor, or (2) provide cooperation.

2.5.1 The judge or the prosecutor interrupting the defendant

2.5.1.1 SAY NOTHING MORE THAN NECESSARY

The judge or the prosecutor usually does not allow the defendant to give explanations, so a considerable number of interruptions take place in the *because* clause or clauses elaborating causes for what was said or done, as in:

Example 9

D: They told me over the phone that we would go fortune telling.
P: They told you to go fortune telling?
D: Yes, yes. At that time, I didn't know it would be a crime. I thought we would just wander about, like itinerant entertainers or craftsmen, telling fortunes for people.
P: Yeah.
D: Because my family was badly off (started sobbing), ‖because my child was disabled.
P: ‖You just answer my questions honestly. Do not talk that much about things irrelevant with this case. Tell honestly those facts related to this case, will you? How many times did you get involved in the swindling?

2.5.1.2 PRESS FOR INFORMATION AND CONFESSION: SAY WHAT I NEED.

When the defendant hesitates or is slow in providing answers, the judge or the prosecutor will interrupt the defendant and urge him/her to give the answer to the question, leaving the defendant no time or opportunity to think of a way to avoid the question, or think of an excuse, or say anything irrelevant, or give more information than required:

Example 10

P: Whose car was it?
D: It was his, I guess.
P: Who is the owner of the car?
D: The owner of the car, the owner of the car is---‖
P: ‖Is the car yours?

2.5.1.3 KEEP THE DEFENDANT ON TRACK

Keep what you say to the point.

Example 11

D: ------ But later, at the end of 1997, I resigned from my post, and in 1998 Wang XX of the new leadership told me that the second loan contract▲
J: ▼*Defendant, please keep to the facts of this case, keep to the facts of this case, ok? The prosecutor asked you to talk about the facts of this case*▲
D: ▼I have finished the first loan contract. Now as for the second loan contract▲
J: ▼*Keep to the facts of the case.*
D: I am talking exactly about the second loan agreement▲

J: ▼*Did you hear me, defendant?*
D: Yes, I do.

2.5.1.4. CONDEMNATION

The judge interrupts the defendant to blame, criticize or condemn him/her.

Example 12

J: On the, on the loan agreement you signed, in the name of what did your company get the loan?
D: In the name of perhaps circulating funds, that is, a loan used to develop business.
J: What?
D: I---specifically, used to develop business. As for the forms, I didn't fill them in because the financial department did it. They only asked me to give my signature. After I asked▲
J: ▼*They only asked you to give your signature. Look at what you've done!* It was such a large sum of money, didn't you go over it?
D: I did. I had a look and it seemed to me that it was several years ago, perhaps it was the circulating fund.

2.5.2 The defendant interrupting the judge or the prosecutor

There are two main reasons for the defendant to interrupt the judge or the prosecutor. The first is to show his/her eagerness to provide the required information, as illustrated by the following, where the defendant interrupts his/her interlocutor at an appropriate place; that is, what is inserted is in syntactic agreement with the interrupted utterance:

Example 13

P: For such a large sum of investment---just now you said you didn't even have a meeting to discuss it, right? *According to what you said, to your* ▲
D: ▼*superior in charge*▲
P: ▼*you reported it, right?*
D: Right.

The second reason for the defendant to interrupt the judge or the prosecutor is to insist with his/her own topic in his/her previous turn, giving explanations or defending him/herself: this is usually by the defendants who do not plead guilty:

Example 14

P: In your opinion, you should not be held responsible for any problem that arose in the operation of this business, should you?
D: Well, it is not that I should not be held responsible for any problem at all, but that I simply couldn't imagine those problems at the time.
P: But just now you said▲
D: ▼*We did take every measure possible to prevent*▲

P: ▼Just now you made it very clear that according to the regulations of the company this business should have been discussed at a meeting and put on file, is that right?
D: Yes, according to the regulations.
P: But you did not follow the regulations, did you?

3. Discussion and conclusions

It is amply evident from the above analysis that interruption is a very important indicator of power or the power relationship in Chinese criminal courtroom discourse. Power or the power relationship is seriously imbalanced in criminal courtroom interaction. This imbalance exists in the following ways: (1) the judge or the prosecutor interrupts most and the defendant is the most interrupted; (2) interruptions of the defendant's utterances predominantly take place in the beginning or the middle, while interruptions of the judge's or the prosecutor's utterances mostly take place towards the end, near or at TRP; (3) the judge or the prosecutor can successively interrupt the defendant while the reverse is seldom true; (4) when the judge or the prosecutor and the defendant interrupt each other, it usually ends with the former interrupting the latter; (5) when the judge has to interrupt the prosecutor, s/he tends to use a meta-interruptive speech act which is least disruptive; when s/he interrupts the defendant or the defence lawyer, s/he tends to adopt a meta-interruptive speech act which is less polite; and (6) the judge or the prosecutor uses interruption to control or to scold the defendant, while most interruptions by the defendant are cooperative or efforts in continuing the floor.

Current findings have important implications for the study of both power and discourse. Locher (2004) summarized some points of consensus in recent studies on power and language in terms of the following: (1) the exercise of power may occur in any kind of situation where two or more people interact, (2) power is (often) expressed through language, (3) power is relational, dynamic and unstable, (4) the interconnectedness of language and society can also be seen in the display of power, (5) the exercise of power involves a latent conflict and clash of interests, which can be obscured because of a society's ideologies, and (6) the exercise of power is often accompanied by displays of unmarked or positively marked relational work in order to maintain the social equilibrium and to negotiate ideologies. My findings suggest that the emphasis on the dynamics of power should not be exaggerated in such a way as to obscure the fact that power is inevitably associated with social, political and economic status and institutional roles. Those who are politically, economically or socially privileged are endowed with more power than those who are disadvantaged. If we ignore this, we would be deceiving others as well as ourselves. Consequently, I propose that a critical analysis of imbalance in social interaction and the consequences resulting from the imbalance should remain the focus of critical discourse analysis and other socially-oriented disciplines. This has been shown in the current study where the imbalance in power in terms of interruption might have serious consequences in the way justice or injustice is done to those 'powerless' participants. What is more, the imbalance most often exists in linguistic details, such as interruptions, which tend to be ignored. Therefore, greater attention should be paid to institutional discourse in discourse studies. This does not mean that the study of everyday conversation is already exhausted or unimportant, but rather that linguistic phenomena such as interruption in institutional settings (e.g. courtroom) are significantly more important in social terms than in non-institutional settings.

These findings lend strong support to the view that the exercise of power involves a latent conflict and clash of interests which may be obscured because of a society's ideologies. Interruption in the courtroom is highly strategic and goal-oriented, or more exactly, interest-motivated. What is more, the goals or interests are more often than not conflicting rather than shared. This explains why those classical theories or models such as the Cooperative Principle (Grice 1975) and the Communicative Act Theory (Habermas 1984) turn out to be impotent when applied to institutional discourse (Sarangi 1992, Harris 1995). Therefore, I propose that a new model for discourse analysis, especially institutional discourse analysis, be formulated in such a way as to consider goals and relationships in terms of goals as the core or starting point, which not only addresses communicative action (Habermas 1984) or cooperative interaction, but also strategic action or non-cooperative interaction (Liao 2003a/b, 2005a/b/c, 2009, 2010, 2012).

Appendix 1: Notes for transcription symbols

(1) ▲▼ for simple interruption
(2) |||| for overlap interruption
(3) --- for drawling
(4) (---) for utterance not clear
(5) ------ for omission
(6) ⊥ for repair

References

Adler, M. and Longhurst, B. 1994. *Discourse, Power and Justice*. London: Routledge.

Berger, C. 1994. Power, dominance, and social interaction, in *Handbook of Interpersonal Communication*, edited by M.L. Knapp and G.R. Miller. Thousand Oaks: Sage, 450-507.

Beattie, G.W. 1981. Interruption in conversational interaction, and its relation to the sex and status of the interactants. *Linguistics*, 19, 15-35.

Bilous, F.R. and Krauss, R.M. 1988. Dominance and accommodation in the conversational behaviors of same- and mixed-gender dyads. *Language and Communication*, 8, 183-194.

Bogoch, B. and Danet, B. 1984. Challenge and control in lawyer–client interaction: a case study in an Israeli legal aid office, *Text* 4(1-3), 247-273.

Bourdieu, P. 1991. *Language and Symbolic Power*. Cambridge: Cambridge University Press.

Chimombo, M. and Roseberry, R. 1998. *The Power of Discourse: An Introduction to Discourse Analysis*. Hillsdale, NJ: Lawrence Erlbaum Associates.

Conley, J. 1998. *Just Words*. Chicago: The University of Chicago Press.

Conley, J., O'Barr, W. and Lind, A. 1998. The power of language: presentational style in the courtroom. *Duke Law Journal*, 1375.

Cotterill, J. 2002. *Language and Power in Court: A Linguistic Analysis of the O.J. Simpson Trial*. London: Palgrave Macmillan.

Danet, B. 1980a. 'Baby' or 'fetus'?: language and the construction of reality in a manslaughter trial. *Semiotica*, 32, 187-219.

Danet, B. 1980b. Language in the courtroom, in *Language: Social and Psychological Perspectives*, edited by H. Giles, P. Smith, and P. Robinson. Oxford: Pergamon, 367-376.

Danet, B. and Kermish, N. 1978. Courtroom questioning: a sociolinguistic perspective, in *Psychology and Persuasion in Advocacy*, edited by L.N. Massery. Washington, DC: Association of Trial Lawyers of America, 412-444.

Dindia, K. 1987. The effects of sex of subject and sex of partner on interruptions. *Human Communication Research*, 13, 345-371.

Ehrlich, S. 2001. *Representing Rape*. London: Routledge.

Fairclough, N. 1989. *Language and Power*. London: Longman.

Ferguson, N. 1977. Simultaneous speech, interruptions and dominance. *British Journal of Social and Clinical Psychology*, 16, 295-302.

Foucault, M. 1982. The Subject and Power. *Critical Inquiry*, 8(4), 777-795.

Fowler, R., Hodge, R., Kress, G. and Trew, T. 1979. *Language and Control*. London: Routledge and Kegan Paul.

Froman, C. 1996. *Language and Power*. Atlantic Highlands, NJ: Humanities Press.

Gal, S. 1995. Language, gender, and power: an anthropological review, in *Gender Articulated: Language and Socially Constructed Self*, edited by K. Hall and M. Bucholtz, London: Routledge, 169-182.

Gibbons, J. 2003. *Forensic Linguistics: An Introduction to Language in the Justice System*. Melbourne: Blackwell.

Grice, H.P. 1975. Logic and conversation, in *Syntax and Semantics III: Speech Act*, edited by P. Cole and J. Morgan. New York: Academic Press, 41-58.

Habermas, J. 1984. *The Theory of Communicative Action. Reason and the Rationalization of Society*. Volume 1. Boston, MA: Beacon Press.

Harris, S. 1995. Pragmatics and power. *Journal of Pragmatics*, 27, 117-135.

Hawkins, K. 1991. Some consequences of deep interruption in task-oriented communication. *Journal of Language & Social Psychology*, 10, 185-203.

Holmes, J. 1991. Language and gender. *Language Teaching*, 24, 207-220.

Kedar, L. 1987. *Power through Discourse.* Norwood, NJ: Ablex Publishing Corporation.

Kedar, L., Kollock, P., Blumstein, P. and Schwartz, P. 1985. Sex and power in interaction: conversational privileges and duties. *American Sociological Review*, 50, 34-46.

Lakoff, R. 1990. *Talking Power: The Politeness of Language.* New York: Basic Books.

Li, H.Z., Krysko, M, Desroches, N. and Deagle, G. 2004. Re-conceptualizing interruptions in physician-patient interview: cooperative and intrusive Communication and Medicine: an interdisciplinary Journal of Healthcare, *Ethics and Society*, 1(2), 145-157.

Liao, M.Z. 2003a. *A Study on Courtroom Questions, Responses and their Interaction: A Linguistic Perspective.* Beijing: Law Press.

Liao, M.Z. 2003b. A field report from the Chinese courtroom. *Law and Life*, 6, 1-15.

Liao, M.Z. 2004. *Courtroom Questions, Responses and their Interaction.* Beijing: Law Press.

Liao, M.Z. 2005a. *Trial Communication Strategies.* Beijing: Law Press.

Liao, M.Z. 2005b. The principle of goal and goal analysis: a new way of doing pragmatics. *Rhetorical Learning*, 3, 1-10.

Liao, M.Z. 2005c. The principle of goal and goal analysis: a new way of doing pragmatics. *Rhetorical Learning*, 4, 5-11.

Liao, M. Z. 2009. A study of interruption in Chinese criminal courtroom discourse. *Text & Talk*, 29(2), 175-200.

Liao, M.Z. 2010. A comparative study of Chinese and American criminal sentencing discourse. *ESP Across Cultures*, 7, 105-128.

Liao, M.Z. 2012. Courtroom discourse in China, in *Oxford Handbook on Language and Law*, edited by L. Solan and P. Tiersma. Oxford: Oxford University Press, 395-407.

Locher, M. 2004. *Power and Politeness in Action: Disagreements in Oral Communication.* Berlin: Mouton de Gruyter.

Marche, T.A. and Peterson, C. 1993. The development and sex-related use of interruption behavior. *Human Communication Research*, 19, 388-408.

Mayr, A. 2008. *Language and Power: An Introduction to Institutional Discourse.* London: Continuum.

Ng, S.H. and Bradac, J. 1993. *Power in Language.* Thousand Oaks: Sage Publications.

Okamoto, D., Rashotte, L.S. and Smith-Lovin, L. 2002. Measuring interruption: Syntactic and contextual methods of coding conversation. *Social Psychology Quarterly.* 65, 92-102.

Sarangi, S. and Slembrouck, S. 1992. Non-cooperation in communication: a reassessment of Gricean pragmatics. *Journal of Pragmatics*, 17, 117-154.

Tannen, D. 1994. *Gender and Discourse.* New York/Oxford: Oxford University Press.

Tannen, D. 2003. Power maneuvers or connection maneuvers? Ventriloquizing in family interaction, in *Linguistics, Language, and the Real World: Discourse and Beyond: Georgetown University Round Table on Languages and Linguistics*, edited by D. Tannen and J.E. Alatis. Washington, DC: Georgetown University Press, 50-62.

van Dijk, T.A. 1989. Structures of discourse and structures of power. *Communication Yearbook*, 12, 18-59.

van Dijk, T.A. 1996. Discourse, power and access, in *Texts and Practices: Readings in Critical Discourse Analysis*, edited by R.C. Caldas-Coulthard and M. Coulthard. London: Routledge and Kegal Paul, 84-104.

van Dijk, T.A. 2009. *Discourse and Power.* New York: Palgrave Macmillan.

Wartenberg, T. 1990. *The Forms of Power: From Domination to Transformation.* Philadelphia: Temple University Press.

Watts, R. 1991. *Power in Family Discourse.* Berlin/New York: Mouton de Gruyter.

Weigand, E. and Dascal, M. 2001. *Negotiation and Power in Dialogic Interaction.* Amsterdam/Philadelphia: John Benjamins.

Wodak, R. 1989. The irrationality of power. *Communication Yearbook*, 12, 76-94.

Zimmerman, D.H. and West, C. 1975. Sex roles, interruptions and silences in conversation, in *Language and Sex: Differences and Dominance*, edited by B. Thorne and N. Henley. Rowley, MA: Newbury House, 105-129.

Chapter 3

'For the reasons given above, I consider that the Court should...': A linguistic analysis of argumentation in the opinions of British and Italian Advocates-General at the Court of Justice of the European Union

Judith Turnbull

1. Introduction

The analysis in this chapter is part of an ongoing research into the language, style and rhetoric of judges at the Court of Justice of the European Union (Turnbull 2010, 2011). The study has been investigating to what extent and in what way the 27 judges and eight Advocates-General (henceforth AGs) working in the Court have adapted the conventions of their legal cultures to the new multicultural context. The judges and AGs come from all member states and hence from different legal systems, which can be grouped according to the classical distinction between common law and civil law. The Court is, therefore, to all intents and purposes a melting pot of legal cultures.

The earlier work analyzed the overtly direct and personal expressions of AGs and their expressions of politeness when agreeing or disagreeing with the parties involved in the case. The present study will examine the way AGs organize and present their argumentation by examining the judicial decisions of British and Italian AGs in the Court as representative of the two classes of legal systems. Indeed, the very nature of these systems determines a specific and characteristic style and rhetoric in the drafting of judgments. To quote an Italian jurist, Italian judgments 'are conceived and written as bureaucratic documents ... the formal explanation of an impersonal decision' (Taruffo 1988: 207, my translation). They consist in a linear concatenation of points which are explained individually to justify the final decision and to prove its validity (Scarpa and Riley 2000: 254). In contrast, in common law systems, judgments of the higher courts are one of the main sources of the law, hence the term judge-made law. Furthermore, the oral tradition of English judgments (Charnock 2010) is reflected in their personalized and discursive style, which has been described as 'conversational, combative or rhetorical' (Lord Hope of Craighead 2005: 1). English judgments are less linear and take into consideration all the various arguments presented by the parties, discuss various hypotheses and closely follow the logic behind the reasoning of the judge. In other words, the deductive and abstract approach adopted in Italian judgments which aims to give a rational explanation of the judicial decision to prove its validity (especially on questions of law) is in stark contrast to the rhetoric of English judgments. The latter trace the logical thought processes followed by judges in their reasoning based on facts as much as on questions of law (Scarpa and Riley 2000: 254). This study aims to assess the similarities and differences which can be found in the argumentation of British and Italian AGs in their Opinions.

2. Corpus and methodology

The analysis was made on a corpus of the Opinions of British and Italian AGs of the Court of Justice,[1] rather than the actual judgments of the Court which are the result of a collegiate decision. AGs sit alone in Court, independently of the panel of judges, and present their Opinion, usually in their native language, on the legal solution to the case before the judges deliberate and deliver their judgment. The function or purpose of an Opinion is purely advisory, but in most cases it is followed by the Court. The corpus is made up of 40 Opinions, 20 for each nationality. The Opinions were selected at random and are of varying length, covering a period of ten years. AGs are appointed for a renewable term of six years, so there is not a frequent turnover; as a result, the corpus includes Opinions of four Italian but only two British AGs. Considerable allowance must be given therefore to idiolectal usage and personal preferences of expression.

The study followed a discourse analysis approach and is purely linguistic in its focus. However, argumentation theory provides a useful framework to guide and structure the analysis. Traditionally, research in legal argumentation has been dominated by the logical and rhetorical approaches that analyze argumentation, respectively, as a form of reasoning consisting of premises which lead to a certain conclusion or as an attempt to convince a certain audience (Toulmin 1958, Perelman and Olbrechts-Tyteca 1969). These two approaches would seem to mirror the judgment styles of the Italian and British legal systems. This study, instead, draws on the pragma-dialectical theory of argumentation developed by van Eemeren and Houtlosser (1999, 2006) and Van Eemeren et al. (2008). The theory aims to bridge the gap between these traditions by combining a dialectical view of argumentative reasonableness with a pragmatic view of the verbal moves made in the discourse. To accommodate the rhetorical dimension of argumentation, that is, its persuasive function, the theory evaluates strategic manoeuvring which 'exploits the opportunities afforded by the dialectical situation for steering the discourse

1 All Opinions, including those quoted in this paper, are available online at the Court of Justice of the European Union's website, http://curia.europa.eu/jcms/jcms/j_6/.

strategically in the direction that serves their [the participants'] own interests best' (van Eemeren and Houtlosser 1999: 481). The study of argumentation has certainly a normative as well as a descriptive dimension. However, given the status and authority of the Court and its judges, it can be presumed that standards of reasonableness are maintained.

A primarily qualitative approach was followed, since argumentative text can only be evaluated properly by a careful analysis of the discourse in order to identify and reconstruct the argumentative process and moves. Nevertheless, the ConcApp concordancer and text analyzer was also used to test and confirm hypotheses.

3. The pragma-dialectical model of argumentation applied to AGs' Opinions

Within the pragma-dialectical framework 'argumentation is viewed as a type of communication aimed at resolving a difference of opinion by critically testing the acceptability of standpoints' (van Eemeren et al. 2008: 476). It adopts a model of critical discussion developed by van Eemeren and Houtlosser (1999: 480) which is an analytical description of what argumentative discourse would be like if it were solely and optimally aimed at resolving a difference of opinion. The model is divided into four phases: *confrontation*, in which the difference of opinion is defined; *opening*, which establishes the starting point of the discussion and what the discussion is actually about; *argumentation*, where the arguments are exchanged; and lastly, *concluding phase*, in which the result of the discussion is determined.

The theory can be applied to any type or form of discussion in which parties are interested in resolving a difference in their favour. In the case of judicial opinions, an example of a specific institutionalized form of argumentation (Feteris 2000: 118), the structure and procedure of argumentation are 'simplified'. Firstly, institutional constraints in the context of law courts and procedural rules condition and regulate the 'discussion', guaranteeing the standard of reasonableness. Secondly, there is only one 'voice', that of the judge, who is not directly involved in the difference of opinion, but adjudicates as a third party.

Opinions follow a standard form which has been introduced to eliminate fundamental differences arising from the conventions of different legal systems in the member states (Rega 1997: 118) and are structured in four parts, which also conveniently correspond to the four phases of the discussion model. In Table 3.1, the headings of the various sections in the Opinions written by British and Italian AGs are those that appear most frequently in the corpus, but they vary according to the type of case and the personal style of the AG.

Table 3.1 Structure of opinions

Phase of critical discussion model	British	Italian
Confrontation	Question Relevant legislation (Community and national)	Introduzione Contesto normativo
Opening	Facts and procedures	Fatti, procedimento principale, questioni pregiudiziali
Argumentation	Assessment	Analisi giuridica
Concluding	Conclusions	Conclusioni

Unlike a discussion in other contexts, the confrontation and opening phases in a judicial opinion are easily determined as the questions or issues to be considered are specified in the order for reference to the Court. The judge starts the Opinion by recalling the details and reporting the facts and earlier legal proceedings. The concluding phase is also easily identified as it involves a formulaic declaration of the kind: *I accordingly consider that ... , I therefore take the view that the Court should ... , Propongo pertanto alla Corte di dichiarare ... , Ritengo di conseguenza che ...* . The *Assessment* section of the Opinions proves to be the most complex, as it is here that the judge presents and discusses the arguments submitted to the Court by the parties involved and of those not directly involved in the case, such as that of the Commission or national governments. This section will, therefore, be the object of the present analysis.

Following in the tradition of the civil law system, the different questions raised in the case and hence in the assessment section are dealt with separately and individually. The discussion of each issue follows a general pattern, which also corresponds to the four phases of the critical discussion model (Table 3.2). Firstly, there is a statement about the applicant's case, corresponding to Confrontation, a definition of the question being heard in the Opening, followed by the Argumentation section made up of the presentation of the parties' arguments, the statement of the AG's position (dis/agreement with the parties) and his/her defence of or explanation for the decision; and lastly the Concluding phase in which the opinion of the AG is pronounced.

As the Opinions are written texts reporting on the hearings before the Court and there is no direct confrontation between the AG and the parties involved, the strategic manoeuvring in the text cannot be considered as responses to an opponent's argumentation, but rather as a well-managed structuring of the argumentation to maximize the clarity and the persuasive force of the discourse (Salmi-Tolonen 2005). Van Eemeren and Houtlosser (2006: 383) have identified three aspects of strategic manoeuvring: the 'topical potential', the 'audience-directed framing' of argumentative moves, and the purposive use of 'presentational devices'. Often

Table 3.2 The argumentation (assessment) section of an opinion

Confrontation	Statement about applicant's case
Opening	Defining questions raised
Argumentation	Statement of AG's position *(dis/agreement)* Presentation of the parties' arguments *(+ submissions from the Commission, national governments or others)* Defence of/explanation for decision *(case-law, assessment of arguments, reference to directives, etc.)*
Concluding phase	Conclusion

strategic manoeuvring consists in a combination of the strategic use of all three in an integrated way.

The 'topical potential' is the possible discourse moves available at a particular stage in the discussion which, in the case of Opinions, is obviously limited by the questions and arguments presented by the parties and the fairly rigid structure of the text type. As for the audience, an Opinion is composed, first and foremost, for the panel of judges who will receive it before deliberating its own judgment. The purely advisory nature of the Opinions may to some extent influence the form and force of argumentation adopted by the AGs. Presentational devices are the 'indicators' of argumentative discourse which are used to organize, structure and mark the moves in argumentation (van Eemeren and Houstlesser 2007). 'Indicators' is, in fact, an umbrella term which covers a variety of expressions that do not belong to any specific grammatical categories and may be single words or phrases, as for example *It follows that ...* , *ne discende che ...* . Some of these expressions may be explicit and straightforward, such as *hence*, *in contrast*, *anzitutto*, *pertanto*, whilst others may be less so.

In Opinions, the argumentative moves developed in the course of the discussion are primarily establishing the standpoints of the parties, their acceptance or refusal and criticism by the AG and the burden of proof (in the philosophical sense of providing sufficient warrant). The indicators therefore serve a number of functions and appear to work at two levels – at a macro level to signal the main argumentative moves, such as acceptance or refusal, and at a micro level to direct the internal structure of the reasoning (burden of proof).

The 'macro' indicators of the argumentative moves are usually easily identified; for example, in the case of acceptance we find expressions such as *I agree with*, *I am of the view*, *I accept*, *condivido*, *convengo*. However, there is also enormous variety, especially when there is a need to modify the force of an assertion as in the case of the rejection of an argument (Turnbull 2010: 147-151):

(1) However, I do not think that such a conclusion would be warranted. (C-128/05)[2]
(2) All those arguments, however, manifestly go beyond the scope of the question referred by the national court … (C-347-03)
(3) La tesi, per quanto suggestiva, non convince. (C-27/98)
[This argument, though interesting, is not convincing.]
(4) … mi sembra costituisca un approccio interpretativo piuttosto miope. (C-362/07)
[… seems to me to represent a rather short-sighted interpretative approach.]

At a micro level, indicators signal result or consequence, explain cause and effect, define, emphasize, sequence, concede, compare, exemplify, contrast and add new information. The following are a few examples of micro indicators according to their function.

Table 3.3 Examples of indicators according to function

	English	Italian
1. Indicating result/ consequence	therefore, thus, consequently, hence, accordingly	pertanto, quindi, di conseguenza, perciò
2. Explaining cause/ effect	since, because, given that	dal momento che, perché, poiché, considerando che, in quanto
3. Qualifying/defining	in particular, essentially, specifically	in particolare, in sostanza, essenzialmente, sostanzialmente
4. Contrasting	however, none the less, by/in contrast, rather, but	tuttavia, piuttosto, però, ma, invece, per contro
5. Comparing	while, whereas, on the one/other hand, similarly, equally	da un lato/dall'altro, per un verso/per l'altro verso, mentre, così come
6. Emphasizing/ reinforcing	indeed, in fact, in other words, that is to say	infatti, in effetti, vale a dire, in altri termini
7. Listing/sequencing	first(ly), second(ly), third(ly), finally	(in)anzitutto, in primo/ secondo/terzo luogo, infine
8. Conceding	while, whilst, although, even if, it is true	sebbene, anche se, è vero, certo
9. Adding	moreover, furthermore, besides, in addition	inoltre, altresì, oltre a, si aggiunge che
10. Exemplifying	for example, for instance, by way of example	ad esempio, per esempio

4. Analysis of two texts

The following extracts were taken from the assessment section of an English and an Italian Opinion, chosen partly on the basis of their manageable length. Each

2 The references given in brackets are the case numbers of the Opinions.

text deals with and completes the discussion of one of the questions raised in the case with the AG's position clearly stated. The numbers at the beginning refer to the paragraphs in the original text.

4.1 The British AG's Opinion

(5) *The first ground of appeal*

22. The applicant submits first that the Court of First Instance misinterpreted Article 43(2) and (3) of Regulation No 40/94 in conjunction with Article 15(3) thereof when taking into account use of the VITAFRUT mark by a third party. In particular, the applicant contends that the Court of First Instance misinterpreted the apportionment of the burden of proof provided for in Article 15(1) and (3), took into account non-conclusive (implicit) statements and evidence produced by the opposing party and relied on presumptions instead of solid evidence.

23. Article 15(1) is not relevant to the present case since it is limited to sanctions for non-use of a Community trade mark. I shall assume that the applicant intended to refer to Article 43(2), applicable by virtue of Article 43(3). It is however correct that Article 15(3) is applicable by analogy to opposition proceedings based on an earlier trade mark. That provision states that use of the mark 'with the consent of the proprietor shall be deemed to constitute use by the proprietor'.

24. In essence the applicant's complaint is that the Court of First Instance did not properly examine whether use of the mark by a third party constituted use by the opposing party within the meaning of Article 15(3).

25. I consider that the Court of First Instance correctly examined that question.

26. The Court of First Instance stated that where an opposing party maintains that use by a third party constitutes genuine use 'he claims, by implication, that he consented to that use'.

27. It went on to make two specific points. First, if the use by the third party was without the proprietor's consent, the use would have infringed the proprietor's trade mark right and it would therefore evidently have been in the third party's interest not to disclose evidence thereof to the proprietor. It consequently seems unlikely that the proprietor would be in a position to submit evidence of such use.

28. That approach seems eminently sensible. It would be pointless and contrary to the principles of sound administration and procedural economy for OHIM as a matter of course to require a trade mark proprietor to adduce evidence of consent in such circumstances.

29. The matter would of course be different if the applicant had raised before OHIM the issue of the lack of consent. That however is the Court of First Instance's second point: there was nothing in the documents before it suggesting that the applicant in the present case had done so.

30. The Court of First Instance accordingly concluded that the above factors 'formed a sufficiently firm basis to allow the Board of Appeal to conclude that the earlier trade mark had been used with its proprietor's consent'. I agree with that conclusion and consider that the Court of First Instance did not err with regard to the burden of proof.

31. The applicant makes a further point under its first ground of appeal which I confess to finding some difficulty in following.

32. The applicant states that, according to *KLEENCARE*, the Court of First Instance should have decided itself whether, at the time of its ruling, a new decision with the same operative part as the decision of the Board of Appeal of OHIM could have been lawfully adopted. That court therefore erred in law when stating that OHIM could rely at the time of adopting the decision of the Board of Appeal on the presumption that the proprietor of the VITAFRUT trademark consented to the use of that mark by a third party.

33. Paragraphs 25, 26 and 29 of *KLEENCARE* read as follows:

> 'The case-law shows that … a new decision with the same operative part as the decision under appeal may be lawfully adopted at the time of the appeal ruling.'

34. Those paragraphs essentially concern the powers of the Boards of Appeal to rule on the basis of new facts or evidence which were not before the examiner or other departments of OHIM deciding on the application at first instance. In that context they were explicitly considered and applied by the Court of First Instance in its determination that the first part of the applicant's first plea was admissible. I do not however see how those powers of the Boards of Appeal are relevant to the powers of the Court of First Instance when hearing an appeal from a decision of a Board of Appeal, where there is clearly no continuity of function.

35. I would accordingly dismiss the applicant's first ground of appeal as unfounded.

(Extract from Opinion C-416/04)

The four phases of the critical discussion model can be identified as Confrontation in paragraph 22, the Opening in paragraphs 23-24, Argumentation in paragraphs 25-34, and the Conclusion in paragraph 35. Understandably, the Argumentation section is the longest.

In fact, indicators are used primarily to specify, concede and list in this text. Some are explicit:

(6) … *In particular*, the applicant contends that the Court of First Instance misinterpreted the apportionment of the burden of proof provided for in Article 15(1) and (3) …

(7) It is *however* correct that Article 15(3) is applicable by analogy to opposition proceedings based on an earlier trade mark.

(8) It went on to make *two specific points. First*, if the use by the third party was without the proprietor's consent …

(9) *It went on to make two specific points, First …*

(10) The applicant makes a further point under its first ground of appeal which I confess to finding some difficulty in following … That, however, is the Court of Instance's second point.

But others are indirect indicators, often used to express the AG's position on certain points, thus attenuating his (dis)agreement or criticism:

(11) Article 15(1) *is not relevant to the present case* since it is limited to sanctions for non-use of a Community trade mark. I shall assume that the applicant intended to refer to Article 43(2), applicable by virtue of Article 43(3).

Although the phrase *Article 15(1) is not relevant to the present case since ...* is not actually an explicit indicator, the AG's rejection of Article 15(1) narrows down the issue to be discussed.

In paragraph 28, the AG indirectly confirms his agreement with the Court through the positive evaluative expression of the Court's decision and the negative evaluation of the applicant's argument:

(12) *That approach seems eminently sensible. It would seem pointless and contrary to the principles of sound administration ...*

It is interesting to note that in (25), beginning the Argumentation section, the AG expresses his position in agreement with the Court of First Instance's argument, and therefore in disagreement with the applicant, before going on to explain the reasons that led to this decision. Judges in the English legal system announce their decision at the end of a judgment, so that there is a kind of tension which builds up as they move through the various stages of their reasoning, but AGs declare their position towards the beginning of the assessment section in Opinions and then go on to defend it, as in the civil law tradition.

4.2 The Italian AG's Opinion

The second text is taken from an Italian Opinion and deals with the third question to be raised in the case, and although it concerns a separate point of law it is nevertheless contingent upon the decision about an earlier question. The extract is presented here in the English translation provided on the Court of Justice's website.[3]

(13) *The third question*

100. By the third question, the referring court asks, in substance, whether in a dispute between private parties a national court may disapply a provision of domestic law (here Article 67 of the 1998 Law) that is contrary to a Community directive. In this particular case, that would be so as to allow the national court to apply other national rules compatible with that directive (here Collective Agreement No 24 of 1975).

101. The question can, of course, be relevant only if the Court identifies a possible issue of compatibility between the Belgian legislation and Directive 98/59.

102. It seems to me, however, that stating the question in terms of possible disapplication, and hence in terms of the possible horizontal direct effect of a directive, represents an unnecessary complication of an issue that can be resolved much more simply.

103. As already discussed at length above, there is no doubt but that the national law can, in the case at hand, be interpreted in two different ways. On the first interpretation, which alone gives rise to questions of compatibility with Community law, the 1998 Law substantially reduced the protection afforded to individual workers in cases of collective

3 The original Italian text is in Appendix 1.

redundancies. A second interpretation, on the other hand, holds that the 1998 Law did not in any way circumscribe the rights already conferred on workers under existing rules, and in particular under Collective Agreement No 24. That second interpretation gives rise to no potential issue of compatibility with Community law.

104. Consequently, since the potential points of incompatibility of the Belgian legislation with Community law relate to only one of the two possible interpretations of the national law, it is clear that a declaration of such incompatibility by the Court could, at most, oblige the national court to follow the second interpretation. In other words, it would be a matter not of disapplying a national provision but simply of interpreting national law in conformity with Community law, in accordance with the established case-law of the Court to that effect.

105. I note that the parties to these proceedings, including the workers concerned, have in fact suggested to the Court an approach along the lines of what is proposed here.

106. Therefore, since as stated above I consider the interpretation of the 1998 Law as imposing restrictions and conditions on all individual actions against collective redundancies (and not only on those seeking reinstatement or suspension of the notice period) to be contrary to Community law, it is my view that the referring court should follow the other interpretation, according to which the conditions mentioned in Article 67 of the 1998 law apply only to actions for the specific remedies introduced by that law.

107. As originally formulated, in terms of the possible disapplication of a provision of domestic law, the question referred by the national court should therefore not even receive a reply. But by rephrasing it in order none the less to provide useful guidance to the national court, I propose that the Court should declare that, where there are two possible interpretations of a national law, in this case the Law of 13 February 1998 on measures in favour of employment, one of which is in conflict with Community law, the national court is bound to follow the one which does not entail points of incompatibility with Community law. (C-12/08)

The division into the four phases of the discussion model appears to be more complex in this text, though it can be roughly outlined as paragraph 100 corresponding to Confrontation, paragraphs 101 and 102 the Opening, paragraphs 103-106 the Argumentation stage and paragraph 107 the Concluding phase, in which the AG makes a formal declaration of the position he wishes to propose to the Court. However, the AG criticizes the way the question of compatibility between Belgian law and the directive has been presented as *an unnecessary complication* in 102. In this way, he indirectly rejects the applicant's case and, untypically, the expression of the AG's position is brought forward from the Argumentation phase in order to define the question better.

The AG appears to be first and foremost concerned with specifying and defining the legal point in question. Twice in the Confrontation phase the AG uses expressions to highlight and qualify the meaning of the national judge's request to the European Court, *in substance* and *in this particular case*. He then makes two specifications in paragraphs 101 and 102 to define the question and to establish the starting point of the discussion, but without actually using specifying indicators.

In the Argumentation stage (paragraphs 103 to 106), the AG goes on to explain how the question can be dealt with more simply. As in the British AG's text, clarity is of utmost importance. Since this is the third issue to be raised in the case, the AG refers back to what has already been explained at length, though he still spells it out very carefully and emphatically:

(14) ... *there is no doubt but that the national law can, in the case in hand, be interpreted in two different ways.*

He then very clearly lists two possible interpretations of the law, *on the first interpretation*, and then *a second interpretation*, introduced by the contrastive *on the other hand* and makes his statement even clearer by reiterating the point with the emphatic contrastive form:

(15) *In other words, it would be a matter not of disapplying a national provision but simply of interpreting national law in conformity with Community law...*

At this point, the AG further reinforces his position by referring to the parties' arguments (105) which proposed a similar solution; this is indicated by *in fact* in the English translation, but is expressed twice in Italian with *in effetti* and *di fatto*. In (106) the AG then draws his conclusion, *therefore*, by dismissing the first interpretation giving the explanation *since* it contrasts with Community law and finally he explicitly states his position that the judge should follow the other interpretation.

In the Concluding phase, he repeats his rejection of the question in the terms set by the judge and recommends the Court to nevertheless provide a useful suggestion with the contrastive indicators *but* and *none the less* by giving an alternative approach.

5. Discussion

The analysis of the two extracts shows how the well-defined organization of the texts fits very closely into the critical discussion model. As the sole adjudicating party, the AG steers the argumentation in a direct and linear manner. In fact, both British and Italian AGs make extensive use of indicators to present their argumentation in a very clear and precise manner, as is wont in all legal discourse, and to guide the reader through the text by specifying, listing/sequencing and contrasting arguments and thus highlighting the internal structure of the argumentation. The analysis of these two texts also suggests that British AGs may use indirect indicators more than Italian AGs.

The extensive use of indicators by both nationalities is confirmed by the results obtained in the quantitative analysis shown in Table 3.4 for one- and two-word indicators.

Table 3.4 The most frequent explicit indicators (normalized per 10,000 words)

British	no. of occurrences	normalized	Italian	no. of occurrences	normalized
however	177	20.30	infatti	240	21.20
therefore	134	15.40	in particolare	162	14.31
but	111	12.76	ma	154	13.60
thus	86	9.88	quindi	146	12.90
since	73	8.39	dunque	124	11.96
rather	62	7.12	invece	103	9.10
in particular	55	6.32	in quanto	101	8.92
because	44	5.05	tuttavia	101	8.92
moreover	42	4.82	pertanto	100	8.83
accordingly	41	4.71	comunque	78	6.89
although	39	4.48	inoltre	64	5.65
essentially	38	4.37	però	64	5.65
indeed	37	4.25	in effetti	42	3.71
in any event	35	4.02	peraltro	41	3.62
finally	33	3.80	anzitutto	40	3.53
in fact	30	3.45	poiché	39	3.44

It must be pointed out, however, that these results cannot in any way be considered conclusive because of the variety of possible indicators, which may be single-word expressions, phrases or even longer expressions. For example, a set of indicators frequently used by both British and Italian AGs to emphasize the importance of a point are cleft and pseudo-cleft structures, but their exact form will vary according to the content and therefore will not be easily captured in a quantitative analysis:

(16) In other words, it is the effect of the redefinition rather than the fact that it is a redefinition which will determine whether it must be notified or not. (C-267/03)

(17) What is at issue is whether the way in which Austria has derogated from the latter requirements is, or is not, permissible. (C-128/05)

(18) Come vedremo in seguito, invece, è proprio questa la via che deve essere, a mio avviso, percorsa per dare una risposta … . (C-200/02)
[As we shall see below, that is precisely the course which, in my opinion, should be followed in replying ...]

(19) In una tale prospettiva, quel che conta ai fini della valutazione preventiva è, quindi, *l'intera ricaduta* dell'attività … . (C-392/96)
[In this context, what counts for the purposes of prior assessment is therefore the *full impact* of the operation …

Furthermore, a one-to-one comparison can be misleading as, for example, the function of explaining cause is fulfilled basically by two indicators in the English subcorpus *since* and *because*, whilst in the Italian it is expressed by a number of expressions, *perché*, *poiché*, *in quanto*, *dal momento che*, *visto che*, and so on.

Even grouping indicators according to function is a complex process because the same word may have different functions: for example, *however* may be concessive, but also contrastive.

However, a few general observations can be made on the use of presentational devices. In line with the general impression of the need for clarity and precision which emerged from the analysis, the British AGs show a slightly greater tendency to list and sequence arguments than Italian AGs, who appear to be more concerned about defining and qualifying the legal points of the case. Functions such as comparing, contrasting, exemplifying and adding do not show significant differences, though tentatively we can say that there is a tendency of the AGs to use indicators of consequence or cause with different frequency (Table 3.5).

Table 3.5 Frequency of indicators grouped according to function (normalized per 10,000 words)

Function	British		Italian	
	total occurrences	normalized	total occurrences	normalized
Listing/ sequencing	112	12.8	133	11.75
Qualifying/ defining	116	13.3	254	22.4
Consequence	355	40.7	315	27.8
Cause	158	18.1	268	23.6

Furthermore, the number of occurrences for the single items would seem to suggest that these indicators, which can be classified generally as discourse markers, may actually be more frequent in Italian than in English. As noted above, the English version of the Italian Opinion used *in fact* once whereas the original used two indicators *di fatto* and *in effetti.* Particularly striking is the difference in occurrences of *infatti* 240 (21.20) and *in fact* 30 (3.45). This may be so because at times indicators in Italian act as fillers, as in the following example:

(20) Parimenti infondata mi sembra anche la censura relativa al difetto di motivazione della sentenza impugnata. Il Tribunale spiega infatti in modo certamente succinto ma chiaro, al punto 153, i motivi per cui ritiene che l'AGL deve essere qualificata come tassa indiretta ...
[Similarly unfounded, in my view, is the submission that the judgment under appeal is not sufficiently reasoned. In paragraph 151 of that judgment, the Court of First Instance in fact explains, succinctly but clearly, the reasons why it considers that the AGL must be classified as an indirect tax.]
(C-487/06)

Although many similarities can be found in the argumentation of British and Italian AGs, there is one aspect that particularly distinguishes the two. Indeed, the (im) personal style of judgments in their domestic legal culture can be perceived in the Opinions (Turnbull 2010). The number of occurrences of first-person expressions in the assessment section of the Opinions shown in Table 3.6 suggests that Italian Advocates have adopted a more personal approach to writing judicial opinions than in their domestic culture.

Table 3.6 Number of occurrences of first-person pronouns and adjectives (normalized per 10,000 words)

	British		**Italian**	
Singular	**absolute value**	**normalized**	**absolute value**	**normalized**
I	301	34.6	366	32.3
my	89	10.2	106	9.3
me	83	9.5	151	13.3
Plural				
we	-	-	25	2.2
our	1	0.1	13	1.1
us	2	0.2	22	1.9

A closer look at the two extracts above, however, will reveal a different distribution and function of personal expressions in British and Italian Opinions, which reflect the different styles used in judgments. In both cases, the AG feels obliged to 'rewrite' or 'reinterpret' the question/argument brought before the Court. The way each one deals with it seems to reflect their domestic style of judgments. The British AG takes direct and personal responsibility in the reinterpretation by saying *I shall assume that the applicant intended to refer to Article 43(2), applicable by virtue of Article 43(3)* and also reinforces his opinion by specifying his personal view, *I agree with that conclusion and consider that the Court of First Instance did not err with regard to the burden of proof.* In contrast, the Italian AG uses nominalizations and impersonal expressions such as *it is clear that*, *it would be a matter* to explain how the question can be interpreted and dealt with in a simpler manner.

(21) Consequently, since the potential points of incompatibility of the Belgian legislation with Community law relate to only one of the two possible interpretations of the national law, it is clear that a declaration of such incompatibility by the Court could, at most, oblige the national court to follow the second interpretation. In other words, it would be a matter not of disapplying a national provision but simply of interpreting national law in conformity with Community law, in accordance with the established case-law of the Court to that effect. (C-12/08)

In fact, the only personal expressions in the text signpost the argument (Turnbull forthcoming), *Come ho infatti già ampiamente indicato in precedenza, osservo che*, *come ho indicato sopra*, which interestingly are translated into English as two impersonal expressions and only one personal expression, *As already discussed at length above, I note that* and *as stated above* respectively. It is not so much the number of personal expressions as the involvement and commitment implicated in the expressions that distinguishes the styles.

However, it must be said that British AGs at times also follow a more impersonal, bureaucratic style with passive forms, nominalization and impersonal expressions, which may be considered as more befitting the Italian style (Turnbull 2009).

(22) ***This aspect has not been discussed*** before the Court in great detail, and it would not be appropriate to express a definitive view which should be based on a full appreciation of national circumstances. However, ***the contested amendment appears to mean*** that the rule precluding reimbursement where the burden of the tax has been passed on applies to all categories of claimant but one: those who have brought proceedings before the Verfassungsgerichtshof challenging a tax declared unconstitutional by that court.

If it is the case that entitlement to benefit from *Anlaßfallwirkung* is confined to those bringing challenges under national constitutional law, then the rules governing reimbursement of taxes found incompatible with national law might be more favourable, in that regard, than in the case of taxes found incompatible with Community law.

For the amendment to comply with the principle of equivalence, ***it would be necessary*** either for the benefit of the exception to be extended to all those who have challenged a tax found to be incompatible with Community law or for the exception to be abolished entirely. (C-147/01)

6. Concluding remarks

Although the institutions of the European Union aim at a homogeneous discourse to create unity and harmonization within the community, it would appear from the analysis of the Opinions of British and Italian AGs that there are many differences, as well as similarities, in the way the AGs draft these documents. The multilingual and multicultural context of the Court seems to favour the production of hybrid texts, in the sense that they are the result of a mixing and infiltration of various linguistic and cultural conventions (McAuliffe 2009).

The comparative analysis of argumentation in British and Italian AGs' Opinions has been made adopting the theoretical framework of the pragma-dialectical argumentation theory. The four phases of the critical discussion model outlined by van Eemeren and Houtlosser can be easily identified in the Opinions. Indeed, the ease with which the Opinions fit the model reflects their fairly rigid structure that arises from the institutional constraints of legal discourse in the European context, and there is one standard format regardless of the nationality of the author.

One overriding characteristic of both Italian and British Opinions is the extreme clarity and precision of the exposition of the argumentation. The presentational devices used by the AGs can be categorized into similar functions for both nationalities, though there is a very wide variation in their actual linguistic realization, which enables each AG to modify the force of his/her assertions as required. Nevertheless, it has been seen that the British tend to list and sequence their arguments explicitly, whilst Italians give greater attention to qualifying and defining the legal points of the case, perhaps reflecting the emphasis given in their domestic legal cultures to facts and questions of law respectively.

Another similarity in the Opinions is that the AG generally expresses his/her agreement or disagreement with the applicant's case towards the beginning of the Argumentation section, thus following in the civil law tradition. This leads to an explanation or justification of the decision, rather than a building up of arguments towards the announcement of the judicial decision at the end of common law judgments. The greater use of indicators of consequence and cause by British and Italian AGs respectively is perhaps again a reflection of their domestic legal cultures.

It would appear that there has been a certain amount of accommodation to the civil law tradition by the British AGs, with a more structured and well-defined textual organization and bureaucratic style. However, there is one particular feature of the Italian AGs' texts which represents a distinct change in style and rhetoric, namely the extensive use of personal expressions. The frequency of the expressions may in part be explained by the single authorship of the texts, but also by the greater freedom experienced by Italian AGs in the European court, so much so that even examples of humour and irony can be found in the Italian Opinions. And yet the use made by Italian AGs is different, insofar as these expressions usually organize the text and argumentation rather than indicate a personal comment or opinion about the issues being discussed.

All in all, the basic difference between the British and Italian AGs, therefore, remains the more personal and involved style of the former as opposed to the more neutral manner of the latter. And so it would seem that we are still some way from European harmonization.

Appendix 1

The original text of the Italian AG's Opinion

C-*Sulla terza questione*

100. Con la terza questione il giudice del rinvio chiede in sostanza se, nell'ambito di una controversia tra soggetti privati, un giudice nazionale possa disapplicare una disposizione interna (qui l'art. 67 della legge del 1998) contraria ad una direttiva comunitaria. Ciò,

nel caso specifico, al fine di poter applicare un'altra norma nazionale compatibile con la predetta direttiva (qui il contratto collettivo n. 24 del 1975).

101. La questione, naturalmente, può essere rilevante soltanto qualora la Corte ravvisi un possibile problema di compatibilità tra la normativa belga e la direttiva 98/59.

102. Mi sembra tuttavia che porre la questione in termini di possibile disapplicazione e, quindi, di possibile effetto diretto orizzontale di una direttiva rappresenti un'inutile complicazione di un problema che può essere risolto in modo molto più semplice.

103. Come ho infatti già ampiamente indicato in precedenza, non vi sono dubbi sul fatto che il diritto nazionale può, nel caso in esame, essere interpretato in due modi differenti. Secondo una prima interpretazione, la quale è l'unica a poter presentare problemi di compatibilità con il diritto comunitario, la legge del 1998 avrebbe sostanzialmente ridotto la tutela riconosciuta ai singoli lavoratori in caso di licenziamento collettivo. Viceversa, una seconda interpretazione ritiene che la legge del 1998 non abbia in alcun modo limitato i diritti già riconosciuti ai lavoratori sulla base delle precedenti disposizioni e, in particolare, del contratto collettivo n. 24. Tale seconda interpretazione non presenta alcun possibile problema di compatibilità con il diritto comunitario.

104. Di conseguenza, poiché i possibili profili di incompatibilità con il diritto comunitario della normativa belga si connettono ad una sola delle due interpretazioni possibili del diritto nazionale, è evidente che l'eventuale affermazione di tale incompatibilità da parte della Corte potrebbe, al più, obbligare il giudice nazionale a seguire la seconda interpretazione. In altri termini, si tratterebbe non di disapplicare una norma nazionale, ma semplicemente di dare al diritto nazionale un'interpretazione conforme al diritto comunitario, seguendo la costante giurisprudenza della Corte in tal senso.

105. In effetti, osservo che le parti nel presente procedimento, ivi compresi i lavoratori interessati, hanno di fatto suggerito alla Corte una soluzione in linea con quella qui proposta.

106. Pertanto, dal momento che, come ho indicato più sopra, considero che l'interpretazione della legge del 1998 secondo la quale essa porrebbe limiti e condizioni per tutti i ricorsi individuali contro i licenziamenti collettivi (e non solo per quelli diretti ad ottenere la reintegrazione o la sospensione del termine di preavviso) contrasti con il diritto comunitario, ritengo che il giudice del rinvio dovrà qui seguire l'altra interpretazione, ai sensi della quale le condizioni indicate all'art. 67 della legge del 1998 si applicano soltanto alle domande dirette ad ottenere gli specifici rimedi introdotti da tale legge.

107. Così come concepita, in termini di possibile disapplicazione di una norma interna, la questione posta dal giudice del rinvio non dovrebbe dunque neppure ricevere una risposta. Riformulandola tuttavia al fine di fornire comunque un'indicazione utile al giudice nazionale, propongo alla Corte di dichiarare che, tra due interpretazioni possibili di una norma interna, in questo caso la legge 13 febbraio 1998, recante disposizioni a favore dell'impiego, una delle quali contrasti con il diritto comunitario, il giudice nazionale è tenuto a seguire quella che non presenta profili di incompatibilità con il diritto comunitario stesso. (C-12/08)

References

Feteris, E. 2000. A dialogical theory of legal discussions: Pragma-dialectical analysis and evaluation of legal argumentation. *Artificial Intelligence and Law*, 8, 115-135.

Lord Hope of Craighead 2005. Writing Judgments. Annual Lecture, Judicial Studies Board. [Online] Available at: www.jsboard.co.uk/downloads/annuallecture-2005-proof-220305.pdf. [accessed: 20 January 2009].

McAuliffe, K. 2009. Hybrid Texts and Uniform Law? The Production of a Multilingual Jurisprudence by the Court of Justice of the European Communities. [Online] Available at: www.allacademic.com [accessed: 10 September 2009].

Perelman, C. and Olbrechts-Tyteca, L. 1969. *The New Rhetoric: A Treatise on Argumentation*. Notre Dame: Notre Dame Press.

Rega, L. 1997. La sentenza italiana e tedesca nell'ottica della traduzione, in *La lingua del diritto. Difficoltà traduttive. Applicazioni didattiche*, edited by L. Schena. Rome: CISU, 117-126.

Salmi-Tolonen, T. 2005. Persuasion in judicial argumentation. The Opinions of the Advocates General at the European Court of Justice, in *Persuasion across Genres*, edited by H. Halmari and T. Virtanen. Amsterdam: John Benjamins, 59-61.

Scarpa, F. and Riley, A. 2000. La fisionomia della sentenza in Inghilterra e in Italia: un'analisi orientate alla traduzione, in *Traduttori e Giuristi a Confronto. Interpretazione, traducente e comparazione del discorso giuridico.* Vol. 1, edited by L. Schena and R.D. Snel Trampus. Bologna: CLUEB, 227-291.

Taruffo, M. 1988. La Fisionomia della Sentenza in Italia, in *La Sentenza in Europa. Metodo, Tecnica e Stile. Atti del Convegno Internazionale per l'Inaugurazione della Nuova Sede della Facoltà, Università degli Studi di Ferrara, Facoltà di Giurisprudenza*. Padova: CEDAM, 180-214.

Toulmin, S. 1958. *The Uses of Argument*. Cambridge: Cambridge University Press.

Turnbull, J. 2010. Harmonisation of the law and legal cultures in the EU, in *Researching Language and the Law*, edited by D. Giannoni and C. Frade. Bern, Peter Lang, 135-154.

Turnbull, J. 2011. The language of EU judges. *Rassegna Italiana di Linguistica Applicata*, 1-2, 225-243.

van Eemeren, F.H. and Houtlesser, P. 1999. Strategic manoeuvring in argumentative discourse. *Discourse Studies*, 1(4), 479-497.

van Eemeren, F.H. and Houtlesser, P. 2006. Strategic maneuvring: a synthetic recapitulation. *Argumentation*, 20, 381-392.

van Eemeren, F.H., Houtlesser, P. and Snoeck Henkemans, A.F. 2007. *Argumentative Indicators in Discourse*. Dordrecht: Springer.

van Eemeren, F.H., Houtlesser, P. and Snoeck Henkemans, A.F. 2008. Dialectical profiles and indicators of argumentative moves. *Journal of Pragmatics*, 40, 475-493.

Arbitration

Chapter 4

International commercial arbitration: A protected practice*

Vijay K. Bhatia

In this chapter I would like to argue that international commercial arbitration practice is a protected practice in two ways. Firstly, a practice that is colonized by litigation experts and hence primarily dominated by lawyers, judges and other legal experts; and secondly, a practice that is controlled by a limited number of established legal experts, and hence largely denied to a wider community of legal experts, in particular to junior and non-initiated practitioners. Bhatia, Candlin and Gotti (2012) have discussed protectionism of the first kind in considerable detail; in this chapter, I would like to give substance to the second kind of protectionism which does not encourage the institution of arbitration to open the practice to new and less experienced members of the arbitration community, legal as well as non-legal experts. However, before offering the main argument, I would like to give a brief introduction to the institution and practice of international commercial arbitration to resolve cross-border disputes.

1. International commercial arbitration

International commercial arbitration was proposed by the United Nations Commission on International Trade Law (UNCITRAL) and established by the United Nations General Assembly by its Resolution 2205 (XXI) of 17 December 1966 to promote harmonization of international trade law. The UN Commission also proposed a model law on international commercial arbitration, which was subsequently adopted by the United Nations General Assembly on 21 June 1985, and was recommended for adoption as the UNCITRAL Model Law on International Commercial Arbitration. The UN recommended its adoption by individual member states. The Model Law was intended to promote the adoption of arbitration as an alternative to litigation to resolve international commercial disputes in global contexts. It was also expected that a uniform adoption would

* This work is supported by a grant from the RGC (Hong Kong SAR) project No. 9041191 (CityU 1501/06H) entitled *International Commercial Arbitration Practice: A Discourse Analytical Study*. For details, see the website: http://www.english.cityu.edu.hk/arbitration/.

lead to the integration of the arbitration processes and procedures across different legal jurisdictions and systems. Since it was meant to be a non-legal practice, which was viewed as an 'alternative' to litigation practices which are invariably jurisdictional, there was a belief that even if participants in international commercial arbitration cases came from different linguistic, ethnic, cultural, jurisdictional and even technical backgrounds, speaking different languages, the arbitration process would be independent of any legal constraints based on jurisdictional, socio-cultural and political influences.

In this context, it is interesting to note that although international commercial arbitration, as envisaged in the United Nations' original proposal, has become a popular alternative dispute resolution mechanism for cross-border commercial disputes, it is far from its other expectation as an 'alternative' to litigation. Since arbitration depends on the disputing parties' agreement to resolve disputes through private adjudication, it allows considerable freedom to parties in their choice of arbitration tribunal, arbitration institution, processes and procedures, as well as the choice of legal experts as their representatives to present their case to the tribunal. Unfortunately, most disputing parties are tempted to choose legal experts as arbitrators and also as their representatives to conduct arbitration on their behalf, in spite of the fact that the practice of international arbitration has developed in a manner to resolve the disputes with little interference by the courts. Thus the parties or their representatives, often legal counsels, present a dispute to an independent arbitration tribunal to resolve and order a decision, known as award in arbitration, which is legally binding, and is generally non-appealable in a court of law.

The main advantage of arbitration, therefore, is that it is like litigation in effect, even though it is decided by a neutral arbitration tribunal instead of a judge; but unlike litigation, it is generally informal, expedient, economical, private and confidential in nature, and at the same time it gives sufficient freedom to disputing parties in the way it is actually conducted. The main benefits of arbitration as an 'alternative to litigation' therefore are speedy resolution of disputes, economy of cost, preservation of privacy and confidentiality of the parties, and yet the enforceability of awards is just like that of a legal judgment. Arbitration is thus a form of private adjudication, and yet the final award has the same power of enforcement as that of a court judgment. In addition, with relatively little interference from courts, it allows parties considerable freedom as to the choice of language, seat of arbitration, the number of arbitrators, and even the rules of arbitration. To make these decisions possible, they also get assistance from independent arbitration centres, especially in their choice of arbitrators, rules of arbitration, infrastructural requirements, such as the informality of court settings, recording facility, and the production of documents.

Although the outcome of arbitration is considered final and enforceable across jurisdictions and regions, parties at dispute often look for opportunities to go to court if and when the outcome is not favourable to them. To make this strategically possible, they often choose legal experts as their counsels and arbitrators rather than specialists in the area of dispute, as they are likely to be more accomplished in exploiting opportunities to challenge the award, if necessary. It is also the case that most companies are advised by their legal departments to choose arbitrators, and they invariably suggest tried and tested legal experts, whom they often refer to as 'a safe pair of hands', meaning that they are more likely to give a favourable award. This leads to a large-scale involvement of legal experts, team of lawyers as legal counsels, and senior or even retired judges as arbitrators, which tends to make arbitration very similar to litigation. In this context, Marriott (2005, The Arbitration Act 1996) remarks:

> Although the 1996 Act gave arbitrators very considerable power over the running of an arbitration and greater confidence in their autonomy, my sense is that they are not really producing radically new procedures more efficient and prompt than hitherto. The English passive tradition dies hard and self-interest is a dominant factor. The practitioners dominate the arbitral processes in the same way as they have dominated litigation, and to the same end.

It is interesting to note that partly because of the training of lawyers in litigation practice, which is understandable, they often tend to consider arbitration the same as litigation. Nariman (2000: 262) goes even further to emphasize that 'International Commercial Arbitration has become almost indistinguishable from litigation, which it was at one time intended to supplant.' Kerr (1997), in a similar fashion, claims that international arbitration seems to have acquired the pejorative sobriquet of *arbitigation*, which signals large-scale 'judicialization' of arbitration. However, this issue of colonization will not be discussed in this chapter. The more relevant issue for us here is the second issue of what Marriott (2005) calls 'self-interest' amongst the established members of the international legal community, which tends to make arbitration what we refer to as a 'protected practice'.

This overwhelming influence of litigation over arbitration results in an increasing mixture of discourses (Bhatia 2004, 2012) and contested professional identities (Bhatia, Candlin and Gotti 2012) as arbitration becomes, as it were, 'colonized' by litigation practices, threatening to undermine the integrity of arbitration practice. Another significant consequence of this trend is that international commercial arbitration has come to be regarded as a protected and somewhat closed practice, dominated by what is often referred to as *the old boys' club*. The main thrust of this chapter is to identify and discuss some of the main factors that have led to the present state of arbitration practice as a 'protected practice' and its implications for the development of international arbitration practice as an independent and non-judicial alternative to litigation to settle cross-border commercial disputes. Let me point out some of the main factors that make arbitration a protected practice.

2. Judicialization of arbitration

As mentioned earlier, the overwhelming involvement of legal experts in arbitration is one of the major factors making arbitration very similar to litigation. In this context, it is interesting to note that Price Waterhouse Coopers (2006) conducted a comprehensive survey of some of the main stakeholders in arbitration practice, particularly from the corporate sector. The study revealed that there was a serious need for 'a wider pool of arbitrators, with specialization or expertise in the subject matter of the dispute', in particular their specialization in the industry sector, their regional or country experience, and their cross-disciplinary expertise, e.g. their technical or financial background. The study conclusively demonstrated that arbitrators with these skills would be more likely to save their corporations time and money. Unfortunately, the appropriation of arbitration practice by litigation experts seems to have continued, skilfully controlled and dominated by a relatively small number of legal practitioners. Since it is a relatively small practice as compared to litigation, it has not opened up to a large number of experts in arbitration, especially young entrants, and has been dominated by retired judges and other senior legal experts.

One of the adverse consequences of this kind of monopolistic tendency in arbitration practice is that it does not encourage arbitration to develop as an institution; firstly because arbitration is by its very nature considered a private arrangement, and hence the proceedings and awards are often kept confidential, which restricts access to arbitration practice to only those who are involved in it. It is most often denied even to legitimate researchers and new entrants to the profession, thus limiting exposure to the realities of good practices, which can and often does hinder the development of the institution of arbitration. The only way new entrants to the profession can get access to such practices is by acting as associates to established senior practitioners. There are two major factors that have encouraged and contributed to this kind of protectionism: lack of transparency in arbitration practice as a consequence of the confidentiality requirement about how arbitration is conducted in practice, and non-availability of discoursal data, written as well as spoken, including the final outcome of the process of arbitration. Let me give more substance to these two aspects of arbitration practice.

3. Transparency in arbitration practice

The issue of confidentiality of information in arbitration has been given considerable attention in the available literature; the views are somewhat divided, especially on disclosure for different purposes and contexts in which such decisions are taken. Often the hearing is held *in camera* and all the documents presented during the hearing and also the documents resulting from the hearing, including the award itself, are kept confidential. There seems to be a general agreement among legal scholars, judges, and arbitration practitioners that there is a duty of confidentiality to be observed, which implies that parties in dispute shall not disclose any information in and about the arbitration process, including the award, to any third parties not involved in the process. Confidentiality in this context refers to the protection from disclosure of all the discursive data, spoken as well as written, relating to, submitted or presented during or resulting from an arbitral proceeding, to outsiders who are not participating or involved in the arbitral proceedings.

It is interesting to note that although the UNCITRAL Rules provide for the confidentiality of the arbitration proceedings as well as that of the award, Article 32.5 does allow the award to be made public with the consent of both parties. Similarly, the New York Convention on the Recognition and Enforcement of Foreign Arbitral Awards 1958, and the European Convention on International Commercial Arbitration 1961, do not envisage any absolute duty of confidentiality. Even in actual practice, courts in different jurisdictions have similarly refrained from accepting an absolute duty of confidentiality. In this context, Fortier (1999: 131) rightly observes that the principle 'at least in the absolute form in which it is generally understood by most parties, is more truism than truth', and some of the issues concerning 'the nature and scope of the principle, in law, to its utility, in practice, to its formulation as a rule of arbitral procedure, are highly contentious.' Brown (2001: 969), in a similar manner, asserts that although a 'presumption of confidentiality – whether implied or explicit – exists between the parties to an international commercial arbitration, there is a disconnect between that presumption and the frequent realities of disclosure and publicity imposed by courts' (see Bhatia, Candlin and Sharma, 2009 for a more detailed account of some of the issues involved in confidentiality in arbitration practice). The present situation seems to be that the duty of confidentiality in arbitration is not absolute in all cases, and need not be assumed as such, but should be negotiable in the beginning of any arbitration process. However, in practice, most arbitrators and legal counsels treat it as assumed without any intention or effort to negotiate the requirement of confidentiality. The most damaging effect of such an assumption of absolute confidentiality is that it encourages a lack of transparency in all aspects of the arbitration process and documentation, thus depriving the institution of arbitration of valuable access to discursive data which can be crucial for the training of new arbitrators, and hence for the development of the institution itself, if the purpose of the institution is to open it up to a wider choice of informed and well-trained arbitration experts. On the other hand, if the intention is to protect or restrict the institution from a wider pool of experts, confidentiality can be viewed as a valid tool to achieve that end.

4. Non-availability of arbitration awards

One of the important purposes of publishing awards is to educate potential stakeholders and also the providers of arbitration services. Referring to this issue, Rix (2006: 42) points out:

> The more that arbitration awards are final and supplant and avoid any visit to the courts, the more commercial parties have, it seems to me, a real and justifiable interest in being able to discover for themselves how arbitration tribunals in general and individual arbitrators or boards of arbitrators in particular, decide and perform.

He further points out,

> They should not be simply in the hands of their legal advisers, who give them anecdotal information. Moreover, the legal advisers themselves should be in a position where they can advise their clients on an informed basis about the principles applied by and performance of arbitrators.

Rix identifies the choice of arbitrators as a very important issue. He rightly emphasizes that parties should have enough of objective, rather than what he calls 'anecdotal', information not only about the background of arbitrators, but also about how they have conducted arbitration in their previous cases, as is the case in litigation. Moreover, there is also the matter of accommodating public interest in the review of arbitration proceedings, which can only be served by the introduction of considerable transparency and disclosure of information regarding such arbitral proceedings and awards. In the context of this chapter, then, there appears to be an established case for making some elements of the arbitral proceedings more transparent and free from the obligation to observe confidentiality. The UNCITRAL Notes on Organizing Arbitral Proceedings (Note 32) encourages parties to include in a *confidentiality* agreement only those elements of the proceedings that are necessary for individual cases. It makes it clear that

> [a]n agreement on confidentiality might cover, for example, one or more of the following matters: the material or information that is to be kept confidential (e.g. pieces of evidence, written and oral arguments, the fact that the arbitration is taking place, identity of the arbitrators, content of the award); measures for maintaining confidentiality of such information and hearings; whether any special procedures should be employed for maintaining the confidentiality of information transmitted by electronic means (e.g. because communication equipment is shared by several users, or because electronic mail over public networks is considered not sufficiently protected against unauthorized access); circumstances in which confidential information may be disclosed in part or in whole …

This provision clearly establishes a need to negotiate, even if selectively, elements or aspects of arbitration that need to be kept confidential, rather than assuming an absolute duty of confidentiality in all cases. Rogers and Cadwallader (2006: 38) explain this view, when they point out:

> [a]rbitral decision-making in the past occurred in a virtual black box ... Instead of formal transparent rules, arbitrators crafted proceedings based on their culturally defined professional experiences and (their) sense of what was equitable and just. As a consequence of these conditions, parties had little ability to peek at the inner workings of the decisional machine. Even if they could, the number of skilled arbitrators and recognized institutions were few, so there was no basis for comparison shopping.

Similarly, Naimark and Keer (2002) point out that confidentiality should not be one of the most valued aspects of international commercial arbitration and in their study less than 10 per cent of their subjects they interviewed had indicated confidentiality as one of the important aspects of arbitration.

However, it must be pointed out that the situation today is somewhat different. A series of reforms have made international commercial arbitration relatively more transparent, meaning that the rules that regulate decision-making are more readily available to interested parties who, in this instance, are the users of the system. At the same time, a growing number of voluntary and involuntary disclosures provide increased information to the users, as well as to the general public, about numerous individual cases. While the disclosures are generally made for reasons other than to advance transparency, the information they provide inevitably illuminates, to some extent at least, the inner workings of the international commercial arbitration system. The parties can impose a contractual obligation of non-disclosure for the researchers before admitting them as observers in arbitral proceedings. Moreover, the ICC International Court of Arbitration regularly publishes its awards after they have been adequately sanitized to remove identifying information, which are then made available for comment by academics, practitioners, and other experts. Publication of awards, they claim, encourages a wider public interest in the transparency of arbitral proceedings. The advantage of having a repository of awards can hardly be overemphasized. Such disclosures could be used as educational samples during the course of training of arbitrators. It could also lead to the development of the law and practice of arbitration and the encouragement of consistency by future arbitrators in reasoned international awards. These collections of awards can have persuasive value in allowing arbitrators to collectively share experiences and can be used as examples by potential parties and future arbitrators. This sharing of experiences and the greater transparency that would ensue could then set the basis for allowing arbitrators, practitioners, and academics to understand, discuss, and provide constructive criticisms of awards. This in turn will greatly assist in improving arbitration itself as a workable and reliable dispute resolution system. The advantages of making the whole process transparent are manifold. Firstly, transparency can help produce more consistent resolutions of disputes arising out of similar disputes. International business practices often give rise to a number of related disputes involving different parties, and participants involved in arbitration can benefit from the proceedings and awards made earlier. Secondly, discursive data, whether written or spoken, can be useful in the training of new arbitrators. If such data is not accessible, new entrants to the field will continue to rely on anecdotal information, which may be marginally useful in explaining broad principles of arbitration, but not necessarily to handle the complexities of real practice. Moreover, confidentiality may not be conducive to controlling the quality of service provided by individual arbitrators. By imposing a general or even implied duty of confidentiality, we tend to make it more difficult to evaluate the quality of services provided to corporate stakeholders, which eventually is not much of a help to them if they need to decide between arbitration or litigation. The only alternative they may have will be to go by the advice of their legal experts, which is not the best alternative but is the dominant practice today.

The requirement of absolute duty of confidentiality also has a more negative effect on the development of arbitration as an institution in developing countries that are in the process of establishing arbitration institutions and making their own rules of arbitration. In order for those newly established institutions to be more persuasive in attracting clients, it would be helpful to them if they can make their awards more widely accessible to potential corporate clients in an attempt to inform and convince them of the quality of arbitration they provide. It is just not enough to enlist experienced arbitrators on their websites, especially when it is well known, and indeed likely, that most of these arbitrators will be engaged elsewhere, and hence may not be personally available to arbitrate in cases from such newly established jurisdictions. In consequence, it is more than likely that a dispute will be arbitrated by local arbitrators or by relatively less experienced arbitrators, thus undermining the reputation of such new arbitration centres.

5. Concluding remarks

Public access and transparency tends to encourage quality control in the decision-making process, enhancing its legitimacy. Similarly, disclosure of information can enable parties and other stakeholders to make evidence-based and informed choices for arbitration as an alternative to litigation. Although it is possible to make a distinction between transparency and disclosure of information, in practice these constructs are not always easy to distinguish. Disclosure of information creates favourable conditions for the monitoring of decision-making in arbitral proceedings. Taken together, they have great potential for monitoring decision-making and, at the same time, protecting public interest and creating a body of jurisprudence in the system of arbitration as an effective alternative to litigation.

The important question remains, however: 'which elements of arbitration practice must necessarily be kept confidential, and which ones need to be more transparent'? It is against this background of confidentiality requirements, and the challenges to them, and the clear advantages of greater transparency that this study may be of some practical value. However, to achieve this, access to arbitration proceedings and procedures, and discursive data, both written and spoken, is essential. Such access can be both carefully monitored and selectively negotiated in terms of its data, keeping in mind the number of texts, both written and spoken, that are produced during and at the conclusion of arbitration practice, and the contexts in which they are done and are likely to be useful to other stakeholders, including those interested in research and training in arbitration. However, if such accessibility to what Goffman (1959) calls the 'on-stage' performance of arbitrators and other participants involved in the negotiation of commercial disputes is completely denied, as is often the case in many jurisdictions, it is difficult to imagine how arbitration practice can be made more transparent and hence less protected. In order to train new entrants to the field, it is crucial to identify what Scollon (1998) refers to as 'critical sites of engagement' and critical moments of interaction during crucial stages of arbitration. Real and authentic examples of evidence from practice are necessary in any form of practitioner training, including arbitration. Hence on the part of the profession, this would amount to a missed opportunity if the intention is to have access to prevalent practices in international commercial arbitration contexts, to create favourable conditions for the future development of the professional skills of its future members and practitioners, and to ensure that a transparent arbitration process remains an effective, popular, and reliable alternative to litigation for corporate stakeholders internationally.

In conclusion, I have made an attempt to argue for greater transparency in the processes and procedures used in arbitration practices. At the moment there seems to be no independent means of conducting a critical inquiry into the good practices of arbitrators because, the chapter argues, arbitration practice is closely guarded by the invocation of an absolute duty of confidentiality, which is often viewed as 'given' rather than negotiable. Unlike courtroom practices and proceedings which are open to the public and which provide court judgments that are readily available in published form, arbitration proceedings are held in private and the procedural details about the trials and their outcomes, including the arbitration awards, remain confidential (Bhatia, Candlin and Sharma 2009). It must be conceded that privacy and confidentiality, in some cases, help firms to protect trade secrets and financial dealings from competitors, but in many cases it may not be necessary for the parties to impose a duty of absolute confidentiality; in fact, it may be helpful in many cases to make the process more transparent in the public domain. Redfern and Hunter (1991) also point out that investigating arbitration practice is not easy. Arbitration awards are not always accessible; even information on procedural aspects of arbitration comes from 'narratives of experience' from some of the participants. The important question that comes to mind is 'to what extent is this veil of secrecy and confidentiality in the process of arbitration a necessary requirement to serve the corporate stakeholders, and make arbitration attractive?' Alternatively, one may tend to agree with Marriott (2005) when he claims that arbitration has become a commercial practice to serve the 'self-interest' of some of the established members of the international legal community.

References

Bhatia, V.K. 2004. *Worlds of Written Discourse: A Genre-based View*. London: Continuum.

Bhatia, V.K. 2010. Interdiscursivity in professional discourse. *Discourse and Communication*, 4(1), 32-50.

Bhatia, V.K., Candlin, C.N. and Gotti, M. (eds) 2012. *Discourse and Practice in International Commercial Arbitration: Issues, Challenges and Prospects*. Farnham: Ashgate Publishing.

Bhatia, V.K., Candlin, C.N. and Sharma, R., 2009. Confidentiality and integrity in international commercial arbitration practice. *Arbitration*, 75, 2-13.

Brown, A.C. 2001. Presumption meets reality: an exploration of the confidentiality obligation in International Commercial Arbitration. *American Uniform International Law Review*, 16(4), 969-1025.

Fortier, Y.L. 1999. The occasionally unwarranted assumption of confidentiality. *Arbitration International*, 15(2), 131-140.

Goffman E. 1959. *The Presentation of Self in Everyday Life.* Garden City, NY: Doubleday-Anchor.

Kerr, M. 1997. Concord and conflict in international arbitration. *Arbitration International*, 13(2), 121-144.

Marriott, A. 2005. *Litigate, Arbitrate, Mediate – Frustrate? Breaking the Dispute Deadlock*, Clayton UTZ Lecture. Online at http://www.claytonutz.com/ialecture/2005/transcript_2005.html [accessed: 15 July 2011].

Naimark, R. and Keer, S. 2002. What do parties really want from International Commercial Arbitration? *Dispute Resolution Journal*, 57(4), 78.

Nariman, F.S. 2000. The spirit of arbitration. The tenth annual Goff lecture. *Arbitration International*, 16(3), 261-278.

Price Waterhouse Coopers 2006. *International Arbitration: Corporate attitudes and practices*. Published in collaboration with Queen Mary, University of London. Online at http://www.pwc.com/arbitrationstudy [accessed: 6 June 2010].

Redfern, A. and Hunter, M. 1991. *Law and Practice of International Commercial Arbitration*. 2nd Edition. London: Sweet and Maxwell.

Rix, B. 2006. Three addresses in St Petersburg: conference April 4, 2006: international arbitration, yesterday, today and tomorrow. *Arbitration*, 72, 227.

Rogers, C.A., and Cadwallader, R.C. 2006. Secrecy and transparency in Dispute Resolution: transparency in International Commercial Arbitration. *Kansas Law Review*, 54, 1301.

Scollon, R. 1998. *Mediated Discourse as Social Interaction: A Study of News Discourse*. New York: Longman.

Chapter 5
Arbitration across genres: From 'private resolution' to 'public war'

Isabel Corona

1. Introduction

International commercial arbitration (henceforth ICA) is defined as a dispute resolution technique, alternative to court action, whose main objective is to obtain a fair and private resolution of disputes between two commercial enterprises by an impartial third party, without the unnecessary expense or delay typically associated with litigation.

In line with this description of what ICA is, there has been a belief that arbitration proceedings are both private and confidential, and that the duty of confidentiality arises from the very nature of arbitration. Confidentiality has thus been listed as one clear advantage of arbitration over litigation to resolve international commercial disputes. However, in the last decade, the global demand for information and the new media technologies have reached arbitration and have brought in a new perspective which has led to a degree of discrepancy between that presumption of confidentiality and the frequent realities of disclosure and publicity (see for example Bhatia et al. 2009, Beechey 2009, Burn and Pearsall 2009). The present work shows evidence that the facts of arbitration are not as confidential now as they used to be, and that this publicity of arbitration is producing an interesting construction of arbitration in the public sphere.

This chapter is concerned with the recontextualization of the discourse of international commercial arbitration across genres. More specifically, it focuses on the last two genres that signal the publicity of arbitration: the press releases produced by the corporations and the resultant news reports. The analysis will show that the concept of arbitration has undergone a transformation from being considered a private non-legal dispute resolution device to being perceived as a transnational war fought in the public eye and as a professional practice indistinguishable from litigation.

The present study combines elements of both critical genre analysis and cognitive semantics. From the former, and as a point of departure developed in the next section, it takes up Bhatia's (2004, 2008) framework for critical genre analysis to help understand the nature and function of professional, corporate, and institutional discursive practices. The framework adopts a multiperspective methodology which, taken here as a top-down process, includes professional culture, professional practices, discursive practices, genres and, ultimately, texts with the purpose of describing and explaining professional discourse.

Furthermore, this study also takes a more cognitive approach to discourse analysis. My intention is to show that arbitration discourse undergoes a conceptual transformation in its path through the genre chain, from the corporate press release to the news report. In doing so, I take van Dijk's (e.g. 1993, 1995, 1998) notion of 'social cognition' – or the way people construe mental models of events and process the information related to them, as the 'interface' (Koller 2005) between the concept of arbitration on the one hand and discourse and genre on the other. The purpose of this line of enquiry is to unveil the force of conceptual metaphors and other rhetorical devices characteristic of media discourse not only as rhetorical devices or generic resources put to use in situated professional practice such as news reporting, but also as cognitive phenomena with sociocultural implications. As van Dijk (1998: 41) states, '[d]iscourse meanings derive from mental models of events, controlled by context models'.

The data gathered as evidence of the re-articulation processes come from the corporate websites and the international media coverage pertaining to ten international commercial arbitration cases filed at various arbitral institutions and from different parts of the world.

The material gathered is freely accessible on the Internet. Table 5.1 lists the ten cases, indicating who claimant and respondent were in each case, the seat of arbitration, the duration of the process and the outcome. The facts and events of the disputes have been reconstructed through the fragmentary information provided by the corporate websites, the news reports from local and international newspapers and news agencies, some law firms' websites, and various blogs with comments and reflections from observers. Of the ten cases traced, five had a final award, one was suspended, one was terminated 'without prejudice', another can be presumed to have been withdrawn or terminated as a consequence of a takeover, though no textual evidence has been gathered, and, at the time of writing, two cases are still pending. The length of time of the arbitration processes varies substantially, from five months to four years. Five of the cases also had ongoing lawsuits in different jurisdictions coexisting at the time of the arbitration proceedings.

This chapter is structured as follows. Firstly, it sketches the corporate context in which arbitration practice is the topic entity and the professional genres involved which make up a specific genre chain that turns the private issue into a public one. Secondly, it focuses on the corporations' press releases to explore the when and how of disclosure of the arbitration event; that is, which are the critical moments and how they are presented to shareholders and the media. Section three shows the conceptual mapping of arbitration in the resultant news reports. The chapter concludes with some reflections upon the sociocognitive impact of the resemiotization of arbitration.

Table 5.1 International commercial arbitration cases analyzed in the study

Case number	Arbitration cases: Claimant vs. respondent	Tribunal	Duration of process	Outcome
1	S&N vs. Carlsberg and Heineken	Arbitration Institute of the Stockholm Chamber of Commerce	October 2007-April 2008/ 5 months	Takeover
2	Danone vs. Wahaha	Arbitration Institute of the Stockholm Chamber of Commerce	May 2007-Sept 2009/ 29 months	Pullout and award
3	Dominion Sky Angel vs. EchoStar	American Arbitration Association	January 2004-Oct 2004/ 9 months	Award claimant successful
4	Vodacom vs. Congolese Wireless Network	ICC in Brussels	April 2010-	Ongoing
5	Agfa-Gevaert vs. AgfaPhoto	ICC in Frankfurt	October 2005-Sept 2009/4 years	Award
6	Bahrain Asphalt Establishment (BAE) vs. Gamuda-WCT	ICC in Qatar	March 2010-	Ongoing
7	Rio Tinto vs. Ivanhoe	British Columbia ICA Centre in Vancouver	July 2010-Dec 2010/ 5 months	Suspended
8	Sonatrach vs. Repsol and Gas Natural	UN Arbitration Court in Geneva	August 2007-Dec 2009/ 16 months	Award claimant successful
9	Archangel Diamond vs. AGP	Arbitration Institute of the Stockholm Chamber of Commerce	2006-Oct 2009/ 3 years	Terminated 'without prejudice'
10	Andersen Consulting vs. Andersen Worldwide and Arthur Andersen	ICC in Paris	December 1997-August 2000/ 31 months	Award claimant successful

2. From confidentiality to publicity: The genre chain

Let us see now how the disclosure of arbitration process works in corporate practice. When two corporations decide to work together, they have a contract between them to regulate their business relationship, which may include a clause typically reading as follows:

> All disputes, controversies or claims arising from or relating to the contract will be resolved by binding arbitration in accordance with the applicable rules of [...] then in effect.

Other specifics, such as the arbitration institution, can also be stated in the clause. This is a typical professional practice articulated in a particular discursive practice by means of a genre, the contract, and a specific piece of text, the clause. This text is confidential.

If some kind of controversy arises, one of the parties (the claimant) in the business contract may decide to submit the dispute to arbitration. In this case, the arbitration procedure is clearly established. Arbitration is initiated by a Request. Once arbitrators (one or three) are appointed, the claimant sets out a Statement of Claim with the matter in dispute and the remedy sought. The other party (the respondent), in another Statement (of Response), admits or denies the claim. After evidence is exchanged and presented to the arbitrators, the parties put forward their case in a private hearing, after which the arbitrators make a decision by means of an enforceable award.

The two parties, partners in the business relationship, have thus become claimant and respondent in an arbitration case, and have entrusted their lawyers with the task. These lawyers, as the companies' counsels, may also be dealing with lawsuits coexisting with the arbitration process. As stated earlier, half of the ten cases that comprise the corpus also had ongoing litigations. This circumstance of having lawyers as counsels who have to deal with parallel litigation and arbitration cases, together with the preference for the choice of legal experts as arbitrators, as Bhatia et al. (2008) have demonstrated, accounts for a growing tendency to choose litigation procedures to conduct arbitration and is believed to be compromising the spirit of arbitration as a non-legal practice.

At this initial stage, we have two professional cultures intertwining: legal and corporate, producing mixed professional and discursive practices, texts and genres in the arbitration process. This is what has usually been considered as confidential in arbitration practice.

However, while arbitral institutions tend to preserve privacy of hearings and of internal operations of the arbitral tribunal, corporations, as part of their professional culture, are bound to communicate their doings. This is typically articulated in the discursive practice of the public announcement or press release. The press release is one of the channels that corporations use to control communication between the corporate elite on the one hand and the more peripheral shareholders and the general public on the other. Their purpose is to publish news about the company and to present the company in as favourable a light as possible. Press releases tend to take the generic structure of news reports and thus serve as pre-cooked texts to be used by journalists in their institutions. This is what Jacobs (1999) refers to as the 'pre-formulating' function of the press release genre. It not only facilitates text production at the other end of the communicative chain – in an age when time and costs are permanent constraints – it also helps convey the desired corporate image. Fairclough (2006) understands this phenomenon as one of the effects of globalization, as a re-articulation of relations between different fields, such as business and the media:

> [T]hink of [...] how business corporations and governments have embraced public relations and increasingly produce media discourse 'for' the media through their 'communications' departments.

This added 'communicative' task is not entrusted to lawyers, but to public relations personnel of the corporation, with their specific professional activities realized in public announcements which re-articulate the professional practices being carried out by the companies' counsels-lawyers in the arbitration process and reformulated into oven-ready news reports. At this stage of the process, the arbitration event becomes partially public. But we could reasonably say that it is still 'controlled' by the corporations.

Then, a third professional culture comes on stage, the mass media: press, radio, television and the Internet. In a globalized world, all the media are potential mass media. The arbitration event then becomes totally public. Figure 5.1 displays the main genres in this specific genre chain and the professional practitioners involved, signalling the cline from confidentiality to publicity.

From the corporate press release produced by public relations personnel to the media reader, there is a transformation of meanings and discourses in the processes of 'mediation' (Fairclough 2006) by the media. This process is shaped by multiple factors: first, by the varied discursive practices deployed in the new multimodal media genres in general and the genre conventions of journalistic practice in particular: editorials, comments, news items, or interviews, to name the best known; second, by the specific historical, social and cultural discourses at a national scale, or the local expectations of a dispute between 'one of us' and 'one of them', what van Dijk (1998 and elsewhere) has described as 'the ideological square', a strategy of polarization for positive ingroup description and negative outgroup description, in our case the local representation of the transnational arbitration process; and third, by the extent to which the media complies with a tactical use of the publicity of the arbitration process by the parties involved and acts – for whatever reasons – as a vehicle of specific corporate strategies. All these extra-textual factors shape discourses and genres and give a public version of reality, in our case, of arbitration.

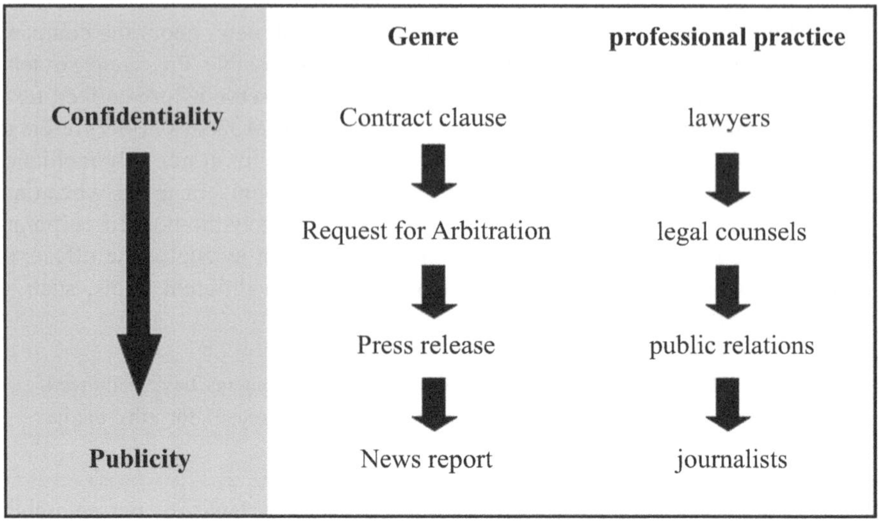

Figure 5.1 From privacy to publicity: A genre chain and its professional practices in arbitration

Focusing on the textual level of analysis, it has been widely acknowledged that media discourse is particularly rich in rhetorical tropes to describe and interpret events. In this line, Macdonald (2003: 9) states that '[w]ords and images, by defining and labelling phenomena, frame the terms in which we think about these'. One crucial role of the media is to construct versions of reality by making use of more reader-friendly semiotic resources. At word level, the most common of these are metaphors, metonyms and also puns or wordplay in more popular media. As we shall see in section three, for the recipients of media texts dealing with arbitration cases, the metaphoric expressions and the use of metonymy account for much of the resemiotization of arbitration. But prior to that, it is necessary to describe the critical moments of disclosure by the corporations through their press releases.

3. The moments of disclosure by the corporations

The disclosure of the arbitration case may be for many reasons, from legal requirements to other more strategic tactics, when confidentiality provisions have not been explicitly regulated by the parties. This discussion falls outside the scope of the present chapter. What is of interest here is when and how disclosure takes place. The corporations' public performance shows a number of critical moments, summarized here as four distinct phases: the pre-arbitration scenario, the actual filing for arbitration, the ongoing process and the final outcome.

Phase 1. The pre-arbitration scenario

The disclosure may be substantiated by the announcement of a decision made by a corporation in relation to the joint business in dispute or by a premature 'leak' to the media revealing the controversy, which makes the whole issue public, including the subsequent arbitration case. The attitudes of the corporations in this pre-arbitration scenario show considerable variation and can, if only partially, be inferred from the discourse strategies they use. They range from apparent reluctance to disclose the fact of arbitration to tactical exposition of facts which make the decision unavoidable, or even to warn the other party, through the media, of their plans. For example, in *Danone vs. Wahaha* (case 2), partners of a joint venture operating in China since 1996, Danone feels compelled to react to the news that appeared in the media (my italics):

> Further to recent articles that appeared in the Chinese press, Groupe Danone confirms that it is *in discussions* with Mr Zong, its partner in the Danone Wahaha joint ventures. (Groupe Danone 2007a)

However, the choice of the word 'discussions' is a form of mitigation, of softening the fact – to be unveiled by Danone in a subsequent press release – that then they were actually asking Wahaha for 'legal actions'; that is, to stop using the trademark 'Wahaha' outside the joint venture which, apparently, was not done and led to Danone's decision to file for arbitration (Corona 2011a).

In the case of *Vodacom vs. Wireless Congolese Networks* (case 4) – both partners of a joint venture operating in the Democratic Republic of Congo – the former is preparing the arbitration scenario in the press release entitled 'Vodacom Congo shareholder dispute' (Vodacom 2010a), where it states that 'discussions [...] have thus far proven unsuccessful', and that 'relations with our minority shareholder are combative and dysfunctional'.

A more expressive attitude is revealed in two other examples. In the early stages of what would develop into the *Scottish & Newcastle vs. Carlsberg* arbitration case (case 1), Scottish & Newcastle (hereafter S&N) was facing a hostile takeover bid from Carlsberg, its partner since 2002 in a joint venture running a top Russian brewer. S&N's strategy was to warn Carlsberg against the takeover by means of the following statement made by its CEO to the *Daily Mail* (Ebrahimi 2007): '[i]t is like an army, you don't publicise it until the last moment', which refers to the filing for arbitration that S&N announced in a press release shortly afterwards. In *Danone vs. Wahaha*, Wahaha's chairman's response to Danone's announcement of arbitration was in turn the announcement of another arbitration to be filed in China, but lexicalized in the form of a threat: '[w]e will utilize the legal weapon to get justice' (Wahaha Group 2008). In both cases, the linguistic metaphors *army* and *weapon* draw on the conceptual metaphor of ARBITRATION IS A WAR;[1] the pre-arbitration scenario is thus represented as the preparations for a battle.

Phase 2. The filing for arbitration

The express announcement made by a corporation that is actually filing for arbitration tends to be highly formal and formulaic:

> The Vodacom Group will be initiating arbitration proceedings under ICC rules in Brussels. (Vodacom 2010b)

> S&N has today initiated formal arbitration proceedings. (Scottish & Newcastle 2007a)

> Rio Tinto refers Ivanhoe's Shareholder Rights Plan to arbitration. (Rio Tinto 2010)

Reluctance to disclose the actual procedure can also lead to omitting the very term that defines it, that is, 'arbitration', as in the press release entitled 'Danone announcement on the Wahaha Dispute', which made the filing of arbitration public and reworded the term as 'appropriate proceedings':

> Danone has commenced appropriate proceedings today. (Groupe Danone 2007b)

It is also interesting to see that when it is the respondent who discloses the filing, the wording varies, as in the case *Bahrain Asphalt Establishment* (BAE) *vs. Gamuda-WCT* (case 6). The arbitration was filed by BAE against Gamuda-WCT's joint venture in Qatar for the cost overruns as a result of delays in completion of the sub-contract works for the joint venture's project, which involved the construction of a new motorway in Qatar. The arbitration claim is made public on Gamuda's website: 'Request for arbitration by Bahrain Asphalt Establishment B.S.C.' (Gamuda 2010) where the choice of 'request' is both the appropriate technical term and a strategic choice, since cases have to be accepted before the process is initiated, and Gamuda expresses its standing on the issue in the body of the announcement:

> Gamuda is of the opinion that the request for arbitration by BAE is premature as the preconditions stipulated in the arbitration clause have not been met.

1 Following the conventions of studies in metaphor, metaphoric expressions or linguistic metaphors are represented here by *italics* as surface-level realizations of underlying conceptual metaphors, represented here IN SMALL CAPS.

The same announcement appeared in the official financial report 'Gamuda Berhad (29579-T) Quarterly Report On Consolidated Results For The Financial Quarter Ended 31 January 2010', where the arbitration was included in the section entitled 'litigations'. Expert reports from various investment research groups reproduced the company's statement, with identical wording, on the following days. At the time of writing, no more information has been made public.

Phase 3. The ongoing arbitration process

There are wide variations in the way corporations tackle the ongoing case. In high-profile cases such as *Scottish & Newcastle vs. Carlsberg* (Corona 2012), publicity is part of the strategy and thus their press releases act as a dialogue between the parties, as if both parties were playing to the gallery:

> S&N's legal claims are spurious, without merit and a distraction to advancing discussions. (Carlsberg Group 2007)

> We are confident of our legal position, we have a robust case. (Scottish & Newcastle 2007b)

S&N's determined attitude and openness would continue throughout the process:

> S&N welcomes date for arbitration award. (Scottish & Newcastle 2008)

The dichotomy discussion-arbitration is also a recurrent discourse. In two of the ten cases explored (cases 2 and 9), the arbitration process was temporarily interrupted. This is how the corporations Danone and Wahaha (case 2), under pressure from their own countries, France and China, announced the suspension through the linguistic metaphor 'peace talks', which draws again on the conceptual metaphor of ARBITRATION IS A WAR (italics my own):

> Complying with the expectations of both Chinese and French governments, both Wahaha Group and Groupe Danone agree to finish antagonism and return to *peace talks*. (Groupe Danone 2007c)

When the suspension proves to no avail, as in case 9, corporations announce their return to arbitration:

> Archangel Diamond Corporation announces that the Stockholm commercial arbitration against OAO Arkhangelskoe Geologodobychnoe Predpriyatie is re-commencing in accordance with a new timetable agreed with the Tribunal. (Archangel Diamond Corporation 2009a)

More generally, corporations tend to give updated news on the critical moments of the process. The formality and careful wording of the different stages is exemplified in the following press release delivered by Ivanhoe Mines (case 7), entitled 'Ivanhoe Mines delivers response and initiates counter-claim in arbitration proceeding with Rio Tinto' (Ivanhoe Mines 2010a). The opening paragraph makes the announcement. The second and third paragraphs develop the two main pieces of information stated in the first, and the fourth gives information about the date for the hearing. The language used owes much to the legal register in the use of technical concepts and lexis, and it was most probably dictated by the corporation's legal counsels (Corona 2011b):

> Robert Friedland, Executive Chairman and Chief Executive Officer of Ivanhoe Mines, announced today that Ivanhoe Mines has delivered a statement of defence and initiated a counter-claim as part of an ongoing arbitration proceeding launched by Rio Tinto on July 9, 2010.
>
> The statement of defence rejects Rio Tinto's claim that the shareholders' rights plan approved by Ivanhoe Mines' shareholders on May 7, 2010, breached Rio Tinto's contractual rights under its agreements with Ivanhoe Mines.
>
> The counter-claim contends that Rio Tinto has breached its covenants in its private placement agreement, signed with Ivanhoe Mines in October 2006, not to engage in activities that could affect control of Ivanhoe Mines without Ivanhoe's permission.
>
> An independent arbitrator has scheduled hearings of the claim and counter-claim between January 18 and February 5, 2011.

The ongoing process can hardly be controlled by the corporations, despite their efforts to keep the proceedings confidential. This reality accounts for the announcements corporations feel compelled to make when the media takes the lead and makes comments on the ongoing dispute. The following examples are a case in point. In the first example, we can see that the corporation Ivanhoe Mines is far from pleased with the way the media is dealing with the ongoing arbitration. In contrast with the language used in the previous example, the press release is highly evaluative, rating the information as 'false', 'misleading', ' conjecture' and 'blinkered speculation' (italics my own):

> Alert Issued About False and Misleading Statements Published by the Australian and Business Spectator
>
> Editors and journalists are advised that stories published in The Australian newspaper on September 15, 2010, and on the Business Spectator website on September 14, 2010, contained *false and misleading information* concerning Ivanhoe Mines and the rapidly advancing Oyu Tolgoi mine development project.

> Flouting fundamental, fair journalistic practice, none of the *instances of conjecture and blinkered speculation presented as facts* were checked with Ivanhoe Mines in advance of publication. (Ivanhoe Mines 2010b)

The same can be said of Agfa-Gevaert's (case 5) reaction to some information published by the media, and this shows its intention to disclose as little as possible about the ongoing dispute, claiming confidentiality of the proceedings:

> The German and international press have published varying reports on legal disputes [...] Afga-Gevaert has meritorious positions in current lawsuits and disputes and will prosecute its claims vigorously. Agfa-Gevaert respects confidentiality and will limit its comments on the proceedings accordingly. (Agfa-Gevaert 2006)

One of the presumed advantages of arbitration is that the proceedings are considered to be shorter than litigation. The truth of the matter is that arbitration cases may take just as long, with lengthy delays. Because of the uncertainty involved and the time invested, this phase 3 is the weakest period for the corporations to keep information under control, or at least to manage satisfactorily the ups and downs of the process. Certainly some corporations are more successful than others.

Phase 4. The end of the process

The conclusion of arbitration has various possible scenarios. The expected one is the final judgment or award, although the tribunal may issue partial ones if the claim contains several matters. Furthermore, the parties may reach an agreement prior to the rendering of the award, in which case the proceedings may be declared as 'terminated', as in case 9 where Archangel Diamond Corporation (2009b) announced the event as such: 'Archangel Diamond Corporation Stockholm arbitration terminated'; they can be declared 'suspended', as in *Rio Tinto vs. Ivanhoe* (case 7) in which a new financial agreement led to a temporary interruption of the case: 'Ivanhoe Mines and Rio Tinto agree to suspend arbitration proceeding for 6 months' (Ivanhoe Mines 2010c).

The final result is more likely to be made public by the successful party, as in the examples below:

> Arbitration panel rules in favor of Dominion Sky Angel. (Sky Angel 2004)

> Andersen Consulting wins arbitration case; will formally separate from Arthur Andersen. (Andersen Consulting 2000)

When both parties announce the outcome of arbitration, we can observe what van Dijk (see, for example, 1998) describes as the 'ideological square' strategy at work. In *Agfa-Gevaert vs. AgfaPhoto* (case 5) the respondent, AgfaPhoto, won the case, but Agfa-Gevaert mitigated the result, focusing on the circumstance of being a 'partial' award; that is, relating to only part of the claims which had been brought, and omits the result:

> ICC International Court of Arbitration issues partial award in trademark arbitration relating to AgfaPhoto. (Agfa-Gevaert 2007)

In contrast, AgfaPhoto's text clearly specifies the result and ignores the fact that it was a partial award:

> AgfaPhoto holding wins trademark dispute with Agfa-Gevaert. (AgfaPhoto 2007)

The same strategy is applied by Repsol, one of the respondents in the *Sonatrach vs. Repsol and Gas Natural* case, where the Spanish companies, Repsol and Gas Natural, lost the case against the Algerian company, Sonatrach, which meant that they were pulled out of the gas exploitation project in the North African country. But this is what they announced:

> The Gassi Touil arbitration proceeding is without compensation to any party. (Repsol 2009)

The headline of the press release cannot be said to be untrue: they did not have to pay damages for delays, but the key issue was the termination of the contract and thus the end of their business there. Repsol emphasized its positive result and ignored, by textual silence, the negative one.

The case *S&N vs. Carlsberg* (case 1) virtually 'disappeared' when Carlsberg eventually took over S&N. An identical press release appeared in both corporations' websites: 'Scottish & Newcastle enters into discussions with Carlsberg and Heineken' (Scottish & Newcastle 2008, Carlsberg Group 2008). There was no further specific mention of it on the corporations' websites. An arbitration case which had produced 42 press releases in five months, 22 from S&N and 20 from Carlsberg respectively, did not deserve a single word once the desired result (a very profitable acquisition) had been reached.

Similar behaviour is observed in *Danone vs. Wahaha*. Four hours after Danone had agreed to pull out of the joint venture, the award was rendered. Only the announcement 'Danone and Wahaha reach an amicable settlement' (Groupe Danone 2009, Wahaha Group 2009) appeared on their websites, and Danone, the 'winner' in the case, omitted the positive arbitration outcome altogether.

To summarize the dominant trend in the lexical expressions for the conceptualization of arbitration when disclosure takes place on the corporate side, we could reasonably argue that, at word level, press releases display specific rhetorical devices. With the exception of two high-profile cases (*S&N vs. Carlsberg* and *Danone vs. Wahaha*), they tend to start, by the very concept of 'discussions' in the pre-arbitration phase, to be referred to as 'disputes' in both the filing and the arbitration process or with the technical term 'arbitration' in particular, when specific information has to be released. In phase 4, if there is an apparent end to the dispute, we see a semantic softening in the graduation scale by going back to 'discussions', or to the antonym of 'dispute' – 'agreement' – when the issue is settled before the award. When an award is rendered, 'wins' or 'rules in favour' + 'arbitration' are the preferred formulae. When the arbitration proceedings are no longer relevant, they are ignored; that is, there is textual silence.

4. The resemiotization of arbitration in the media

There are two dominating trends in media reports of arbitration which in all probability are not exclusive to this field: one that literally reproduces corporate discourse and one that recontextualizes information. The new information technology has undoubtedly maximized the former. To take just one example, the press release posted by Archangel Diamond (case 9) on the corporation's website to announce the termination of arbitration (Archangel Diamond Corporation 2009b) prompted 15 identical postings on different websites. It is the latter practice that is of interest here. The resemiotization of arbitration brings particular metaphors and other rhetorical devices to bear in the interpretation of arbitration events from the press releases as source texts.

'The essence of metaphor', Lakoff and Johnson (1980: 5) explain, 'is understanding and experiencing one kind of thing in terms of another'. That is, metaphor consists in relating different semantic domains of experience. Richardson (2007: 66) argues that 'certain types of metaphors are associated with specific genres of journalism', and gives as the most significant example the use of metaphors of war in sports reporting. There is also substantial research that has pointed out that business media discourse is permeated by metaphors (see, for example, Greco 2009; Koller 2005, 2009; White 2003; White and Herrera 2009). Business media journalists seem to draw mostly on the same range of metaphoric conceptualizations of business practice as evolutionary struggle, with MATING, FEEDING and FIGHTING as the most dominant metaphors (Koller 2005).

Let us see how the news reports on the cases explored recontextualize arbitration, following the same phases outlined in the previous section.

The pre-arbitration phase (phase 1) is represented as a pre-war scenario in the following headline from the *Daily Mail* (italics my own):

> S&N *mobilises to fight* Danes. (Ebrahimi 2007)

In the body of the text, it reinforces the confidentiality of the strategic defensive move where arbitration is still a 'secret plan' (italics my own):

> S&N is hatching *secret plans* to fend off a hostile takeover bid from Continental rival Carlsberg. (Ebrahimi 2007)

The incipient dispute between Vodacom and Congolese Wireless Network (case 4) is lexicalized with an idiomatic expression (italics my own):

> Vodacom DRC shareholders *lock horns*. (*TeleGeography* 2010)

The idiom 'to lock horns' means to argue and it is etymologically based on the same literal meaning of two animals fighting. It could be considered a dead metaphor, but its use here to refer to an incipient dispute on African soil helps it recover the source domain of the reader's background knowledge and combines it with the target domain (pre-arbitration) to create a live metaphor of fight.

At this stage, we can also find low-scale near-synonyms[2] of the incipient dispute, such as 'row', that is, 'a noisy argument' (italics my own):

> Vodacom, Congo partners to meet over capital *row*. (*Reuters* 2010a)

> *Row brews* over Russian beer pact. (*BBC News* 2007)

In the second example, which refers to two brewing companies (case 1), the headline plays with polysemy, with the meanings of 'brew' as 'make beer' and 'be imminent' to construe a homographic pun.

We have seen how the announcement of arbitration proceedings, i.e. phase 2, by the corporations tends to be lexicalized using the technical term 'arbitration', and it can be duly reproduced in the media literally:

> Vodacom plans arbitration proceedings over Congo unit. (Kew and Kavanagh 2010)

> Ivanhoe to support Rights Plan in Rio Tinto arbitration. (McKinnon 2010)

> Algeria takes gas disputes to UN arbitration court. (*Magharebia* 2007)

However, when the technical word is not specified; i.e., it is an arbitration case, the use of the metonym 'court' brings ambiguity to the message. Metonymy is defined by Chandler (1994: Glossary of Key Terms, Metonymy) as a function which involves 'using one signified to stand for another signified which is directly related to it or closely associated with it in some way.' In this case, the arbitration proceedings are substituted by the institution or organization sometimes referred to as the Court of Arbitration.

2 I take here Edmonds and Hirst's (2002) definition of near-synonyms as words being very similar but not identical, with peripheral concepts making significant distinctions.

Bid target S&N takes Carlsberg to court. (*Evening Standard* 2007)

Sonatrach will take Gassi Touil Partners to court. (*Petroleum Africa* 2007)

Rio, Ivanhoe heading to court. (Chambers 2010)

This particular kind of metonymic substitution focuses on the legal, adversarial aspect of arbitration and thus frames the way the reader thinks about it, as a lawsuit that takes place in court. Similarly, the legal action verb 'sue' in the headline below reinforces this ambiguity and makes it indistinguishable from litigation:

Danone set to sue Wahaha over breach of contract. (*South China Morning Post* 2007)

The ongoing arbitration stage, or phase 3, is by far the most prolific in terms of media output. In contrast to the corporations' reluctance to provide general information on the ongoing dispute through their press releases, the media keeps the dispute public. The metaphoric expressions or linguistic metaphors shown in the examples below (in italics) are all surface-level realizations of the underlying conceptual metaphor of ARBITRATION IS A WAR:

Double agents in a *cold war*. (Kemp 2007)

S&N seeks Russian resolution in Carlsberg *war*. (Jameson and Walsh 2007)

A Chinese company *fights* its French partner. (Barboza and Kanter 2007)

Danone *strikes back* at Wahaha. (*People's Daily* 2007)

S&N awaits bid *battle* verdict. (Wiggins 2008)

Christian TV Networks *Battle* for the Heavens. (Olsen 2003)

Danone's Chinese Food *Fight* Gets Messier. (Kwok 2007)

[In] the ongoing *feud* [...] Vodacom is still *fighting the fight*. (Francis 2011)

[Ivanhoe's] *battle* with Rio Tinto for control of Mongolia's Oyu Tolgoi mine is continuing. (Hotter 2010a)

[A] financial *fisticuff*. (Jones 2010)

Ivanhoe defiant in Rio *stoush*. (Hotter 2010b)

If 'row' was the near-synonym for the imminent dispute in phase 1, other more potent synonyms appear in the midst of the dispute, as linguistic intensifiers. In a semantics of graduation (Martin and White 2005), the conceptual metaphor of ARBITRATION IS A WAR gives way to a range of linguistic expressions, with a cline clearly upscaled, instantiated mainly by *battle* and *fight*, but also by *feud, strike back, fisticuff* or *stoush* (Australian slang for 'a violent fight').

In the last phase of the arbitration case, or phase 4, the possible scenarios outlined in the previous section also have a particular recontextualization. Thus, the final award is again worded as 'suit', or 'lawsuit'; that is, as a litigation process (my italics):

> Dominion Sky Angel wins EchoStar *suit.* (*Christian Examiner* 2004)

> News & information site regarding the dominion sky angel/echostar dish network *lawsuit.* (*DBSTalk* 2004)

In the second case, the text opens as follows: 'After more than a year of litigation, an arbitration panel has unanimously ruled ...' where both processes are used as being the same practice and thus having the same meaning. Otherwise, it is often left unclear:

> Court overrules Agfa's termination of AgfaPhoto trademark agreement. (*Forbes* 2007)

> Gassi Touil project: Sonatrach wins case against Spanish companies. (*Algeria News* 2009)

When the arbitration is clearly specified, it is portrayed as a war to be won or lost:

> Arbitrator's ruling goes against accounting arm: consultants *win battle* of Andersen. (Martin 2000)

The conceptual metaphor of ARBITRATION IS A WAR is again present when arbitration is 'suspended', in the case *Rio Tinto vs. Ivanhoe* (case 7) (my italics):

> Rio Tinto and Ivanhoe *bury the hatchet.* (Bouw 2010)

> Ivanhoe and Rio Tinto *call truce* over financing pact. (*Reuters* 2010b)

As we have seen, some of the cases explored seem to have 'abandoned' the arbitration proceedings, and there is a softening of the terms used. For example, the 'war' between Scottish & Newcastle and Carlsberg (case 1) vanishes into thin air to be replaced by negotiation, with the expression 'in talks' (my italics):

> Scottish & Newcastle *in talks* on Carlsberg-Heineken takeover. (*AFP* 2008)

More remarkably, the arbitration case is accorded less newsworthiness, only to appear at the end of the report to state that it has disappeared from the corporations' press releases. It is then referred to as a 'spat', that is, a brief and petty quarrel, with a clear downscaling of the issue (italics my own):

> Thursday's statement gave no update on the ongoing *spat* between S&N and Carlsberg. (*AFP* 2008)

As we can see, the overall representation of an event can be conceptualized as more important or less important by means of the lexical item chosen.

To summarize the results of the exploration of the construct of arbitration in news reports, we could argue that because of the specific semantics determined by the generic influences of media practices, which make use of a combination of metaphor and metonymy, the overall representation shows significant differences if compared with the formulation of arbitration produced in the press releases. Cockcroft and Cockcroft (2005: 169) contend that metonymy employs a principle of structural association while metaphor functions on a principle of semantic association. Following this line, we could arguably assert that the media discourse of arbitration structurally associates, as a professional practice, with litigation, and is semantically conceptualized as a corporate war. In other words, the use of metonymy accounts for the confusion with litigation, while the use of metaphor reinforces the concept of arbitration as war.

5. The sociocognitive impact of the new construct of arbitration

I started this chapter with the definition of commercial arbitration as a dispute resolution device, originally meant to be carried out confidentially so that corporations could wash their 'dirty linen' in private. How confidentiality is currently understood and applied depends on multiple factors: on the law of the seat of arbitration, the rules of the arbitral institution or on the contractual provisions made by the parties but, increasingly so, on the way corporations deal with their arbitration processes in the public sphere.

The aim of this chapter has been to enhance understanding of the discourse of arbitration on the corporations' messages to the general public and the media's re-articulation of those messages as a consequence of globalization of information. Bearing in mind that informing shareholders and the general public that the corporation is involved in arbitration is not good news,[3] we can understand the general trend towards reluctance – with some remarkable exceptions – to relinquish details of the processes and towards making announcements to respond to media

3 It has been observed that shares fall after announcements of arbitration.

outputs. Corporations themselves refer to media reports, sometimes criticize them, or regret having to discuss matters through them, although they willingly promote their positive arbitration outcomes. We have seen how, in general, the corporations tend to stick to the term 'arbitration', and refer to it as a 'dispute' or replace it with 'discussions' whenever possible, while, in contrast, the media construe a more metaphorical definition of what arbitration is and how the process is to be understood. Koller (2005: 206) states that 'any discourse is cognitively structured by the metaphors prevailing in the respective discourse domain'. In the process of mediation, as 'movement of meaning from context to context, culture to culture, institution to institution' (Silverstone 1999: 13) and – I would add – genre to genre, the dominant metaphor in the media discourse of arbitration consists mainly in equating arbitration processes with transnational wars.

The model established by journalists has an impact on discourse, on the readers' cognition and on the wider social scenario where arbitration is represented as defensive-aggressive, threatening and searching for victory over rivals. The prevailing metaphoric scenario found in media discourse on arbitration helps sustain this social practice as a fight for dominance, making it hard to preserve arbitration within the more desirable limits of concepts such as ARBITRATION IS NEGOTIATION. It has also been observed that high-profile cases tend to increase the adversarial tension.

The main effect of both associations is that they construe arbitration as an adversarial procedure, portraying disputing parties as enemies. These findings strengthen the thesis sustained by Bhatia et al. (2008) that arbitration is becoming indistinguishable from litigation as an adversarial mechanism to settle disputes.

Acknowledgements

I would like to acknowledge project FFI2009-09792, funded by the Spanish Ministerio de Ciencia e Innovación (Secretaría de Estado de Investigación).

References

AFP 2008. *Scottish & Newcastle in Talks on Carlsberg-Heineken Takeover*. [Online, 17 January]. Available at: http://afp.google.com/article/ALeqM5gaJ1GCn-Lmpo__up7wwaYQ155oSw?index=0 [accessed: 18 February 2009].

Agfa-Gevaert 2006. *Agfa-Gevaert on Disputes with AgfaPhoto and AgfaPhoto Employees* [Online, 23 May]. Available at: http://agfa.com/en/co/news_events/press_archive_months/press_releases/CO_200605 [accessed: 3 February 2010].

Agfa-Gevaert 2007. *ICC International Court of Arbitration Issues Partial Award in Trademark Arbitration Relating to AgfaPhoto* [Online, 11 December].

Available at: http://agfa.com/en/co/news_events/pres_archive_months/press_releases/CO20071211_AP_UK.jsp [accessed: 3 February 2010].

AgfaPhoto 2007. *AgfaPhoto Holding Wins Trademark Dispute with Agfa-Gevaert* [Online, 13 December]. Available at: http://www.prnewswire.co.uk/cgi/news/release?id=215171 [accessed: 3 February 2010].

Algeria News 2009. *Gassi Touil project: Sonatrach Wins Case against Spanish Companies* [Online, 29 November]. Available at: http://news.marweb.com/algeria/ecomonics/gassi-touil-project-sonatrach-wins-case-against-spanish-comp [accessed: 12 November 2010].

Andersen Consulting 2000. *Andersen Consulting Wins Arbitration Case; Will Formally Separate from Arthur Andersen* [Online, 7 August]. Available at: http://www.thefreelibrary.com/ersen+Consulting+Wins+Arbitration+Case%3B+Will+Formally+Separate...-a06390106 [accessed: 9 April 2010].

Archangel Diamond Corporation 2009a. *Archangel Diamond Corporation Announces Update on the Status of Arbitration and Litigation* [Online, 7 March]. Available at: http://findarticles.com/p/articles/mi_pwwi/is_200903/ai_n31468875/?tag=content;selector-search [accessed: 3 June 2010].

Archangel Diamond Corporation 2009b. *Archangel Diamond Corporation Stockholm Arbitration Terminated* [Online, 23 October]. Available at: http://diamondinvestingnews.com/1526-archangel-diamond-corp-stockholm-arbitration-terminated.html [accessed: 3 June 2010].

Barboza, D. and Kanter, J. 2007. A Chinese company fights its French partner. *The New York Times* [Online, 13 June]. Available at: http://www.nytimes.com/2007/06/13/business/worldbusiness/13danone.html [accessed: 14 October 2009].

BBC News 2007. *Row Brews over Russian Beer Pact.* [Online, 24 October]. Available at: http://news.bbc.co.uk/2/hi/business/7103004.stm [accessed: 14 February 2009].

Beechey, J. 2009. Foreword. Confidentiality in arbitration. *ICC International Court of Arbitration Bulletin. Special Supplement*, 3.

Bhatia, V.K. 2004. *Worlds of Written Discourse: A Genre-based View*. London: Continuum.

Bhatia, V.K. 2008. Towards critical genre analysis, in *Advances in Discourse Studies,* edited by V.K Bhatia et al. London: Routledge, 166-177.

Bhatia, V.K., Candlin, C.N. and Engberg, J. 2008. Concepts, contexts and procedures in arbitration discourse, in *Legal Discourse across Cultures and Systems*, edited by V.K. Bhatia et al. Hong Kong: Hong Kong University Press, 3-31.

Bhatia, V.K., Candlin, C.N. and Sharma, R. 2009. Confidentiality and integrity in international commercial arbitration practice. *Arbitration*, 75, 2-13.

Bouw, B. 2010. Rio Tinto and Ivanhoe bury the hatchet. *The Globe and Mail* [Online, 10 December]. Available at: http://www.theglobeandmail.com/globe-investor/rio-tinto-and-ivanhoe-bury-the-hatchet/article1829557/ [accessed: 20 February 2009].

Burn, G. and Pearsall, A. 2009. Exceptions to confidentiality in international arbitration. *ICC International Court of Arbitration Bulletin*. Special Supplement, 23-38.

Carlsberg Group 2007. *Carlsberg Response to Statement by Scottish and Newcastle*. [Online, 31 October]. Available at: http://www.carlsberggroup.com/media [accessed: 21 February 2009].

Carlsberg Group 2008. *Scottish & Newcastle Enters into Discussions with Carlsberg and Heineken* [Online, 17 January]. Available at: http://www.carlsberggroup.com/media. Company Announcement 4/2008 [accessed: 20 February 2009].

Chambers, M. 2010. Rio, Ivanhoe heading to court. *The Australian* [Online, 15 September]. Available at: http://www.theaustralian.com.au/business/rio-ivanhoe-heading-to-court-over-mongolian-project/story-e6frg8zx-1225922985519 [accessed: 12 November 2010].

Chandler, D. 1994. *Semiotics for Beginners* [Online]. Available at: http://www.aber.ac.uk/media/Documents/S4B/ [accessed: 20 November 2008].

Christian Examiner 2004. *Dominion Sky Angel wins EchoStar suit* [Online, 20 October]. Available at: http://www.christianexaminer.com/Articles/Articles%20Oct04/Art_Oct04_07.html Dominion Sky Angel wins EchoStar suit [accessed: 20 July 2010].

Cockcroft, R. and Cockcroft, S. 2005. *Persuading People: An Introduction to Rhetoric*. New York: Palgrave MacMillan.

Corona, I. 2011a. Arbitration recontextualized. *World Englishes*, 30(1), 129-140.

Corona, I. 2011b. Confidentiality at risk: the interdiscursive construction of International Commercial Arbitration. *Discourse & Communication*, 5(4), 355-374.

Corona, I. 2012. Confidentiality vs publicity: the impact of international arbitration in the media. A case-study, in *Discourse and Practice in International Commercial Arbitration: Issues, Challenges and Prospects*, edited by V.K. Bhatia, C.N. Candlin and M. Gotti. London: Ashgate Publishing.

DBSTalk 2004. *News & Information Site Regarding the Dominion Sky Angel/Echostar Dish Network Lawsuit* [Online, 13 September]. Available at: http://www.dbstalk.com/archive/index.php/t-32998.html [accessed: 21 July 2010].

Ebrahimi, H. 2007. S&N mobilises to fight Danes. *Daily Mail* [Online, 9 September]. Available at: http://www.dailymail.co.uk/money/markets/article-1613813/SN-mobilises-to-fight-Danes.html [accessed: 12 February 2009].

Edmonds, P. and Hirst, G. 2002. Near-synonymy and lexical choice. *Computational Linguistics*, 28(2), 105-144.

Evening Standard 2007. *Bid Target S&N Takes Carlsberg to Court*. [Online, 31 October]. Available at: http://www.thisismoney.co.uk/money/markets/article-1615532/Bid-target-SN-takes-Carlsberg-to-court.html [accessed: 24 February 2009].

Fairclough, N. 2006. *Language and Globalization*. London: Routledge.

Forbes 2007. *Court Overrules Agfa's Termination of AgfaPhoto Trademark Agreement* [Online, 13 December]. Available at: http://www.forbes.com/feeds/afx/2007/12/12/afx4429700.html [accessed: 3 February 2010].

Francis, L. 2011. Save Vodacom DRC. *ITWeb Financial* [Online 10 January]. Available at: http://www.itweb.co.za/index.php?option=com_content&view=article&id=39976:save-vodacom-drc [accessed: 15 April 2011].

Gamuda 2010. *Request for Arbitration by Bahrain Asphalt Establishment* [Online, 11 March]. Available at: http://www.gamuda.com.my/newsroom.html [accessed: 26 March 2011].

Greco, S. 2009. Metaphoral headlines in business, finance and economic magazines. *Linguistica e Filologia*, 28, 193-211.

Groupe Danone 2007a. *Groupe Danone Confirms Being in Negotiations with its Chinese Partner in Beverages, Mr Zong* [Online, 10 April]. Available at: http://phx.corporate-ir.net/phoenix.zhtml?c=95168&p=irol-news&nyo=0 [accessed: 11 October 2009].

Groupe Danone 2007b. *Danone Announcement on the Wahaha Dispute* [Online, 9 May]. Available at: http://phx.corporate-ir.net/phoenix.zhtml?c=95168&p=irol-news&nyo=0 [accessed: 11 October 2009].

Groupe Danone 2007c. *Joint Statement between Hangzhou Wahaha Group and Groupe Danone* [Online, 21 December]. Available at: http://phx.corporate-ir.net/phoenix.zhtml?c=95168&p=irol-newsArticle&ID=1089603&highlight= [accessed: 11 October 2009].

Groupe Danone 2009. *Groupe Danone and Wahaha Group Reach an Amicable Settlement* [Online, 30 September]. Available at: http://phx.corporate-ir.net/phoenix.zhtml?c=95168&p=irol-newsArticle&ID=1336626 [accessed: 11 October 2009].

Hotter, A. 2010a. Ivanhoe sticks to shareholders' plan as arbitration continues. *Dow Jones Newswires* [Online, 17 August]. Available at: http://www.tradingmarkets.com/news/stock-alert/ivhmf_rtp_dj-ivanhoe-sticks-to-shareholders-plan-as-arbitration-continues-1114773.html [accessed: 12 November 2010].

Hotter, A. 2010b. Ivanhoe defiant in Rio stoush. *The Australian* [Online, 18 August]. Available at: http://www.theaustralian.com.au/business/ivanhoe-mines-defiant-in-rio-tinto-stoush/story-e6frg8zx-1225906568347 [accessed: 12 November 2010].

Ivanhoe Mines 2010a. *Ivanhoe Mines delivers response and initiates counter-claim in arbitration proceeding with Rio Tinto* [Online, 26 October]. Available at: http://www.ivanhoemines.com/i/pdf/2010Oct26-NR.pdf [accessed: 12 April 2010].

Ivanhoe Mines 2010b. *Alert Issued About False and Misleading Statements Published by the Australian and Business Spectator* [Online, 15 September]. Available at: http://www.ivanhoemines.com/s/The_Facts.asp [accessed: 12 April 2010].

Ivanhoe Mines 2010c. *Ivanhoe Mines and Rio Tinto agree to suspend arbitration proceeding for 6 month* [Online, 8 December]. Available at:

http://www.ivanhoemines.com/i/pdf/2010-12-08_NR.pdf [accessed: 12 April 2010].

Jacobs, G. 1999. *Preformulating the News*. Amsterdam/Philadelphia: John Benjamins.

Jamelson, A. and Walsh, D. 2007. *The Times* [Online, 5 December]. Not Available. [accessed: 28 May 2009].

Jones, C. 2010. Vodacom awaits DRC outcome. *ITWeb Financial* [Online, 11 May]. Available at: http://www.itweb.co.za/index.php?option=com_content&view=article&id=33002:vodacom-awaits-drc-outcome&catid=260&Itemid=59 [accessed: 30 May 2010].

Kemp, K. 2007. Double Agents in a Cold War. *The Sunday Herald* [Online, 24 November]. Available at: http://www.sundayherald.com/misc/print.php?artid=1857567 [accessed: 28 May 2009].

Kew, J. and Kavanagh, M.J. 2010. Vodacom plans arbitration proceedings over Congo unit. *Bloomberg* [Online, 7 April]. Available at: http://www.businessweek.com/news/2010-04-07/vodacom-to-initiate-arbitration-proceedings-over-congo-unit.html [accessed: 2 May 2010].

Koller, V. 2005. Critical Discourse analysis and social cognition: evidence from business media discourse. *Discourse & Society*, 16(2), 199-224.

Koller, V. 2009. Missions and empires: religious and political metaphors in corporate discourse, in *Metaphor and Discourse*, edited by A. Musolff and J. Zinken. London: Palgrave MacMillan, 116-134.

Kwok, V. 2007. Danone's Chinese food fight gets messier. *Forbes Asia Magazine* [Online, 14 June]. Available at: www.forbes.com [accessed: 16 October 2009].

Lakoff, G. and Johnson, M. 1980. *Metaphors We Live By*. Chicago: University of Chicago Press.

Macdonald, M. 2003. *Exploring Media Discourse*. London: Arnold.

McKinnon, J. 2010. Ivanhoe to support Rights Plan in Rio Tinto arbitration. *Dow Jones Newswires* [Online, 12 July]. Available at: http://www.foxbusiness.com/markets/2010/07/12/updateivanhoe-support-rights-plan-rio-tinto-arbitration/ [accessed: 12 November 2010].

Magarebia 2007. *Algeria takes gas disputes to UN arbitration court* [Online, 26 September]. Available at: http://www.magharebia.com/cocoon/awi/xhtml1/en_GB/features/awi/newsbriefs/general/2007/09/26/newsbrief-05 [accessed: 23 March 2010].

Martin, J.R. and White, P.R.R. 2005. *The Language of Evaluation*. London: Palgrave MacMillan.

Martin, M. 2000. Arbitrator's ruling goes against accounting arm: consultants win battle of Andersen. *The New York Times* [Online, 8 August]. Available at: http://www.nytimes.com/2000/08/08/business/worldbusiness/08iht-consult.2.t.html [accessed: 29 April 2010].

Olsen, T. 2003. Christian networks battle over Dish Network. *Christianity Today* [Online, 1 July]. Available at: http://www.christianitytoday.com/ct/2003/julyweb-only/7-14-22.0.html?start=2 [accessed: 19 July 2010].

People's Daily 2007. *Danone strikes back at Wahaha* [Online, 10 May]. Available at: http://english.peopledaily.com.cn/200705/10/eng20070510_373375.html [accessed:11 October 2009].
Petroleum Africa 2007. Sonatrach will take Gassi Touil partners to court [Online, 10 September]. Available at: http://www.petroleumafrica.com/en/newsarticle.php?NewsID=4470&format=print&PHPSESSID=465f6959363307d1d5499597b5a8fb28 [accessed: 23 March 2010].
Repsol 2009. *The Gassi Touil arbitration proceeding is without compensation to any party* [Online, 27 November]. Available at: http://www.repsol.com/es_en/corporacion/prensa/notas-de-prensa/ultimas-notas/27112009-gassi-touil.aspx [accessed: 25 January 2010].
Reuters 2010a. *Vodacom, Congo partners to meet over capital row* [Online, 6 April]. Available at: http://www.abndigital.com/page/news/top-business-stories/462397-Vodacom-Congo-partners-to-meet-over-capital-rowv [accessed: 2 May 2010].
Reuters 2010b. *Ivanhoe and Rio Tinto call truce over financing pact* [Online, 12 December]. Available at: http://tengerfinancialgroup.com [accessed: 2 March 2011].
Richardson, J.E. 2007. *Analysing Newspapers*. London: Palgrave.
Rio Tinto 2010. *Rio Tinto refers Ivanhoe's Shareholder Rights Plan to arbitration* [Online, 9 July]. Available at: http://www.riotinto.com/media/18435_media_releases_19362.asp [accessed: 18 January 2011].
Scottish & Newcastle 2007a. *S&N has today initiated formal arbitration proceedings* [Online, 31 October]. Available at: http://archive.scottish-newcastle.com/sn_acq/acquisition [accessed: 20 February 2009].
Scottish & Newcastle 2007b. *Scottish & Newcastle Plc BBH Arbitration Update* [Online, 20 November]. Available at: http://archive.scottish-newcastle.com/sn_acq/acquisition [accessed: 20 February 2009].
Scottish & Newcastle 2008. *Scottish & Newcastle enters into discussions with Carlsberg and Heineken* [Online, 17 January]. Available at: http://archive.scottish-newcastle.com/sn_acq/acquisition [accessed: 20 February 2009].
Silverstone, R. 1999. *Why Study the Media?* London: Sage.
Sky Angel 2004. *Arbitration panel rules in favor of Dominion Sky Angel* [Online, 13 September]. Available at: http://www.dbstalk.com/archive/index.php/t-32998.html [accessed: 15 July 2010].
South China Morning Post 2007. *Danone set to sue Wahaha over breach of contract*, 11 April, B3.
TeleGeography 2010. Vodacom DCR Shareholders lock horns 2010 [Online, 9 January]. Available at: http://www.telegeography.com/products/commsupdate/articles/2010/01/08/vodacom-drc-shareholders-lock-horns/ [accessed: 2 May 2010].
van Dijk, T.A. 1993 Principles of critical discourse analysis. *Discourse & Society*, 4(2), 249-283.

van Dijk, T.A. 1995 Discourse semantics and ideology. *Discourse & Society*, 6(2), 243-289.

van Dijk, T.A. 1998. Opinions and ideologies in the press, in *Approaches to Media Discourse*, edited by A. Bell and P. Garrett. Oxford: Blackwell, 21-63.

Vodacom 2010a. *Vodacom Congo shareholder dispute* [Online, 6 January]. Available at: http://www.vodacom.com/news_article.php?articleID=566&pid=ir_news_media_releases2 [accessed: 2 May 2010].

Vodacom 2010b. *The Vodacom Group will be initiating arbitration proceedings under ICC rules in Brussels* [Online, 7 April]. Available at: http://www.vodacom.com/news_article.php?articleID=566&pid=press_ir [accessed: 2 May 2010].

Wahaha Group 2008. *Wahaha and Danone Gaming on 'Emotions, Reasoning and Laws'* [Online, 22 August]. Available at: http://en.wahaha.com.cn/news/company/2008/08/22/wahaha962.html [accessed: 12 October 2009].

Wahaha Group 2009. *Danone and Wahaha Group reach an amicable settlement* [Online, 7 December]. Available at: http://en.wahaha.com.cn/news/company/ [accessed: 11 October 2009].

White, M. 2003. Metaphor and economics: the case of growth. *English for Specific Purposes*, 22(2), 131-151.

White, M. and Herrera, H. 2009. How business press headlines get their message across: A different perspective on metaphor, in *Metaphor and Discourse*, edited by A. Musolff and J. Zinken. London: Palgrave MacMillan, 135-152.

Wiggins, J. 2008. S&N awaits bid battle verdict. *The Financial Times* [Online, 3 January]. Available at: http://www.ft.com/coms/s/79a3f5dc-ba68-11dc-abcb+ [accessed: 20 February 2009].

Chapter 6

Arbiter→Arbitration: Genesis of a functional word*

Natale Rampazzo

1. The resolution of disputes in Ancient Rome

Clifford Geertz (1983) argued that, according to Max Weber, human beings are animals suspended in webs of significance they have spun for themselves.[1] Some strands of those webs deal with disputes that are entangled with other cultural, social, political, economic, legal, and linguistic strands, and any historical question must be taken into account in order to define the correct meaning of each phenomenon.

Alternative dispute resolution procedures outside litigation appear to be ordinary practices in less organized and institutionalized societies: self-help, negotiation and arbitration provide in themselves different progressive degrees in an imaginary scale running from private autonomy to public authority intervention. Normally, if the parties are able to settle their dispute themselves by negotiating an agreement, by turning to a mediator or an arbiter authorized to render a decision between them, the community will not interfere unless it is called upon in the enforcement stage against a party who has consciously departed from the agreed solution.

It is difficult to perceive the consciousness of ancient Romans as regards the real legal nature of the procedures they used to settle their own interests in a private matter. The complexity of the issue will inevitably be simplified in this short synopsis as further details may be found in the main literature. In those times, (voluntary) arbitration can be said to constitute the process (other than litigation) by which the parties disputing on the existence or the scope of their individual rights submitted the controversy to a third party appointed by themselves. This process was potentially adjudicative and led to an award outside the arranged settlement between the parties, as in mediation. In the relevant civil procedure of the Republican Age (*legis actiones*, actions based on the law, and *formulae*) until Imperial times, the contending parties went to the *praetor* appointed for a term

* This chapter is a modified version of the presentation given at the Conference '*The Language of Law: pulling together different strands and disciplines*' on 19th June 2010.

1 'Der Mensch ein Wesen ist, das in selbstgesponnene Bedeutungsgewebe verstrickt ist' (Geertz 1983: 9).

of one year, whose competence was *iurisdictio* (i.e. authorized to speak, declare, state the law or the principles applicable to a specific issue). The *praetor* had to identify the terms of the dispute, and, by agreement among the parties, to appoint a *iudex*, a layman who was able – but also obliged (except in statutory cases of exemption from the duty) – to make assessments and valuations about the reported facts and end the procedure by giving a verdict (*iudicatio*).

In the first Republican period there were three possible types of 'cognitive' action.[2] The first consisted of taking an oath on the entitlement of the swearing person to a thing or a credit (*legis actio sacramento*); in the second, the plaintiff made a request to the *praetor* (*postulatio*) in a strictly prescribed form, whereupon the *praetor* would assign (*datio*) the judge (*iudicis arbitrive postulatio*; 'by application for a *iudex* or *arbiter*'), usually for having the debtor breach a formal promise, the *stipulatio*. The third was the *legis actio per condictionem* (literally 'by giving notice'), brought only for a specific thing or a sum of money. Only citizens of Rome could make use of the *legis actiones*, but from 242 BC another *praetor* was appointed (yearly) as Rome became the centre of Mediterranean business, in order to deal with claims where one or more parties were not citizens. Before a decision could be given, the plaintiff issued an oral summons to his opponent, bidding him to appear before the *praetor* (*in ius vocatio*).

The new procedural system, in force until the second half of the fourth century AD, was based on *formulae*. The procedure was divided into two phases respectively managed by the *praetor* (*in iure*) and the *iudex* (*apud iudicem*). The key position was held by the *praetor*, who oversaw the preliminaries before the hearing and had the discretionary power to grant the *formulae* necessary to the finalization of the judicial procedure. If, on the basis of a short description of facts, *the praetor* felt that the complaint was determined and substantially supported by evidence and therefore deserved attention, he granted a *formula* by formally giving the action to the plaintiff. It was for the *praetor* to order the *iudex* to proceed according to such description and the hypothetical solution provided by the drafted *formula*. This was published in an annual edict and could also be applied to other similar cases. *Arbitri* also took part in the bipartite procedure: as mentioned above, the magistrate, with the agreement of the parties, selected a number of *arbitri* (but normally just one) who would hear the litigants at a subsequent meeting. They were mainly involved in connection with claims brought by the *legis actio per postulationem*, specifically used, under authorization by statute, in cases where the demanding party sued on a formal verbal contract called *stipulatio* or when a dispute concerned an inheritance or the division of property, but also boundary controversies (*actio finium regundorum*) and damages caused by rain water (*actio pluviae arcendae*). The majority of such questions required a high level of technical skills in order to make a proper assessment of property values and boundary lines. Here, it could be argued that the *arbitri* shared their considerable

2 See Gai 4.12 and Roebuck and de Loynes de Fumichon (2004: 70-80).

discretionary powers also with the *agrimensores* acting several times beside the judge whom they counselled about difficult matters requiring specific expertise.

2. The origins of the word 'arbiter'

The initial problem in approaching the study of antiquity and 'dead languages' is whether to give in to the temptation of building concepts and categories using modern words belonging to a different legal system, which cannot clarify what ancient lawyers really meant when they talked about arbitration. This methodological issue is well known to ancient scholars rather than Roman lawyers themselves. They often switched from one word to another without regard to lexical consistency, as in the case of *iudex* and *arbiter*, which are mutually interchangeable in the same document, and describe the same person and/or the same function. In other words, ancient scholars did not shape the difference between *iudices* and *arbitri*,[3] as Ulp. 13 *ad ed.*, D. 4.8.13.2[4] wrote while also giving a brief description of the procedure: 'a person is held to have accepted appointment as *arbiter* where he has undertaken to be *iudex* for the parties and promises that he will end the dispute by his award' or again: 'the parties are to choose someone to be *iudex* in an arbitration', or 'a *iudex* appointed *ex compromisso*': P.S. 5.5a.1[5]. This was possible in the eye of the

3 On this topic Cicero's perspective is particularly striking (*pro Mur.* 12.27): *Iam illud mihi quidem mirum videri solet, tot homines, tam ingeniosos, post tot annos etiam nunc statuere non potuisse utrum 'diem tertium' an 'perendinum', 'iudicem' an 'arbitrum' 'rem' an 'litem' dici oporteret*, where the rhetorician said that it was remarkable that so many ingenious men after so many years remain still undecided as to whether one should say, 'two days hence' or 'the day after tomorrow', 'judge' or 'arbitrator', 'cause' or 'case'.

4 *Recepisse autem arbitrium videtur, ut Pedius libro nono dicit, qui iudicis partes suscepit finemque se sua sententia controversiis impositurum pollicetur. Quod si, inquit, hactenus intervenit, ut experiretur, an consilio suo vel auctoritate discuti litem paterentur, non videtur arbitrium recepisse* [Moreover, a person is held to have undertaken to arbitrate (as Pedius says in his Ninth Book), when he has accepted the role of judge and promises to settle the controversies of the parties by his award. But if, as he says, the arbiter has intervened in an attempt to see whether the parties are ready to end the dispute by his advice or authority, he is not held to have undertaken to arbitrate: adapted translation from Watson (1985)].

5 *Res iudicatae videntur ab his, qui imperium potestatemque habent vel qui ex auctoritate eorum inter partes dantur, itemque a magistratibus municipalibus usque ad summam, qua ius dicere possunt, itemque ab his, qui ab imperatore extra ordinem petuntur. Ex compromisso autem iudex sumptus rem iudicatam non facit: sed si poena inter eos promissum sit, poena re in iudicium deducta ex stipulatu peti potest* [Actions-at-law are decided by those who have the authority and power to do so, or by the authority of persons selected by the parties themselves, and likewise by municipal magistrates up to the amount for which they have the legal right to render judgment; and by those who have been appointed by the Emperor out of the regular order. Moreover, a judge appointed in a case involving a joint promise does not render a final decision, but if a penalty has been promised

lawyers perhaps because *iudex* and *arbiter* were both appointed by the *praetor* or by the parties and neither of them was a professional officer charged with the settlement of disputes. An arbiter was also a kind of *iudex* who applied equity, through means of *bona fides*, rather than law, strict law (*ius strictum*). Cicero (*pro Roscio com.* 4.10-11) remarks on this point: 'A *iudicium* is for a certain sum, arbitration for an uncertain. We come before the *iudicium* with the expectation that we shall either win or lose the whole amount in question; we go to arbitration on the understanding that we shall end up neither with nothing nor as much as we asked for. ... What is the formula before a *iudex*? Exact, clear-cut and explicit: "If it appears that 50,000 sesterces are due" ... What is it in an arbitration? Mild, moderate: "As much should be awarded as is the more fair and proper". That man admits he is asking for more than is owed to him but says that he will be more than satisfied with whatever he gets from the arbitrator. So one has confidence in his case, the other has not'. Of certain importance to the issue is also a passage of Seneca minor's *de beneficiis* (3.7),[6] where the philosopher claims that in a trial the issue is confined and the judge, unlike the *arbiter*, does not have unlimited discretion. So a party with a precisely defined case would be better off going to a *iudex*, since the formula constrains him and sets limits he may not exceed. The *arbiter* instead has complete freedom of conscience and can add to or take away from the claim. He has, furthermore, the power to deliver judgment according to the dictates of humanity and mercy rather than law and justice. These sources underline an important feature of Roman law: its judicial way of ascertaining and attributing the entitlement to obtain something from someone seems largely dependent on the opinion of jurists or lawyers. They gave advice to judges and public officers on the law to be applied, but did not usually serve as judges or legislators themselves; they held legal authority in the community, while the judge was a private individual appointed to evaluate the circumstances of a situation and the *praetor* the public gatekeeper of civil law. The main aim of a respected lawyer was to be and act as a *bonus vir*; this way of approaching matters based on

---

by the defendants, and the case is afterwards brought into court, the penalty can be claimed under the relevant action].

6 *Quaecumque in cognitionem cadunt, conprendi possunt et non dare infinitam licentiam iudici; ideo melior videtur condicio causae bonae, si ad iudicem quam si ad arbitrum mittitur, quia illum formula includit et certos, quos non excedat, terminos ponit, huius libera et nullis adstricta uinculis religio et detrahere aliquid potest et adicere et sententiam suam, non prout lex aut iustitia suadet, sed prout humanitas aut misericordia inpulit, regere* [Those things which form the subject of a judicial inquiry can be distinctly defined, and cannot afford unlimited licence to the judge; wherefore a good cause is in a better position if it comes before a judge than before an arbitrator, because the words of the law tie down a judge and define certain limits beyond which he may not pass, whereas the conscience of an arbitrator is free and not fettered by any rules, so that he can either give or take away, and can arrange his decision, not according to the precepts of law and justice, but just as his own kindly feeling or compassion may prompt him].

common sense and good faith[7] rather than technical expertise was the distinctive feature of solving disputes other than by an *arbiter compromissarius*. There are, in fact, similar procedures intended to remove the state of uncertainty concerning both the elements of a contract and the rights arising from it: for example, the so-called *arbitratus boni viri*.

The second problem is the lack of legal sources for the origins and the Republican age that makes a reliable reconstruction of the exact juridical meaning of the word and of the phenomenon impossible. We may therefore turn our attention to literary sources in order to obtain appreciable results for our analysis: authors such as Plautus, Terence or Cato the Elder and, of course, the aforementioned Cicero, allow us to perceive at least something, just as Roman comedy scenarios, though largely dependent upon Greek models, may be revealing in some way. But first, it may be worth turning our attention to the origin of the word *arbiter*. In actual fact, terminologically speaking, most legal theorists assume that this *terminus* was coined in Italy as a compound *ar-bit-(t)er*, from *ad* ('towards') + *baeto/bito* ('go')+ *ter* (someone doing something – and not 'having done' as suggested by the ending *tor*); it means literally 'one who goes to' a place and may end a dispute by giving evidence there (as an eye-witness, a *testis*), 'one who looks into or examines', consequently 'a judge in equity'. The word was actually connected with calling bystanders to witness infringements of property rights (*endoplorare* as mentioned in the Twelve Tables). Doubts raised by linguists about this position are based on the fact that *baeto* (and *bito)* contains a long vowel; the 'i' in *arbiter* is short but in Latin cannot be made a compound word by shortening the vowel of its root. A more audacious etymology has been put forward by Martino.[8] He proposed a kind of Italo-Semitic compound whose primary element is the root *rb*, well known in the eastern world with the sense of 'mediate as guarantee', 'security', or 'dealer', placing the matrix of the institution in the business relations of merchants who traded in the Mediterranean in the sixth century BC (Phoenicians and others whose mother tongue was not Indo-European). The term was then consolidated in Roman vocabulary. It is possible that the words coming from *arbit* are a relic of an original linguistic mélange, developed as a means of communication between two or more groups that did not have a language in common. The Semitic root *rb* can be explained as 'a third party dealing between buyer and seller in commercial matters' and later also in private matters. An economic substratum can also be found in the similar oriental word *arrabon* (in classical Latin *arrha*), a sort of guarantee, consisting in the previous delivery of a sum of money or a token to bind both parties to a deal.

7 This is the criterion regulating business life in ancient Rome just as much as daily life. There was a form of procedure called *bonae fidei iudicia* where the judge had to possibly condemn the defendant to pay 'whatever he ought to give or do in accordance with good faith'. See Roebuck and de Loynes de Fumichon (2004: 51-52).

8 Martino (1986: 59-72) for his argument, and for the collection of the various opinions (1986: 11-26).

The word *arbiter* was not used only for 'dispute solvers'. It might also have been used in the case of contracting parties who wished an arbiter to settle the terms of the contractual partnership, such as the proportion to which profits and losses were to be divided. In a case in which profits were unequally assigned, the jurist Proculus (5 *ep*. D. 17.2.76)[9] pointed out that there were two kinds of *arbitri*: the first has complete freedom and the decision he renders has to be abided by, whether it is fair or not, while the second may decide within the limits of discretion of a *bonus vir*,[10] i.e. of an exemplar of superior moral character. Thus, his *sententia* must conform to the qualities usually appreciated of a good and reasonable man, otherwise it is void. Also from this fragment it can be easily argued that the word in itself is ambiguous: it was used to mean different things. For example, in Cato's *de agri cultura*, the character of a *vir bonus* often emerges whose *arbitratus* is binding for the parties since he adopts a standard of judgment which may be considered objective: what is subjective is the personal expertise in also adapting quantitative criteria to the state of facts. Something uncertain does not at first lead to a dispute but rather to the necessity for clarification: if a ladder is to be returned after use but has been broken, the parties who did not regulate this eventuality have to keep to the decision of a third impartial party and therefore a fair deduction will be made by the arbitration of a *vir bonus*.[11] Again, it is well known that wine cannot be sold if it has become sour or musty; the purchaser has to taste it within three days under the arbitration of a reasonable man (*de agr.* 148.1). It might be concluded that the role of a *vir bonus* is to decide on a specific and foreseeable issue in a contract, as can also be seen from the later evidence of *Digesta*,[12] where a *vir bonus* in a conditional contract is called to settle whether the condition is satisfied or not before the sale is executed.

Turning back to Roman comedy (which was widely dependent on Greek models),[13] it could be of interest to deepen our understanding of its content.

9 *Arbitrorum enim genera sunt duo, unum eiusmodi, ut sive aequum sit sive iniquum, parere debeamus (quod observatur, cum ex compromisso ad arbitrum itum est), alterum eiusmodi, ut ad boni viri arbitrium redigi debeat, etsi nominatim persona sit comprehensa, cuius arbitratu fiat* [There are, in fact, two kinds of arbitrators. the first we are obliged to obey whether he is fair or unfair; this principle applies in cases where people go to an arbitrator having made a mutual promise to abide by his decisions. The other is one whose decision must be made to conform with the judgement of a good man, even if the person by whose decision the matter is to go forward is expressly identified: transl. by Watson 1985].

10 On the case see, e.g., Stein (1995: 225-226). This is one of the possible conceptual abstractions made by lawyers and rhetoricians to set a model of diligence and virtue (such as the *pater familias*). See Cicero, *de off.* 3.19.

11 Cato de agr. 144.2: *si* [*scalae*] *non erunt redditae, aequom <viri boni> arbitratu deducetur*; see also 145.3 about the contractual arrangements for pressing olives.

12 Ulp. 28 *ad Sab.* D. 18.1.7 pr.

13 This peculiarity has often caused difficulties for scholars in approaching genuine Roman elements. But I think that a playwright follows his audience no less than the opposite: in order to entertain and amuse, the scenes and the story needed to be clear and

In the Plautine era, remedies were applied such as *bonae fidei iudicia* and the *actiones in bonum et aequum conceptae* (actions framed on considerations of what is right and fair) noted before, in which the defendant was condemned to give whatever amount of money seemed right and fair (*bonum et aequum*). This kind of formulation (very common in the relevant period) evokes extreme freedom of judgment for the person charged with settling the dispute, which could lead to an arbitrary decision.[14] On the contrary, the term *arbiter* appears rarely in the comedies of Plauto, where it is often connected with the idea of fairness (*Cas.* 966;[15] *Rud.* 1004, 1016, 1038-1044; *Truc.* 629[16] and Terence *Heaut.* 498-501). This has led to clashes between legal historians, optimistically arguing that private arbitrators existed in the second century, and Latin literature scholars, maintaining that the addition of *aequus* to *arbiter* in the Plautine *loci* is due more to an alliterative effect than to a significant example of arbitration. This is because it is not rare to find persons acting as arbitrators or mediators in comedy scenes without being mentioned as *arbitri* in a technical sense. But it does seem plausible that a concept is not always revealed by the presence of the word used to depict it. For instance, in Plautus' *Curculio* (701-703),[17] Phaedromus interferes in the dispute between a soldier and a pimp concerning the return of a sum of money used to purchase a would-be slave. He enters the scene asking for permission to arrange a solution: *animum advortite, si possum hoc inter vos componere* and stating that his opinion had to be followed by the parties, almost making the arbitration dependent on these promises: ... *dicam meam sententiam,/siquidem voltis quod decrero facere.* The answer is: *tibi permittimus*. The *iudicium* made by Phaedromus, who was himself an involved party aiming to marry the slave girl Planesium, is frustrating for Cappadox who is condemned to give back the money and compelled to do so by threat of physical violence,[18] a way of enforcing the 'award'. It is in fact present both during the arbitration (707, 713) and after the verdict is rendered (718, 723, 725-727). In *Rudens*, the wording is even clearer: it dealt with a classic situation requiring the intervention of a third party, determining the entitlement to the disputed thing (a chest fished out of the sea): the situation requires a sequester or an arbiter, otherwise there is no way out: [Trachalio] *tu istunc hodie non feres, nisi das sequestrem aut arbitrum/quoius haec res arbitratu fiat*, and some lines below

---

understandable to common people: this gives meaning and success to a non-hermetic performance, which seeks public appreciation and aims to excite through irony.

14 See Paul. Fest. *de verb. sign.* p. 15: *arbiter dicitur iudex, quod totius rei habeat arbitrium et facultatem.*

15 *Nunc ego te cum aequom arbitrum extra considium captavero.*

16 *Abo domum ego te cum, bellator, arbitrum aequom ceperim.*

17 Phaed. Now attend to me, both of you, if I can arrange between you. You let him go. Procurer, come you this way. I'll pronounce my opinion, if indeed you are ready to abide by what I shall decide you should do. Therap. We leave it to you.

18 The element of violence and intimidation by expressing the will to apply to the authorities (hence the threat of a raw or an institutionalized force), as preliminary to the recourse to arbitration, is not rare: Scafuro (1997: 178, 424-453).

(1018) again: *aut ad arbitrum reditur aut sequestro ponitur.*[19] The alternative is between entrusting somebody with the chest or appointing a third party in order to perform the settlement. [20] Arbitration is also seen as a peaceful way to treat the disputes such as ibid. (1041-1042): Gripus: 'although I know for certain that the thing is mine, I'll go along with it, rather than fight you now'.[21] And then, to the qualities of the *arbiter*: 'though you're calling me before an arbiter I don't know, if he will bring faith into play, however unknown he is I'll know him and, if not – though known – he will be my most distant acquaintance'.[22] This passage perfectly describes the proper features of an *arbiter*; he must follow the criterion of good faith which becomes a common ground of mutual acknowledgement: the *boni viri* rely upon this essential quality, bound by a code of honour to act in a proper way according to ideals of fairness.

In Terence (*Heaut.* 498-501), there is the representation of a typical arbitration dealing with boundary disputes: Menedemus: *paulum hoc negoti mi obstat: Simus et Crito/vicini nostri hic ambigunt de finibus:/me cepere arbitrum: ibo ac dicam, ut dixeram/operam daturum me, hodie non posse eis dare.*[23] The litigants have appointed a neighbour in order to settle the controversy between them or, rather, they have 'caught' him – this is the meaning of *capere* – and, after his 'acceptance' (i.e. *accipere*, coming from *capere* with the addition of *ad*, signifying to agree with the choice) usually described, in the legal sources, with the word *receptum* (again from *capere* by adding the particle *re-*, denoting a positive attitude towards a proposal, a plan, a suggestion), he has to carry out an activity program consisting of finding out the best answer to the question. It is hard to doubt the connections among the evidence examined: in each, the appointment of an arbiter is expressed with a *captio. Operam dare* (or *praestare* or *praebere*) is the content of the performance required from the *arbiter* according to the given (and accepted) task. He feels free to postpone the accomplishment of the obligation, but only by communicating his will to the parties, stating his intentions with a verbal act (*dicere*). As Scafuro (1995) argues, this evidence is not to be underestimated[24] in the reconstruction of the arbitral environment and characteristics in the second

19 'You shall not carry that off this day, unless you find a trustee for it, or an arbitrator, by whose opinion this matter may be settled' … 'or it is referred to arbitration, or it is placed in safe keeping'.

20 About the roles of *arbiter* and *sequester* see Broggini (1957: 120) and Wlassak (1895: 408-411).

21 *Quamquam istuc esse ius meum certo scio,/fiat istuc potius, quam nunc pugnem tecum.*

22 *Quamquam ad ignotum arbitrum me appellis, si adhibebit fidem,/etsist ignotus, notus: si non, notus ignotissimust.*

23 'There's a little bit of business getting in my way. Our neighbours Simus and Crito are in dispute about their boundaries. They have taken me as arbiter. I am going to tell them that the job they are giving me I cannot do for them today.'

24 Scafuro (1995) also argues, inter alia, that 'where arbitral figures are designated in Roman Comedy and are recognizable as private arbitrators, the scenarios are dependent

century BC. The various pathways mentioned must be put together like *tesserae* or pieces of a jigsaw: the dependence on Greek models is structural and substantial but cannot in itself exclude the Roman distinctiveness of the legal materials used in the plot. Summarizing, it could be stated that in the comedies of Plautus and Terence the terms *iudex* and *arbiter* have different technical meanings: the former to mean judge or (in Terence) private arbitrator, and the latter to mean both the judicial system and the third party to an arbitration. The use of arbitration scenarios is not random as Scafuro claims;[25] but in any case not so frequent as is usually thought.

3. The elementary moments of the arbitration process and their linguistic features

The main phases of an arbitrary dispute settlement were the *compromissum* (reference), binding the parties like a contract, the *receptum arbitri* (undertaking of reference), i.e. the approval of the convention by the third party, and the *sententia* (award) given by the arbiter. Arbitration was possible on any private matter except for delicts, which involved *infamia* or issues concerning the freedom of a person.

Compromissum

During the second century BC, the noun *compromissum* acquired a technical meaning: the combination of two mutual promises to comply with an arbitration and to submit to the arbitrator's award was usually endorsed by a penal clause. This served as a balance of two opposites: if the law ignored the arbitration as such, it would be completely ineffective, while if regulated too closely arbitration would become a pale reflection of the legal process with all its disadvantages. The *Digest* gives us a functional definition: *compromissum* is to be brought into a category analogous to judgments and is aimed at putting an end to lawsuits.[26] At least that is the most common interpretation of the sentence '*ad finiendas lites*', which could be rather considered in the sense of trying to give the right context of a controversy by describing the facts and organizing the legal framework in which they have to be evaluated. However, from a structural perspective, a *compromissum* seems to contain (or to be supported by) a number of promises: to appoint an arbiter, to commit the matter to him, to take part in the process, to perform what is required by the arbiter even before the award, or to pay a penalty in default of performance of any of those promises.

---

upon Greek originals'. And these figures have sometimes no specific label, nor their activities, miscellaneously depicted as *iudicare, conciliare pacem, componere*.

25 See at pp. 472-474.

26 D. 4.8.1 (Paul. 2 *ad ed.*): *compromissum ad similitudinem iudiciorum redigitur et ad finiendas lites pertinet*.

Examples of Roman private *compromissa* come from a very limited area, namely Pompeii and Herculaneum. The first are the so-called *Tabulae Pompeianae Sulpiciorum* which survived the eruption of Vesuvius in 79 AD, as edited by Camodeca,[27] and concerned the activities of a powerful family of Puteoli, the *Sulpicii*, who managed business throughout the Campania region. The reading of a chain of tablets, dated 55-56 AD (TPSulp. 34-39),[28] allows us to define the structure of a *compromissum* and the fulfilling of the substantial and procedural obligations descending from it. It could be stipulated before or after the beginning of a trial and contained a standardized formula in which the *promissor* expressed his willingness not only to cooperate towards the correct execution of the arbitral orders (*operam praeberi*), but also to perform the duties ascertained by the arbiter (*pecuniam dari*).[29] This combination is also present in a fragment of a classical lawyer, Javolenus (quoting Cassius, another jurist operating in the age of the documents – D. 4.8.39 pr.: *ad solutionem pecuniae aut operam praebendam*), and therefore may be proof of the diffusion of a modelled prescriptive language. In order to enhance the efficacy of the mutual promises, a penal clause could also be stipulated. According to other tablets, the *Tabulae Herculanenses* 76 (reporting facts that occurred in 68-69 AD) resorted to the usual conditional sentences: *si quid adversus ea factum erit sive quid ita factum non erit*,[30] followed by the penalty. In these formulations, the pattern of the sanctions established in the public legislative acts was embodied.[31]

> *In controversia quae est inter L. Cominium Primum et L. Appuleium Proculum de finibus fundi Numidiani qui est L. Comini Primi et fundi Strataniciani qui est L. Appulei Proculi ... de ea controversia ita stipulati sunt itaque pacti: quod Ti. Crassius Firmus arbiter ex compromisso inter L. Cominium Primum heredemve eius palam coram utroque praesenti sententiam prove sententia dicat dicive iubeat et dum ante K. Februarias primas sententiam dicat dicive iubeat diemque compromissi proferat proferrive iubeat: si quid adversus ea factum erit sive quid ita factum non erit HS M probos recte dari dolumque malum huic rei arbiterioque abesse afuturumque esse.*

27 Camodeca (1999: 103-111).

28 Camodeca (1992: 124-129).

29 Thus Camodeca (1999: 105). It is also possible that *opera* and *pecunia* were the descriptions of the possible objects the debtor was compelled to give.

30 See D. 45.1.71, Ulp. 13 *ad ed.*: *cum, quid ut fiat, stipulemur poenam, sic recte concipiemus: 'si ita factum non erit', cum quid ne fiat, sic: 'si adversus id factum sit'* [Whenever we stipulate for a penalty in order that some act may be performed, we express ourselves properly as follows, 'If it is not done in this way'. If, however, the penalty is for some act not to be performed, we should express it as follows, 'If anything contrary to this is done'].

31 For example in the *lex Quinctia de aquaeductibus* (Front. *de aq.* 129; FIRA, I, 14): *si quid ... fecerit ... centum milia ... dare damnas esto*; *qui adversus ea quid fecerit* ... The translations of the following are taken from Roebuck and de Lyones de Fumichon (2004) with some adaptations.

[In the dispute between L. Cominius Primus and L. Appuleius Proculus about the boundaries of the Numidian land of L. Cominius Primus and the Stratanician land of L. Appuleius Proculus, ... in respect of that dispute they have by stipulation and pact agreed as follows: that Ti. Crassius Firmus should be arbiter *ex compromisso* between L. Cominius Primus and his heir and L Appuleius Proculus and his heir and should render his award or order his award to be rendered, openly in his presence and in the presence of each other, before the first day of February next, and may postpone that day when he renders his award or orders it to be rendered or orders it to be postponed, and if anything shall be done or fail to be done, against these agreements, 1,000 sesterces shall be properly paid, fraud being absent from this matter and arbitration and to be so in the future.]

The analysis of this type of document (as supplemented by the editors) provides a real picture of the arbitration procedure concerning the obligations of the parties and, inter alia, the regulatory powers of the arbiter giving an order to appear with specific indications of time and space of the hearing (TPSulp. 35: *diem ad audiendum dare*; *adesse eos iubere*: establish a date; order to come to the defined place). The scope of the powers held by *arbitri* depended on the terms of the *compromissum*: it was their source and could involve a simple issue or a series of issues (in this case it was called *plenum*) concerning the relationships between the parties involved.

Receptum arbitri

Receptum arbitri is the three-headed contract the parties made with the appointed *arbiter*. He could be freely selected by the parties, but the choice fell on someone included in a proper list. He had to comply with specific requirements concerning the capacity of acting with other people: he could not be under the age of puberty, insane, deaf or dumb, or of course a slave.[32] No formalities were required, but the *arbiter* was supposed to sign at the bottom of the *compromissum*. It is one of the *recepta* set out in the 4th Book of Justinian's *Digest*, including contracts by which the party receiving something is bound to return it. Unlike the bankers or the shipmasters, the arbiter's duty was not to give back a material object, but to discharge an undertaking to deal with a dispute.

The function of the *receptum* was to commit the arbiter to fulfil all the duties which the *compromissum* required of him: i.e. to set the place, date and time of the hearing, to make interlocutory orders for accomplishing his task, to render an award (*sententiam dicere*: literally to speak the award, with all the performative – and institutional – effects implied in the verb *dicere*). This was to be done with genuine discretion, i.e. the *arbiter* was meant to evaluate the matter without being

32 Ulp. 13 *ad ed.* D. 4.8.9.1: *Sed neque in pupillum neque in furiosum aut surdum aut mutum compromittetur, ut Pomponius libro trigensimo tertio scribit.*

influenced by the parties in the arbitration or by third parties. In cases where the arbiter did become involved, e.g. if the parties agreed on a certain solution to the issue entrusted to the arbiter, the effect was to make the award void.[33] However, the *arbiter* had undertaken an honorary public office and should perform it as one of the duties inherent to private citizens under the above-mentioned directive power of the *praetor*. Sometimes the complications connected with the due discharge of his obligations could lead the arbiter even to hide himself (in this case, the praetor would fine him[34]), otherwise he could be excused from acting due to circumstances such as illness, duties of public office, an emergency pertaining to private affairs, or inconsiderate behaviour of the parties (excessive delay in answering his convocation, insults).[35]

An example of a *receptum* is given by very corrupted tablets (*Tabulae Herculanenses* 81: and also, according to the past doctrine,[36] 77) as in both of them appear the technical terms, respectively *recepit* and *recepi*.[37]

Sententia

The inscription from Histonium[38] shows an arbitration *ex compromisso* of a boundary dispute held in 19 AD. The conceiving and drafting of the award may have required the assistance of a skilful consultant charged of measuring the land. The text reads as follows:

> *C. Helvidius Priscus, arbiter ex compromisso inter Q. Tillium Eryllum procuratorem Tilli Sassi et M. Paquium Aulanium actorem municipi Histoniensium, utrisque praesentibus iuratus sententiam dixit in ea verba, quae infra scripta sunt: rell.*
>
> [Gaius Helvidius Priscus, arbiter *ex compromisso* between Quintus Tillius Eryllus, attorney of Tillius Sassius, and Marcus Paquius Aulanius, acting on behalf of the municipality of Histonium, in presence of both of them, having taken the oath pronounced his award in these words written below: [follows a brief description of the facts].]

---

33 Paul. 13 *ad ed.* D. 4.8.19 pr.: ... *si sic fuit in arbitrium compromissum, ut certam sententiam dicat, nullum esse arbitrium, nec cogendum sententiam dicere Iulianus scribit libro quarto digestorum.*

34 Paul. 13 *ad ed.* D. 4.8.32.12: *Si arbiter sese celare temperaverit, praetor eum investigare debet, et si diu non paruerit, multa adversus eum dicenda est.*

35 All these grounds of exemption are provided in D. 4.8.9, 10, 11pr., 15, 16 pr. and 17.1.

36 Arangio-Ruiz, Pugliese Carratelli (1955: 451-452), followed by Ziegler (1971: 81, 152) and Talamanca (1958: 2).

37 Camodeca (1994) 144, has proven that the TH 77 is the fragmentary testimony of a formal interrogation concerning the fulfilment of the obligations derived from the award.

38 CIL IX 2827 = Dessau 5982; FIRA III 509 Nr. 164.

Another epigraphic source (TH 79) confirms the 'ritual' structure of an award based on the warning that the written form was optional – at least until the constitution of Valentinian, Valens and Gratian in 374 AD (CTh. 4.17.1)[39] – and the decision of the arbiter derived its effects directly from the spoken expression:

> *Ti. Crassius Firmus arbiter ex compromisso inter L. Cominium Primum et L. Appuleium Proculum de finibus fundi Numidiani et fundi Strataniciani ... ae et dirimendis et dinoscendis et qui sint pali caesi adhibito mensore L. Opsio Herma at M. Nonium P—m ut causa patelat L. Opsio Hermae mensori, inter L. Cominium Primum et L. Appuleium Proculum coram sententiam dixit.*
>
> [Titus Crassius Firmus, arbiter in the compromissum between Lucius Cominius Primus and Lucius Appuleius Proculus about the boundaries between the Numidian land and the Stratanician land which are to be distinguished and divided and for which pegs have been cut according to the survey of Lucius Opsius Herma and Marcus Nonius ... he declared his award between Lucius Cominius Primus and Lucius Appuleius Proculus in their presence.]

Another example of the important expression *sententiam dicere*[40] comes from the first century, namely 87 BC: the so-called Tabula Contrebiensis, a well-preserved bronze tablet found near Zaragoza in Spain.[41] This bronze records the settlement of a dispute concerning the right of a community to make a canal or channel water through the public and private land of another community. There are two different 'courts' involved in this issue: the senate of a third community about the main question of the existence of that right (a proper public arbitration concerning the *an*) and a board of five men – appointed from the magistracy of this community – committed with the assessment of the countervalue to be given under the condition of the above-mentioned existence (*quantum*). This board made an evaluation of the whole matter and then pronounced the opinion (*sententiam deixerunt*): 'Whereas

39 Roebuck and de Loynes de Fumichon (2004: 181). From the text of the constitution cited below, we can be sure only that the provision was made for the judgments passed by a provincial judge, but it could be also be generalized: *Statutis generalibus iusseramus, ut universi iudices, quibus reddendi iuris in provinciis permittimus facultatem, cognitis causis ultimas definitiones de scripti recitatione proferant. Huic adicimus sanctioni, ut sententia, quae dicta fuerit, cum scripta non esset, ne nomen quidem sententiae habere mereatur, nec ad rescissionem perperam decretorum appellationis sollemnitas requiratur* [Codex Theodosianus 4.17.1 = Codex Iustinianus 7.44.3: We order by our general laws that all judges whom we have invested with the power of dispensing justice in the various provinces, after having heard the cases, shall render their final decision in writing. We add to this law that any judgment rendered without having been reduced to writing shall not be worthy of the name, and the formality of an appeal shall not be required for the annulment of such a wrongful decree].

40 Among several examples, the technicality of the term is well attested in the legal ancient sources also for this matter, from the 8th title of the 4th Book of the *Digest*.

41 Richardson (1983) 33-34.

the right of judgment is ours, in the matter which is the subject of this action we give judgment in favour of the Salluienses' (l. 15).

Once the *arbiter* had rendered the award, *arbiter esse desierat*, he was released from the undertaken duties;[42] that is, when he pronounces it with the intention that the parties as a result give up their dispute completely. If the submission is concerned with several issues, unless he settles all matters in dispute, he is not considered as having rendered his award.[43] This has to be final (defining all the questions) and complete (inherent to each one of those). An arbiter may make a decision on actual disputes existing between the parties at the time they made the *compromissum* but not those that arose later (D. 4.8.46, Paul. 12 *ad Sab.*).[44] In this regard, it is important to stress the role of the praetor: he was charged with an administrative function of supervising the procedure and enforcing the acts of the arbitration, mainly by ensuring the payment of the agreed penalty in case of a partial performance of the required actions by the parties involved. But his intervention was crucial, at least from the second century BC onwards, in cases where an *arbiter*, though accepting the reference from the parties, then refused to act, i.e. to render an award, even after investigating the dispute. From a comparative perspective, it is worth mentioning that a *iudex* in the ordinary process was also compelled to give a decision.[45] It appears a priority to protect the good faith of the parties[46] relying on a *receptum* which produced the expectations the dispute would be solved and thus the *praetor* forced the arbiter to express his binding point of view on the question. In the edictal words: *qui arbitrium pecunia compromissa receperit eum sententiam dicere cogam.*[47] The sanction provided against a reluctant *arbiter* was probably just a fine, which sounds comparatively feeble against the tough language used in the praetorian order.

The lawyers were anxious to ensure that the *arbiter* adhered rigorously to the terms of the *compromissum*, but they avoided at the same time any kind of

42 D. 4.8.19.2, Paul. 13 *ad ed.*

43 D. 4.18.9.1, Paul. 13 *ad ed.*: *Dicere autem sententiam existimamus eum, qui ea mente quid pronuntiat, ut secundum id discedere eos a tota controversia velit, sed si de pluribus rebus sit arbiterium receptum, nisi omnes controversias finierit, non videtur dicta sententia, sed adhuc erit a praetore cogendus* [We must consider that an arbiter renders a decision, when he does so with the intention that the entire matter in controversy shall be settled. But where arbitration with reference to several matters is involved, unless he disposed of all that are in controversy, he will not be held to have made an award, and he can still be forced by the praetor to act].

44 *De his rebus et rationibus et controversiis iudicare arbiter potest, quae ab initio fuissent inter eos qui compromiserunt, non quae postea supervenerunt.*

45 D. 50.5.13, Ulp. 23 *ad ed.*: *Qui autem non habet excusationem, etiam invitus iudicare cogitur.*

46 Some scholars go beyond this and imagine even a necessity of data protection deriving from the disclosures made by the parties themselves who could 'have revealed the most intimate personal detail and secrets': Stein (1995: 219).

47 Lenel (1927: 130-131). See also Ziegler (1971: 24-25).

interference in the content of the award, even if the arrangement was unfair. That is understandable if we see the statutory correspondence between the text of the reference and the plan of action to which all the parties must stick, including the *arbiter*, after having 'received' the *compromissum*.

There are two noticeable differences between ancient and modern arbitration practice. The first concerns agreements to arbitrate future disputes, as the Romans allowed only a *compromissum* of existing disputes. The second is that during Roman times, as mentioned above, parties who reached a settlement on their own were not allowed to insert it in the award. In fact, if a dispute was referred to an arbiter upon terms that he delivered a certain award, the arbitration was void.

History goes on and teaches us, first of all, that looking to the future for answers to our problems could be inspired by a critical study of the solution to the problems given by other law-making systems. Forward to the past.

References

Arangio-Ruiz, V. and Pugliese Carratelli, G. 1955. Tabulae Herculanenses V, in *Parola del Passato* 10, 448-477.

Broggini, G. 1957. *Iudex Arbiterve. Prolegomena Zum Officium des Römischen Privatrichters*. Köln-Graz: Böhlau.

Camodeca, G. 1992. *L'Archivio Puteolano dei Sulpici* I. Napoli: Jovene.

Camodeca, G. 1994. Riedizione del trittico ercolanese TH 77+78+80+53+92 del 26 gennaio 69, in *Cronache ercolanesi*, 24, 137-146.

Camodeca, G. 1999. *Tabulae Pompeianae Sulpiciorum* I. Roma: Quasar.

Edzard, D.O. 1991. Arbiter, ein punisches lehnwort?, in *ZSS RA* 108, 286.

Geertz, C. 1983. Dichte Beschreibung. Bemerkungen zu einer deutenden Theorie der Kultur, in *Dichte Beschreibung. Beiträge zum Verstehen kultureller Systeme*, Frankfurt am Main, 7-43.

Kaser, M. and Hackl, K. 1996. *Das Römische Zivilprozessrecht*. München: Beck.

Lenel, O. 1927. *Das Edictum Perpetuum. Ein Versuch zu seiner Wiederherstellung*. Leipzig: B. Tauchnitz.

Marrone, M. 2003. Sull'arbitrato privato nell'esperienza giuridica romana, in *Scritti giuridici*, edited by G. Falcone. Palermo: Palumbo, 609-628.

Martino, G. 1986. *Arbiter*. Roma: CNR.

Mélèze-Modrzejewski, J. 1952. Private arbitration in the law of Graeco-Roman Egypt, in *Journal of Juristic Papyrology* 6, 239-256.

Richardson, J.S. 1983. The 'tabula Contrebiensis': Roman law in Spain in the early first century B.C., in *Journal of Roman Studies*, 73, 33-41.

Roebuck, D. and de Loynes de Fumichon, B. 2004. *Roman Arbitration*. Oxford: HOLO Books.

Stein, P. 1995. Roman Arbitration. An English perspective, in *Israel Law Review* 29, 215-227.

Talamanca, M. 1958. *Ricerche in Tema di Compromissum*. Milano: Giuffrè.

Watson, A. 1985. *The Digest of Justinian*. IV. Philadelphia: University of Philadelphia Press.

Wlassak, M. 1895. Arbiter. *Paulys Realencyclopädie der Classischen Altertumswissenschft* II/1, 408-411.

Ziegler, K.H. 1971. *Das Private Schiedsgericht Im Antiken Römischen Recht*. München: Beck.

Mediation

Chapter 7
Restorative Justice, a comparative analysis of discursive practices: Dialogistic exchanges in the USA and Italy

Lucia Abbamonte[1] and Flavia Cavaliere[2]

1. Introduction

Restorative Justice (RJ), with its notion of dealing with the causes of crime by changing behaviours, has captured imaginations around the world (Tickell and Akester 2004); not only within the boundary of legal domains, but also in the fields of social studies and contiguous areas. RJ has developed out of several movements of the past three decades aimed at guaranteeing the victims' rights, making justice less formal and more substantial, and relieving the judicial system of some of its burden. RJ was also inspired by traditional ways of administering justice as practised by native North Americans and other aboriginal populations.

The practices of RJ revolve around the process of mediation conducted through a sequence of dialogues between mediators and victims, mediators and offenders, then mediators and all people involved in the harmful event. Such dialogistic exchanges can be of great sociolinguistic/pragmalinguistic interest and also of cross-cultural relevance insomuch as RJ is practised – with more-sensitive variations – in Australia, New Zealand, the United States, as well as in Austria, Norway, England, Wales and other European States. RJ began as an experiment to seek alternatives to criminal prosecution and conventional sentencing, especially where aboriginal populations were involved. The Correctional Service of Canada started to introduce RJ programs in many of its prisons in 1974, and in 1996 the Church Council on Justice and Corrections was set up to compile a list of community-based responses to crime, the majority of which were restorative initiatives. RJ is now widely applied in North America and is attracting growing attention from governments. In the UK, the practice was introduced in the 1980s and then implemented in the 1990s: it has profoundly changed the youth justice system and is increasingly influencing the treatment of adults. In 1989, the New Zealand government enacted the *Children, Young Persons and their Families*

1 Lucia Abbamonte's contributions to this chapter are Sections 3, 4.2, and 5.

2 Flavia Cavaliere's contributions to this chapter are Sections 1, 2, and 4.1.

Act; Australia followed with the implementation of family group conferencing in several jurisdictions.

Since RJ is neither an originally European Union (EU) notion nor easily compatible with highly formalized legal systems, its application in Italy is still tentative and limited (Abbamonte and Cavaliere 2012). Nonetheless, following the EU Guidelines (CEPEJ: 2007,13) concerning mediation in penal matters, the Italian criminal justice authorities are developing programs for cooperation with mediation services in order to reach victims and offenders more effectively.

What does RJ actually consist of? RJ is a process whereby parties with a stake in a specific offence collectively resolve how to deal with the aftermath of the offence and its implications for the future. A salient issue concerns terminology: do the same terms convey the same meanings in different areas? Are mediation and reconciliation restorative? According to Bazemore and Walgrave (1999: 48), RJ can be defined as 'every action that is primarily oriented towards doing justice by repairing the harm that has been caused by a crime.'

Furthermore, are RJ practices the best possible choice? When considering instantiations in different countries, the scenarios can be substantially different. No monolithic approach is to be found. Rather, blended approaches are quite common: such approaches operate within the traditional criminal legal system, but they also have components that function independently. Other practices mainly rely on community involvement and minimize punishment and policing orientation. Moreover, some initiatives try to directly address the social conditions in which violence arose, while others do not.

Nonetheless, some basic values/commitments are shared: the declared aims of RJ essentially involve 'restoring relationships, with establishing or re-establishing social equality in relationships' (Llewellyn and Howse 1998: 1). RJ engages the victim, the offender, and the community in a search for solutions that promote repair, reconciliation, and encourage a sense of agency. Such practices take place outside the courtrooms in reassuring environments. A major emphasis is laid on the victims' needs, on constructive healing processes and on the safety of survivors, whereas the focus in ordinary criminal justice is on offenders and on lawbreaking as a concept. Active involvement of all parties and acceptance of responsibility leading to positive transformation of offenders together with prevention of future harm are the recognized goals, rather than 'retributive' sentences and harsh punishment.

Such solutions are construed through dialogistic exchanges that take place in sessions where mediators – first separately, then collectively – discuss the issues with victims, offenders and supporters. The communicative and negotiatory skills of mediators play a pivotal role in these exchanges where features of affectual intensity and force are displayed within the context of (socio)legal interactions.

Legal language discursive practices in relation to text-internal and text-external factors (Bahtia 2010) have attracted growing critical attention, especially as far as intertextuality and interdiscursivity is concerned (Tessuto 2011, 2012).

However, integrated studies of professional and socio-cultural practices in Restorative Mediation in a discourse-analysis perspective have not been carried out as yet. The present research aims at filling the gap by initiating such cross-disciplinary investigation. In our study, we analyzed qualitative samples of legal mediation linguistic exchanges from a cross-cultural perspective by comparing US and Italian texts. As a consequence of differences in legislation about privacy in the US and in Italy, there is a significant difference in the availability of data in the two countries (see below in Sections 3 and 4.2). Thus, such data could only be analyzed qualitatively and required a special focus on different socio-cultural attitudes. Texts were evaluated in their contextual implications in the light of Critical Discourse Analysis (CDA), particularly of the Appraisal Framework (Martin and White 2005, 2007; Bednarek 2010) and of the notion of interdiscursivity.[3]

2. Background

The basic assumptions of RJ are based on the belief that the origins of crime lie in social conditions and relationships within the community; prevention is therefore dependent on communities – in conjunction with local and central government – taking some responsibility for resolving these conditions. The process of re-establishing relationships and reintegrating individuals into the communities and societal groups often entails transformation of both parties involved. Therefore, RJ is often referred to as 'transformative justice'; shared beliefs, values and principles play an essential role in establishing and sustaining restorative practices in various countries – i.e. in initiating a fruitful journey of exploration and of continuous improvement. In a supportive environment, it is reasonable to predict that restorative practices can make a positive difference when responding to crime or other harmful behaviour, as meaningful contextualized alternatives to Retributive Justice processes.

2.1. Restorative Justice vs. Retributive Justice philosophies

In Zehr's perspective (1990), RJ entails a 'Changing Lenses' philosophy, aimed at facilitating dialogue between all those affected by the wrongdoing or conflict, while encouraging those responsible for the harm to become accountable for their

3 Interdiscursivity accounts for a variety of discursive processes and professional practices, often resulting in mixing, embedding, and bending generic norms in professional contexts. More importantly for our discussion here, interdiscursivity can be viewed as appropriation of semiotic resources (which may include textual, semantic, socio-pragmatic, generic, and professional) across any two or more of these different levels, especially those of genre, professional practice and professional culture. Appropriations across texts thus give rise to intertextual relations, whereas appropriations across professional genres, practices and cultures constitute interdiscursive relations (Bhatia 2010).

actions. All those affected should be given the opportunity to share their stories, their feelings and their needs in order to find mutually acceptable ways forward.

The basic differences between RJ and traditional Retributive Justice are effectively schematized in the following table (Leung 1999):

Table 7.1 RJ and Retributive Justice perspectives

Retributive Lens	Restorative Lens
Blame-fixing central	Problem-solving central
Focus on past	Focus on future
Needs secondary	Needs primary
Battle model; adversarial dialogue normative	[Non-confrontational dialogic model; Affectual values displayed][4]
Emphasizes differences	Searches for commonalties
Imposition of pain considered normative	Restoration and reparation considered normative
One social injury added to another	Emphasis on repair of social injuries
Harm by offender balanced by harm to offender	Harm by offender balanced by making right
Focus on offender; victim ignored	Victim's needs central
Victims lack information	Victim and offender are key elements
Restitution rare	Restitution normal
Victim's 'truth' secondary	Victim's suffering lamented and acknowledged
Action from state to offender; offender passive	Offender given role in solution
State monopoly on response to wrongdoing	Victim, offender, and community roles recognized
Offender has no responsibility for resolution	Offender has responsibility in resolution
Outcomes encourage offender responsibility	Responsible behaviour encouraged
Rituals of personal denunciation and exclusion	Rituals of lament and reordering
Offender denounced	Harmful act denounced
Offender's ties to community weakened	Offender's integration into community increased
Offender seen in fragments, offence being definitional	Offender viewed holistically
Sense of balance through retribution	Sense of balance through restitution
Balance righted by lowering offender	Balance righted by raising both victim and offender
Justice tested by intent and process	Justice tested by its fruits
Justice as right rules	Justice as right relationships
Victim-offender relationships ignored	Victim-offender relationships central
Process alienates	Process aims at reconciliation
Response based on offender's past behaviour	Response based on consequences of offender's behaviour
Repentance and forgiveness discouraged	Repentance and forgiveness encouraged

4 Our addition.

Retributive Lens	Restorative Lens
Proxy professions are the key actors	Victim and offender central; professional help available
Competitive, individualistic values encouraged	Mutuality and cooperation encouraged
Ignores social, economic, and moral context of behaviour	Total context relevant
Assumes win-lose outcomes	Makes possible win-win outcomes

As highlighted above, the RJ perspective is holistic and its practices are based on both empathic and mediatory linguistic exchanges; it actually endeavours to attend to victims' needs – material, financial, emotional, and social – and considers those personally close to the victims. Another key objective is to prevent re-offending by reintegrating offenders into the community, thereby avoiding the escalation of legal justice and the associated costs. One further reason why the interest in RJ continues to grow among nation states and communities is probably the resulting limitation of costs.

2.2 Restorative Justice models

The aftermath of crime cannot be fully resolved without the involvement of parties; flexible, balanced justice measures need to be adopted to respond to specific requirements, personal needs and possibility of action in each case. Partnership and common objectives between legal/statutory bodies, agencies/associations and the community are essential. The most important single factor of RJ practices is interdiscursive negotiation.

On the one hand, offenders should be made to understand that their behaviour has had unacceptable consequences while, on the other, victims should have an opportunity to voice their experiences and express their needs in order to participate in finding the best way for offenders to make amends (Johnston and van Ness 2007).

A common European objective is to recreate a working community that supports the rehabilitation of offenders and victims and plays an active role in preventing crime, partly by empowering those involved in conflictual or harmful situations. Within the EU context, differences arise in individual Member States due to differing socio-legal frameworks, professional and organizational cultures, and crime policies. Relevant questions are whether RJ practices should be conducted by legal professionals (within the justice system) or by Non-Governmental Organizations (NGOs), and what sort of training the operators should receive.

In northern European countries, the culture of community orientation and pragmatic negotiation are shared behavioural modalities, together with more concrete, inductive reasoning in jurisprudence, especially where crime prevention is concerned. Expert culture, involving lay judges and volunteers, is a widely used option for implementing social services activities at a local level (see Table 7.2), whereas the situation is different in Italy and Spain.

Table 7.2 European RJ landscape

France	England/ Wales, Austria, Germany, Czech Rep	Belgium, Portugal, Netherlands	Central and eastern EU countries (highly centralized state structures)	Southern European countries (Italy and Spain)
justice de proximité	NGOs	victim support /concerns	probation services	fragmentation
prevention	probation services	probation services	NGOs	projects in Italian cities
victim support	social/legal services		volunteers	interaction between ordinary judges and social services
probation services	courts, charities			

RJ is also in line both with the United Nations principles regarding the use of programmes in criminal matters that focus on the restorative process and outcome, and with European Union guidelines. According to the Council of Europe Recommendation (99)19, mediation is defined as 'Any process whereby the victim and the offender are enabled, if they freely consent, to participate actively in the resolution of matters arising from the crime through the help of an impartial third party (mediator).'

Mediation is also the focus of European Union Council Framework Decision 15 March 2001 on the position of victims in criminal proceedings (Art. 10), which encourages an implementation of RJ and common objectives:

> 1. Each Member State shall seek to promote mediation in criminal cases for offences which it considers appropriate for this sort of measure;
> 2. Each Member State shall ensure that any agreement between the victim and the offender reached in the course of such mediation in criminal cases can be taken into account.

The common core is the mediation process which relies mainly on dialogical exchanges, whose practices can be grouped into four main general types (Umbreit, Vos and Coates 2006):

1. Victim-offender mediation (VOM)
2. Family/Community/Group conferencing
3. Sentencing/healing circles
4. Others, e.g. local community-based programs that help victims and offenders to participate together in crafting an appropriate response to the offence.

More specifically, victim/offender mediation (VOM) or conferencing/reconciliation/dialogue draws on direct mediation facilitated by one or two mediators/facilitators and, occasionally, through a third party who carries information back and forth (shuttle mediation).

In wider group conferencing such as family/community groups, support persons (parents or friends) for victims and/or offenders are often present (on average from six to ten persons), as well as additional participants from the community.

Peacemaking/repair of harm/sentencing/healing circles can involve an even wider community of member participation than those gathered for conferences, either as interested persons or as additional circle-keepers/facilitators. The process involves the use of a talking piece (e.g. a stone, a shell, a plum) that is passed around the circle to designate who may speak.

Besides basic knowledge of the criminal justice system, such programs need to include common principles concerning the ethics and attitude of the mediators. As Umbreit and Burns have already highlighted (2002), an approach to mediation needs to be rooted in social work practice rather than in legal principles and procedures – a humanistic mediation, as they defined it. In their perspective, the client-centred, dialogue-driven practice of humanistic mediation needs to be integrated within the transformative/healing aspects of social work intervention.

Moreover – and this is a particularly relevant aspect to the present study – they need to employ appropriate skills and techniques of communication with victims, offenders and others engaged in the mediation process, as well as expert knowledge about the possible (negative) reactions/responses of victims and offenders (Kloosterhuis 2012). To borrow Bhatia's term (2010), mediators' communicative skills have to be interdiscursive in order to be effective across multifaceted, even contrasting cultures, and multifunctional professional contexts (i.e. legal, social, and psychological at the same time).

Such conferencing groups usually rely on a script, although some are more open-ended. In many cases, the recordings of these meetings are available online, the point of 'going public' being that restoration of social balance is viewed as a collective aim and achievement, which needs some kind of positive reinforcement at community level. Showing the positive values that can emerge from these mediated interactions apparently helps to endorse the effectiveness of RJ group conferencing and practices, and to further promote their use. However, a different scenario is found in Italy where, on the contrary, meetings are strictly confidential and privacy is the key word. The sessions are generally led by either social workers or (para)legal professionals who interact with the victims and offenders, first separately, then together. No one else is allowed (except, occasionally, the parents of underage victims/offenders), and no form of recording is ever made available to anyone. The mediators keep their own notes to themselves, and only tell the judges whether the mediation has been successful or not.

In sum, two main mediation models can be identified (Table 7.3):

Table 7.3 Main mediation models

Social work model	Independent mediation model
Offender focus	Victim and offender focus
Objectives	*Objectives*
Rehabilitation	Equal, neutral service
Prevention	Working with volunteers
Education	
Mediation style: more direct and professionalized	*Mediation style*: facilitation

The EU 2007 guidelines highlight the fact that the lack of RJ awareness in many Member States among the judiciary, public prosecutors and other criminal justice authorities, among victim support organizations and offenders, among legal professionals and the general public is one of the main obstacles to the development of mediation schemes.

3. Aims and analytical tools

The aims of this pilot study were to analyze qualitative samples of such exchanges from foreign contexts and to compare them with samples from similar Italian initial practices. The aim was to evaluate, from a cross-cultural perspective, the negotiation of challenging social relationships, in the light of CDA and AF interactive frames – i.e. a versatile set of tools for Applied Discourse Studies. To better highlight those discursive features, fine-grained discourse analysis was required; consequently, we needed qualitative rather than quantitative data for our investigation. Furthermore, owing to the different attitudes and legislation about privacy in the US and in Italy, there is a significant difference in the availability of data in the two countries (see Section 4.2).

Interdiscursive practices inevitably play a fundamental role in contemporary societal exchanges – a clear example of what Fairclough has defined as the *technologization* of discourse, which 'takes on greater significance in the world of providing and consuming services' (Jaworski and Coupland 2008: 4). Also, from Candlin's (2009) perspective, the study of language in the context of professional communication can 'foreground a problem-orientation, deeply embedded in methodological and analytical challenges, so that research outcomes are made practically relevant' (2009: 8).

Discourse and dialogistic exchanges, in the Bakhtinian sense,[5] are the most important single medium in RJ negotiations, based mainly on meetings between victims and offenders, where the professional discursive skills of mediators ('circle-keepers' or 'facilitators') are essential to the development of such sessions.

The language of mediators in the light of Appraisal Framework (Attitudinal Positioning) identifies them as being equally partial, non-judgemental, emotionally articulate and empathic; they have to empower the stakeholders to an equal extent in order to promote mutual respect, collaboration and the valuing of others. They also have to display conflict management skills highlighting the values of integrity, honesty and trust. According to their various typologies, these meetings are defined as 'Youth Justice Conferencing' or 're-integrative shaming' and take place in circles known as 'peacemaking circles', 'restorative justice circles', 'repair of harm circles' or 'sentencing circles'. Many group conferencing programs rely on scripts, and both in these scripts and in the recordings of authentic meetings a wide array of interactional moves and strategies is displayed, with Attitudinal positioning ranging from positive to Negative Affect and/or Judgement.

The comprehensive Appraisal Framework (Martin and White 2007) is particularly suitable for the evaluation of Attitude – a key notion in our analysis. Its multidimensional model can be conveniently schematized as follows:

New insights into the category of Affect are conveyed in Bednarek's works (2008, 2009, 2010), which distinguish between Portraying and Creating, or Invoking and Provoking Emotion. The notions of in/security (anxious/confident) – dis/satisfaction (fed up/absorbed) – un/happiness (sad/happy) and surprise/beliefs/ counter-expectation – are also outlined in detail and considered in the light of shared cultural construal in a given Ambience.[6] While Martin and White categorize irrealis as dis/inclination (e.g. wanting vs. fearing), Bednarek reinterprets it in terms of un/willingness (wanting vs. not wanting); more specifically, future states or existing ones are categorized in terms of realis (like) vs. irrealis (want), applicable to all categories of affect. She reassigns a number of emotions to these

5 For Bakhtin, language necessarily has a dialogic dimension. Whatever is said always exists in response to things that have been said before and in anticipation of things that will be said in response: we never speak in a vacuum. Every word is refracted through a host of other antagonistic idioms. Moreover, the porous and unpredictable nature of language is a token of human freedom, as opposed to the *monologism* of dictatorships (such as Stalinism). Linguistic exchanges are dynamic, relational and engaged in a process of endless re-definition of the world. Certain uses of language maximize the dialogic nature of words, while others attempt to restrict their poly-vocality.

6 See also Bednarek (2006: 32-33, 41-43) where she classified further evaluative standards:

- important–unimportant evaluation in terms of significance
- genuine–fake evaluation in terms of genuineness and truth
- expected–unexpected evaluation in terms of expectedness
- possible–not possible evaluation in terms of possibility
- necessary–not necessary evaluation in terms of necessity.

Table 7.4 Appraisal framework schema

Attitudinal Positioning	Intertextual Positioning	Engagement and Dialogistic Positioning
Affect implies a positive/negative assessment of people, places, things, state of affairs, and is concerned with emotional response and disposition. It is typically realized through mental processes of reaction such as: • ideational metaphor: reactions may be realized as nouns – e.g. His fear was obvious to all; • either positive or negative categories (*love* vs. *hate*, *please* vs. *irritate*, *be bored* vs. *be intrigued, realis* vs. *irrealis*); • *gradation*: each meaning is located along a *sliding scale* of force or intensity, from low to high: *like, love, adore*; *to be troubled by*. Judgement analyzes meanings which serve *to evaluate* human behaviour positively and negatively by reference to a set of *institutionalized norms.* It can be either *explicit* or *implicit* and is divided into two broad categories: • social esteem: normality/tenacity/capacity; • social sanction: veracity/propriety. Appreciation relates to positive and negative assessments of material objects, but also of artefacts such as works of art, texts.	Intertextual positioning comes to the foreground when a writer/speaker chooses to quote or reference the words or thoughts of another, either endorsing or dis-endorsing them. • 'Attribution', 'intertextuality' or, after Bakhtin, 'heteroglossia' are other traditional labels. • Writers can also remain neutral; in any case, the criterion is of (implied) relevance to their ongoing communicative purposes. • Source specification and Textual integration (insertion vs. assimilation) make clear the degree to which the attributed material is integrated or assimilated into the text itself.	Engagement and Dialogistic positioning means that every word/utterance is refracted through a host of other (antagonistic) idioms. The concept of 'dialogism' is inspired by the works of Bakhtin/Voloshinov: speakers/writers engage in a 'dialogue' to the extent that they respond to other speakers/writers or anticipate possible responses. The rhetorical resources by which speakers/writers adjust and negotiate the arguability of their utterances can be grouped under headings such as: *attribution, (modality, hearsay, concession, polarity), evidentiality, hedges, boosters and metadiscursives.*

categories: for example, fearing is categorized as irrealis-insecurity. Furthermore, behavioural surge (laugh, weep) is opposed to mental disposition (like, dislike) and graded along an intensity cline: low (like) – median (love) – high (adore). She also foregrounds Martin and White's notion of reactivity (2005: 46-49): reaction to other (the boy liked the teacher/the teacher pleased the boy) vs. undirected mood (the boy was happy). Of particular relevance to our analysis is her 'Bridging' opinion (Judgement and Appreciation) and emotion (Covert/Overt Affect). Bednarek seems to suggest that a holistic interpretation of Appraisal categories needs to take into account the resulting contextual polyphony (blends, fusing, conflation, collocation).

In her 2008 *Emotion Talk across Corpora*, Bednarek also outlines overt roles not only for the Emoters (the persons who experience the emotion) but also for Triggers (the entities, situations or events that the emotion is caused by or directed towards), thus widening the explicit focus of analysis on the type of attitudinal target or attitudinal assessment considered.

4. Materials

A closer look into RJ practice entails considering the Restorative Conference Facilitator Script (O'Connell, Wachtel and Wachtel 1999), which we analyzed as a reference text for the case studies proposed (see Tables 7.5 and 7.6). It is organized into the following phases:

I. Preamble for all participants
II. Dialogues with Victim (and supporters)
III. Dialogues with Offenders (and supporters)
IV. Reaching-an-Agreement
V. Closing.

4.1. United States data

Here, we analyzed the prescribed mediator/participant interlocutions (Johnstone and Van Ness 2007) outside Italy, in the light of Key Affectual-Judgemental values.

Table 7.5 Mediator's script

Script [Trigger]	Values/Positioning	Emoter	Addressees
Welcome … I will be facilitating this conference … Thank you all for attending.	Positive Involvement	Mediator	Participants
This is difficult for all of you	Evoked Judgement	Mediator	Participants
An opportunity for all of you to be involved in repairing the harm	Positive Involvement	Mediator	Participants
This conference will focus on an incident which happened	Detached/Impersonal Stance	Mediator	Participants
How that unacceptable behaviour has affected others	Explicit Judgement	Mediator	Participants
We are not here to decide whether (offender name/s) is/are good or bad.	Non-judgemental	Mediator	Participants
I must tell you that you do not have to participate in this conference and are free to leave at any time, as is anyone else. If you do leave, the matter may be referred to court	[Dialogistic] Argumentative–Stanceless face of the Law	Mediator	Participants
This matter, however, may be finalized if you participate in a positive manner and comply with the conference agreement	Positive constructive involvement	Mediator	Participants
Who do you think has been affected by your actions? How have they been affected?	Evoked distress	Mediator	Offender
What was your reaction at the time of the incident? How do you feel about what happened?	(Frame-construal) Professional detachment and Affect (tense-time shift)	Mediator	Victim
What has been the hardest thing for you? How did your family and friends react when they heard about the incident?	Judgement Evoked distress	Mediator	Victim

Script [Trigger]	Values/Positioning	Emoter	Addressees
What did you think when you heard about the incident? How do you feel about what happened?	(Frame-construal) Professional detachment and Affect (tense-time shift)	Mediator	Offender and Victim supporters
What has been the hardest thing for you? What do you think are the main issues?	Affect/Judgement Appreciation	Mediator	Offender and Victim supporters
Is there anything you want to say at this time?	[Dialogistic] Argumentative	Mediator	Offender
What would you like from today's conference?	Affect	Mediator	Victim
Before I prepare the written agreement, I'd like to make sure that I have accurately recorded what has been decided. Before I formally close this conference, I would like to provide everyone with a final opportunity to speak. Is there anything anyone wants to say?	[Dialogistic] Argumentative– Stanceless face of the Law	Mediator	Participants
Thank you for your contributions in dealing with this difficult matter. Congratulations on the way you have worked through the issues. Please help yourselves to some refreshments while I prepare the agreement.	Positive constructive involvement	Mediator	Participants

Let us now move from this reported (slightly shortened) script, where the main value positioning has been highlighted, to the case studies. The following is an example of community conferencing for a burglary case (Minnesota, US). The first step is the offender's preparation.

The third step is the direct victim/offender meeting-mediation.

Table 7.6 Offender's preparation. Conferencing – burglary case (Minnesota, US)

Offender's preparation [Evoking Triggering Situations]	Values/Positioning	Emoter	Addressees
What happened in your perspective? Some friends and I were looking for something to do, we were kind of short of cash … somebody rolled up the idea of breaking into a home	[Dialogistic] Professional stance Frame-construal, Evoking Triggering Situations	Mediator Offender	Offender Mediator/ Offender supporters
They all pointed fingers at me saying I should do it … I guess the pressure was too great for me … so I did it … I took TV, some jewelry and some cash …	Self-excusing, empathy raising, 'broken narrative'	Offender	Mediator/ Offender supporters
How do you feel about that? It's been really hard, I am so angry, so embarrassed … I feel like … people think, maybe I didn't raise him right and I feel really sad	[Dialogistic] Professional stance Negative Affect: reaction to other, mental disposition	Mediator Mother	Offender/ supporters Mediator/ Offender
What happened in your perspective?	[Dialogistic] Professional stance	Mediator	Victim
It was just awful, I didn't … I couldn't believe it was happening to me again in my own home … I had come in … I just knew something wasn't right … it just (2) was awful	Negative, explicit Affect– Fear/Anger, irrealis-insecurity	Victim	Mediator/ Victim supporters

The second phase is the victim's preparation.

Table 7.7 Victim's preparation. Conferencing – burglary case (Minnesota, US)

Victim's preparation	Values/Positioning	Emoter	Addressees
As a member of the community … how does it make you feel	[Dialogistic] Support/ implicit Affect	Victim supporter (male)	Victim/ Mediator
We can't protect each other … we don't feel safe anymore	Negative Judgement/ Affect–Fear, irrealis-insecurity	Victim supporter (female)	Victim/ Mediator

Table 7.8 Victim/offender mediation – (VOM) meeting. Conferencing – burglary case (Minnesota, US)

VOM Meeting [Evoking Triggering Situations]	Values/Positioning	Emoter	Addressees
I want to thank you both … ask you to talk respectfully … you have a chance to tell your own story … ask any questions How did you feel then …?	(Frame-construal) Equally partial, professional stance	Mediator	Offender and Victim
Walked into my home and it was just destroyed … just a mess … and this awful feeling the whole time … that someone was going to jump out and hurt me …	Negative Affect–Fear/ Judgement, Negative Appreciation, surprise/counter-expectation	Victim	Offender and Mediator
It just hasn't got any better … it's not my home anymore … it's not a place I don't feel safe … why did you do that? You just don't know how awful it is … You just couldn't ... You just had no idea of what you'd left … You walked away with the TV and some money but … the effect is well beyond that	Negative Affect–Fear/ Judgement Dialogistic–surprise/beliefs/ counter-expectation	Victim	Offender and Mediator
I … didn't know the effect was that … I am sorry I upset you … that you don't feel safe in the house	Negative Affect–Shame –Regret/Judgement– Acknowledgement	Offender	Victim and Mediator

As highlighted in the tables, the Mediator as Emoter displays positive attitudes oriented towards constructive involvement. She also evokes distressing situations in a detached manner, occasionally adopting the stanceless face of the law. She is in turns argumentative and, rather than being explicitly judgemental, she triggers the offender's self-judgement as a necessary step in the process of personal transformation, which includes experiencing shame, regret and acknowledgement.

The Offender as Emoter displays negative affectual emotions when narrating the event, and the dominating feelings are fear, anger, irrealis/insecurity, and dislike.

The victim also voices Negative Affect, especially fear, insecurity and surprise, but her negative Judgement is definitely explicit as well as her Negative Appreciation of the event.

4.2. Italian data

In Italy, the existing forms of family, civil and criminal mediation are subdivided into *Conciliazione* (when the court has already issued a sentence) and *Mediazione Penale* (when legal proceedings have not yet begun: Articles 9, 28, c. II D.P.R. 448/88).

The VOM centres were established for the first time in the early 1990s within the juvenile criminal justice system. Such a system is functionally connected with, and somewhat dependent on, a complex network of subjects and institutions such as the national and local social services, the judicial police for juveniles, voluntary work associations, and rehabilitation communities, where the juvenile offenders may be placed for the term of their sentence (probation, rehabilitation, etc.) (Mestitz 2000, 2002).

By and large, the goals and values are the same as elsewhere and the mediators are mainly social workers. Such practice has been gaining ground (to some extent) in many Italian cities in the last decade, despite many obstacles, such as the lack of awareness/information about RJ mediation, the difficulty of interaction with the judiciary system, and disparities in training and qualifications of mediators, not to mention the emphasis on privacy, which is not in the true, collective spirit of the RJ philosophy. In Italy the preparatory meetings are one-to-one interactions, and when the mediation takes place no lawyers, community members, or recordings are allowed (see above). The only types of data that could be collected by interviewing the mediators were the following:[7]

1. the standard texts of the 'getting-in-touch' letters from the mediator to the victim/s (or to supporter/s);
2. rough scripts both of the telephone call that follows the letter, and of the *mediation sessions*;

7 Dr. Maria Luisa Liberatore and her team of the *Servizio Conciliazione e Mediazione Penale* – Naples – kindly helped us with their useful and enlightening information.

3. the texts of institutional letters from the mediators to judges (consisting only of a few 'formulaic' phrases to communicate the final results of the mediation).

If the offender opts for RJ, the process of mediation begins in writing: the mediation team sends a letter to the victim/s. The letter types range from *Evento luttuoso* (death) or *Episodio* (event – the offence is not specified) to *Episodio di cui è stata vittima sua figlia* (event to which your daughter fell victim).

The following are samples taken from letters where the Key Affectual-Judgemental values are highlighted:

Table 7.9 Letter phrases

Frequent phrases from the letter [Evoking Triggering Situations]	Values/ Positioning	Emoter	Addressees
Gentile Famiglia, ci permettiamo di disturbar La per chiedere la Sua attenzione su qualcosa che ha a che fare con l'episodio di cui è stata vittima sua figlia (Dear Family, we dare to disturb you to ask for your attention on something related to the event to which your daughter fell victim)	(Frame-construal) Extreme politeness Hedging Evoked distress	Mediator	Victim + SuS Victim + Supporters VSupporter
La gravità del reato subìto presuppone particolari attenzioni e sostegno per riuscire a superare un'esperienza così dolorosa (The seriousness of the crime requires particular attention and support for you to be able to overcome so painful an experience)	Explicit-negative Judgement/ Appreciation Affect/Involvement Empathy/	Mediator	Victim + Supporter
Questo Servizio Le propone uno spazio d'ascolto (This office is proposing you a listening service)	(Frame-construal) Professional stance/ detachment	Mediator	Victim + Supporter

Frequent phrases from the letter [Evoking Triggering Situations]	**Values/ Positioning**	**Emoter**	**Addressees**
L'autore del reato ha riconosciuto la sofferenza causataLe e ha richiesto di poter manifestare il proprio rammarico per quanto commesso (The offender is now aware of the pain he caused you and is willing to express his regret for what he did)	Explicit Judgement/ Appreciation Positive Affect – Evoked Involvement	Mediator	Victim + Supporter
L'incontro Le dà la possibilità di elaborare ed esprimere ciò che sente rispetto quanto accaduto (To meet him will enable you to work through your grief and to express what you feel about what has happened)	Positive Involvement/ Explicit Judgement/ Appreciation	Mediator	Victim + Supporter
Offrire la sua disponibilità non è un obbligo. E' una Sua libera scelta. (Your willingness is not an obligation. It is a free choice)	(Frame-construal) Professional stance/ reassuring	Mediator	Victim + Supporter
La Conciliazione è un rapporto strettamente riservato. Tutto quanto emergerà dall'eventuale incontro rimarrà a conoscenza solo dei diretti interessati. (Mediation is highly confidential. Everything that happens or emerges during this proposed meeting will remain the exclusive knowledge of the participants)	(Frame-construal) Professional stance/ reassuring	Mediator	Victim + Supporter
Nei prossimi giorni un operatore del nostro ufficio la contatterà telefonicamente per sapere se lei è disponibile ad un eventuale incontro. (Within a few days you will be contacted by a social worker who will ask you whether you agree to the meeting)	(Frame-construal) Professional stance	Mediator	Victim + Supporter

Professional encouragement and a degree of formality, although blended with positive affect, are recognizable in the standard letters texts. Victims are reassured that the choice to accept the mediation is totally voluntary and that the sessions will be highly confidential. They are informed that a social worker will contact them in the next few days by phone. The next step in the procedure is the phone call.

Table 7.10 Phone call phrases

Frequent phrases from the telephone call [*Evoking Triggering Situations*]	**Values/ Positioning**	**Emoter**	**Addressees**
Avete ricevuto la nostra lettera circa ... ? (Did you receive our letter about … ?)	(Frame-construal)	Mediator	Victim/ Supporter
Vorremmo invitarLa/vi per discutere … (We would like to invite you to discuss …)	Involvement	Mediator	Victim/ Supporter
E tu dove diavolo eri quando mi rapinavano??!! (But where the hell were you while I was being robbed ??!!)	Explicit-negative Judgement/ Appreciation	Victim	Mediator

It is during the telephone conversation that the victim decides whether to accept the mediation, hence the social worker needs to be tactful and persuasive. However, victims' reactions can sometimes be negative. Then the actual interview takes place:

Table 7.11 Phrases from the interview

Phrases from the interview [Evoking Triggering Situations]	**Values/ Positioning**	**Emoter**	**Addressees**
Entra, io sono ... mi chiamo ... Dove vuoi sedere? (Please, come in … My name is … Where would you like to sit?)	Positive involvement	Mediator	Offender
Vuoi parlare? Cosa ricordi? (Do you feel like talking? What do you remember?)	(Frame-construal) Professional detachment [Evoking Triggering Situations]	Mediator	Offender
Puoi parlare liberamente, tutto resterà segreto (You can talk freely, everything will be kept secret)	(Frame-construal) /reassuring	Mediator	Offender

Phrases from the interview [Evoking Triggering Situations]	Values/ Positioning	Emoter	Addressees
Cosa hai provato? (What did you feel?)	Empathy	Mediator	Offender
Ti sei reso conto? (Did you realize?)	Evoked Judgement	Mediator	Offender
Ma perché? Che ho fatto? (Why so? What did I do?)	Cognitive Gap/ Distancing	Offender	Mediator
[presentazione] Come ti senti? Vuoi parlare? Qui sei al sicuro ... (How do you feel? Do you want to talk? Here you are safe …)	(Frame-construal) Empathy/ Empowerment	Mediator	Victim
Cosa ricordi/hai provato? (What do you remember? What did you feel?)	Empathy	Mediator	Victim
Sento che provi ancora rabbia ... (I can feel you still feel rage …)	Implicit Judgement/ Appreciation	Mediator	Victim

The mediators' attitude is mainly empathic and positive involvement is displayed when they try to engage the interlocutor in the exchange. No authentic samples either of victims' or of offenders' discourses are available, but a common (young) offenders' reaction is reported: in the cases where they were guilty of trying to give back stolen goods to their legitimate owners and get 'reasonably' paid for that restitution, the offenders did not feel they had actually committed a blatant crime.[8]

5. Discussion and conclusions

Interdiscursive practices shaped in legal contexts have captured growing attention from legal language scholars, although integrated studies of both professional and socio-cultural practices have not been carried out yet. Our investigation into Restorative Mediation aimed at providing new cross-disciplinary insights in a discourse-analysis perspective. Drawing on the Appraisal Framework resources, we compared qualitative samples of US and Italian legal mediation linguistic exchanges, focusing on different socio-cultural attitudes. Such a cross-disciplinary perspective allowed us to include legal/professional contexts, thus widening the field of investigation to the arenas where such situated meanings were produced.

As our linguistic data show, successful mediators need to be active, open-minded, non-judgemental, good listeners and emotionally articulate, so as to empower stakeholders and to encourage them to find a way forward. Mediators should be able to modulate the polyphony of voices and (local) cultures in order to enhance positive Affectual values in a reassuring environment. From a CDA

8 In southern Italian slang, this crime typology is referred to as '*cavallo di ritorno*' (a returned horse).

perspective, the key notion appears to be the salience of the mediators' professional interdiscursive skills, which need to be formalized to a certain extent, in view of the increasing technologization and commodification of discourse. The attitudes of US and Italian mediators emerge as basically similar. Nonetheless, some lingua-cultural differences are apparent, especially in the resort to bureaucratic language, which is decidedly more prominent in Italian mediators' discourse, together with the use of longer sentences and subjunctives, especially in written texts and preparatory scripts.

In some countries, VOM is also implemented from primary school to manage (not so) minor conflicts: its achievement depends on community awareness and appraisal of the restorative values involved. RJ sessions are actually *loci* of care that rely heavily on the notion of community, social solidarity, and are collective in their essence. When planning RJ programs, some basic universal values should never be understated: sensitivity to the victims' needs; attention to the material and/or psychological harm done to both victims and the community; engagement of victims, offenders, and all supporters in the healing process and in determining solutions for repairing the harm; and emphasis on accountability and restoration/transformation, rather than retribution. Furthermore, the process needs to be a voluntary and holistic interaction, rather than the outcome of an opportunistic choice. The people engaged need to trust the feasibility of alternative resolutions to the bureaucracy of courts and dreariness of prisons.

On the other hand, the role of cultural differences and crime typologies is not to be overlooked in assessing the appropriateness of programs. Besides, apart from the local variety of RJ models and applications, a striking difference surfaces when the issue of privacy is considered. While RJ procedures and outcomes in the US, Australia, New Zealand, Canada, northern EU countries and the UK are openly available on the web, in Italy, confidentiality is the all-pervading notion.

Such an emphasis on privacy, which envelops every single aspect of Italian mediatory exchanges, is definitely not in the spirit of RJ – and definitely not in line with contemporary Italian attitudes to matters of privacy in many instantiations. Indeed, privacy concerning RJ practices seems rather to echo the expression of the monoglossic language of bureaucracy. Whereas globally the language of mediation dialogistically refers to shared values and visions, and is better understood in terms of Affect, Judgement and Appreciation, in Italy the lack of publicity and dissemination together with a certain *penchant* for bureaucratic language seems to make these exchanges more opaque.

References

Bednarek, M. 2008. *Emotion Talk across Corpora.* London/New York: Palgrave Macmillan.

Bednarek, M. 2009. Language patterns and attitude. *Functions of Language*, 16(2), 165-192.

Bednarek, M. 2010. Emotion-talk and emotional-talk: cognitive and discursive perspectives, in *Language and Social Cognition. Expression of the Social Mind* (*Trends in Linguistics. Studies and Monographs* 206), edited by H. Pishwa. Berlin: Mouton de Gruyter, 395-431.

Bednarek, M. 2010. Polyphony in APPRAISAL: typological and topological perspectives. *Linguistics and the Human Sciences*, 3(2), 107-136.

Bhatia, V.K. 2004. *Worlds of Written Discourse*. London and New York: Continuum.

Bhatia, V.K. 2010. Interdiscursivity in professional communication. *Discourse & Communication* 4(1), 32-50.

Bhatia, V.K., Cheng, W., Du-Babcock, B. and Lung, J. (eds). 2009. *Language for Professional Communication: Research, Practice & Training*. The Hong Kong Polytechnic University/City University of Hong Kong/Asia-Pacific LSP and Professional Communication Association: Hong Kong SAR China.

Candlin, C.N. 2009. Preface to Bhatia, V.K., Cheng, W., Du-Babcock, B. and Lung, J. (eds). *Language for Professional Communication: Research, Practice & Training*. The Hong Kong Polytechnic University/City University of Hong Kong/Asia-Pacific LSP and Professional Communication Association: Hong Kong SAR China, 6-10.

Fairclough, N. 2001. *Language and Power*. 2nd Edition. London: Longman.

Hunston, S. and Thompson, G (eds.) 2000. *Evaluation in Text: Authorial Stance and the Construction of Discourse*. Oxford: Oxford University Press.

Jaworski, A. and Coupland, N. 2008. *The Discourse Reader*. London/New York: Routledge.

Kloosterhuis, H. 2012. The logic of indirect insulting in legal discussions. A speech act perspective. *Explorations in Language and Law*, 1, 69-82.

Martin, J. and White, P. 2007. *The Language of Evaluation: Appraisal in English*. London/New York: Palgrave/Macmillan.

Tessuto, G. 2011. Legal problem question answer genre across jurisdictions and cultures, *English for Specific Purposes*, 30/4, 298-309.

Tessuto, G. 2012. *Investigating English Legal Genres in Academic and Professional Contexts*. Newcastle upon Tyne: Cambridge Scholars Publishing.

White, P.R. 2005. *Appraisal: the Language of Attitudinal Evaluation and Intersubjective Stance*. Available at http://www.grammatics.com/appraisal [accessed: 30 June 2011].

Restorative Justice References

Abbamonte, L. and Cavaliere, F. 2012. Restorative Justice and mediation – the healing power of language. *Explorations in Language and Law*, 1, 110-123.

Bazemore, G. and Walgrave, L. 1999. Restorative juvenile justice: In search of fundamentals and an outline for systemic reform, in *Restorative Juvenile*

Justice: Repairing the Harm of Youth Crime, edited by G. Bazemore and L. Walgrave. Monsey, NY: Criminal Justice Press, 45-74.

Blecher, N. J. 2011. Sorry justice: Apology in Australian family group conferencing. *Psychiatry, Psychology, and the Law*, 18(1), 95-116.

Choi, J. and Severson, M. 2009. What! What kind of apology is this?: the nature of apology in victim offender mediation. *Children & Youth Services Review*, 31(7), 813-820.

Giliberti, C. 1990. *Victim Impact Statements in Canada. Volume 7. A Summary of the Findings*. Ottawa: Department of Justice Canada.

Harris, S. 2002. *Principles and Values of Restorative Justice.* Restorative Justice Week 2002 Resource Kit. Ottawa, Ontario: Restorative Justice and Dispute Resolution Branch, Correctional Services Canada.

Henley, M., Davis, R. and Smith, B. 1994. The reactions of prosecutors and judges to victim impact statements. *International Review of Victimology*, 3, 83-93.

Johnstone, G. and Van Ness, D. 2007. *Handbook of Restorative Justice*. Cullompton, Devon: Willan Publishing.

Lazaro, J. and Marques, F. 2008. What to do with these victims? *British Journal of Community Justice*, 6(2), 93-99.

Leonard, L. and Kenny, P. 2011. Measuring the effectiveness of restorative justice practices in the Republic of Ireland through a meta-analysis of functionalist exchange. *The Prison Journal*, 91(1): 57-80.

Leung, M. 1999. The origins of Restorative Justice. Alberta, Canada: Canadian Forum on Civil Justice. Available at http://www.restorativejustice.org/articlesdb/articles/362 [accessed: 28 July 2011].

Llewellyn, J. and Howse, R. 1999. Restorative Justice – a conceptual framework. Paper for the Law Commision of Canada. Available at http://hdl.handle.net/10222/10287 http://www.restorativejustice.org/articlesdb/articles/39 [accessed: 10 June 2011].

Mastropasqua, I. 2010. Juvenile criminal mediation in Italy: current and future perspectives, in *European Best Practices of Restorative Justice in Criminal Procedure*, edited by M. Gyokos and K. Lanyi. Ministry of Justice and Law Enforcement: Budapest, Republic of Hungary, 152-160.

Mestitz, A. and Ghetti, S. 2002. Juvenile magistrates and victim-offender mediation centres: communication system. *Paper to the II Conference of the European Forum for Victim-Offender Mediation and Restorative Justice: Restorative Justice and its Relation to the Criminal Justice System*, Oostende, Belgium, 10-12 October.

Mestitz, A. and Ghetti, S. 2004. What do prosecutors and judges think about victim-offender mediation with juvenile offenders? (What do Italian judges and prosecutors think about victim-offender mediation?). *Paper to the III Conference of the European Forum for Victim-Offender Mediation and Restorative Justice: Restorative Justice in Europe: Where are we heading?*, Budapest, Hungary, 14-16 October.

O'Connell, T., Wachtel, B. and Wachtel, T. 1999. *Conferencing Handbook: The New Real Justice Training Manual*. PA: Piper's Press.

Roberts, J.V. 2002. *The Use of Victim Impact Statements in Sentencing: A Review of International Research Findings*. Ottawa: Policy Centre for Victim Issues, Department of Justice Canada.

Roberts, J.V. and Erez, E. 2004. Communication in sentencing: exploring the expressive and the impact model of victim impact statements. *International Review of Victimology*, 10, 223-244.

Rogers, L. and Erez, E. 1999. The contextuality of objectivity in sentencing among legal professionals in South Australia. *International Journal of the Sociology of Law*, 27, 267-286.

Tickell, S. and Akester, K. 2004. *Restorative Justice: The Way Ahead*. London: Justice.

Umbreit, M.S. 2001. Restorative justice, in *Encyclopedia of Crime and Justice* edited by J. Dressler. New York: Macmillan Reference.

Umbreit, M.S. and Burns, H. 2002. *Humanistic Mediation: Peacemaking Grounded in Core Social Work Values.* St. Paul, MN: Center for Restorative Justice and Peacemaking, School of Social Work, University of Minnesota.

Umbreit, M.S., Vos, B. and Coates, R. 2006. Responding to hate crimes through restorative justice dialogue. *Contemporary Justice Review*, 9(1), 7-21.

Zehr, H. 1990. *Changing Lenses: A New Focus for Crime and Justice*. Waterloo: Herald Press.

Chapter 8
Participants' relationships in online dispute resolution: Legal discourse as social practice

Olga Denti and Michela Giordano[1]

1. Introduction

Alternative Dispute Resolution (ADR) involves extra-judicial dispute resolution methods, such as negotiation, mediation and arbitration. Online Dispute Resolution (ODR) performs alternative dispute resolution procedures through electronic means to solve disputes which arise both in online and offline environments.

The analysis of two websites, the MediationRoom and ECODIR, providing ODR, and of the transcript of a dispute mediation kindly provided by the Chamber of Arbitration of Milan, will try to unveil how participants' relationships unfold and may be enhanced by the presence of technology aiming at transmitting communication but not necessarily re-creating or trying to resemble face-to-face interaction. In a previous study (Denti and Giordano 2010), the general 'architecture' of the two websites MediationRoom and ECODIR was investigated in order to show the relevance of considering texts, images, charts and symbols synergically as a way of conveying both verbal and non-verbal communication more intelligibly for the layperson, within the genres of mediation and of electronic texts. Efficiency, cost-effectiveness, time-saving, parties' involvement in achieving the final agreement, less formality and greater flexibility in rules and procedures, privacy, and fewer jurisdictional problems represent some of the advantages that ODR practices share with those of ADR.

In particular, ODR procedures are even faster, since communication between the parties and between them and the neutral, i.e. the impartial and independent mediator, is simplified by electronic devices. The collection, transmission and storage of information are less complex and less time-consuming than in ADR.

---

1 While this chapter has been jointly planned and drafted, Olga Denti is responsible for the sections 'Participants as parties: Interaction and exchange', 'Building rapport through technology: ECODIR, The MediationRoom and Risolvionline', and 'Genre structure in online mediation', whereas Michela Giordano is responsible for the sections 'Email and threaded discussions: Moves, building blocks and regulatory principles', and 'A mediation transcript from RisolviOnline: An analysis'.

Distance and logistical barriers are reduced, deterritorializing online procedures and, consequently, relationships. One of the drawbacks of ODR is the loss of face-to-face interaction which leaves the floor to coldness and impersonality. Moreover, the lack of physical meetings brings about a certain physical distance which in turn may produce a lack of confidentiality and security.

The absence of non-verbal cues, of paralanguage features, of the 'human touch' as Kaufmann-Kohler and Schultz (2004: 15-16) define it, influences meaning, emotion conveyance, and the understanding of the other party's intentions and goals. According to Katsh and Rifkin (2001: 73-90), in order to be successful, any ODR system should have the 'right' combination of the three fundamental factors or 'building blocks': Convenience, Trust and Expertise, which stand for accessibility and participation facilitation, including financial and logistical factors, legitimacy and value. Of course, each participant may need different degrees of one or the other, but they must all be present since they will affect the choice of one website rather than another.

2. Data and methodology

ECODIR (http://www.ecodir.org) originates from a university project supported by the European Commission and the Irish Department of Enterprise, Trade and Employment. It is meant to solve, by electronic means, disputes between consumers and sellers. The ECODIR site offers assisted negotiation and mediation. The process starts as a negotiation process and, if the parties fail to find an agreement, a mediation phase follows. If even this procedure falls short, the mediator issues a recommendation which is not binding, unless otherwise stated by the parties. As the website itself recites on the homepage: '[t]he 3-step process is designed to maximize the chances of parties reaching a quick and mutually beneficial settlement.'

The MediationRoom (http://www.themediationroom.com), instead, a service provided by The Claim Room.com Ltd, Liverpool, UK, facilitates the resolution of disputes through fast, cheap and less damaging procedures than litigation might otherwise provide. It exploits a 'pioneering software' employed by 'courts, government bodies, leading companies, business associations, law and business schools and mediation companies worldwide', as the website homepage welcoming introduction explains.

This site also offers assisted negotiation and mediation. The mediator communicates with the parties, who can be assisted by lawyers, either separately or jointly. An expert can be consulted for advice and anonymous comments may also be taken into account.

RisolviOnline (http://www.risolvionline.com) is a service offered by the Milan Chamber of Arbitration that allows commercial disputes to be resolved simply and economically. RisolviOnline may be used both by individual consumers/users and by enterprises. A solicitor may act as a representative for a consumer or enterprise. 'All disputes of a commercial nature may be submitted to RisolviOnline irrespective of their financial value or the nationality of the parties involved.' The webpage also refers to the role of the 'neutral mediator who is an expert in conflict management in an informal and confidential environment', and to the tools employed 'discussing the problem in real time by means of a chat line or by means of a discussion forum.'

In terms of the type of discourse they represent, as pointed out in Denti and Giordano (2010), ODR websites can be recognized as a 'mixed or embedded genre' (Bhatia 2008: 161-162, Bhatia 2002: 10-12) of legal language, as they combine some aspects of the genres of both Alternative Dispute Resolution and of online transactions, exploiting information technology devices and methods. The genre of the mediation process, articulated into moves (Swales 1990), goes through a series of changes influenced by technology and online communication. Therefore, textual aspects are synergically integrated with visual or 'text-external factors', as well as different discursive practices with professional ones (Bhatia 2008: 161-162). This leads to 'interdiscursivity', i.e. the 'appropriation of semiotic resources across genres, professional practices and disciplinary cultures' (Bhatia 2008: 162).

Taking these factors into account, the present study focuses on the roles carried out by each party participating in ODR and on the relationships between them.

3. Participants as parties: Interaction and exchange

In ODR, the disputants try to solve a problem that has arisen either online or offline. The mediator (Third party) controls the verbal and non-verbal tools, the technology or Fourth party, i.e. email, chats, etc., the 'new presence at the table' (Katsh and Rifkin 2001: 93), through which information is exchanged and interactions occur. The website provider, the Fifth party, supplies the technology, i.e. all communication devices, and the technique to implement online mediation: 'the provider of the site offers e-mediation as a total concept: the e-mediation tools and e-mediator are included in the e-mediation service' (Bol 2005).

More specifically, in order for ODR to be accepted and developed, disputants must feel comfortable in using online tools for the process to work optimally. Disputants may be two individuals or large organizations, groups or affiliations.

Third parties are the neutrals and their expertise entails information management: in mediation, mediators try to manage the flow of information and the message-exchanging process between each party and between the parties and themselves; in arbitration, information management involves receiving information, evaluating it and reaching a judgment.

The role of mediators is of great significance, as it involves language skills to build confidence and trust with and between the parties. Moreover, they must understand what the parties are aiming at and make sure they comprehend the whole process, especially if emails, which lack voice and tone inflections, are used as a means of communication. The Risolvionline website states that 'The mediator does not decide who is right and who is wrong. He/she simply helps parties to initiate a dialogue and to work together to reach an agreement.'

The Fourth party works and assists the traditional Third party in managing the stream of information. The Fourth party 'helps coordinate agents such as people and data in dynamic virtual environments', and is 'the product of the whole conceptual and cognitive environment created when a choreographed dispute resolution production takes place' (Gaitenby 2006). However, as Marquardt (2001) observes, if the Fourth party is becoming more and more important, does it mean that the 'human touch' is not indispensable anymore? Does it mean that mediators and negotiators are heading for extinction?

Last but not least, the Fifth party can be identified as the e-mediation website or e-mediation technique provider (Bol 2005), or as the online courts (Pappas 2008). According to the latter, online courts play the instrumental role of providing legitimacy and trust while exercising control.

One of the most controversial issues in approaching an ODR procedure is the choice of the tool and media to be employed in order to provide the most fluid process of interaction among the disputants. This choice involves, first of all, the adoption of either synchronous or asynchronous communication. In the former, such as chat rooms, instant messaging and videoconferencing, all parties are present and interact at the same time. This entails that the parties must quickly answer and exchange messages, and the qualities of face-to-face conversation are partially kept, including the inability to hide feelings and emotional reactions. In the latter, as in emails, case message boards or web-based exchanges, parties communicate at times that are convenient to them. In this case, they are in control of when to answer and have more time to reason and to consult others. With reference to the sites under investigation here, ECODIR mainly employs emails while the MediationRoom makes use of emails, tele- and videoconferencing. Risolvionline prefers real time means such as chat lines and discussion forums.

When more text is involved, complex ideas can be explained better and details can be preserved. Strings of email messages become threaded discussions which keep a record of an entire line of conversation. Images, graphics and animations, instead, can show patterns and changes over time (Katsh and Rifkin 2001: 42).

Another choice regards the right balance between reliance on humans (Third party) and reliance on technology (Fourth party), i.e. the mediator's approaches, strategies and skills used to bring the parties to an agreement juxtaposed to the tools that allow information exchange and sharing, discussion, storing, scheduling, evaluation and enforcement. The extent to which these tools are combined will be relevant in order to build and maintain trust in the transactions.

4. Building rapport through technology: ECODIR, The MediationRoom and Risolvionline

The application of multimodal tools through digital devices helps to make the message clearer and more intelligible, and improve participants' relationships. Of course, this must be accompanied by the simplification of the text through the avoidance of those features of legal English which are usually troublesome to decode for a non-expert who might otherwise get confused and frustrated and decide to look for another ODR provider.

Observing the websites under scrutiny, titles and headings seem to aid understanding through the use of informative, precise, unambiguous words and labels, leading the visitors to what they are looking for. Section titles are also presented as questions such as 'What is mediation?', 'Why mediate?', and 'Why Online?'. These linguistic features make the text easier to understand and more comprehensible for the layperson. Technical terminology and legal jargon are often explained and defined in dedicated sections, thus establishing a transparent and reliable environment that allows users to feel at ease and favourably disposed and not threatened or deceived by ambiguity or unclear meanings and concepts.

The presence in the three sites of sections dedicated to *Policies* helps build trust between the provider and users: confidentiality, integrity, security and privacy are dealt with to make the reader feel safe during the ODR procedure. They will not be concerned about data corruption or interception, or about third parties reading personal information. For example, ECODIR declares that 'Personal information is never sold to third Parties and never used for commercial purposes or revealed except in accordance with this Policy' for the uses required within the procedure, and that all third parties are bound by a confidentiality agreement (*Privacy* page). The MediationRoom has a *Privacy Policy* section as well, including references to information privacy and use within the procedure and for the uses described, to non-responsibility towards other sites (*Hyperlinks*) not directly managed, and to copyright (*Copyright Notice*). Risolvionline states that, 'the Administration Office and the online mediator undertake not to disclose to third parties any knowledge acquired during the proceedings. The parties are bound not to disclose to third parties the circumstances of the online mediation attempt, nor the facts and the information acquired during the proceedings, and not to create and keep copies of the communications relative to the proceedings.'

The web page is an example of modern multimodal text (Baldry 2000: 41), combining different traditional semiotic resources, such as rhetorical devices, structures of advertising discourse, colloquialisms along with graphs, charts and images to catch attention and enhance understanding and persuasion. The text thus appears as less formal and less loaded, therefore easier to understand.

Hyperlinks can be considered as textual-mapping devices as suggested by Bhatia (1993: 141); discursive strategies which have a text-cohering function relating one aspect of the text to another text. They reduce the information load at a particular point in the website, fragmenting the content and distributing it spatially and visually into various levels. Again, the transparency and clear organization of the elements within the website allow the service provider and its users above all to create a bond of reciprocal reliance, by perceiving good intentions and shared purposes on the part of the others.

In particular, the building of trust and rapport is carried out at different levels. The first level is in the presentation of the site, therefore in the relationship between the potential disputant/user and the Fifth party. ECODIR employs a very straightforward and clear layout providing the explanation for the procedure through numbered steps and through graphs. The MediationRoom, instead, presents a video through which the website founder, shot in a warm and almost familiar setting, explains the advantages of the procedure. Another video on the website provides a guided example of the procedure. Therefore, more technological interactive tools are employed and less text is present. Risolvionline is even more schematic and concise than ECODIR. This might make some people feel less taken care of, but it could meet the needs of someone requiring a quick and straight-to-the-point approach.

The human presence in the MediationRoom contributes to creating a closer relationship with the user. The navigation of the site is also important. In all three sites, most windows open within the same browser. Therefore linear, objective, rational relationships develop from the information stated to the information to be given. The clarity and ease of navigation makes the user feel safe and confident, as less effort is required to decode and act upon information.

In addition, the three sites build trust through knowledge and experience. For example, each site provides mediators' personal data and references. This enables users to verify their expertise in mediation endowing them with additional precious information which enhances a sense of trust.

The choice between faster or slower tools of communication can affect the kind of interactions created between disputants and Third party, but it can also be affected by their preferred means of communication. Therefore, while videoconferencing may be required by disputants who need eye contact and active listening, or by others with poor writing skills, email and threaded discussions might be chosen by parties who wish to be able to go back and re-read the text if necessary.

Reading and writing skills become essential especially with reference to the neutral's tasks. Mediators must be able to interpret the text and answer even more quickly than disputants in order to avoid ambiguity, confusion, frustration and, consequently, disputants' loss of trust if they have to wait too long for a reply.

Not only personal attitudes but also one's cultural background play a key role in approaching the different possibilities.

5. Genre structure in online mediation

In order to identify the organizational and communicative function of online mediation, the procedure analyzed has been compared to Swales' CARS model on research article introductions (1990: 140-174). His four rhetorical moves have been identified as the structure of the process. They have been utilized as the starting point for the analysis. Then other moves and submoves have been identified, more specific to the genre under scrutiny.

In particular, the first move corresponds to the Opening and includes four steps: mediators verify whether the parties are set and ready to negotiate, reassure them on their neutral role and on the respect of confidentiality, explain the rules of the procedure, and make sure the parties are willing to undergo online dispute mediation.

The second move entails the Presentation of the case. In the first step, the mediator solicits the parties to present their positions and requests, while in the second he/she invites them to summarize their legal positions and to confirm the information reported. The latter is characterized by the use of tentative verbs and hedging expressions on the part of the neutral. The third step aims at clarifying the objectives, i.e. verifying what outcome the parties expect to reach.

The third move identifies the Search for solutions. The mediator helps the parties to find a solution through cooperative behaviour, coping with conflicts and emotional outbreaks. Cooling-off periods help greatly. Different strategies may be employed at this stage. One possibility is to raise their awareness of the costs of traditional litigation. Another is to carefully and calmly listen to them without interrupting, gauging their anger, providing explanation, and making it no one's fault. Dealing with emotions is a very difficult task, as they are bound up with the parties' frustration and have a strong influence on them. Moreover, especially when emotionally driven, parties tend to ignore the rules of regular turn-taking, forgetting about the basic conventions of mediation.

Another technique is to give a party an assignment, such as writing and summarizing what they want, while negotiating with the other party in private sessions. Interaction in private sessions aims at disclosing facts, concerns, interests, offers, reassuring the parties about confidentiality, making them feel they all have been taken care of and understood. By communicating proposals as hypothetical suggestions, the neutral tries to facilitate consensus.

Another strategy is represented by the use of rephrasing (or reframing) and intertextuality. This may help to change a totally unacceptable proposal into an acceptable one.

Move four is the Ending move. The neutral makes sure the parties know and understand the terms of the agreement, presenting them in a balanced way in order to reach a solution shared by all of them.

Technology both positively and negatively influences the realization of the four moves. Sometimes messages are not well synchronized, there may be failure of communication or the online environment does not facilitate the natural flow of negotiations. According to the means of communication chosen, the parties must wait patiently for their turn. In addition, technology favours economy of language which, however, does not help the mediator's task.

6. Email and threaded discussions: Moves, building blocks and regulatory principles

The four moves introduced – Opening, Presentation of the case, Search for solutions and Ending – are of course the general scaffolding structures of a mediation process. Several submoves are then utilized in order to carry on with the discussion and reach a mutually satisfactory solution. It is worth remarking that ODR seeks a solution rather than blame. A win-win solution would be the ideal result since revenge is not the focus of the dispute (Katsh and Rifkin 2001: 25).

Among the various technological devices utilized within ODR, email programs are capable of supporting communication between multiple parties (Rule 2002: 49), but interaction can become confusing with many participants exchanging numerous messages. Being the first online resource most people become familiar with, email is considered 'the lowest common denominator of online tools' (Katsh and Rifkin 2001: 120). Email can certainly be convenient, but 'as time passes and more and more messages are exchanged [...] a burden is placed on users to manage and organize them efficiently' (Katsh and Rifkin 2001: 120).

Threaded discussions, as a string of messages placed one after another (Rule 2002: 49), is one of the most frequently used ways in which the ODR process can be carried out to find out how both the Third and the Fourth parties cooperate to help disputants find a solution. Threaded discussions allow for a scrupulous and prompt examination of all the parties' contentions and proposals for possible settlements which emerge from the debate. A record is generally kept of all exchanges to build feedback, to recreate the chronology of communication, and to investigate what pragmatic strategies have been used and whether improvement is possible.

The transcript under scrutiny was kindly provided by the Chamber of Arbitration of Milan, Italy. The messages (*threads*) exchanged in private sessions between each party and the mediator were not obtainable. In addition, the two parties do not seem very aware of the discussion environment and how threaded messages work, so that some messages refer to previous messages addressing a different point, making the discussion a little difficult to follow. Therefore, a precise reconstruction of the entire online talk, with all the moves and submoves, including those that pertain to the messages exchanged in private emails and synchronically in forums, is not possible at this stage. Nevertheless, the threaded discussion occurring between the parties and the neutral is straightforward and easily comprehensible since, being a private transaction, newcomers were not foreseen and nobody else was allowed to join the discussion apart from the parties themselves.

As the analysis of the original transcript will show in the following paragraph, the various moves in the threaded discussion are strictly linked to the building blocks of any ODR system, to the core regulatory principles and to some indispensable skills on the part of the Third party practitioners. The building blocks identified by Katsh and Rifkin (2001: 73) – Convenience, Trust and Expertise, as explained earlier – allow the ODR system to 'facilitate access and participation, have legitimacy, and provide value.' Similarly, the core regulatory principles identified by Kaufmann-Kohler and Schultz (2004: 108-121) 'ensure a better quality of justice in ODR processes', covering requirements existing for offline dispute resolution processes and adding specific conditions to consider the use of technology. The principles are Transparency, Independence and Impartiality, Speed, Accessibility, Fairness and the more or less Binding character of outcomes.

Mediating with parties in an online environment is very different from mediating in face-to-face settings and the level of interactivity online is not the same as in in-person meetings. As a consequence, there are some fundamental skills that a mediator must master and which are influenced not only by the structural moves of the discussion, but also by the three building blocks of ODR and by the regulatory principles mentioned above, all of which must be borne in mind. Such skills as building and maintaining trust, using verbal and non-verbal communication, managing emotions, active listening, exploiting questions and reframing techniques (Katsh and Rifkin 2001: 147-155) are critical to all dispute resolution practices offline, but 'the context of online disputes creates different challenges for their use and mastery' (Katsh and Rifkin 2001: 147). The skills mastered by neutrals are of course crucial if the final aim of the mediation is enhancing the *relationships among parties* in order to help them find a solution that can satisfy all rather than fostering conflict and escalation of negative feelings towards each other.

7. A mediation transcript from RisolviOnline: An analysis

The dispute is about a pair of handmade, made-to-measure leather shoes. The following excerpt (1) shows the email opening the mediation, through which the mediator establishes contact with both disputants, clarifying his role: expertise and transparency are the credentials of the provider and of the service being offered.

> (1) Opening
> Mediator 09 dec 2008 19:01
> Dear Mrs. G. and Mrs. R.,
> Good evening.
> First of all I would like to thank for your kind participation to this mediation process.
>
> I just would like to introduce myself. My name is XX., I am Italian and have been appointed by the RisolviOnline service to manage this mediation.
>
> As a mediator therefore I will assist both of you to find a solution to the problems occurred. I am not going to be requested then to decide the matter. You can count on me as a neutral and independent professional to help you to discuss everything about the dispute and eventually reach a mutual and satisfactory settlement.
>
> The entire procedure will be confidential.

As far as operations are concerned, please remember that any time reference is to be intended to Continental time (1 hour later than GHT).

Moreover please make sure to check your e-mail account periodically (i.e.: daily) for new messages. Please let me know in case of your not being able to check your e-mail account for more than two days.

Then this mediation is now open.

MEDIATOR

Through the first email, 'the process is explained, ground rules are laid out, and the tone for future conversations is set' (Katsh and Rifkin 2001: 187), just as in face-to-face mediation. Trust is earned through the mediator's behaviour and, in particular, through the language he uses. Firstly, he introduces himself and his role in the mediation. Then he claims his neutrality, underlining that he is not bound to decide on the matter. Impartiality is expressed through the mediator's commitment to assist the parties in reaching a mutually satisfactory solution.

Confidentiality and security are ensured by the statement that the entire procedure will be confidential. Convenience is expressed through reference to continental time. According to the principle of accessibility, the mediator makes sure that both parties have equal access to the process in order to facilitate participation. The final sentence: 'This mediation is now open' confers authority and legitimacy to the procedure.

Following the mediator's opening letter, in excerpts (2) and (3) both Party 1 (K.G.) and Party 2 (the Shoe Shop) thank the mediator for his assistance. Party 1 wants to be sure that the neutral possesses all the details in order to carry on the process, to assure expertise in managing the information the parties are going to provide.

(2) Re: Opening

G. 10 dec 2008 21:12

Dear Mediator,

Thank you for your opening letter, and your assistance to try and resolve our problem.

I would like to know if you have all the details of the dispute from both parties or do we need to submit all of our individual information.

In response to your query, I. & I (K.) can access our E-mail account on a daily basis, with the exception of this Saturday & Sunday (13th & 14th December) when we will be visiting I.'s family in W. (60 kms distance).

We appreciate your information with regards to the time difference [...].

Thanking you once again.

K. G.

(3) Re: Opening

(shoe shop) 11 dec 2008 16:06

Good afternoon everybody,

> Thank you from Shoe shop. We appreciate your support. We are able to access our email on a daily basis.
> (shoe shop).

Both parties make reference to accessibility and explicitly assert their ability to participate using the technological tool the mediator has proposed. Both parties acknowledge the convenience of the email medium since it can be used at their ease considering the time difference. Friendly, gregarious participants might become very good at building rapport even in an online environment. This is what the Shoe Shop party tries to do first. Greetings are normally intended to establish a friendly relationship and this is what the sentence *Good afternoon everybody* does more than the cold and formal businesslike salutation *Dear Mediator* in the first party's email.

During the mediation process, in excerpt (4) the mediator invites both parties to get back to the forum to continue the open discussion there: reference to other media used in the website shows that the process is being conducted through asynchronous communication and synchronous communication at once.

> (4) Discussion
> MEDIATOR 26 dec 2008 18:17
> Mrs. G. and Mrs. R.
> I would like to get back to forum in order to enable an open discussion on what happened and what solutions could be achieved.
> First of all, may I ask you how is important for you to really assess the precise conduct of the parties involved in the dispute? In other words would you prefer to concentrate on what happened and why that happened or rather to focus on viable solutions to settle the matter?
> Thank you for your reply.
> MEDIATOR

In excerpt (4) shown above, the mediator questions the parties on how important it is for them to assess the other party's conduct. Here he takes advantage of the reframing techniques (Katsh and Rifkin 2001: 154) that help neutrals to change the way parties see an issue, sometimes helping to modify their point of view by removing emotions and judgement. The mediator prefers to leave to the parties the choice between discussing what caused the dispute and focusing on viable solutions to settle the matter. Asking questions and inviting parties to clarify their perspectives aims at avoiding ambiguity and misinterpretation.

> (5) Re: Opening
> (shoe shop) 28 dec 2008 14:01
> Dear Mr MEDIATOR and Mrs G.

In answering to Mr MEDIATOR's question we'd like to say that we think it is definitely better to look for a solution, therefore we are open to discuss.

Happy new year to all of you!

D. R. (shoe shop)

In the excerpt above, once more the party Shoe Shop tries to establish a friendly environment for the interaction, avoiding businesslike behaviour, but rather wishing 'Happy New Year' to all participants. As underlined earlier, friendly participants might be very good at building rapport and avoiding conflict even in an online environment where personal interests are discussed and called into question.

In the following extract (6), the mediator is facilitating the exchange of ideas on how to find a possible solution. He suggested using the forum again to discuss in real time in order to facilitate an open exchange in communication, and now he elicits ideas and proposals from the two parties to make them feel active in the solution of the dispute. He puts forward his own proposals, addressing parties individually but openly, again showing neutrality and impartiality, trying to identify the parties' interests and understand their positions.

(6) Re: looking for a solution
MEDIATOR 03 feb 2009 09:46
Mrs. G. and Mrs. R.,
I invited both of you to open forum in order to facilitate an open exchange in communication.

Please feel free to jot down some ideas regarding a possible solution to the dispute arisen.

To Mrs. R.: "Will you consider the refund of the money paid a possible action ?"

To Mrs. G.: "Would you be interested in receiving some valuable "Made in Italy" article in substitution ?"

Regards, MEDIATOR

At a certain point in the threaded discussion, as shown in excerpt (7), Party 2 (Shoe shop) writes in Italian since the person who normally participated in the exchange is currently abroad. This represents a halt in the process, since Party 1 believes the message in Italian might be a confidential message between Party 2 and the mediator.

(7) Re: Opening
(shoe shop) 19 apr 2009 00:01
Signori buonasera,
mi dispiace ma posso rispondere solo in italiano in quanto non conosco così bene l'inglese per poter esprimere quanto desidero e mio marito, che parla correntemente l'inglese, è fuori Italia per lavoro.

Dunque spero che possiate tradurre per la sig.ra G. […]
(shoe shop)[2]

In excerpt (8), where the topic of the threaded discussion becomes 'Re-start', the mediator, impartial and transparent, re-starts the discussion by translating the message in excerpt (7) from Italian into English. Mediators need to make sure all participants can speak the language being used or provide a translator if necessary. This assures impartiality by not showing bias toward any of the parties. From now on in the threaded discussion, the mediator will provide a translation when necessary, sometimes rephrasing certain statements to soften demands, and to remove an excessively emotional language.

(1) Re-start
MEDIATOR 25 jun 2009 10:41
I try to translate the message by shoe shop which seems to have halted the discussion:
'As said before we manufactured twice the pair of shoes to Mrs. G […]'
We hope that Mrs G. could possibly accept our offer to settle the matter.
Thanks R.
MEDIATOR

In excerpt (9), the topic of the discussion changes again, becoming 'Offer': the Mediator facilitates the exchange of communication by translating the alternative offer made by the Shoe Shop owner to the customer:

(1) Offer
MEDIATOR 01 jul 2009 11:34
Translation for Mrs. G.:
(message from Mrs. R.)
"Our offer is as follows:
a bag for a lady in hand-made leather. Mrs. G. may select two or three bags by viewing pictures via e-mail and different leathers both in colours and kind (suede/goat/veal). This is our offer, reasons were expressed in previous messages. Even in English, Mrs. G.s mother language.
Commercial value of the bag we are offering is the same as shoes'. We frankly think this is a reasonable solution.
R."
MEDIATOR

2 'Dear Sirs, good evening. I am sorry but I can write only in Italian since I do not speak English as well as I would like to, and my husband, who speaks fluent English, is currently abroad on business. Therefore, I hope you can translate this message for Mrs G.'

Excerpt (10), though containing the refusal of the alternative offer, is not directly linked to the new topic above, 'Offer', but it resumes the old topic which pertained to the opening of the discussion. In a firm and even forceful manner, Party 1 (K.G.) refuses the offer of a bag in place of a refund, even using capital letters to write the sentence 'I DO NOT WANT A BAG'. Capital letters in an online environment mean 'shouting' and Party 1 seems to be willing to openly show their disappointment, writing an angry email in order to clarify their position once more.

(1) Re: Opening
G. 06 jul 2009 15:47
First of all yes we have received all the e-mails at our new e-mail site ixxxxx@yyyy.com, we have been away the last few days so have not been able to view most recent e-mails. In answer yet again to the recent offer, I DO NOT WANT A BAG, no matter what the cost or quality, if I had wanted a bag we would not have gone to a shoe shop. What I wanted was a nice pair of handmade, made to measure shoes, what I got was 2 pairs of shoes, neither of which fitted me. The first pair being to tight and painfull across the front (on both occasions) and the second pair was OK across the front but too big and kept falling off my heel, WHICH WAS EXPLAINED WHEN WE RETURNED THEM to the shop having been promised a refund for the shoes.
[...]
The offer of having a bag made seems to me to fly in the face of common sense, they are having to go to the time and expense of making this bag (which I do not want) rather than give me a refund for the same amount as the cost of the bag!
Regards. G.

After various attempts at mediation, the fixed timeframe for the overall process has elapsed. Even a high quality handmade bag has been offered to replace the shoes or to avoid a refund, but in excerpt (11) the mediator declares the closing of the mediation proceedings since the parties have not reached an agreement.

(1) Closing of the mediation
MEDIATOR 23 jul 2009 02:38
Dear Mrs. G.,
considering that no effective improvement has been achieved recently in the mediation, I herewith intend to declare the closing of the proceedings. Unfortunately the outcome is negative and an agreement has not been reached by the parties.
I appreciate that both you and Mrs. R. have made great efforts to find a solution to the dispute, but the positions still remain significantly distant.
Also taking into account the long time elapsed, I think that this mediation can then be terminated.

> I'm sending you the mediation record which I ask you to kindly complete with your address data and send to RisolviOnline secretary office.
>
> [...]
>
> Best regards
>
> MEDIATOR

Notwithstanding the active listening and negotiation provided to both parties, the outcome is negative. The conflict between the parties has been characterized by actions and counteractions, and the mediator himself has utilized a series of subsequent moves and submoves. Nevertheless, the parties' positions remain significantly distant. The mediator's last move in this procedure is therefore that of conducting the process assessment, declaring the mediation closed and managing the last formalities to officially end the mediation process.

8. Conclusions

Transcripts are certainly useful to gain an understanding of how online mediators use language to make screen-to-screen communication efficient, focusing on building trust, providing expertise, managing emotions and promoting active listening between the parties.

Improving information exchange in ODR websites can prevent the escalation of conflict and assist in its resolution (Zondag and Lodder 2005). The balance between Third party (reliance on humans) and Fourth party (reliance on technology) can bring about new forms of social interaction, new social practices and new genres: online models do not need to simply copy or reproduce offline approaches. With the progress of technology, ODR will spread.

Threaded discussions in mediation are developing as a specific genre with specific moves and submoves (opening, developing ground rules, discussion, re-start, eliciting proposals, perspective taking, evaluating options for settlement, cooling-off periods especially after flaming, i.e. the exchange of angry emails, reaching an agreement, ending or closing). Rule (2002: 75) suggests that mediators take advantage of what he calls 'reusable language' such as some types of formulas, statements, passages, well-phrased questions and reframing techniques taken from the mediation exchanges, crucial for motivating the parties towards a resolution or for clarifying their positions.

Cultural issues do have a key role in the choice of the right combination of tools and additional interpersonal skills are required from Third parties when disputants come from different cultural backgrounds: the cultural aspect in ODR relationships and interactions, which has not been dealt with in the present study, would certainly deserve further investigation.

Primary sources

The ECODIR website. Available at: http://www.ecodir.org [accessed: 30 September 2011].

The MediationRoom website. Available at: http://www.themediationroom.com [accessed: 30 September 2011].

The RISOLVIONLINE website. Available at: http://www.risolvionline.com [accessed: 30 September 2011].

References

Baldry, A. (ed.) 2000. *Multimodality and Multimediality in the Distance Learning Age*. Campobasso: Palladino Editore.

Bhatia, V.K. 1993. *Analyzing Genre. Language Use in Professional Settings*. London and New York: Longman.

Bhatia, V.K. 2002. Applied genre analysis: a multi-perspective model. *IBÉRICA*, 4, 3-19.

Bhatia, V.K. 2008. Genre analysis, ESP and professional practice. *English for Specific Purposes*, 27 (2), 161-174. Available at: http://www.sciencedirect.com [accessed: 30 September 2011].

Bol, S.H. 2005. An analysis of the role of different players in e-mediation: the (legal) implications, in *Second international ODR Workshop (odrworkshop.info)*, edited by J. Zeleznikow and A.R. Lodder. Tilburg: Wolf Legal Publishers, 23-29. Available at: http://cli.vu/pubdirectory/233/manuscript.pdf [accessed: 30 September 2011].

Denti, O. and Giordano, M. 2010. ODR websites: bringing legal texts closer to ordinary citizens? *ESP Across Cultures*, 7, 25-44.

Gaitenby, A. 2006. The fourth party rises: evolution of environments of online dispute resolution, in *The Symposium on Enhancing Worldwide Understanding Through Online Dispute Resolution, University of Toledo Law Review*, 38 (1), Fall 2006.

Katsh, E. and Rifkin, J. 2001. *Online Dispute Resolution: Resolving Conflicts in Cyberspace*. San Francisco: Jossey-Bass.

Kaufmann-Kohler, G. and Schultz, T. 2004. *Online Dispute Resolution: Challenges for Contemporary Justice.* The Hague: Kluwer Law International, Schulthess.

Marquardt, R.R. 2001. Settling disputes online: just another tool, or are negotiators, mediators and arbitrators approaching extinction? Available at http://adrr.com/adr4/sdo.htm [accessed: 30 September 2011].

Pappas, B.A. 2008. Online court: online dispute resolution and the future of small claims. *UCLA Journal of Law and Technology*, Vol. 12 (2), Fall 2010. Available at: http://www.lawtechjournal.com [accessed: 30 September 2011].

Rule, C. 2002. *Online Dispute Resolution for Business: B2B, E-commerce, Consumer, Employment, Insurance, and other Commercial Conflicts*. San Francisco: Jossey-Bass.

Swales, J.M. 1990. *Genre Analysis. English in Academic and Research Settings*. Cambridge: Cambridge University Press.

Zondag, B. and Lodder, A.R. 2005. Towards the development of generic Computer Assisted Dispute Resolution based on Conflict Theory, in *Proceedings 3rd ODR workshop*, Brussels. Available at: http://ODRworkshop.info [accessed: 30 September 2011].

PART II
Issues

Identity

Chapter 9

Negotiating legal identity online: Narratives of drug use

Hugo Bowles and Valeria Moretti[1]

This chapter explores how legal identity is negotiated in online discourse practices by analyzing Internet narratives concerning drug use. Previous studies of the virtual discourse of drug use such as the collection by Murguia et al. (2007) use ethnographic and survey-based methods as well as qualitative analysis to assess Internet forum users' participation, intentions and attitudes to psychoactive substance use and the role of the virtual environment in shaping them. Results are interpreted from the perspective of the social psychology of individuals and groups (Barratt: in press) or from a legal perspective in terms of implications for public policy (Gatson: 2007).

By contrast, the present study examines the linguistic construction of the posts themselves using the perspective of interactional sociolinguistics to look at the way posters' orientations to legality are expressed through their narrative styles and what this can tell us about the virtual discourse community. The first half of the chapter examines the issue of personal legal responsibility for online talk and how it can be claimed or avoided by choosing a particular level of anonymity (section 1) or narrative strategy (section 2); the former is construed as a legal question which relates to online criminal behaviour and the latter as a linguistic one relating to the interactional choices available to narrators in establishing distance between themselves and the events they are recounting. It is argued that when illegal activities are involved, the question of legal responsibility is resolved through negotiation of an online 'legal identity'. This negotiation is illustrated in the second half of the chapter by a case study (section 3) involving a corpus of posts from an Internet forum in which posters produce potentially self-incriminating narratives of drug use. These posts are analyzed in terms of the markers of self-reference and the narrative strategies and 'tellability' features used in the stories. Conclusions regarding narrative legal identity are drawn in section 4.

1 Hugo Bowles is responsible for section 2 and Valeria Moretti for section 3. The rest of this chapter was planned and written together.

1. Legal responsibility and Internet anonymity

In addressing the question of online anonymity, this section examines the classification of anonymity (1.1), types of anonymity on the Internet (1.2) and anonymity in relation to criminal behaviour online (1.3).

1.1 Classifying anonymity

Although anonymity is generally understood as not having one's identity known to others, there are a number of ways in which it can be defined. Within the behavioural social sciences, anonymity has been classified by Burkell (2006) in terms of: 1) identity protection, 2) visual anonymity, and 3) action anonymity. The first of these categories – identity protection – is the basic interpretation of the term anonymity. Being anonymous simply means being unidentified. The second category – visual anonymity – refers to a state of being unseen and particularly having the face unseen; the wearing of a disguise in public places, for instance, is a case of visual anonymity. Finally, action anonymity is related to the extent to which people feel responsible for their actions or feel known by their actions even when they are not identified; for example, you can feel embarrassed about something people have seen you do even if nobody knew it was you who did it. Thus, according to Burkell (2006: 202), individuals can feel known 1) by name (or other unique identifier), 2) by being seen, and 3) by history of action.

1.2 Types of Internet anonymity

How are these three social forms of anonymity reflected in online discourse practices? One of the most common and least complicated ways of obtaining true anonymity on the Internet is by making use of an anonymity service. These services can be connected directly to specific newsgroups on the usenet or can service the Internet globally by making use of remailers, which forward electronic material to other network addresses making sure that the information showing where the message originated and the identity of the sender is no longer attached to the email. In this case, the user is truly anonymous because he or she is not known by name, by being seen or by history of action.

Another type of anonymity, often called 'pseudonymity', involves the use of remailers which give each user an anonymous ID. This means that the anonymity of the user in terms of name and face is preserved but the user remains reachable by other users and is ultimately traceable. In terms of Burkell's categories described above, a pseudonym allows one to be known by history of action while remaining unnamed and unseen. Overall, the flexibility of anonymous and pseudonymous modes of operation means that there are fewer links between anonymity by name, by face and by history of action when people are online (Kim 2010).

The link between the kind of anonymity chosen by Internet users and their actual participation has been studied as 'social anonymity', a term referring to the way in which an individual *perceives* his or her anonymous status. As Barratt (2011: 159) notes, an individual's perception of the anonymity of online interaction produces social psychological effects which in turn can affect his or her online participation. There is a link, for example, between a greater perception of anonymity and greater self-disclosure online (Joinson and Paine 2007); the more anonymous Internet users feel, the more they tend to reveal about themselves. However, if users are totally anonymous then they may not be perceived as genuine by other users. In resolving this tension between self-disclosure and trustworthiness, members of socially marginalized organizations often prefer a pseudonymous format because it is ultimately traceable and its users are ultimately accountable for their actions (Barratt 2011). They thus feel able to interact without revealing their true identities while being more confident that the users with whom they are interacting are genuine members of the same social group.

1.3 Anonymity and online crime

Having outlined the various ways in which anonymity can be achieved on the Internet, we now turn to the relationship between anonymity and the law in cases when anonymity is used as a defence against criminal charges connected with Internet activity. It distinguishes between Internet communication used in the organization of criminal activity and verbal crime itself (e.g. hatespeech, personal threats, libel, disclosure of trade secrets and personal information) in which the Internet communication actually constitutes the illegal activity.

1.3.1 Organization of illegal activity

In cases in which Internet communication involves more than one individual, the Internet is used for 'association' in that activity. Defendants may be entitled to claim that anonymity is part of the right to freedom of association and that interference with the right to Internet anonymity can therefore be regarded as an interference with the right to association. This is certainly the case when the association does not involve illegal activity. In US case law, the courts will usually deny the right to anonymous association if a group is seeking illegal goals such as kidnapping, terrorism and financial scams. There are cases in which the distinction between lawful goals and unlawful ones is not always clear-cut. For example, in the case of file-sharing, although copyright holders are entitled to discover the identity of illegal sharers, courts need concrete evidence of illegal activities if identities are to be revealed.

1.3.2 Anonymity and verbal Internet crime

An area in which the issue of anonymity with regard to speech has created considerable difficulties is the tort of libel in which the right to free speech and the right not to be defamed come into conflict. If comment that is possibly libellous appears on a website, a plaintiff who feels that he or she has been libelled cannot sue the website itself since hosting websites are immune from liability related to 'user-generated comment' (UGC) under Section 230 of the Communications Decency Act. One strategy is for a lawyer to send a 'cease and desist' letter to the website asking for the offending message to be removed. The response of some service providers is to remove the information automatically, while the terms and conditions of other websites do not allow them to comply without a court order requiring them to do so.

Alternatively, a plaintiff may wish to identify the writer of the message to sue for libel in order to obtain damages. A successful libel action has to demonstrate the following: publication of the libellous statement, falsity, libellous content, injury and fault. The anonymity or pseudonymity of a screen name makes it particularly difficult to prove fault since plaintiffs may need to know whether or not the defendant knew the libellous content to be false. As Stiles (2002) has suggested, it is difficult to prove a defendant's state of mind without knowing his or her identity. Identification of the plaintiff is therefore not just a formal requirement if a libel case is to proceed but a substantive one.

How is the identity of an anonymous Internet user established by the plaintiff? Under US law, since computer logs can reveal the names of Internet users, a 'John Doe' lawsuit can be filed against unknown defendants. This empowers the plaintiff to subpoena the host website to provide the IP address of the person posting the comments. From there, the plaintiff can determine the ISP. Because the Cable Communications Policy Act prevents the ISP from disclosing personally identifying information about Internet users to non-governmental entities without a court order, the plaintiff will need to obtain a court order allowing the ISP to be subpoenaed for the identity of the poster. Subpoenas may or may not be granted since ISPs may argue that revelation is in breach of privacy laws. Defendants may also invoke the First Amendment and their right to free speech. It is therefore a decision of the courts as to whether or not to protect the anonymity of defendants being sued for libel. In sum, not knowing who a defendant is extends the legal process because identification is a matter of 'discovery' and requires a court order. This extra difficulty in finding out who defendants are in order to establish whether it is worth proceeding against them means that few plaintiffs want to sue anonymous defendants for libel under US law.

Under UK law, the situation is broadly similar. ISPs in the UK are protected from legal proceedings by the 2002 EC Directive on Electronic Commerce Regulations, according to which removal by ISPs of defamatory material on request exempts them from prosecution. However, USG websites that involve moderators may be more liable to prosecution if they choose not to remove offending material. This is because the so-called 'publication rule' states that every time a defamatory comment is viewed, there is a new publication of that comment. Website hosts may therefore be guilty of 'secondary defamation' because they are facilitating the publication of defamatory material by a third party. This secondary defamation is compounded by the number of viewings of the material on the website.

2. Legal responsibility and narrative strategy

We now turn to specifically linguistic ways in which legal responsibility for online discourse can be maintained or avoided. These are discourse strategies that aim to position the author of the online discourse in relation to the discourse itself. Although such linguistic strategies can cover a number of discourse areas, this chapter will focus specifically on online narratives. What do Internet users write when they describe and discuss their own illegal activities?

2.1 The interactional dilemma of all narratives

Before looking at the specific positioning strategies a narrator might adopt, it is important first to outline the interactional dilemma which all narrators face, irrespective of the legal/illegal nature of the events they are recounting.

Telling a story about oneself might seem to be a relatively straightforward, everyday activity which presents little interactional difficulty to the teller. In reality, as narrative analysts have noted, storytelling is a delicate discourse enterprise because narrators are caught up in what Labov has described as a storytelling paradox (Labov 1997). On the one hand, tellers need to entertain their audiences and keep them interested in what they are being told; their narrations therefore have to be about what Labov calls 'reportable' events. On the other hand, storytellers also have to be believed by their audiences/readers and are therefore obliged to maintain credibility throughout the storytelling process. However, these two requirements, or 'tellability conditions', work against each other because the most interesting stories are usually the ones that are hardest to believe. The expression used by Labov to describe the paradox – 'as reportability increases, credibility decreases' – is illustrated as a diagram in Figure 9.1.

Given the nature of the paradox, storytelling becomes an exercise in strategic navigation between the competing needs of listeners. Toolan (2001: 176) has written of how narrators have to 'work their way between the Scylla of the "so what?" question (by making their stories not uninteresting) and the Charybdis of the "I don't believe you!" reaction (by making their stories not incredible)'.

However, when making a public confession online, there is clearly a risk of Internet users incriminating themselves. So as well as facing the same demands

REPORTABILITY ⟷	**CREDIBILITY**
Keeping the story interesting (avoiding the 'so what?' response)	Keeping the story believable (avoiding the 'I don't believe you' response)

Figure 9.1 Labov's storytelling paradox
Source: Labov 1997

of reportability or credibility as any other storyteller, narrators of illegal activities also have to avoid self-incrimination. Like the boredom and scepticism of an audience/reader, self-discrimination is a discursive obstacle and public narration of illegal activity is an additional burden on the poster. Section 3 below is a case study in how narrators deal with this difficult task.

2.2 Strategies for narrating illegal events

When stories involve illegal activities, writers may wish to distance themselves from them in order to avoid self-incrimination. There are three possible strategies that the narrator might adopt:

1. distancing from the narrated events
2. distancing from the act of narration
3. distancing from the agent of the narrated event.

Each of these strategies will be examined in turn. The formula for self-incriminating narrative that will be used in the analysis is '*x* says that *x* did *y*', where *y* is an illegal event. Each of the strategies involves a variation on this formula.

*2.2.1 Distancing from the narrated events (*x *says that* x *did* z*)*

The first strategy is to admit responsibility for the narration but to distance oneself from the narrated illegal events. In a narrative such as '*x* did illegal event *y*', *x* might claim that he or she did not do illegal event *y* but did *z* instead. In this case, the argument is 'it wasn't me because it didn't happen like that; this is how it happened ...'.

This kind of defence produces the 'what really happened' scenarios of courtroom discourse whose asymmetries have been frequently discussed in the sociolinguistic literature on legal testimony (Eades 2008, Heerey 2000, Tiersma 1999). In these situations, different versions of the facts are presented by prosecution and defence with each side aiming to provide a convincing narrative favourable to its own case. In terms of drug use, 'distancing from the narrated events' was the strategy adopted by Bill Clinton when he was accused of smoking marijuana as a student. By saying 'I didn't inhale', he is claiming that the events went differently from the way they were alleged to.

*2.2.2 Distancing from the act of narration ('not-*x *says that* x *did* y*')*

The second strategy is to admit that the narrated events took place ('*x* did illegal event *y*') but to deny responsibility for the narration itself (i.e. to turn the '*x* said' part of the formula into 'not-*x* said'). In this case, the argument is 'yes, that's the way things went but it's not my story'. How can a narrator deny responsibility for the story in this way? According to Goffman (1981: 144-145), talk is carried out by taking up a particular role or stance in relation to other speakers, so analysis in terms of Goffmanian interaction needs to examine the particular participant role(s) that the narrator adopts to distance him/herself from the narration. Goffman outlines four possible roles for the narrator:

author	=	the person who is selecting the words of the utterance
animator	=	the actual producer of the utterance
principal	=	the person whose beliefs or attitudes are being expressed in the utterance
figure	=	the agent, protagonist in a scene, character in a story

In order to have full interactional responsibility in Goffman's terms, a person has to be the author, animator and principal of the talk or writing in question, and in order to avoid responsibility, a narrator has to detach him or herself from one of these categories. For a poster on a drug forum, this can be done in a number of ways:

i. To deny that you are the *author*; for example, a poster could claim 'I didn't select the words; someone dictated the post to me and I just copied it down'.
ii. To deny that you are the *principal*; for example, a poster might say 'I selected and typed the words but I was writing the words on behalf of someone else'. This might be called the ghost-writer's defence when a writer claims to be putting him/herself into someone else's shoes.
iii. To deny that you are the *author or principal*: a poster might claim that he/she typed the words but was forced to do it by someone else. Here the poster is admitting to being the animator but not the author or principal. It is the defence of someone who claims to have written a document under duress.
iv. To deny that you are the *author*, *principal* or *animator*; in this case, the poster disclaims any responsibility by saying that he/she did not select the words, did not type them and they were not written on his/her behalf. In this case the claim is one of identity theft. A poster on a website might claim that might someone had stolen their password and avatar to write something illegal.

Thus, by applying Goffman's categories, we can see how, when crimes involve language use, it is possible to say 'it wasn't me' by denying personal responsibility for the speech acts themselves. You are admitting that the events of the incriminating story happened in the way they are told but casting doubt on the identity of the teller.

*2.2.3 Distancing from the agent of the narrated event ('*x *said that not-*x *did* y*')*

The third strategy is for the narrator to admit responsibility for the narration (*x* said) and to admit that *y* took place but to deny that he/she was the agent of the events. This can be paraphrased as the 'it wasn't me who did it' defence. In

Goffmanian terms, we are therefore dealing with the manipulation of the 'figure'. The figure is the character in the story and by not identifying him or herself with the character in the story (i.e. by turning *x* into not-*x*), the writer is able to disclaim responsibility for the actions.

2.3 Summary: legal identities in narratives

As Bamberg (2006) has suggested, any kind of storytelling activity involves a narrator taking up a position in relation to the story being told. Regarding the question of legal identities, we argue in this section that when illegal activities are publicly narrated by their perpetrators, writers' orientations to legality are likely to surface. When narrating potentially criminal events, narrators have to reconcile 'telling a good story' for the benefit of the website discourse community with 'telling a legal story' for personal self-protection (2.1). This means that the narrator has to negotiate a complex legal identity in the narrative by establishing distance between him/herself and the events being recounted (2.2). The next section will present a case study and analysis of this kind of discourse.

3. A case study in orientations to legality in online narrative

This section examines narrators' choices and orientations in relation to legality by looking at a corpus of narratives posted on a forum for drug users, in which posters describe their use of illegal psychoactive substances. The drug forum was chosen because it is a pseudonymous website, and although users may assume different identities, they are all ultimately traceable. Since total anonymity is not guaranteed, the dilemma for the poster writing about his/her own drug use is, if he/she wishes to avoid a criminal charge, how to write about the illegal activities without admitting responsibility for them. The data and analytical method are described in 3.1 and the results are analyzed in 3.2.

3.1 Data and method

The narrative data to be analyzed is taken from the website www.drug-forums.com – an online community concerned with the exchange of information on psychoactive substances. Previous research on this website (Schifano et al. 2006) addressed, from a purely medical perspective, the way the Internet is used as a resource for finding new drugs and the development of new drug-using trends. Here we focus on posts in the forum section of the website dealing with a range of drug-related topics, looking in detail at a 16-post thread from the *Ethnobotanicals (Natural Drugs)* section of the *Various Drugs* category, entitled 'Ever had a pleasant salvia trip?', over a two-month period (02/09/09 – 31/10/09).

Legal identities expressed in the posts were analyzed in two ways. The first of these involves the way in which narrators position themselves in relation to the forum's own rules. As Chua (2009) has shown, regulation of speech on the Internet is an important factor in the creation of a group identity. The Forum Rules (below) set out the forum's own orientation to legality by dictating recommended narrative strategies to prospective posters:

> It is not allowed to post that you are going to do or have done any illegal activity or that you have used any illegal drugs. Hypothetical stories or questions are allowed. It is allowed to describe your dreams. It is allowed to describe the actions of your pet or AFOAF (A Friend Of A Friend). Creative writing is welcomed.
>
> Because it is not possible for staff to keeping track of every members location and because most drugs are illegal somewhere, we consider confessing to any drug use to be self incrimination.

Figure 9.2 Forum Rules

In terms of the strategies set out in 2.0, the poster is being encouraged to adopt strategy 2.3 (*x* said that not-*x* did *y*). It is not clear if the forum is making these statements in order to protect itself from being sued under the laws relating to the publication of illegal activity or to protect its posters or both.

These Forum Rules show two orientations to legality. First, in the phrase 'it is not allowed to post that you are going to do or have done any illegal activity', the forum is stating its own publication rule. It also makes a statement about its linguistic policy ('we consider confession to any drug use to be self-incrimination') and the assumption on which this policy is based ('most drugs are illegal somewhere'). Second, it has a recommended policy for posters. This policy is explained in the terms used for giving permission ('it is allowed that') as well as through explicit encouragement ('creative writing is welcomed'). The suggestion is that posters can disclaim responsibility for illegal drug use by turning an autobiographical anecdote ('**I** did *y*') into a third-person story about someone else ('**X** did *y*'). The rules recommend that posters use the expression 'my pet' or acronyms such as AFOAF ('a friend of a friend') or SWIM ('someone who isn't me') instead of the deictic pronoun *I*. Given these two orientations, our analysis looked at the extent to which each poster complied with the forum's policy by analyzing the markers of self-reference they used.

The second mode of interactional analysis was to analyze the 'tellability' of the narrative, i.e. the narrator's involvement of the reader in the narrative. The term 'tellability' was introduced into narrative analysis by Sacks (1992) to justify the extended turn with which storytellers establish a story's point and value by giving their reasons for telling it and engaging the audience's attention. Storytellers therefore deploy narrative features in different ways depending on how far they want to show their own personal involvement and enhance that of the reader. To describe these features, narrative analysts have adopted different sets of descriptive categories, of which the best known are 'evaluative categories' (Labov 1972) and 'involvement strategies' (Tannen 2007). These are claimed to enliven narrative by 'creating a sense of concreteness, particularity and familiarity' and sending 'messages of rapport and intimacy to the audience inviting their involvement with them' (Georgakopoulou and Goutsos 1997: 136). Narrative analysis of the posts on the drug forum thus involved examining the kind of involvement strategies employed by posters in their use of particular features of tellability. Tellability features were classified in terms of the two main purposes for which they are discursively used: to maintain the reader's attention and to mark the writer's attitude to what he/she is narrating. The way in which a narrator involves readers at a cognitive level in the construction of meaning is through *sense-making devices*. These require readers to participate imaginatively in the story by creating their own mental picture of the narrated events. The writer's presentation of imagery and detail is an important part of this process, as is the use of direct speech, metaphor and hyperbole. The way that speakers/writers signal their attitude to the narrated events and to the storytelling itself is by using *attitude markers*. These include markers of intensity, emotion, interactional remembering and story formulation (Norrick 2000).

3.2 Results

The results are described in terms of markers of self-reference, indicating the level of compliance with the forum's own rules and markers of tellability, attesting the narrator's attempt to involve the reader of the forum in the narrated illegal events.

3.2.1 Markers of self-reference

The interactional structure of the thread, which has a total of 16 posts of different lengths, is shown in Table 9.1. The name of the poster is given at the top of each column and the number of words in each post is shown in the first row. Row two shows whether the poster used the first or third person to refer to themselves and row three the exact term used.

Table 9.1 shows that 13 out of 16 posters described their experience in the third person using the SWIM acronym, one poster used the acronym JOSH and two posters used the first person *I*; one of the two corrected *I* to SWIM at the end of the post.

3.2.2 Markers of tellability in the posts

In order to illustrate posters' use of markers of tellability, we look first at a typical example of a narrative post. In this post, *Rawbeer* describes his experience of using the herb salvia:

Table 9.1 Markers of self-reference

	Space cadet	Chronix	Matthijs	Saybin 1	Rhyn	Saybin 2	The pieman	Dying tomorrow
Number of words used in post	135	43	44	121	86	78	87	180
1st person or 3rd person	3rd	3rd	3rd	3rd	3rd	3rd	3rd	3rd
Term for self-reference	SWIM	SWIM	SWIM	SWIM	SWIM	SWIM	SWIM	SWIM

	Mr Mackey	Halothanatos	Soujla	Nacumen	Neti neti	Cory in Japan	Wybie	Raw beer
Number of words used in post	153	56	84	132	88	76	57	139
1st person or 3rd person	3rd	3rd	3rd	3rd	1st + 3rd	1st + 3rd	3rd	3rd
Term for self-reference	SWIM	SWIM	SWIM	SWIM	I/SWIM	I/SWIM	JOSH	SWIM

RAWBEER: Re: *Ever had a pleasant Salvia trip?* 31-10-2009 19:30

Only once has SWIM had a good salvia trip. It was while he was on mescaline...he had some left over and packed it in the bong, and whoa! He was watching a movie with some friends and this is all hard to describe...his friends speech became visible, like golden wiring coming from their mouths and connecting in the center of the room to form this fantastic image. And it was impossible to differentiate between the movie and the room, it was as if both had merged...and then it was over, before SWIM could really make sense of it. Brief, confusing, uninformative, (he's heard this said of DMT too) but certainly pleasant. He's never been able to try it again – salvia has been banned in his neck of the woods.

Figure 9.3 Narrative post

Rawbeer's post contains a considerable number of sense-making devices. As regards metaphor and visual imagery, the detail of 'packed it in a bong' and 'speech became visible' as well as the two similes 'like golden wiring coming from their mouths' and 'as if both had merged' combine to draw the reader into the writer's narrative world. The term 'whoa' – what Goffman (1981) would call a response cry – is used here in the manner of direct speech with the writer talking directly to the reader. *Rawbeer* also makes use of hyperbole – 'fantastic', 'never', 'impossible' – signalling his direct investment in what he is writing. As regards markers of attitude, *Rawbeer* uses a number of markers of emotion ('confusing', 'pleasant') to describe his experience as well as markers of intensity ('only', 'all', 'really', 'certainly') which, like hyperbole, serve to signal personal investment in the experience. *Rawbeer* also uses a story formulation ('this is all hard to describe') to show his own interest in the storytelling process. Overall, *Rawbeer*'s post is a 'high involvement' narrative which employs a great many tellability features to gain the reader's interest in the post.

The level of involvement of each of the posts on the thread has been analyzed in terms of the sense-making devices and attitude markers that are deployed in them and the level of involvement they aspire to. The results for each post are shown in Table 9.2 (sense-making devices) and Table 9.3 (markers of attitude).

Tables 9.2 and 9.3 show that most of the posts adopt a high involvement strategy, either by using sense-making devices or by using markers of speaker attitude, and in many cases both. Only the posts by *Chronix* and *CoryinJapan* can be said to show low involvement.

Table 9.2 Sense-making devices

SENSE-MAKING DEVICES	**Space cadet**	**Chronix**	**Matthijs**	**Saybin 1**	**Rhyn**	**Saybin 2**	**The pieman**	**Dying tomorrow**
Imagery + detail + direct speech	ripped apart piece by piece, someone laughed at her fear		entity	Rips out to kill him		into another galaxy	in the dark, nice music, drop the bong	bustling party, white knuckles
Simile/ Metaphor	Like waking up from a dream				salvia land, it's like the real world and salvia world combined, kill your ego	galaxy		
Hyperbole	all, completely, ripped	no, best		never, out to kill		fucking, full-blown, so far off		Bustling, stupid, terrifying, MUST
SENSE-MAKING DEVICES	**Mr Mackey**	**Haloth anatos**	**Soujla**	**Nacumen**	**Netineti**	**Cory in japan**	**Wybie**	**Raw beer**
Imagery + detail + direct speech	Bathed in holy light	Smoking a bowl of terror			No one listened to her lessons, 'pay attention in class'		Travelling circus. The Beatles – being for the benefit of Mr Kite	Packed it in the bong, speech became visible, whoa!
Simile/ Metaphor	bathed in holy light, gauntlet of terror	like smoking a bowl of terror, the whole world is mocking		world opening	Like waking up from a dream awakening into reality. He was salvia	Salvia kicks ur ego's ass	Part of a travelling circus	Like golden wiring coming from their mouths

Table 9.3 Attitude markers

ATTITUDE MARKERS	Space cadet	Chronix	Matthijs	Saybin 1	Rhyn	Saybin 2	The pieman	Dying tomorrow
Intensity	completely	no	mostly	only, no, never	only	full-blown so		long before so, any
Markers of emotion	scary terrifying	anxiety or fear	positive	positive negative feelings, pissed off	scared	fucking awesome can't stop fucking laughing, laughs a bunch	'pleasant', mellow	Bad, terrifying, fear, enjoy
Markers of IR + SF		best way to say it						
ATTITUDE MARKERS	**Mr Mackey**	**Haloth anatos**	**Soujla**	**Nacumen**	**Netineti**	**Cory in japan**	**Wybie**	**Raw beer**
Intensity	always, really, fucking, such, no, everything	fuck knows, never, whole, everyone	everyone, only	purely, truly, only, no	only	only		only, all, really, certainly
Markers of emotion	bizarre, unsettling, strange	terror	buzz bad, beautiful	Pleasant, trippy euphoria	bad feeling, mad, scared	bad	nice, pleasant	confusing, pleasant
Markers of IR + SF					SWIM remembers smoke		Just forgot to add	This is all hard to describe

4. Discussion

The most interesting question that arises from the fact that posters use high involvement strategies relates to Labov's paradox. The effect of a high involvement strategy is to heighten the 'maintaining interest' side of the storytelling process. What is unusual about these high involvement posts is that they are not counterbalanced by attempts to maintain credibility. Most narratives with only high involvement, i.e. aimed exclusively at maintaining interest, will invite a sceptical response from readers. So when extraordinary events are recounted, narrators will usually pay attention to their stories' creditworthiness while telling the story. In the case of the drug-forum posts, however, the credibility of the bizarre stories is never contested by other posters even though they are recounted without any attempt to make them seem credible. In fact, the more involving and the more 'incredible' the reportable events are, the more acceptable the story seems to be within the drug forum. If this were fictional writing, this kind of acceptance by the reader would be the norm. Readers of fiction accept exaggeratedly high involvement because, knowing that the recounted events are not true, they will suspend their disbelief. In the case of the posters' narratives, however, there is no suspension of disbelief and readers accept the 'incredible' (most reportable) events as highly credible. In this respect, posters' narratives succeed in breaking Labov's paradox because the same event can be both highly reportable and highly credible. How is this possible in a non-fictional context such as a drug forum?

We suggest that the main reason for the acceptance of the 'incredible' is the high degree of affiliation that is created between posters in the reading and writing of posts. Affiliation is usually created in forums through posters overtly supporting other posters. However, this is not the case in the posts we analyzed. Table 1.4 shows the low levels of speaker support given to posters by other posters.

Table 9.4 shows that only two of the 16 posts make reference to other posts, either directly, as when *Dying Tomorrow* writes 'like Rhyn said', or indirectly as when *Souila* quotes *Halothanatos*' post. Furthermore, only four of the posts make a general reference to posters (e.g. 'as others have said'). Another symptom of the lack of speaker support is the absence of markers of agreement. Only two examples were found ('ya' and 'ok'). This general lack of evidence of mutually supportive interaction raises the question of how affiliation is achieved across the discourse community.

The main way in which poster affiliation seems to be achieved is through posters adopting a similar narrative style. The first similarity is the almost universal use of the SWIM (or other) acronym. Since SWIM is used by most of the posters, it carries with it the implicature 'you know it's me really'. Thus, as well as avoiding self-incrimination, the function of SWIM appears to be a stylistic choice – a wink to the other posters, an in-joke designed to show that despite the detached, fictional nature of the prose, the poster is still very much a part of the community. SWIM is a constant reminder to writers and readers that they are indulging in 'knowingly illegal' discourse and this tacit knowledge serves to bind them together.

Table 9.4 Speaker support

MARKERS OF SPEAKER SUPPORT	*Space cadet 135*	*Chron Ix 43*	*Matt Hijs 44*	*Saybin 1 121*	*Rhyn 86*	*Saybin 2 78*	*The pieman 87*	*Dying Tomorrow 180*
1. Specific reference to others	0	0	0	0	0	0	0	1 like Rhyn said
2. Implicit reference to others	0	0	0	0	0	0	0	0
3. General reference to others	anyone there?	0	0	as other swims said	0	ya, SWIM also noticed	0	0
4. Markers of agree or disagreement	ok	0	0	0	0	ya	0	0
MARKERS OF SPEAKER SUPPORT	*Mr Mackey 153*	*Halothanatos 56*	*Soujla 84*	*NacUmen 132*	*NetiNeti 88*	*Cory In japan 76*	*Wybie 56*	*Rawbeer 139*
1. Specific reference to others	0	0	0	0	0	0	0	0
2. Implicit reference to others	0	0	1 Halothanatos	0	0	0	0	0
3. General reference to others	0	0	0	0	0	I agree with you all	0	0

Secondly, the tables show that posters' use of markers of tellability is fairly homogeneous. Fourteen out of 16 posters describe their experiences in a 'high involvement' style and they are all strongly reliant on markers of intensity and emotion; it seems to be a characteristic of these narratives that posters feel the need to mark up the intensity of their experience rather than the description itself. Where experiences are described in detail, imagery and metaphor are both prominent features of the narratives. Only two out of 16 posts fail to produce a metaphor or an image to describe their experience. Overall there seems to be a distinct pattern of tellability marking which is adhered to by posters, and we would argue that this stylistic homogeneity helps to bind the discourse community together.

These results on narrative style can be linked to the findings of Barratt (2011) in which 'perceived legal risk' was an influence on the extent to which Internet users participated in discussion of drug use in online forums. The two risks identified by Barratt's participants were 'police and/or other official organisations monitoring Internet forums for information which could lead to drugs-related arrests, and the potential for entrapment if forum users interacted with strangers through an Internet forum.' Her study also highlighted linguistic strategies used for risk-avoidance, which included 'masking personal identifiers', 'never discussing current or future usage', 'followed forum rules' and 'restricting the level of detail and content'. These strategies tally closely with our own results, particularly the use of SWIM and the third person, the use of the past tense and the Forum Rules. Our study also expands on Barratt's finding concerning restricted detail and content. We suggest that the restriction only applies to certain areas. Our forum interaction goes into considerable detail about the personal experiencing of the drug-taking event but is restricted in the sense that it fails to give details about the facts themselves (e.g. what happened, when and where).

5. Conclusion: A 'knowingly illegal' narrative identity

Three main conclusions can be drawn from this chapter. First, the linguistic markers produced by posters confirm social psychological studies that 'legal risk', i.e. the avoidance of self-incrimination, is an important factor in interactional behaviour in online drug forums.

Secondly, the choice of pseudoanonymous formats indicates that posters are willing to take a legal risk in order to maintain the credibility of their posts. Sections 1 and 2 have shown that the Internet user can choose between formats providing total anonymity, which enables him or her to elude legal responsibility, or pseudonymity which does not exclude legal responsibility but allows the user to remain unseen and unnamed during interaction. This difference has consequences for the reception of online narratives because totally anonymous posts lack credibility within online discourse communities. Users of pseudonymous forums and discussion groups are regarded as more responsible for what they write because their identities are ultimately traceable. In this case, legal responsibility acts as a guarantee of linguistic credibility.

Thirdly, at the level of narrative, we argue that the narration of potentially illegal events presents a particular interactional problem for pseudonymous users and that the avoidance of self-incrimination is an *additional tellability condition* which is in competition with other tellability conditions such as reportability and credibility. Reconciling these different positions produces an unusual narrative style, which is set out in the four tables describing the case study. On the one hand, Table 9.1 shows that the stories are projected as third-person fiction and Table 9.4 that there is very little overt mutual support between posters. These two factors combine to distance the writer from the reader. On the other hand, Tables 9.2 and 9.3 show that the tellability of the stories remains high and draws the reader into the narrative. The forum reader is thus presented with stories which have many of the characteristics of fiction because they are at the same time both distancing and involving. Paradoxically, however, these hybrid, fiction-like narratives are widely accepted as non-fiction within the forum. This acceptance suggests that the drug-forum discourse community is strongly affiliative and that, stylistically, this affiliation is achieved not in the traditional fashion through overt speaker support but in a non-standard way through the adoption of a similar narrative style, producing a 'knowingly illegal' group identity.

We conclude that orientations to legality/illegality are important features of the online discourse of drug use and that these orientations are part of a larger, more complex narrative identity. Pseudonymity obliges posters recounting illegal events to resolve the interactional problem of competing tellability conditions (credibility, reportability and avoiding self-incrimination) by using third-person markers of self-reference and a high involvement style. This produces a uniform narrative style which enhances the affiliation and intimacy between posters and creates a 'knowingly illegal' narrative identity across the virtual discourse community.

References

Bamberg, M. 2006. Stories: big or small. Why do we care? *Narrative Inquiry*, 16 (1), 139-147.

Barratt, M. 2011. Discussing illicit drugs in public Internet forums: visibility, stigma, and pseudonymity. In *C&T '11 Proceedings of the 5th International Conference on Communities & Technologies* (29 June-2 July 2011, Brisbane, Australia), edited by J. Kjeldskov and J. Paay. New York: ACM, 159-168.

Burkell, J. 2006. Anonymity in behavioural research: not being unnamed, but being unknown. *University of Ottawa Law & Technology Journal*, 3, 89-203.

Chua, C.E.H. 2009. Why do virtual communities regulate speech? *Communication Monographs*, 76, 234-261.

Eades, D. 2008. Telling and retelling your story in court: questions, assumptions, and intercultural implications. *Current Issues in Criminal Justice*, 20(2), 209-230.

Gatson, S. 2007. Illegal behavior and legal speech: internet communities' discourse about drug use, in *Real Drugs in a Virtual World: Drug Discourse and Community Online*, edited by E. Murguía, M. Tackett-Gibson, and A. Lessem. Lanham, MD: Lexington Books, 135-159.

Georgakopoulou, A. and Goutsos, D. 1997. *Discourse Analysis*. Edinburgh: Edinburgh University Press.

Goffman, E. 1981. *Forms of Talk*. Philadelphia, PA: University of Pennsylvania Press.

Heerey, P. 2000. Storytelling, postmodernism and the law. *The Australian Law Journal*, 74(10), 681-691.

Joinson, A. and Paine, C. 2007. Self-disclosure, privacy, and the internet, in *Oxford Handbook of Internet Psychology*, edited by A. Joinson, K. McKenna, T. Postmes, and U-D Reips. Oxford: Oxford University Press, 237-252.

Kim, M. 2010. The right to anonymous association in cyberspace: US legal protection for anonymity in name, in face and in action. *SCRIPTed*, 7(1), 51-70.

Labov, W. 1972. *Language in the Inner City: Studies in the Black English Vernacular*. Philadelphia, PA: University of Philadelphia Press.

Labov, W. 1997. Some further steps in narrative analysis. *Journal of Narrative and Life History*, 7 (1-4), 395-415.

Murguía, E., Tackett-Gibson, M. and Lessem, A. (eds.). 2007. *Real Drugs in a Virtual World: Drug Discourse and Community Online*. Lanham, MD: Lexington Books.

Norrick, N. 2000. *Conversational Storytelling*. Amsterdam: John Benjamins.

Sacks, H. 1992. *Lectures on Conversation*. Edited by G. Jefferson. Oxford: Blackwell.

Schifano, F., Deluca, P., Baldacchino, A., Peltoniemi, T., Scherbaum, N., Torrens, M., Farrè. M., Flores, I., Rossi, M., Eastwood, D., Guionnet, C., Rawaf, S., Agosti, L., Di Furia, L., Brigada, R., Majava, A., Siemann, H., Leoni, M., Tomasin, A., Rovetto, F. and Ghodse, A.H. 2006. Drugs on the web; the psychonaut 2002 EU project. *Progress in Neuropsychopharmacology and Biological Psychiatry*, 30, 640-646.

Stiles, A. 2002. Everyone's a critic: defamation and anonymity on the internet. *Duke Law and Technology Review*, 4, 1-6.

Tannen, D. 2007. *Talking Voices*. Cambridge: Cambridge University Press.

Tiersma, P. 1999. *Legal Language*. Chicago, IL: University of Chicago Press.

Toolan, M. 2001. *Narrative: A Critical Linguistic Introduction*. London and New York: Routledge.

Recontextualization

Chapter 10
Ethical particularism and contextualist interpretation in impossible attempts

Ross Charnock

Dancy's theory of unprincipled ethics has been largely ignored in jurisprudence, partly because of the apparent contradiction inherent in the concept of a law without rules. However, this model corresponds closely to legal practice in cases where the law is unclear or where there are no directly applicable rules to follow. In cases of impossible attempts, for many years there were no clear legal rules at all. The fact that recent efforts to clarify the applicable law have been unsuccessful corroborates the idea that the particularist approach may be more generally applicable. It may be relevant in all cases where there is room for disagreement. However, there are important differences between the problems raised in legal interpretation and in ethics.

1. Introduction

The relation between ethics and the law is fundamental in jurisprudence, yet many jurists remain unfamiliar with the arguments presented in Dancy's (2004) theory of 'Ethical Particularism'. Although moral principles may exist in theory, Dancy shows that they cannot function like fixed rules, and that attempts to apply them to particular cases may do more harm than good. He claims that ethical behaviour cannot be guided by appeal to abstract moral principles corresponding to Kantian categorical infinitives, but that the relevant principles can only function as general guides to behaviour, which may or may not apply in particular circumstances.

Although he is not primarily concerned with the application of his theory to the law, the questions he raises are clearly relevant to jurists. His theory applies in cases where the law is unclear, where there is room for judicial discretion or where the precedents are contradictory.

Although the idea of a law without rules or principles may seem at first sight a contradiction in terms, there are many legal problems for which there is no established law. It is useful to take as examples cases of impossible criminal attempts. These raise questions that go beyond mere dishonest intent, which is not punishable in itself, and concern rather steps taken preparatory to the commission of a crime. The attempt may be seen as criminal in itself, even where the crime has not actually been committed. However, it is unclear whether this should still be so where the act envisaged is physically impossible, or where the intended crime happens to be unknown to the law.

The most significant nineteenth-century cases in this field appear to have been decided mainly on intuitive grounds. The results were often contradictory, and thus appear to confirm, or at least to corroborate, the unprincipled thesis. Although attempts have been made in more recent cases to clarify the law, both through precedent and through statute law, the relevant principles remain unclear to the point of being indeterminate. In *Anderton vs. Ryan* (1985), Lord Bridge presented the situation thus:

> It is sufficient to say of subsection (2) that it is plainly intended to reverse the law, originally declared in Collins (1864), mistakenly thought to have been overruled by Brown (1889), but reaffirmed in Smith's case, that the pickpocket who puts his hand in an empty pocket commits no offence. (*Anderton vs. Ryan* HL 1985, *per* Lord Bridge)

This shows at the very least a lack of clarity in this area of the law. However, the theory of particularism may apply more generally whenever there is room for disagreement.

2. Ethical particularism

In ordinary language, an unprincipled person is generally considered to be one who has no moral standards. The idea of an ethics without principles therefore appears counter-intuitive. However, Dancy (2005: 1) rejects this 'naive view':

> Moral Particularism, at its most trenchant, is the claim that there are no defensible moral principles, that moral thought does not consist in the application of moral principles to cases, and that the morally perfect person should not be conceived as the person of principle.

He is concerned to show firstly that morality does not require principles and secondly that the imposition of fixed principles may actually do harm (2004: 2). His radical argument is that, on the holistic view, moral principles are not just impractical but theoretically impossible. This claim is generalized to apply to all putative moral principles.

On the practical level, no rules can be universally applicable, because they cannot fully take into account the infinite complexities of life. And theoretically, because all rules must be interpreted according to the unpredictable features of the particular case, they cannot be stated in advance. If this is true, then all moral judgement must be case by case.

The practical argument clearly applies to the law. It has been recognized since the time of Aristotle that although law is universal, 'about some things it is not possible to make a universal statement which shall be correct' (*Nichomean Ethics* V, 10). In his 'Discours préliminaire' to the French *Code Civil* (1804), Portalis points out the impossibility of providing for all possibilities. Even Blackstone seems to admit that too scrupulous an adherence to rules and principles may constitute a danger for the legal system. Having expressed his belief in the (near) perfection of the English criminal law, he admits (1765: Bk4, Ch1) that: '... even here we shall occasionally find room to remark some particulars, that seem to want revision and amendment', and further suggests that these imperfections 'have chiefly arisen from too scrupulous an adherence to some rules of the antient common law' (Blackstone, 1765: Bk 4, Ch 1). However, the existence of exceptions to rules does not in itself prove, as the particularists claim, that the principles involved can never be fully stated or intelligently applied.

Moral principles are often found to be in contradiction with each other, as in the Kantian example in which the obligation to tell the truth conflicts with the imperative of saving life. However, legal principles may also contradict each other, as when the right of free speech contradicts the right to privacy. Indeed, one of the principal functions of the judge is to balance conflicting rights

Jurists clearly have no difficulty in taking a particularist view of legal principles, as opposed to strict rules of law. These are merely persuasive whereas rules of law, like Dancy's moral principles, are binding on the judges and function as strict imperatives. Legal principles come into play in particular contexts, and are often helpful in deciding on the best interpretation of a given law. They therefore fit well with the particularist system of ethics. A more difficult question is whether strict legal rules (or laws) should be seen, as in particularist ethics, as unnecessary or harmful. In an ideal world, laws should apply uniformly, independently of context. If this ideal can be shown to be not just impractical but actually impossible, then the particularist view must be accepted as a plausible alternative in legal reasoning.

3. Legal rules: Impossible attempts

The idea of 'impossible attempts' raises fundamental problems in the criminal law. One of the basic rules in this field is that the criminal act (*actus reus*) and the criminal intent (*mens rea*) must both be present before an accused can be convicted of a crime. This rule is essentially subjective, because it makes conviction depend crucially on the intent, even where the criminal act is complete.

Where the act has not been completed, an individual may still be found guilty of an attempt. Uncontested examples are attempted murder where the victim survived the shooting, or attempted rape where the act was interrupted through the timely intervention of the police. In such cases, the accused was clearly attempting to commit the crime. The question is less obvious where the accused could not possibly have succeeded in committing the intended crime. In a Sherlock Holmes story, for example, the villain shot at the great detective's reflection in a mirror. When invited to press charges for attempted murder, the great detective magnanimously refused.

An attempt was made in *Doctor No* to kill James Bond by shooting him while he slept. The attempt failed because the intended victim was not in the bed at all, and so his mysterious enemies had merely shot his mattress. Yaffe (2011) evokes cases of attempted murder in which the victim turned out to be already dead. In such cases, it is clearly not sufficient to apply the classic legal test as to whether or not the accused has done something 'more than merely preparatory'.

Impossible attempts may be divided into two categories. In the first, the criminal act is incomplete, as in the examples mentioned above. In the second type of case, the accused may have actually completed the act envisaged, only to find that it was not illegal after all. In such cases, although he/she cannot be found guilty of committing an act which was not technically a crime, he/she may nevertheless be guilty of the attempt. Here, there is no longer any pretence of objectivity.

In *R vs. Goodchild* (1846), Mary Goodchild was found guilty of attempting to procure an abortion. She could never have completed the act because the young woman who submitted to the process turned out not to be pregnant after all. The highest judges in the land (including Lord Denman C.J., Tindal C.J., Pollock C.B., and Parke B., among others) considered the case on appeal and stated that: 'All were of opinion that under this indictment, the fact of the woman not being pregnant, at the time of the instrument being used, was immaterial' (*per* Parke B.). No clear reasoning is given in the report. However, the judges may have been influenced by the fact that the young woman later died, though from unrelated causes.

The opposite result was obtained in *R vs. M'Pherson* (1857). Here, the accused entered private property with the intention of stealing certain goods, but as these were not in the house at the time, it was held on appeal that he could not have 'attempted' to commit the felony charged. In this case, Cockburn C.J. tried without success to distinguish between 'intent' and 'attempt':

> There is a difference between intending to do a thing and attempting to do it. A man goes to a place intending to commit a murder, but when he is there he does not find the man he expected to find. How can he be said to have attempted to commit the murder? He merely attempts to carry an intention into effect. (*R vs. M'Pherson* 1857, *per* Cockburn C.J.)

Bramwell B.'s concurring judgment in the same case was based on an invented analogy. He suggested that no one would be convicted of attempted murder for striking a block of wood, even if in the dark he thought he was striking a man, and intended to kill him. Similarly, if a pickpocket puts his hand into an empty pocket, he could be said to be attempting to steal whatever was in the pocket at the time. In consequence, if there was nothing in the pocket, then he was attempting to steal nothing. Therefore he could not be guilty of a criminal attempt because what he was attempting to do did not amount to a crime.[1]

1 'The argument that a man putting his hand into an empty pocket might be convicted of attempting to steal, appeared to me at first plausible; but suppose a man, believing a

The case of a pickpocket putting his hand into an empty pocket actually occurred a few years later in *R vs. Collins* (1864), heard by the same judge. In view of his previous remarks, Bramwell B. was obliged to hold that the accused could not be convicted. His original *obiter dicta* was thus elevated to the status of *ratio decidendi*, and became binding on later judges.

However, as the decision in *Collins* was found unworkable, this precedent was overruled, in *R vs. Brown* (1889), by simple assertion, no argument being included in the case report. Here the accused had attempted to commit the 'unnatural act' of bestiality, by trying to rape a duck. Although this act was physically impossible, the prisoner was nevertheless found guilty of criminal attempt. Lord Coleridge clearly took a dim view of the matter.[2] He may have been influenced by the distasteful behaviour of the accused, by the circumstance that this was clearly not the first time he had indulged in such behaviour, or by the inference of unnecessary suffering to animals. The legal question raised but not answered was whether a mere attempt to perform something impossible could amount to a criminal attempt.[3] A different view was taken more recently in *R vs. Higson* (1984), when Colin Higson's wife complained to the police about his having (courageously) succeeded in having sexual relations with a Pyrenean mountain dog.[4]

In *R vs. Ring* (1892), an early case of mugging in the London tube, although nothing was actually stolen, the overruling of *R vs. Collins* was confirmed, without argument but by authoritative assertion.[5]

The contrary view was taken in *R vs. Williams* (1893) in which, in spite of having actually completed the act of rape (on a girl only nine years old), the young John Williams could not be found guilty, because according to the law as it then

---

block of wood to be a man who was his deadly enemy, struck it a blow intending to murder, could he be convicted of attempting to murder the man he took it to be?' (*R vs. M'Pherson* 1857, *per* Bramwell B.)

2 'The prisoner was convicted before me upon his own confession at the last assizes for the county of Essex, on an indictment charging him with an attempt to commit unnatural offences with domestic fowls. The depositions shewed that in all probability the offence had been habitual with him, and had resulted in the death of several of the birds, and serious injury to several others, who were found torn and bleeding apparently from the effects of the attempted penetration.' (*R vs. Brown* 1889, *per* Coleridge C.J.)

3 This case went to appeal on the grounds that according to an unpublished precedent, a duck was not an animal. The appeal was rejected without argument.

4 Leggat J. held that probation was more appropriate than a sentence of imprisonment because: 'When all is said and done, it is the appellant and indeed his wife, and not the dog, who need help.' (*R vs. Higson*, 1984).

5 'This conviction must be affirmed. The case was stated to ascertain whether or not *Reg. vs. Collins* is good law. That case was overruled by the decision in *Reg. vs. Brown*, a case decided by five judges, and since this case will also be decided by five judges, one of whom was one of the judges who decided *Reg. vs. Brown*, the learned judge who stated the case will have the satisfaction of knowing that now nine judges hold that *Reg. vs. Collins* is bad law.' (*R vs. Ring* 1892, *per* Coleridge C.J.).

stood, no such crime could be committed by a boy of only 13. In the opinion of Coleridge C.J., this was a legal rather than a physical impossibility, and it was not open to the court to convict the boy of an attempt simply because he could not have been convicted for the act itself.

In these cases, rather than follow a fixed rule, the judges seem to have been taking account of the particular circumstances, which are especially important where there is no clear rule to be applied. Dancy's claim is that no rule can be devised which would not lead inevitably to renewed problems. The question thus arises as to whether the particularist theory applies not just in ethics but also in the law.

4. Particularism in the law

In ethics, it is often assumed that to guide his/her conduct, the individual derives rules from past experience. In the particularist system, this is known as the subsumptive option (Dancy 2004: 3), in which moral thought and judgement is seen as the subsumption of the particular case under some universal principle. Dancy claims that this task is not just difficult but impossible. Because new distinctions arise in new, previously unenvisaged cases, there can be no universal principles.

The subsumptive option corresponds well to the common law system based on precedent, in which the judges are expected to find an applicable rule which fits adequately with earlier decisions. However, in the law as in ethics, the results are often incoherent because of the new distinctions which inevitably arise. Different judgments have been given in apparently similar cases and the results often seem contradictory. Dancy argues that in any case no putative principles can be assumed to be generally valid, and that strict application of precedent would necessarily lead to injustice in particular situations.

As a matter of definition, if rules applied generally then a feature that is a reason for a decision in one case would remain a reason for a similar decision in another. Such features would preserve their practical relevance in all circumstances. However, a particularist (or 'holist') considers (Dancy 2004: 3) that a new context can affect the ability of a feature to make a difference in the new situation. Given that (Dancy 2004: 27) 'a feature that is a reason in one case may be no reason at all, or an opposite reason in another', it follows that there can be no general solution.

There are two well-known solutions to this problem. On the one hand it may be argued that a complete statement of the relevant legal rules would implicitly include rule-governed exceptions (thus, properly understood, the duty to help would never conflict with a duty not to inflict pain). Indeed, Dancy admits that it is at least plausible to make exceptions to take account of such cases. Kant's categorical imperative may thus be rejected, for example when it is possible to save a life by lying instead of telling the truth. However, this tactic is not sufficient. Given that there will also be exceptions to the exceptions, attempts to provide for all possible circumstances, or to include even readily predictable exceptions in the statement of a given rule would quickly lead to unmanageable complexity. In any case, as Dancy points out, this kind of exception cannot be specified in advance. The fact that the rule must be adapted in response to particular cases is precisely the point.

The second possible solution proposed by those who favour a general rather than a particularist solution involves sorting the different rules into a hierarchy by ascribing to them some kind of moral weight, so as to construct a hierarchy of norms. Indeed, judges do frequently 'weigh' the relative importance of conflicting rights. However, once the hierarchy is accepted as part of the law, the law itself imposes a correct solution. Nevertheless, Dancy rejects what he calls this 'kitchen scales' approach, pointing out (2004: 26) that the features involved may have greater or lesser weight in different circumstances and that it is not possible to specify in advance which of the competing considerations should dominate. Further, the approach proposed fails to account satisfactorily for feelings of hesitation or regret where, even though the rule comes down on one side or the other, it appears that there is still something to be said on both sides.

Dancy (2004: 18, 81) thus acknowledges the possibility of non-monotonic reasoning in ethics, so that a feature that counts in favour of a certain act in a given situation may be less favourable or even have the opposite effect in another. The same applies in the law. In certain circumstances, it is clearly wrong for individuals to insist on their strict legal rights. They may even be stopped from doing so. Similarly, a contractual promise may be a good reason to keep your word, but it is no longer a valid reason if the contract was obtained under duress. It may even be a reason to breach the contract if it involves illegal activity. Given the possibility of change of polarity, there can be no universal rule.

It is sometimes argued that a legal system is necessary in all modern societies and that fixed rules are essential, because they constitute the common ground required for conflict resolution. It may be accepted that debate is possible without at least a tacit awareness of the basic rules. However, Dancy (2004: 133) points out that, in practice, most moral debate and disagreement concerns the principles themselves. On the legal level, the debate concerns not just the precise form of the rule, but its content; that is, what it implies in any particular context.

McCormick (2005) appears to accept the particularist view in ethics, but nevertheless affirms the necessity for rules in the law. For McCormick (2005: 99), there can be no law without rules. The judges are therefore obliged to take account of a kind of 'master rule book', which alone allows them to present the law as objective and as independent of their personal preferences. Further, the existence of fixed, clear rules simplifies the judicial system and has the advantage of certainty. These arguments are sometimes justified by the fact that the question of what the law is, is logically different from the question of what the law should be. However, this positivist reasoning is also open to objection.

On the one hand, fixed rules of law cannot be justified merely on the grounds that they tend to simplify the task of the judge. If the function of rules was to facilitate the administration of justice then they would become reasons for action in themselves. However, in that case, they may do harm whenever they can be interpreted as justifying dubious behaviour which has not been expressly forbidden. Rules should not be followed simply because of their official status but also because they are just. On the other hand, justice requires that laws, like moral principles, be reinterpreted as necessary in particular contexts. Indeed, reinterpretation is often necessary to avoid injustice or absurdity.[6] Judges are frequently required to provide new, original interpretations of statutes or to 'discover' new distinctions.

Dancy (2004: 134) admits that the particularist may be less predictable than the 'generalist', for example because the former does not always keep his or her promises, whereas the generalist always does so. He points out, however, that legal certainty is often overrated. The fact that it is sometimes necessary to choose between justice and certainty should be seen as a weakness in the legal system rather than as a matter of pride. By hypothesis, the particularist only keeps his or her promises when it is right to do so, and breaks them when to keep them would be wrong. Because the generalist always keeps his or her promises, even when it is wrong to do so, it may reasonably be concluded that the particularist system is more moral than that of the generalist.

5. Rules governing impossible attempts

In more recent cases, attempts have been made both by judges and by Parliament to clarify the law regarding impossible attempts. However, the rules remain unclear.

The question was extensively considered in *Haughton vs. Smith* (1974), in which Roger Smith and others planned to receive stolen goods, and the police hoped to catch them in the act. Unaware that their accomplices had been arrested and that the goods had already been recovered by the police, the accused did in fact take delivery. Their ingenious (and successful) defence was based not on entrapment, but on the fact that, at the time they were received, the goods, being in the possession of the police, had ceased to be stolen goods at all.

Lord Hailsham accepted that: 'if the facts had been as he believed they were, the man would have committed a crime. He intended to commit it. But he took no step towards the commission of a crime because there was no crime to commit.' However, he refused to accept that an act which was otherwise legal (handling goods in the possession of the police) could not be converted into an illegal act (handling stolen goods) simply by virtue of the defendant's mistaken

---

6 *Whiteley vs. Chappell* (1868) is an example of literal interpretation leading to absurdity. In *Garner vs. Burr* (1951) it was decided that a chicken hutch should count as a vehicle. The court of last resort is often able to reach more acceptable results by relaxing the rules, as in *Mandla vs. Dowell Lee* (1983).

belief concerning the status of the goods in question. That would amount to using judicial discretion to manufacture a new criminal offence.[7]

For similar reasons, Lord Reid considered that a guilty verdict would amount to punishment merely for a guilty intention,[8] and that the judges had no right to make such a radical change in the existing rules of law, however deserving of punishment the accused may be. He rejected the theory proposed in *Brown* and in *Ring*, and reinstated *Collins*, affirming that the purported overruling of the earlier case could not be valid as no justification was given:

> No words, unless so general as to be virtually useless, can be devised which will fit the immense variety of possible cases. Any attempted definition would, I am sure, do more harm than good. It must be left to common sense to determine in each case whether the accused has gone beyond mere preparation. (*Haughton vs. Smith* 1974, *per* Lord Reid)

Faced with the unfortunate precedent set in *Haughton vs. Smith*, which allowed morally guilty men to avoid punishment, Parliament intervened to change the law. In passing the *Criminal Attempts Act* (1981), the intention of the legislator was explicitly to disallow the 'impossibility' defence. Unfortunately, as predicted by Lord Reid, the application of the new statute was unclear.

Section 1(1) of the statute relies on the 'more than merely preparatory' rule to distinguish between intention and attempt: 's1(1) If, with intent to commit an offence to which this section applies, a person does an act which is more than merely preparatory to the commission of the offence, he is guilty of attempting to commit the offence.' However, this phrase remains vague to the point of being meaningless.

Section 1(3) provides that the intention of the accused should be determined according to the facts 'as he believed them to be'. However, this also fails to deal with the problem, as the offence itself must be real. No one can be condemned for an imaginary crime. Indeed, if 'the facts of the case had been as he believed them to be' (s1(3)(b)), then the problem would not have arisen in the first place.

---

7 'I do not think that it is possible to convert a completed act of handling, which is not itself criminal because it was not the handling of stolen goods, into a criminal act by the simple device of alleging that it was an attempt to handle stolen goods on the ground that at the time of handling the accused falsely believed them still to be stolen. In my opinion, this would be for the courts to manufacture a new criminal offence not authorised by the legislature.' (*Haughton vs. Smith* 1973, *per* Lord Hailsham).

8 'The theory is really an attempt to punish people for their guilty intention. The man who stabs the corpse may be as deserving of punishment as a man who attempts to murder a living person. The accused in the present case may be as deserving of punishment as he would have been if the goods had still been stolen goods. But such a radical change in the principles of our law should not be introduced in this way even if it were desirable.' (*Haughton vs. Smith*, 1973, *per* Lord Reid).

Further, according to s1(4), the Act applies to offences which 'would be triable' if completed. This rule presumably applies where the facts are as observed in reality, rather than on the basis of a false belief. This means that, by hypothesis, there could be no such 'triable' offence.

More generally, the statute fails to avoid the criticism of Lord Reid in *Haughton vs. Smith* concerning guilt by mere intention. If Parliament intended to introduce such a radical change in the law, it may have been expected to say so expressly.

Unsurprisingly, the new statute was found inapplicable when it came to be interpreted by the House of Lords in *Anderton vs. Ryan* (1985), the first new case on the subject to reach the court. Mrs Ryan was accused of 'handling' a stolen audio-cassette, which she had acquired for a suspiciously low price, though without having been explicitly informed of its provenance. She was acquitted because the prosecution was unable to prove that the cassette had in fact been stolen. According to Lord Roskill, the application of the statute in this case would lead inevitably to absurdity.[9] It was contrary to common sense and gave the impression of asininity.[10] This new decision gave rise to an abundant academic literature (see Hart 1981, Hogan 1985, Williams 1985, Fletcher 1986, Mathis 2004).

Possibly as a result of academic criticism, *Anderton vs. Ryan* (1985) was itself overruled only the following year in *R vs. Shivpuri* (1986), in which two brothers confessed to 'dealing with and harbouring a controlled drug', contrary to the *Misuse of Drugs Act* 1971 3(1). They thought they were illegally importing diamorphine (a variety of heroin or cannabis) from India for a stranger named Desai who had offered them £1000. Unknown to them, the substance was really snuff or 'some similar vegetable matter'. This time, the court found the accused guilty of attempting the crime to which they had confessed, on the clear wording of s1 and s2. Section 3 was explicitly considered irrelevant and ignored. *Anderton vs. Ryan* was overruled. Lord Hailsham reacted characteristically:

> [After the *Criminal Attempts Act*, 1981] I was happily under the impression that my hopes had been realised, and that my carefully prepared speech [in *Haughton vs. Smith*] would henceforth be relegated to the limbo reserved for the discussions of medieval school men. It was therefore with something like dismay that I learned that the ghost of my speech had risen from what I had supposed to be its tomb and was still clanking its philosophical chains about the field, and that the new Act had formed a tilting yard for a joust of almost unexampled ferocity

9 He gave the example of a young gentleman determined upon sexual intercourse with a young lady whom he erroneously believed to be under 16. She was in fact 18. Lord Roskill found it 'impossible to believe that the young gentleman should be found guilty of attempting to have unlawful sexual intercourse with a girl under 16 merely because of his erroneous belief.' (*Anderton vs. Ryan* HL 1985, *per* Lord Roskill).

10 'The language used in the statute is such as to make the attainment of common sense and the avoidance of asininity at the same time almost impossible of achievement.' (*Anderton vs. Ryan* 1985, *per* Lord Roskill).

> between two of the most distinguished professors of English criminal law in the United Kingdom. (*R vs. Shivpuri* HL 1986, *per* Lord Hailsham)

As predicted by the particularist philosophers, and indeed by the Wittgensteinian rule-following considerations, the new statute inevitably failed to resolve the problems raised in cases of impossible attempts. As was pointed out by Lord Reid in *Haughton vs. Smith* (1974), no rule, however formulated, whether in statute or in the common law, could take account of all the contextual features which may be present in any particular case.[11] The problem cannot be avoided by the introduction of more explicit rules of interpretation, intended to guide the interpretation of the rule in new cases, not just because they would fail to solve unenvisaged problems, but also because the new rules must themselves be reinterpreted in each new context. The problem is therefore infinitely recursive.

7. Particularism in other areas of law

The problems associated with adjudication in cases of impossible attempts are not confined to the English common law. Yaffe (2011) mentions the US cases of *People vs. Jaffe* (1906) in which the accused purchased fabric falsely represented as stolen as part of a sting operation, and the more contemporary case of *US vs. Crow* (1999), a 'grooming' case concerning the attempted sexual exploitation of a minor through Internet messages. Crow's defence was that the 'adult' police officer, going under the chat-room pseudonym of 'StephieFL', whom he had admittedly intended to exploit, was not in fact a minor.

Similar problems also arise in other areas of the law. Marital rape, for example, is rarely mentioned in the context of impossible attempts. Yet, until 1991, the problem was precisely that of legal impossibility, as the offence was unknown to the common law. According to the old rule, the husband could not commit rape on his wife because a conviction would require proof of the absence of consent, and this was impossible because the wife had 'constructively consented' during the marriage ceremony. Yet in practice it was often clear that the accused had intended to rape and had carried out his threat. The solution generally adopted, until the precedent was overruled in *R vs. R* (1991), was to consider the act as one of aggression, or trespass against the person.

The theory of ethical particularism predicts that similar difficulties will occur more generally whenever it is necessary to reinterpret established rules in new contexts. This is confirmed by the reasoning given in *Airedale NHS Trust vs. Bland* (1993), which corresponds particularly closely to particularist theory. Following

---

11 'No words, unless so general as to be virtually useless, can be devised which will fit the immense variety of possible cases. Any attempted definition would, I am sure, do more harm than good. It must be left to common sense to determine in each case whether the accused has gone beyond mere preparation.' (*Haughton vs. Smith*, 1973, *per* Lord Reid).

the disaster at the Hillsborough stadium, a young football supporter was reduced to a permanent vegetative state. Bingham M.R. listed the legal principles applicable when considering the question of whether the boy should be kept artificially alive or be allowed to die. These included respect for the sanctity of human life, the fact that medical treatment cannot be imposed without the consent of the patient and the fact that the doctor must comply with his patient's instructions, whether rational or irrational.

However, explicit reference was made in the judgments to the problems raised by attempts to apply fixed principles. In his judgment in the same case, while confirming that no clear rule could be derived either from previous decisions or from the new statute, Lord Hoffman pointed out that the principles to be applied could never be exhaustive: 'But the sanctity of life is only one of a cluster of ethical principles which we apply to decisions about how we should live.' It was also necessary to consider other principles including individual autonomy and the right of self-determination, as well as the closely related principle according to which it is wrong for someone to be treated without respect for his or her value as a person. Most significantly, Lord Hoffman indicated (as observed by the particularists) that the relevant principles are often contradictory and that it is impossible to decide in advance which of them should predominate:

> But what is not always realised, and what is critical in this case, is that they are not always compatible with each other. [...] There is no formula for reconciling this conflict of principles and no easy answer. It does no good to seize hold of one of them, such as the sanctity of life, and say that because it is valid and right, as it undoubtedly is, it must always prevail over other principles which are also valid and right. (*Airedale NHS Trust vs. Bland* HL 1993, *per* Lord Hoffman)

In the same case, Lord Browne-Wilkinson admitted that his own conclusion seemed irrational, though he insisted it was the one imposed by the existing law.[12]

As predicted by Dancy in the field of ethics, and as explicitly affirmed in this legal case, it appears that all moral judgement must depend on the particular circumstances and that there can be no single 'right' answer of general application. Various solutions are available in moral situations apparently governed by similar principles. The variable application of rules to apparently similar legal cases shows that the particularist approach also applies to the law. The point is relevant not just to cases for which there is no applicable rule but to all cases where there is room for disagreement among the judges; that is, to most cases heard on appeal in the higher courts.

---

12 'Finally, the conclusion I have reached will appear to some to be almost irrational. [...] But it is undoubtedly the law and nothing I have said casts doubt on the proposition that the doing of a positive act with the intention of ending life is and remains murder.' (*Airedale NHS Trust vs. Bland* 1993, *per* Lord Browne-Wilkinson).

8. Conclusion: Rules and principles

One objection often made to particularist ethics is that it fails to solve ethical problems. Rather than providing moral certainty, or at least a guide to deciding what is right or wrong, the particularist system merely gives an account of the difficulties involved. The advantage of this approach is that it corresponds to reality. If it were otherwise, then the theory would be directly falsified by observations. It would fail to account for the cases of disagreement and misunderstanding observable in ordinary life. If the law similarly fails to provide certainty, then the particularist theory would be corroborated, if not confirmed, to the extent that it corresponds not just to ethics and morality but also to legal practice.

It is generally admitted that legal decision-making depends not just on the application of fixed rules; it is also influenced by legal principles including, for example, Lord Atkins' celebrated 'neighbour principle' ('no man shall profit from his own wrong', *Donoghue vs. Stevenson,* 1932). These principles are broad, general and unspecific (Hart 1994: 261). As in the particularist theory, they are persuasive rather than binding. Even Dworkinian principles of justice, supposed to establish a determinate 'right answer' even in hard cases, must be interpreted in each new context, and usually appear more indeterminate than the statutes they were supposed to clarify. In Dancy's terms, they are contributory reasons that favour, rather than impose, a certain view.

However, as Hart (1994: 261) points out, there is no sharp contrast between mere legal principles and true rules of law. Indeed, principles are occasionally formalized in an attempt to make them applicable as rules of law, whether in statute, as in the *Forfeiture Act* (1982) (which prevents murderers from profiting from their own wrongs), or in the common law, as in *Donoghue*. However, judges still disagree regarding their application in particular cases.

Conversely, as rules of law must always be interpreted in context, they are in practice no more decisive than legal principles, and similarly fail to provide legal certainty. Like moral and indeed equitable principles, legal rules often conflict with other equally valid considerations. They must be applied case by case. However, if decisions are made case by case then the judge cannot be said to be following a rule at all. In this sense, legal practice corresponds closely to the particularist theory, which denies any useful role for rules or principles.

The significance of this conclusion lies in the fact that it is usually taken as fundamental to the idea of law that it should apply equally to all, at all times. However, if the particularist view is to be preferred, not just in 'hard' cases for purely pragmatic reasons, but for theoretical reasons more generally, then the application of the law must always depend on the circumstances of the case. As fixed rules lead inevitably to injustice in particular cases, the correct result cannot therefore be established merely by formalist reasoning from basic premises but must remain to some extent unpredictable. Particularist ethical theory is, in this respect, closely parallel to that of contextualist semantics, which rejects, for reasons that depend on linguistic rather than moral arguments, the assumption of the existence of a purely literal – that is, acontextual – level of meaning. On this view, the semantics of the law itself must be essentially contextual. This amounts to a denial of the possibility of a purely literal interpretation as a condition of certainty in the law, and constitutes on the contrary a strong argument for the idea of indeterminacy. The linguistic arguments thus strengthen the ethical conclusion. Not only is it preferable in the interests of justice to take account of the particular circumstances, contextual interpretation appears to be necessary in order to reach a proper understanding of the law. Dancy himself points out (2004: 197) the complementarity between his view of ethics and the contextualist theory of semantics, pointing out that 'The whole thing whirls on endlessly, without any fixed points'.[13]

The extension of the theory of particularism to this field thus suggests, perhaps controversially, that legal argument depends essentially on casuistics. A less tendentious conclusion would be to suggest that, in spite of common though idealistic assumptions regarding the certainty of law and its literal meaning, legal practice seems to corroborate new theories in moral philosophy.

References

Aristotle (1925) [350BC]. *The Nicomachean Ethics.* (Trans. Ross). Oxford: Oxford University Press.

Blackstone, W. 1765-1769. *Commentaries on the Laws of England.* Oxford: Clarendon Press.

Charnock, R. 2007. Lexical indeterminacy: contextualism and rule-following in common law adjudication, in *Interpretation, Law and the Construction of Meaning*, edited by A. Wagner, W. Werner and D. Cao. Dordrecht: Springer, 21-47.

Charnock, R. 2013. Hart as contextualist: theories of interpretation in language and the law, in *Current Legal Issues – Law and Language*, edited by M. Freeman and F.M. Smith. Oxford: Oxford University Press, 128-150.

Dancy, J. 2004. *Ethics without Principles*. Oxford: Clarendon Press.

Dancy, J. 2005. Moral particularism. In *Stanford Encyclopedia of Philosophy.* Available at: http://plato.stanford.edu/entries/moral-particularism [accessed: 1 January 2012].

Duff, A. 1996. *Criminal Attempts*. Oxford: Oxford University Press.

Duff, A. 1998. Principle and contradiction, in *Philosophy and the Criminal Law*, edited by A. Duff. Cambridge: Cambridge University Press, 156-204.

Fletcher, G. 1986. Constructing a theory of impossible attempts. *Criminal Justice Ethics*, 53, 53-69.

---

13 For an overview of a contextualist approach to legal interpretation see e.g. Charnock (2007, 2013).

Hart, H.L.A. 1981. The House of Lords on attempting the impossible. *Oxford Journal of Legal Studies*, 1, 149-166.

Hogan, B. 1984. The Criminal Attempts Act and attempting the impossible. *Criminal Law Review*, 584, 589-590.

Kripke, S. 1982. *Wittgenstein on Rules and Private Language*. Oxford: Blackwell.

Llewellyn, K. 1952 [1930]. *The Bramble Bush: On Our Law and Its Study*. New York: Oceania Publications.

McCormick, N. 2005. *Rhetoric and the Rule of Law*. Oxford: Oxford University Press.

Mathis, S. 2004. Criminal attempts: the subjectivism/objectivism debate. *Ratio Juris*, 17(3), 328-345.

Patterson, D. 1990. Law's pragmatism: law as practice & narrative. *Virginia Law Review*, 76, 937-966.

Portalis, J.E.M. 1804. Discours préliminaire, *Code Civil*, Paris: Dalloz.

Recanati F. 2004. *Literal Meaning*. Cambridge: Cambridge University Press.

Sperber, D. and Wilson, D. 2002. Pragmatics, modularity and mind-reading. *Mind and Language*, 17, 3-23.

Travis, C. 1991. Annals of analysis (review of Grice 1989). *Mind*, 398, 237-264.

Williams, G. 1985. Attempting the impossible: the last round. *New Law Review*, 33, 337-348.

Williams, G. 1986. The Lords and impossible attempts, or Quis custodiet ipsos custodes? *Cambridge Law Journal*, 45(1), 33-83.

Wittgenstein, L. 1953. *Philosophical Investigations*. Oxford: Blackwell.

Yaffe, G. 2011. Trying to kill the dead: De Dicto and De Re intention in attempted crimes, in *Philosophical Foundations of Law & Language*, edited by A. Marmor and S. Soames. Oxford: Oxford University Press, 184-216.

Case references

UK Statutes

Criminal Attempts Act 1981 c 47.
Forfeiture Act 1982 c 34.

UK Cases

Anderton vs. Ryan [1985] AC 560.
Airedale NHS Trust vs. Bland [1993] 2 W.L.R 316.
Donoghue vs. Stevenson [1932] AC 562.
Haughton vs. Smith [1974] 2 W.L.R. 1.
R vs. Higson [1984] 6 Cr. App. R20.
R vs. R (Marital Exemption) [1991] 4 All ER 481.
R vs. Shivpuri HL [1986] 2 WLR 988.

Reg. vs. Brown (1889) 24 Q.B.D. 357.
Reg. vs. Collins (1864) 9 Cox C.C. 497.
Reg. vs. Goodchild (1846) 2 Car. &; K. 293.
Reg. vs. M'Pherson (1857) Dears. &; B. 197.
Rex vs. Percy Dalton (London) Ltd. [1949] 33 Cr.App.R. 102, C.C.A.
Reg. vs. Ring (1892) 17 Cox C.C. 491.
Reg. vs. Williams [1893] 1 Q.B. 320.

US cases

People vs. Jaffe 185 N.Y. 497, 78 N.E. 169 (1906).
US vs. Crow (164 F.3d 229 (5th Cir. 1999).

Comprehensibility

Chapter 11

From primary legislation to public presence. The language of gay rights: From legislation to lobbying

Bronwen Hughes and Antonella Napolitano[1]

1. Introduction

Homophobia, hate crimes, discrimination based on sexual orientation, and gay and transgender rights have been the *foci* of ever-increasing legislative and public interest in recent years. There is, however, a discrepancy between the enforceable rights of these discriminated-against categories and the manner in which such rights are conveyed to the public. The issue of discrimination based on sexual orientation is of a particularly delicate nature as it comes up against not only legislative barriers, but also hurdles of a social, cultural, ethical and linguistic nature.

This chapter will explore the way discrimination is dealt with and subsequently fought against in three different ambits: legislative, institutional and public. Our interest was initially triggered by a massive hard-hitting hoarding campaign which Stonewall, the UK gay and bisexual lobbying organization, launched in the summer of 2009 and which had repercussions, both positive and negative, upon the general public.

The Stonewall poster presents a red background with a specular visual effect between the two parts of the message. The initial 'matter-of-fact' statement 'some people are gay' is in white block capitals, the direct imperative 'get over it' is in black block capitals. The two sentences that make up the message encapsulate, in 'catch-phrase' style, the manifold discourses produced by the three ambits mentioned above. As regards the negative repercussions of this hoarding campaign, shortly after its appearance, a number of semiotically similar posters began to appear with slogans such as: 'Some people are gay, kill them!'; 'Some people are Christian and believe buggery is wrong, get over it!'; and the more light-hearted 'Some people are from Wigan, get over it!'. Such repercussions, though in some cases unpleasant, testify to the success of the campaign.

1 Although this chapter was jointly researched and conceived, Bronwen Hughes is responsible for sections 4, 6 and 7 and Antonella Napolitano for sections 1, 2, 3, 5 and 8.

Figure 11.1 Stonewall billboard campaign, 2009

Following a process of reverse engineering, we chose to begin our study by investigating the legislative Acts in the UK which have in some way 'encoded' the prohibition of discrimination over the years. We then decided to look at the way discrimination is dealt with by an institutional body, namely the Crown Prosecution Service (henceforth CPS), the principal prosecuting authority in England and Wales. The CPS is an independent non-ministerial government department responsible for prosecuting criminal cases investigated by the police.

The third aspect of our tripartite study involves the investigation of a Stonewall publication which strictly concerns homophobic hate crimes. Stonewall is a charitable organization which promotes the rights of lesbian, gay and bisexual people in the UK and is renowned for its parliamentary lobbying activities.

2. Aims and methodology

Different disciplinary ambits are characterized by different discursive practices. Drawing on Bhatia's (1993, 2004) studies on genre theory, we have analyzed the lexico-grammatical, rhetorical and discoursal elements employed in the three ambits of study. We observed how, in the context of legislative and institutional texts characterized by a consolidated generic integrity, the emergence of a new hybrid genre may progressively be evidenced in ways that it reaches and benefits the ultimate consumer, in our case being members of the lesbian, gay, bisexual and transgender (henceforth LGBT) community.

We aim to illustrate that not only does language undergo significant modification depending on its context of use, but that there is also a process of reciprocal endorsement whereby the progressive simplification which occurs in the move from the legislative to the institutional and on to the lobbying comes full circle and will, in turn, have an influence on subsequent primary legislation. As Fairclough and Wodak (1997: 258) state, '[A] discursive event is shaped by situations, institutions and social structures, but it also shapes them.'

3. Corpus

Our corpus has been selected on the basis of the tripartite investigation and covers a selection of legislative provisions, two of the CPS institutional publications and the most recent Stonewall publication aimed at the LGBT community.

Table 11.1 The corpus

Primary Legislation (a selection of Acts which create offences and make provisions for crimes related to different forms of discrimination):

1986	Public Order Act
1998	Crime and Disorder Act
2001	Anti-Terrorism Crime and Security Act
2003	Criminal Justice Act
2006	Racial and Religious Hatred Act
2008	Criminal Justice and Immigration Act

CPS booklets which cover Homophobic and Transphobic hate crimes:
CPS Policy for prosecuting cases of homophobic and transphobic crime (2007)
Leaflet introducing the CPS policy for prosecuting cases of homophobic and transphobic crime (2009)

Stonewall publication on Homophobic hate crime:
Blow the whistle on hate crime: A plain English guide on gay hate crime for lesbian, gay and bisexual people (2010)

4. Primary legislation

In terms of genre analysis, our impression is that primary legislation has received and continues to receive ample attention from eminent scholars in the field as regards the specific textual and linguistic features which characterize parliamentary Acts. Phenomena such as their strongly de-contextualized nature, which stems from a need for 'precision, clarity, unambiguity and all-inclusiveness' (Bhatia 1993: 102), or more specific features which are often considered to hinder easy comprehension (sentence length, nominalization, embedded clauses including syntactic discontinuities) together with the many attempts made to bring '[the] content or linguistic form within the area of experience of a particular group of readers' (Bhatia 1993: 145). Indeed, in the course of our investigation of a number of parliamentary Acts, we frequently came across phenomena which hinder understanding for laypersons.

Our investigation has centred on the way in which the language of primary legislation in the field of discrimination has progressively evolved due to the influence of changes in social consciousness and has, over time, conferred a particular identity to certain discriminated-against categories.

We have identified two main strands in our investigation of the evolution of anti-discrimination legislation: hatred and aggravation. The term 'hatred' refers to those laws that have, over time, laid down the penalties for offences involving hatred based on sexual orientation, race or religion. Likewise, the term 'aggravation' refers to those crimes that are rendered more serious by the addition of aggravating circumstances which enhance the culprit's guilt.

Table 11.2 Primary legislation – the two strands of investigation

1986 Public Order Act 2006 Racial and Religious Hatred Act 2008 Criminal Justice and Immigration Act	HATRED
1998 Crime and Disorder Act 2001 Anti-Terrorism, Crime and Security Act 2003 Criminal Justice Act	AGGRAVATION

As regards the hatred strand, the 1986 Public Order Act (c.6, s17) makes provisions to prevent 'the stirring up of racial hatred' and provides a definition of racial hatred.

The 2006 Racial and Religious Hatred Act (c.1 schedule 16, s29A) amends the 1986 Act merely by adding the words 'Hatred against persons on religious grounds'. A definition of religious hatred is provided; however, no other aspects of the 1986 Act are modified, and this is merely a case of amending by insertion.

The 2008 Criminal Justice and Immigration Act (c.4, s74, schedule 16) further amends the 1986 Act by inserting 'Hatred on the grounds of sexual orientation'. Again, a definition of hatred on the grounds of sexual orientation is provided, but there are no further modifications or additions to the original Act.

Table 11.3 Primary legislation on hate crimes

Public Order Act 1986	Racial and Religious Hatred Act 2006	Criminal Justice and Immigration Act 2008
Meaning of 'racial hatred' 17. In this Part 'racial hatred' means hatred against a group of persons defined by reference to colour, race, nationality (including citizenship) or ethnic or national origins. ***Acts intended or likely to stir up racial hatred*** 18. 1 A person who uses threatening, abusive or insulting words or behaviour, or displays any written material which is threatening, abusive or insulting, is guilty of an offence if— (a) he intends thereby to stir up racial hatred, or (b) having regard to all the circumstances racial hatred is likely to be stirred up thereby.	***Hatred against persons on religious grounds*** The Public Order Act 1986 (c. 64) is amended in accordance with the Schedule to this Act, which creates offences involving stirring up hatred against persons on religious grounds. In the Public Order Act 1986 (c. 64), after Part 3 insert— 'Part 3A Hatred against persons on religious grounds'. 29A **Meaning of 'religious hatred'** In this Part 'religious hatred' means hatred against a group of persons defined by reference to religious belief or lack of religious belief.	***Hatred on the grounds of sexual orientation*** 74 Hatred on the grounds of sexual orientation Schedule 16— (a) amends Part 3A of the Public Order Act 1986 (c. 64) (hatred against persons on religious grounds) to make provision about hatred against a group of persons defined by reference to sexual orientation, and 29AB **Meaning of 'hatred on the grounds of sexual orientation'** In this Part 'hatred on the grounds of sexual orientation' means hatred against a group of persons defined by reference to sexual orientation (whether towards persons of the same sex, the opposite sex or both).

The evolution of legal prohibitions on the grounds of discrimination therefore goes from race to religion and on to sexual orientation.

The second strand we have chosen to investigate, denominated 'aggravation', also includes three parliamentary Acts, of which the second two amend the original. The Crime and Disorder Act 1998 (c.37, s28) creates a number of racially aggravated offences. Perpetrators of racially motivated hate crimes can be charged by the police with specific offences such as racially aggravated harassment or assault.

The Anti-Terrorism, Crime and Security Act 2001 (c.24, s36) amends the 1998 Crime and Disorder Act by adding the words 'racially or religiously aggravated offences': this is merely a case of amending by insertion, and the text remains identical from the point of view of the language employed. The Criminal Justice Act 2003 Section 146 introduces 'aggravation related to disability or sexual orientation'; these two categories stand alone and are not 'tagged on' by mere insertion to the previous discriminated-against categories.

Table 11.4 Primary legislation on aggravation

Crime and Disorder Act 1998	Anti-Terrorism, Crime and Security Act 2001	Criminal Justice Act 2003
28. Meaning of 'racially aggravated' (1) An offence is racially aggravated for the purposes of sections 29 to 32 below if— (a) at the time of committing the offence, or immediately before or after doing so, the offender demonstrates towards the victim of the offence hostility based on the victim's membership (or presumed membership) of a racial group; or (b) the offence is motivated (wholly or partly) by hostility towards members of a racial group based on their membership of that group.	36. Meaning of '[racially or religiously aggravated]'— (1) (a) at the time of committing the offence, or immediately before or after doing so, the offender demonstrates towards the victim of the offence hostility based on the victim's membership (or presumed membership) of a [racial or religious group]; or (b) the offence is motivated (wholly or partly) by hostility towards members of a [racial or religious group] based on their membership of that group.	146. Increase in sentences for aggravation related to disability or sexual orientation (1) This section applies where the court is considering the seriousness of an offence committed in any of the circumstances mentioned in subsection (2). (2) Those circumstances are— (a) that, at the time of committing the offence, or immediately before or after doing so, the offender demonstrated towards the victim of the offence hostility based on— (i) the sexual orientation (or presumed sexual orientation) of the victim, or (ii) a disability (or presumed disability) of the victim, or (b) that the offence is motivated (wholly or partly)— (i) by hostility towards persons who are of a particular sexual orientation.

In both the 'hatred' and the 'aggravation' strands, the evolution of legal prohibitions on the grounds of discrimination goes from race to religion and on to sexual orientation.

In order to investigate the manner in which discrimination is dealt with in an institutional ambit, the next step in our tripartite investigation involves an analysis of the two CPS publications which concern the LGBT community.

5. CPS: The *Policy*

Addressor: CPS
Addressee: All members of society
Channel: Informative booklet which promotes the action taken by CPS and all partner agencies.

The CPS *Policy*, among the many CPS publications, serves as a mission statement to clarify the aims of the CPS and the action taken when safeguarding the legal rights of the LGBT community. 'An organization's mission statement establishes the scope, domain and fundamental purpose of the organization and provides a guiding philosophy. It should be a clear, simple statement of the overall purpose of the organization, provide a focal point for objectives, goals and activities and define success for the organization' (Newsom and Haynes 2005: 82).

In the *Policy*, the desire to address society and the call for social change is strongly marked, as is evident in the following excerpts:

> [the *Policy*] *'reflects the changes in legislation and society'*
> 'in an open and democratic society'
> 'unacceptable/not acceptable' [for society]
> 'it is a priority for our society'
> 'if we are to build an open, tolerant and inclusive society.'

Throughout our research, we communicated frequently with Jackie Kerr, CPS's Senior Policy Advisor, Strategy & Policy Directorate. She informed us that although no linguistic experts were employed to assist in the drafting of CPS documents, the language used in the *Policy* was the subject of extensive debate. She also stated that the aim of the *Policy* was 'to let the public know how we make decisions, how we carry out our duties and the service they can expect from us', and that 'the *Policy* is an outward-facing document intended for members of the public'.[2]

Ms. Kerr's emphatic use of the institutional 'we/us' led us to seek tangible evidence in the *Policy* of the manner in which pronoun use can serve as a positioning device which marks addressor/addressee engagement.

---

2 Jackie Kerr, Senior Policy Advisor, Strategy & Policy Directorate, CPS Headquarters in response to a specific e-mail enquiry sent by B. Hughes and A. Napolitano – March 2010.

Pronouns play a crucial role in the building of addressors and addressees' textual identities and, as De Fina states (1995: 384), it is by means of pronouns that 'the speaker expresses both his own presence in discourse, the presence of others and the relationship that he/she entertains with these others.'

Our investigation of the personal and possessive pronouns present in the *Policy* led to the results we have illustrated below:

5.1 Pronouns (personal and possessive)

The pronouns *we/our/us* always refer to the CPS whereas *they/their* refer to the LGBT community. The pronoun *you* is absent throughout the entire document. This can be explained by the fact that the *Policy* is not intended to be a direct form of communication between the institutional body (CPS) and the ultimate consumer (the LGBT community), but rather a mission statement which uses pronouns strategically to 'create an atmosphere of communality and consensuality' (Rounds 1987: 25) between the institutional body and the public at large.

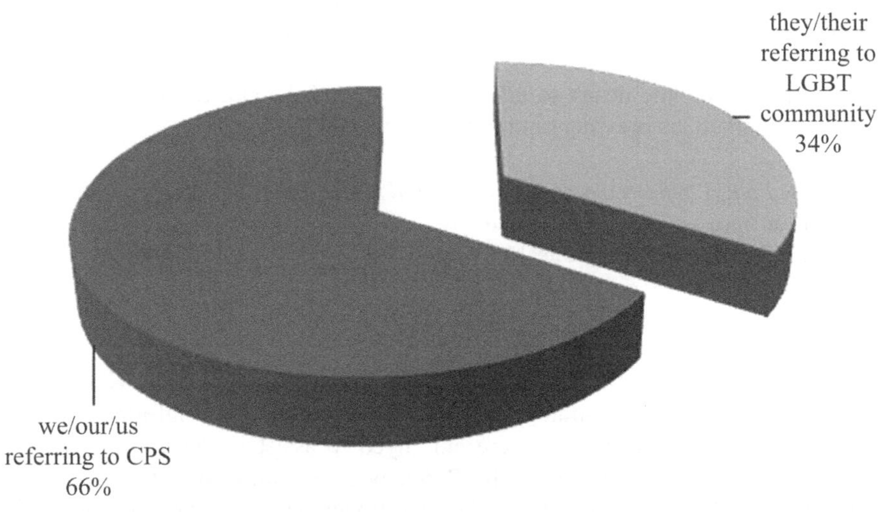

Figure 11.2 Distribution of pronouns in CPS *Policy*

5.2 Lexical items

As mentioned above, the *Policy* not only spells out the overall organizational aims of the CPS, it also promotes a sense of social conscience and the desire to support and uphold the specific legislative needs and concerns of the LGBT community.

We have identified a number of lexical items which indicate both a strong empathetic sentiment and a pledge to commitment. As the terms 'empathy' and 'commitment' are here strictly interrelated, we have chosen the label *empathetic commitment* to describe the manner in which the CPS promotes its actions through the use of words and expressions belonging to a common semantic field. The expression *intensified empathetic commitment* refers to the mechanism through which the CPS not only demonstrates understanding and sympathy for the LGBT category, but also pledges to build on that understanding, and to carry forth its actions accordingly.

In the following table, we list the most recurrent lexical items which convey the CPS' concern for the LGBT community:

Table 11.5 List of empathetic lexical items in the *Policy*

EMPATHY	COMMITMENT	INTENSIFIERS
Undermine	Unacceptable	Firmly
Help	Not acceptable	Fully
Confidence	Assist	Effectively
Securing (the confidence)	Promote	Essential
Encourage	Important to us	Properly
(Our) understanding	All that we can	Very
Support	Playing its part	Strongest
Concerns (noun)	Approach	Prime
Safe	A proactive approach	
Respect	Consideration	
Dignity	All practicable steps	
Vulnerable	To do (our) job well	
Hope	We welcome	
Feel		

Examples of empathy and commitment in context in the *Policy*:

1. [...] we will treat all victims and witnesses with respect and dignity. It is important to us all that those affected by homophobic and transphobic incidents report them and come to give their evidence in court when a prosecution follows [...]
2. Such crimes must be investigated fully and prosecuted firmly.
3. The CPS is fully committed to taking all practicable steps to help victims and witnesses through the often difficult experience of becoming involved in the criminal justice system.
4. We will do all that we can to make giving evidence in court as easy as possible.
5. We want to promote greater confidence in the criminal justice system.
6. Securing the confidence of those affected by homophobic and transphobic crime is an essential part of the CPS' approach to dealing effectively with cases with a homophobic or transphobic element.

5.3 The simplification of legal discourse

The CPS *Policy* is not based on the presumption of shared knowledge within a specific discourse community; it has an informative aim and therefore is devoid of those features which render legal language inaccessible to the general reader – such as excessively lengthy sentences with complex patterns of coordination and subordination, presence of binominal and multi-nominal expressions, complex prepositional phrases, inclusion of archaic and foreign terms (cfr. Melinkoff 1963; Williams 2007). Though some semi-technical legal terms such as 'aggravated' are maintained, they are subsequently clarified and often paraphrased. In most cases, however, the original legal wording is substituted. Whenever the *Policy* touches upon specific legal provisions in the field of homophobic and transphobic crimes, the wording of the provisions is simplified in accordance with the communicative purpose of the entire document (Bhatia 2004: 202). In this simplification process, we have identified the following four features:

a. The *Policy* discards the typical section and subsection layout of the Act.
b. The original Act and specific section from the Act are mentioned.
c. The *Policy* provides a clarified summary of the original section of the Act.
d. The *Policy* employs discursive linkers to create simple cohesive discourse.

These features are exemplified in Table 11.6 below. The left-hand column reports an excerpt from section 146 of the original Act, while the right-hand column, extrapolated from the *Policy*, summarizes and comments upon the original section. With reference to points a) – d) above, it is evident that:

a. The *Policy* presents continuous text and is devoid of the section/subsection layout which characterizes the Act.
b. Section 146 is clearly mentioned in the *Policy*.
c. The *Policy* summarizes what is stated in section 146, leaving out those parts which do not concern sexual orientation.
d. The *Policy* employs discursive linkers (*therefore/because of*) as cohesive devices.

As regards the simplification of the original legal terminology, we have identified the following changes:

[Section 146: 'The court must state in **open court** that ...'
(open court: legal term in opposition with *in camera*)
vs.
CPS *Policy*: 'The court must also state the fact **openly**'.

(use of adverb which simplifies and generalizes the original legal term causing it to lose its legal connotation).

Table 11.6 Simplification of legal terminology in the *Policy*

Section 146 CJA 2003	CPS *Policy*
This section applies where the court is considering the seriousness of an offence committed in any of the circumstances mentioned in subsection (2) (2) Those circumstances are— (a) that, at the time of committing the offence, or immediately before or after doing so, the offender demonstrated towards the victim of the offence hostility based on— (i) the sexual orientation (or presumed sexual orientation) of the victim, or (ii) a disability (or presumed disability) of the victim, or (b) that the offence is motivated (wholly or partly)— (i) by hostility towards persons who are of a particular sexual orientation, or (ii) by hostility towards persons who have a disability or a particular disability. The court— must treat the fact that the offence was committed in any of those circumstances as an aggravating factor. (b) must state in open court that the offence was committed in such circumstances.	Section 146 does not create any new offences; it imposes a duty upon courts to increase the sentence for any offence aggravated by hostility based on a number of factors including the victim's sexual orientation (or presumed sexual orientation). Therefore, when an offender has pleaded guilty or has been found guilty and the court is deciding on the sentence to be imposed, it must treat evidence of hostility based on sexual orientation (or presumed sexual orientation) as something that makes the offence more serious. The court must also state the fact openly so that everyone knows that the offence is being treated more seriously because of this evidence of hostility based on sexual orientation (or presumed sexual orientation).

The generic use of 'everyone' to refer to all concerned can be classed as an 'extreme case formulation' which is employed '[to] propose that some behavior is not wrong, or is right, by virtue of its status as frequently occurring or commonly done' (Pomerantz 1986: 220).

5.4 Modals

The modals *will*, *shall*, *may*, *must*, *can* and *should* are all present in the *Policy*. *Will* and *may*, however, deserve special attention as they distinguish themselves for three specific reasons:

- they outnumber all the other modals: *will* and *may* together make up 65 per cent of the total number of modals present in the *Policy* (see Figure 11.3);
- they take on a meaning which characterizes the text type being investigated – a mission statement rather than a legislative provision;

- their usage belongs more to the sphere of general language than to prescriptive legal English.

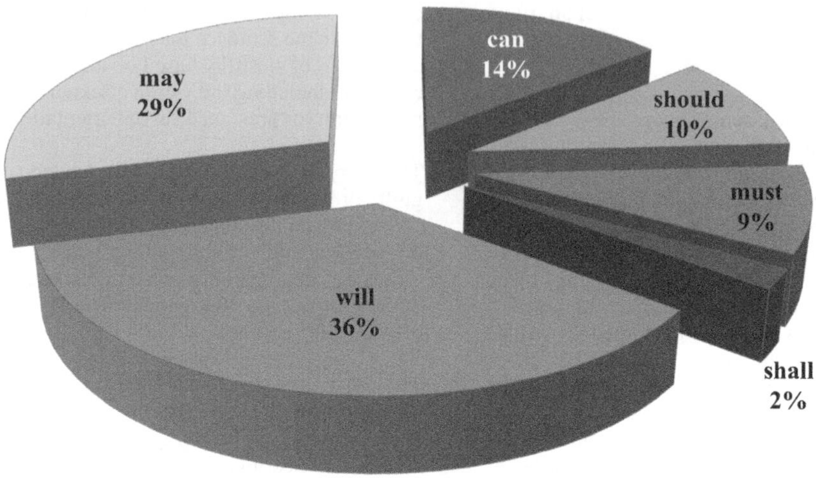

Figure 11.3 Distribution of modals in CPS *Policy*

As regards the modal *will*, the most striking feature we have encountered in our investigation of the CPS *Policy* is its commissive use. This illustrates both the empathy felt towards members of the LGBT community, and the CPS' pledge to commit itself to the hilt. 'Commissives [...] are those illocutionary acts whose point is to commit the speaker (again in varying degrees) to some future course of action' (Searle 1976: 11).

The following are examples of commissive *will* in the *Policy*:

1. We will ensure tailored support
2. We will ensure that...
3. We will manage your care.
4. We will explore all options fully.

The modal *will* can be interpreted as a commissive when it indicates an action to be carried out by members of the CPS themselves – in which case it is a pledge – and as an overlapping commissive/future form when it refers to actions that will be carried out by third parties: in this case, the CPS can merely act as a 'committed guarantor' for actions carried out by another body, but cannot provide a full pledge:

1. We will ensure that an experienced prosecutor supervises the case.
2. We will ask for advice from the LGBT liaison officer.

3. We will continue to work and train with community partners from the LGBT communities.

In the *Policy*, the use of the modal *may*, both in the affirmative and in the negative, indicates epistemic possibility:

1. Some words or phrases used in this document may not be familiar to everybody.
2. People may commit crimes for more than one reason.
3. Those affected by homophobic or transphobic incidents are sometimes reluctant to report them [...] because they may be 'outed', that is their sexual orientation or their trans identity may become known.

This use of *may* confirms the informative rather than legal nature of the document as, in the legal context, deontic *may* confers discretionary power (affirmative) or prohibition (negative) (Williams 2007).

6. CPS: The *Leaflet*

Addressor: CPS
Addressee: Members of the LGBT community
Channel: Informative booklet based on a question/answer dialogical format.

The *Leaflet* is the communicative mode chosen by the CPS to convey the empowering function of legal norms to the ultimate consumer (the layperson belonging to the LGBT community). It bridges the gap between the ideal world of law and the real world of the victims of homophobic hate crimes.

The CPS *Leaflet* presents a brief introduction to the CPS' anti-homophobia guidelines. It is an eight-page booklet in large print destined for rapid consultation by a non-specialized audience made up of members of the LGBT community. In the booklet, there is no direct reference to members of this community as *gays* or *lesbians*, nor is the initialism LGBT ever used. The only terms employed are 'sexual orientation', 'victims of crime', and 'people involved in hate crimes'.

Among the textual features, it would appear that the *Leaflet* presents a clearly delineated structure or cognitive pattern similar to those identified by Bhatia when examining different text-types (2004: 116-121):

- Identifying the topic
- FAQs establishing 'customer' needs
- Answers to FAQs providing product description and product offer
- Establishing CPS credentials
- Soliciting response.

In identifying the topic, the CPS minimally adapts a definition of racial hate incidents and crimes extrapolated from the strongly controversial report into a racially motivated murder in 1999.[3] Not only does this recall the passage in the previously mentioned legal provisions from race to religion and on to sexual orientation, it also makes the CPS *Leaflet* strongly intertextual.

> There is no legal definition of a homophobic or transphobic incident. However, we adopt this definition when applying our policy:
>
> *'Any incident which is perceived to be homophobic or transphobic by the victim or any other person'.*

FAQs are employed to establish an ongoing conversation between the CPS (institutional *we* employed in answers) and a member of the LGBT community (*I* employed in questions).

The question/answer mechanism as a 'conversational device' is fully developed in that the member of the LGBT community states his/her concerns in an open-question form, and receives an answer which assuages his/her concerns by empathetically describing CPS practice in favour of the LGBT community. As Fairclough states: '[...] conversational discourse practices which traditionally belong in the private sphere are being systematically simulated within organizations' (1992: 8).

The member of the LGBT community then goes on to ask a further question which refers directly to the content of the previous answer.

Question:	What if I don't want to go to court?
CPS answer:	We will explore all options fully and offer whatever support we can through our Witness Care Units before we decide whether or not to proceed with a prosecution.
Question:	What do Witness Care Units do?

Direct speech and personal story-telling in discourse are used here as an 'inclusive device' through which the reader is positioned as the 'universal *I*' or 'ideal subject' (Fairclough 2001: 41) and thereby feels that the CPS is catering for his/her specific needs and concerns. This FAQ device functions as a 'simulated face-to-face dialogue' (Fairclough 1992: 98) which 'entails a division between an individual producer or relatively small production team and a body of receivers that is indeterminate in size [...]' (Chouliaraki and Fairclough 1999: 43).

The following are examples of questions which show strong personal concerns:

1. I do not want my sexual orientation or trans identity to become widely known. What safeguards can you offer?

3 Home Office, *The Stephen Lawrence Inquiry: Report of an Inquiry by Sir William Macpherson of Cluny*, Cm 4262–I, February 1999.

2. I am being targeted because of my sexual orientation – what can the court do?

The answers to the FAQs have an informative-promotional objective as, on the one hand, they provide the necessary information to help the victims of homophobic crimes, while on the other they strongly promote the activities of the CPS as an institutional body. This strategic promotional activity is then pursued in the section which establishes the CPS' credentials.

The highly ideological promotional discourse, typical of an advertising genre, is further pursued in the final section of the *Leaflet* which encourages readers to acquire more in-depth knowledge in the field by reading other CPS publications.

Throughout the *Leaflet* we are presented with two communicative devices: the above-mentioned use of FAQs as a user-friendly dialogical tool, and the reformulation of legal wording as a simplification device. Both of these contribute to the construction of a rhetorically simple text (Bhatia 2004).

Examples of the simplification of technical legal expressions are 'aggravating factor' and 'open court' (previously commented upon when investigating the CPS *Policy*), originally found in the Criminal Justice Act 2003, which respectively become 'more serious' and 'openly' (supported by the generic 'everyone') in the CPS *Leaflet*.

Table 11.7 Simplification of legal terminology in the *Leaflet*

Criminal Justice Act 2003 (sc 146)	CPS *Leaflet*
The court— must treat the fact that the offence was committed in any of those circumstances as an **aggravating factor**.	the Court must treat this hostility as something that makes the offence **more serious**.
(b) must state in **open court** that the offence was committed in such circumstances.	The Court must state this **openly** so that everyone knows that this is the case

In contrast with the de-contextualized, impersonal language of legal provisions, the CPS *Leaflet* presents a strongly empathetic tenor, a high 'degree of emotional charge in the relationship between the participants' (Renkema 2004: 47). The content of the legal provision is thus progressively conveyed at an institutional level where recipient and context design (Hutchby and Wooffitt 2005) are of key importance.

Numerous factors such as pronoun use, empathetic terms and modality all contribute to the creation of this discursive genre.

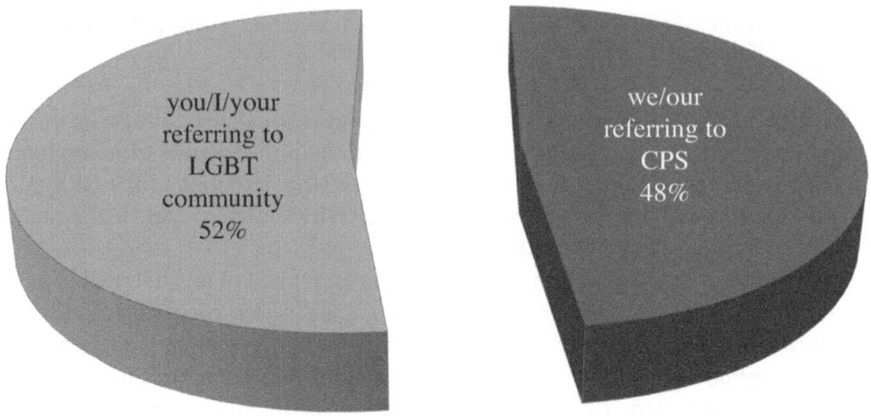

Figure 11.4 Distribution of pronouns in CPS *Leaflet*

6.1 Pronouns (personal and possessive)

The breakdown of personal pronouns, possessive pronouns and adjectives illustrates an equal balance between the *we/our* employed by the addressor (CPS) and the *you, I* and *your* referring to members of the LGBT community.

6.2 Lexical items

Despite the reduced length of the document, we have again identified numerous terms which indicate both a strong empathetic sentiment and a pledge to commitment.

Table 11.8 List of empathetic lexical items in the *Leaflet*

Empathy	Commitment	Intensifiers
Concerns (noun)	All that we can	Best
Support (verb)	Whatever support we can	Fully
Care (verb)	Responsibility	
Whenever possible	Tailored for your needs	
	Ensure	
	(We will) make sure	

The following is an example of empathetic commitment in the context of the *Leaflet*:

1. We recognize these concerns and we will treat all victims and witnesses with dignity. We will do all that we can to make giving evidence in court as easy as possible.

6.3 Modals

As regards modality, the frequency of modals present in the brief *Leaflet* is considerably reduced compared to the *Policy*.

The modals *can*, *may*, and *should* are all used epistemically in a canonical manner and do not in any way characterize the intended message conveyed by the text:

1. what can the court do?
2. the CPS [...] will answer any general queries that you may have.

Again, we find a widespread use of commissive *will*, as was the case in the *Policy*. This use of *will* confirms the CPS's pledge to commit itself to the respectful support of the LGBT community:

1. We will treat all victims with dignity.
2. We will do all that we can.
3. We will explore all options fully.
4. We will try to make sure [...].

There are five occurrences of *must* in the *Leaflet* (see Table 11.9 below), all deontic to indicate procedure. *Must* is only used when there is a reference to the original legal provisions.

Compared to the *Policy* examined above, the *Leaflet* presents a further simplification of the legal language used in the original provisions. It does so in the following manner:

- The section/subsection layout of the original act is no longer present.
- The wording of the original section or subsection of the act is not summarized (as it was in the *Policy*), but rather paraphrased in a simple manner.
- The weight and strength of the original legal provision is conveyed in two ways: deontic *must* is maintained, and the term *court* acquires primary importance by the use of the capital 'C'.

The combination of a number of pragmatic textual devices (simplification, FAQs as a dialogical tool, the selection of a highly interpersonal tenor and the expression

Table 11.9 Use of the modal *must* in the *Leaflet*

Criminal Justice Act 2003	CPS *Leaflet*
The court— **must** treat the fact that the offence was committed in any of those circumstances as an aggravating factor.	the Court **must** treat this hostility as something that makes the offence more serious.
(b) **must** state in open court that the offence was committed in such circumstances.	The Court **must** state this openly so that everyone knows that this is the case

of 'empathetic commitment') all contribute to the shaping of a new form of discourse which conveys the CPS disciplinary culture.

By drawing upon the resources exploited by other social practices (the combination of a discourse of information with one of promotion), the CPS manages to forge a new institutional discursive genre which bridges the gap between the de-contextualized world of legal provisions and the highly contextualized world of 'hands on' information conveyed in the language of the ultimate consumer to be found in Stonewall publications and which we shall now examine.

7. Stonewall's *Blow the whistle on gay hate*

Blow the whistle on gay hate is Stonewall's latest publication on hate crimes. It is an eight-page booklet which exploits a number of semiotic devices (images, contrasting font sizes and types, highlighting, 'post-it' insert effects) with strong visual impact.

Publications that offer advice, support and help on solving problems or carrying out tasks can be placed in two categories: 'self-help' manuals and 'how-to' guides. 'Self-help' manuals tend to give advice on how to solve problems within the emotional sphere and point towards 'personal growth' (e.g. solving eating disorders, getting over depression), and the language employed therein tends to be more 'reactive' than 'proactive' in that readers are encouraged to react to an existing problem. 'How-to' guides, on the other hand, teach readers how to face a new situation.

The *Blow the Whistle* booklet would appear to belong to the 'how-to' category in that it teaches the LGBT community how to combat hate crime by providing a specific 'tool-kit' which includes legislative and terminological information, advice on how to talk about homophobia, and operative information on how to act/react in case of attack.

1. When you get called something in the street [....]
2. When you step into the police station [....]

3. This is what you do.
4. Don't react.

Unlike the CPS booklet, which presents a single linear internal structure or cognitive patterning, the Stonewall booklet appears to adopt a *double-layered structure*.

Each page presents a main text and a 'post-it' insert. The same topic is dealt with on each page, though at different levels of discourse.

The main text, which extends over seven pages, is of a more informational though highly contextualized nature. Each of the following seven topic areas is covered on a separate page:

- Index: list of 'how-to' tips:

  1. How to get yourself out of harm's way.
  2. Who you need to report stuff to.

- Establishing customer needs by contextualizing the scene:

  1. You're walking along, minding your own business, and you hear it [...]
  2. You may have been on the receiving end of a physical homophobic attack.

- Establishing a need for action:

  1. You need to report any homophobic incident.
  2. You still should do something about it.

- Instructions for action:

  1. If you're in real danger you obviously phone 999.
  2. You can also step into a police station and report an incident to the officer on duty.

- Providing legal background and terminology:

  1. A 'homophobic hate incident' is according to the police [...] any non-crime incident which [...]
  2. A hate crime is [...] Any criminal offence which [...]

- Appeal to a social conscience:

  1. Even if you don't care about being heckled in the street, you should still do your bit and report any 'hate incident'.

2. […] you might be preventing something more serious happening to someone else

- Endorsement of institutional backup:

1. You can contact the police, either at the police station nearest to where the incident happened, or by calling a non-emergency number.

The parallel 'post-it' inserted texts, present on all pages except the first and last, serve as a running commentary, in the form of asides, to the main text. They are the expression of Stonewall's in-depth empathetic involvement and reiterate the information given in the main text. The 'post-it' inserts are not self-standing, as is the main text, and can only be understood if one has first read the topic presented on each page.

On the 'Establishing customer needs by contextualizing the scene' page, as a comment to example (30), the 'post-it' insert states:

1. People who spend their time shouting abuse at passers-by are looking for a reaction, which is why it's delicious not to give one.

On the 'Instructions for action' page, as a comment to example (34 and 35), the 'post-it' insert states:

1. 'Yes, there was a time when gay men and lesbians were reluctant to call in the cops. But that was then, this is now'.

The two texts are complementary in that by integrating the two levels of discourse (information-giving and commentary), Stonewall establishes a relationship based on implicit endorsement and mutual trust.

The Stonewall booklet manifests a plurality of discourses and can be classified as a 'hybrid genre' (Bhatia 2004: 112) bringing together an info-advisory discourse and a more pragmatic 'how-to' discourse. It is distinguished by a number of lexico-grammatical and rhetorical devices which contribute to the creation of this new genre.

7.1 From out-group to in-group

The booklet is written by members of the LGBT community for other members of the same community. It is built on the knowledge that both speaker/writer and hearer/reader share a common identity (their sexual orientation), common experiences (homophobic hate crimes and incidents) and even common localities (gay bars, pubs, venues).

This common background serves to mark them as a specific 'in-group' (opposed to the out-group of homophobics). The out-group is clearly delineated by the specific use of offensive language 'faggot', 'dyke' and by specific behavioural traits, *they* 'shout', *they* 'slap', *they* 'punch', *they* 'vandalise', *they* 'break windows' (italics added by authors for additional emphasis).

1. *People* who spend *their* time shouting abuse at passers-by are looking for a reaction. Which is why it's delicious not to give one.
2. More importantly, *they* are often looking for a fight. (italics added by authors).

7.2 In-group markers

The LGBT community constitutes the 'in-group'; their belonging is signalled by the constant use of *situational ellipsis* (Cook 1996) which creates proximity, intimacy and immediacy and presupposes shared knowledge. As Goddard (2002: 107) states: '[...] people who know each other well don't need to be all that explicit about their meanings, because they know the other person will fill in the gap as a result of shared knowledge and shared history.'

1. Been shouted at in the street?
2. Called a faggot or a dyke?
3. Been beaten up?
4. Walked away feeling humiliated?

Notice here the inversion: the discriminated-against community is customarily considered an out-group. Here the out-group has become the homophobic community.

7.3 The conversationalization of legal language

In this booklet, the language and content of primary legislation (section 146 of the 2003 Criminal Justice Act) maintains the original meaning but is expressed in simplified, conversational terms, hence 'aggravating factor' becomes 'a tougher sentence'.

The impersonal term 'court' becomes 'judge' reinforced by 'he' or 'she'.

Table 11.10 Conversationalization of legal language in *Blow the Whistle*

Section 146 Criminal Justice Act 2003	*Blow the Whistle* (Stonewall Publication)
The court— must treat the fact that the offence was committed in any of those circumstances as an **aggravating factor.**	And remember, if a **judge** thinks that it's homophobically motivated, **he or she** can give a **tougher** sentence.

7.4 Endorsement of institutional backup

Throughout the booklet, there is constant reference to the proactive attitude of the police. We feel that the endorsement that Stonewall now grants the police force, after considerable misgivings in previous years, is due to their role as the interface between the LGBT community and that of all legislative and institutional bodies.

Below are some examples of statements that endorse the police force which:

1. should take you seriously.
2. want to help.
3. are as anxious as you are.
4. will listen to what you have to say.

7.5 The imperative as a rhetorical device

A recurrent lexico-grammatical feature which occurs throughout the booklet, both in the main informational text and in the secondary 'post-it' inserted text, is the use of the imperative. All the imperatives have a strong exhortative connotation and spur the members of the LGBT community to action.

1. Blow the whistle on hate crime.
2. Let's blow the whistle on homophobes!
3. Don't let it go!
4. Don't be fobbed off [...].

8. Conclusion

Over the years, primary legislation has attempted to support and protect the LGBT community by prohibiting and punishing anti-discriminatory behaviour. Primary legislation has rarely met with the approval of the LGBT community or the public campaign lobbying groups such as Stonewall. Along the same lines, institutional bodies such as the CPS only started publishing 'committed' anti-sexual discrimination materials as late as 2007.

As regards the issue of discrimination on grounds of sexual orientation, legislative and institutional bodies and parliamentary lobbying groups such as Stonewall have for many years stood on opposite sides of the fence, with the latter strenuously attempting to right a number of legislative 'wrongs' and seek out a more empathetic commitment from the institutions.

Following a brief analysis of the discourse practices that characterize the three ambits of study, we wish to posit that there has been a progressive move towards a new 'hybrid' genre embodied by the latest Stonewall booklet which, through a number of interdiscursive and intertextual devices, encapsulates the initial legislative and institutional message in a linguistic form that is both accessible and empathetic to the ultimate consumer: the LGBT community.

It can also be posited that the language employed when talking about sexual discrimination has followed a similar itinerary. From the de-contextualized language of the parliamentary Acts (Swales 1990, Bhatia 1993) which have been passed over the years, largely thanks to Stonewall's unrelenting pressure, simplified versions of the original Acts (or sections of Acts) in institutional publications have been made available. The 2010 Stonewall guide written in plain English was in fact wholly endorsed by Parliament:

> Gay people have the same rights as everyone else to live in peace and security. Homophobic incidents have no place in a civilized, decent society. There are no extenuating circumstances. I welcome this excellent plain-English guide that encourages gay men and lesbians to report hate crimes. It sends a clear signal that there's no place in a civilized society for such hatred. Gay people should have the same right as everyone else to justice, to live their lives without fear. (Home Secretary Alan Johnson – 31st March 2010)[4]

Besides Parliament supporting and endorsing Stonewall in 2010, we also have Stonewall endorsing Parliament. In fact, the 2010 Equality Act, sections of which became operative in October 2010, takes into account requests put forward by Stonewall as regards both content and language. As for content, all nine discriminated-against categories are brought together in one all-inclusive category under the heading 'protected characteristics'; as for language, the Act is presented in a wholly innovative format totally devoid of cross-referencing, supported by explanatory inserts, background information and case examples.

It can be said that there has been a progressive evolution in the UK towards harmonization in the field of anti-discrimination law and in the linguistic presentation of parliamentary Acts. This is largely due to the constant pressure of extra-parliamentary bodies such as the CPS and parliamentary lobbying groups such as Stonewall.

References

Austin, J.L. 1962. *How to do Things with Words: The William James Lectures delivered at Harvard University in 1955*, edited by J.O. Urmson. Oxford: Clarendon.

Bhatia, V.K. 1993. *Analyzing Genre: Language Use in Professional Settings*. London: Longman.

Bhatia, V.K. 2004. *Worlds of Written Discourse: A Genre-based View*. London: Continuum.

4 Reported in digitaljournal.com on 3 April 2010.

Biber et al. 1999. *Longman Grammar of Spoken and Written English.* Essex: Pearson Education Limited.

Chouliaraki, L. and Fairclough, N. 1999. *Discourse in Late Modernity: Rethinking Critical Discourse Analysis.* Edinburgh: Edinburgh University Press.

Cook, G. 2001. *The Discourse of Advertising.* London: Routledge and Kegan Paul.

De Fina, A. 1995. Pronominal choice, identity and solidarity in political discourse. *Text* 15 (3), 379-410.

Fairclough, N. 1992. *Discourse and Social Change.* Cambridge: Polity Press.

Fairclough, N. 2001. *Language and Power.* 2nd edition. London: Longman.

Fairclough, N. and Wodak, R. 1997. Critical discourse analysis, in *Discourse as Social Interaction. Discourse Studies Vol. 2. A Multidisciplinary Introduction,* edited by T.A. van Dijk. London: Sage, 258-284.

Goddard, A. 2002. *The Language of Advertising. Written Texts.* 2nd Edition. London/New York: Routledge.

Hutchby, I. and Wooffitt, R. 2008. *Conversation Analysis.* 2nd Edition. Cambridge: Polity.

Mellinkoff, D. 1963. *The Language of the Law.* Boston: Little Brown & Co.

Newsom, D. and Haynes, J. 2005. *Public Relations Writing: Form & Style.* Boston: Wadsworth Publishing Co Inc.

Pomerantz, A. 1986. Extreme case formulations: a way of legitimizing claims. *Human Studies*, 9 (2-3), 219-229.

Renkema, J. 2004. *Introduction to Discourse Studies.* Amsterdam: Benjamins.

Rounds, P.L. 1987. Multifunctional personal pronoun use in an educational setting. *English for Specific Purposes*, 6, 13-29.

Searle, J.R. 1976. A classification of illocutionary acts. *Language in Society*, 5, 1-23. Swales, J.M. 1990. *Genre Analysis. English in Academic and Research Settings.* Cambridge: Cambridge University Press.

Williams, C. 2007. *Tradition and Change in Change in Legal English. Verbal Constructions in Prescriptive Texts.* 2nd Edition. Bern: Peter Lang.

Acts of Parliament

Anti-Terrorism Crime and Security Act 2001. (c. 24) [Online]. Available at: http://www.legislation.gov.uk/ukpga/2001/24/contents [accessed: January 2010].

Crime and Disorder Act 1998. (c.37) [Online]. Available at: http://www.legislation.gov.uk/ukpga/1998/37/contents [accessed: January 2010].

Criminal Justice Act 2003. (c. 44) [Online]. Available at: http://www.legislation.gov.uk/ukpga/2003/44/contents [accessed: January 2010].

Criminal Justice and Immigration Act 2008. (c. 4) [Online]. Available at: http://www.legislation.gov.uk/ukpga/2008/4/contents [accessed: January 2010].

Public Order Act 1986. (c.64) [Online]. Available at: http://www.legislation.gov.uk/ukpga/1986/64/contents [accessed: January 2010].

Racial and Religious Hatred Act 2006. (c.1) [Online]. Available at: http://www.legislation.gov.uk/ukpga/2006/1/contents [accessed: January 2010].

Official publications

CPS. 2007. *Policy for prosecuting cases of homophobic and transphobic crime.* [Online]. Available at: http://www.cps.gov.uk/publications/docs/htc_policy.pdf [accessed: January 2010].

CPS. 2009. *Leaflet introducing the CPS policy for prosecuting cases of homophobic and transphobic crime.* [Online]. Available at: http://www.cps.gov.uk/publications/prosecution/homophobic_and_transphobic_hate_crime_leaflet.pdf [accessed: January 2010].

Stonewall. 2010. *Blow the whistle on hate crime: A plain English guide on gay hate crime for lesbian, gay and bisexual people.* [Online]. Available at: http://www.stonewall.org.uk/documents/stonewall_gay_hate.pdf [accessed: January 2010].

Metaphor

Chapter 12

Shaping reality through metaphorical patterns in legislative texts on immigration: A corpus-assisted approach

Ersilia Incelli

People in power get to impose their metaphors.

(Lakoff and Johnson 1980: 157)

1. Introduction

Just as the law pervades many aspects of our lives, metaphors pervade virtually all branches of discourse, often reflecting the attitudes and values of the society that generates them. As claimed by cognitive linguists, our conceptual system is reflected in language patterns, which also involves the systematic use of metaphor (Lakoff and Johnson 1980: 5). The fact that human cognition is profoundly metaphorical in nature has led to an abundance of metaphor research in linguistics, largely restricted to the realms of political discourse (Chilton 1996, Charteris-Black 2006), business discourse (Bowker 2009), and media discourse (Koller 2004), with few studies investigating the status of metaphors in legal discourse.

However, of late, metaphors in law are beginning to be acknowledged in terms of their social implications (Johnson 2006: 845). Because metaphors can provide insights into the way the world is viewed, this makes them possible carriers of ideology (Charteris-Black 2004: 28); they are therefore central to a form of discourse analysis that takes a socio-cognitive approach to how they appear in different types of genre. This also places them within the sphere of Critical Discourse Analysis (CDA), which is concerned with the study of how values and ideologies are represented in texts and how social inequality is constituted in the discourse structure (Fairclough 2001). Such an approach is congruent to the view of Critical Legal Studies (CLS), which challenges accepted norms and standards in legal theory and aims to expose practices in jurisprudence that are contradictory and illogical. Such studies try to eradicate ambiguous laws or redefine them, for example by creating alternative metaphors to substitute 'entrenched metaphors' embedded in society.

In this light, this chapter will hopefully contribute to a growing body of research that explores metaphorical language in its pragmatic, functional and communicative role in the specialized genre of legal speech acts, namely regulative acts in UK statutory laws, and EU regulations and directives on various aspects of immigration. Hence, the approach to the analysis is socio-pragmatic as well as cognitive. For this reason, the chapter also pursues recent contributions that emphasize the compatibility of Hallidayan functional linguistics and cognitive linguistics, re-establishing the importance of syntax in metaphor research (Cabbalero 2002: 46), and confirming a trend in metaphor studies which looks more deeply at metaphor as a linguistic phenomenon and moves beyond Lakoff and Johnson's primary focus on metaphor as 'a matter of thought' (Lakoff and Johnson 1980: 6). Thus, the chapter concentrates specifically on how metaphorical language is realized at a lexico-semantic and grammatical level in legal texts and tries to show that an accurate analysis of metaphor (and metonyms) should relate to linguistic expressions.[1] Arguably, the metaphorical patterns produced reveal the underlying discourse of a government's ideology, policy and principles towards immigration issues.

1.1 Aims and research questions

This work can also be considered as experimental; first of all because metaphor analysis is not a standard methodology of legal analysis, and second because it integrates specific applied techniques of cognitive linguistic theory with a corpus-linguistic approach to legal genre analysis. The aims of the research are therefore two-fold: firstly, to uncover and understand how metaphors are used in the highly specialized genre of immigration law; and secondly, as the corpus was fairly large, to integrate qualitative and quantitative metaphor retrieval techniques, so as to systemically organize the metaphorical patterns and identify their multi-functionality and evolving cognitive scenarios. More specifically, the overall aims are motivated by the following research questions:

a. how are metaphors in the corpora realized at the lexico-semantic grammatical level, and how do they co-occur (e.g. in clusters)?
b. can computer-assisted analysis, combined with qualitative methods, help identify metaphor candidates in the discourse?
c. as a contrastive analysis, do metaphors play different/similar functions in the way they are used in each corpus, with similar/different dominant conceptual metaphors or conceptual schemas?

It is worth pointing out here that, as regulative acts are *fait accompli* documents and the final product of public debate, one might not expect to find metaphorically constructed language in this particular form of legal writing since, unlike the descriptive evaluative language of political or media discourse, statutory writing

1 It is not my purpose here to enter into a detailed account of the distinction between metaphor and metonym, but the presence of metonymic structures is acknowledged throughout the corpus, e.g. *court* for judges; *third country national* referring to non-EU nationals.

is not formulated to persuade, incite judgement, or appeal to the emotions, so that this type of legal discourse should appear (on the surface) neutral. The main purpose, then, was to see whether this type of investigation revealed conceptual metaphorical schemas which lie beneath the surface level of legal reasoning, with underlying overt or covert ideology in the discourse; and whether the legal terms familiar to the legal discourse community are in actual fact conventional metaphors with their etymological roots grounded in conceptual experiential theory (Lakoff and Johnson 1980: 56).

The chapter is organized as follows: after presenting the corpus and corpus-linguistic tools, I describe the theoretical preliminaries followed by the methodological procedure for identifying metaphors. I then discuss the metaphorical realizations found in the corpus and the conceptual schemas they create. Section 6 draws some conclusions as to the pedagogical implications and future research regarding metaphor analysis in legal discourse.

2. The corpora and corpus-linguistic tools for metaphor retrieval

I have carried out my investigation by exploring corpora of almost 400,000 words divided into two data-sets; one consisting of UK statutory laws, totalling 201,560 words, namely seven national Immigration Acts spanning the decade 1999-2009;[2] the second set consisting of 26 European Union Regulations and Directives on immigration over the period 2000-2009, totalling 188,747 words, e.g. *Directive 2003/9/EC, laying down minimum standards for the reception of asylum seekers.* I accessed and downloaded the corpora from the UK government website on UK legislation,[3] and from the EUR-Lex website for European legislation.[4]

Following a framework for corpus-assisted metaphor analysis developed by Hardie et al. (2005), I used *Wmatrix* (Rayson 2003) to retrieve representative lexical items from the semantic domains identified in the corpus and the metaphorical expressions associated with them. This web-based system, with an inbuilt automatic semantic annotation tool (USAS),[5] automatically allocates each word (or multi-word unit) in a text to: (a) a part of speech, and (b) a semantic field, e.g. Law and Order. Although Wmatrix was not originally created for metaphor identification, the semantic fields annotated by USAS can be seen as roughly corresponding to the domains of conceptual metaphor theory (Hardie et al. 2005).

---

2 *Immigration and Asylum Act 1999*; *Asylum and Immigration (Treatment of Claimants) Act 2004*; *Immigration, Asylum and Nationality 2006*; *UK Borders Act 2007*; *Criminal Justice and Immigration Act 2008*; *Border, Citizenship and Immigration Act 2009.*

3 http://www.legislation.gov.uk/all?title=immigration.

4 http://eur-lex.europa.eu/en/index.htm.

5 See www.comp.lancs.ac.uk/ucrel/usas/ for all the semantic tagsets and semantic field divisions.

The procedure using this corpus-linguistic tool is explained in more detail with illustrative empirical data in section 4.

3. Theoretical background

The theoretical approach has its underpinnings in conceptual metaphor theory (hereafter CMT), clearly expounded in Lakoff and Johnson's (1980) seminal work *Metaphors We Live By*. However, since then CMT has been developed and elaborated into several contemporary metaphor theories.[6] I refer here, for the purpose of this study, to the Blending Theory (BT) (Fauconnier and Turner 2002), which extends the cross-mappings of the two conceptual structures in CMT, source domain and target domain, to more input domains (a four-space model) and treats metaphor as a conceptual projection involving these four 'mental spaces' (ibid.: 40). These spaces include two 'input' spaces (associated with the source and target of CMT), 'plus a "generic" space, representing conceptual structure that is shared by both inputs, and the "blend" space, where material from the inputs combines and interacts' (Grady et al. 1999: 101).[7] Figure 12.1 opposite represents Fauconnier and Turner's basic diagram (2002: 46), also reproduced and adapted in Hart (2008: 8). Hart has applied BT in particular to studies on political discourse (c.f. Hart 2008).

Generally speaking, BT is a pragmatic offshoot of CMT and better suited for the complex variables involved in contextual discourse analysis, because the 'mental spaces' encapsulate not only the domain but all the surrounding social and cultural variables which add to the scenario. Fauconnier and Turner (2002: 46) describe the basic diagram as 'really just a snapshot of an imaginative and complicated process'. The model can be applied to the data in this corpus.

Nevertheless, returning to CMT, in order to understand the conceptual metaphors which emerge from the empirical data in the corpora, it is essential to understand the theory of experientialism or 'conceptual embodiment', which affirms that our conceptual structure is directly grounded in bodily and human experience and the physical world we inhabit (Lakoff and Johnson 1980: 56). We know the law refers to words which may have a meaning that can be traced back hundreds of years.[8] These terms probably have historical roots which can be explained by the experientialist theory. In fact, an overwhelming number refer to animal or human activity, or solid objects. For example, *burden of proof* originates

6 See the Open University's Metaphor Analysis Project for an account of contemporary metaphor theories: http://creet.open.ac.uk/projects/metaphor-analysis/index.cfm.

7 See Grady et al. 1999 for a detailed account of CMT and BT as associated conceptual theories at: http://cogweb.ucla.edu/CogSci/Grady_99.html [accessed 15/09/2011].

8 I used the following reference tools: the *online Etymology dictionary* http://www.etymonline.com/; the online *Macmillan dictionary* http://www.macmillandictionary.com/; *The Law Student's Dictionary* (Penner, 2008) for legal terminology.

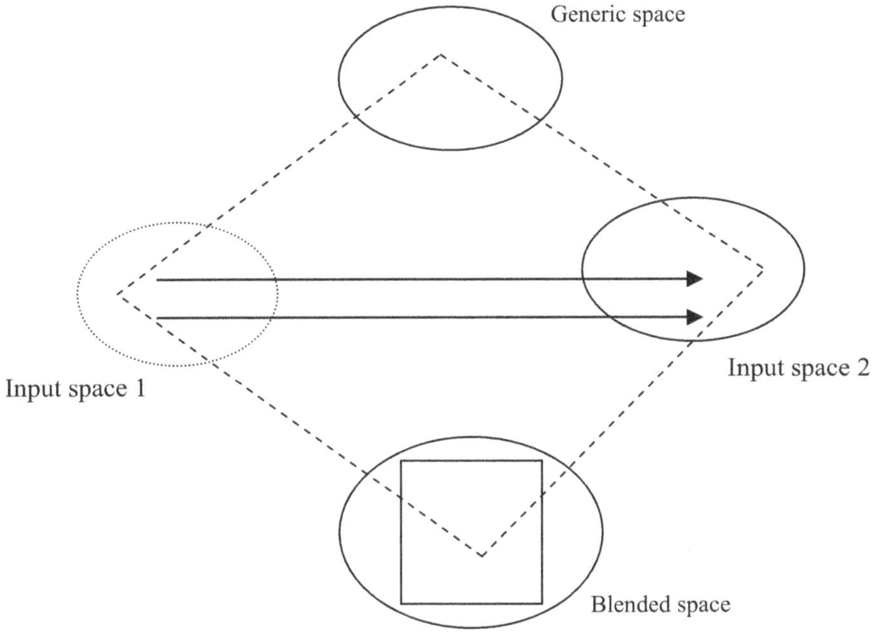

Figure 12.1 Basic diagram for conceptual blending theory
Source: Adapted from Fauconnier and Turner 2002: 46

from the fact that responsibility and problems are portrayed as a 'heavy weight'; *standing arrangements* from the legal (Latin) term *locus standi* meaning a 'place to stand' and be heard, in a fixed physical place; *miscarriage of justice*, perhaps from the injustice and unfairness of a pregnancy which was not carried through to the end; *closure* referring to a bounded agricultural area. These terms appear more frequently in the UK corpus.

3.1. CONTAINER Metaphor[9]

Lakoff and Johnson particularly stress the CONTAINER concept as intrinsic to our conceptual system. The basic orientation of this concept is spatial (and ontological), and sets out reference points for our understanding of relationships with the world.

9 Following conventional notation in cognitive linguistics, deep-level cognitive mappings representing concepts appear in capital letters, conventional metaphors or linguistic expressions are in italics.

> Each of us is a container, with a bounding surface and an in-out orientation. We project our own in-out orientation onto other physical objects that are bounded by surfaces.
>
> (Lakoff and Johnson 1980: 29)

As the container concept (Lakoff and Johnson 1980: 25-32) is a dominant metaphorical schema in the corpora, it is worth elaborating here on its metaphorical construction and the cognitive processes it entails in legal texts. A container schema (see Figure 12.2 below) has an inherent 'logic' or topology consisting of an interior and exterior, defined by boundary (Koller et al. 2008: 308); what is more, the concept of 'into' and 'out of' are blendings of the CONTAINER schema with the SOURCE-PATH-GOAL schema, with the interior as the goal and the exterior representing the source of movement (Johnson 2006: 853). As we are also dealing with 'land areas' in the corpora, this explains the metaphorical mappings of *migration flows.*

These sorts of schemas have entailments, for example the 'categorization' of people, denoting referential strategies for the 'insiders' and 'outsiders', leading to metaphors of INCLUSION and EXCLUSION (Judge 1995). According to Lakoff and Johnson, the conceptualization of CATEGORIES AS CONTAINERS is pervasive throughout our conceptual system, and 'imposes complex hierarchical systems' (Lakoff and Johnson 1999: 20). In the context of legal discourse, the container observation may appear trivial, but its effects on cognitive processes are not, especially in the context of legitimacy and legal reasoning, and the representation of group identity, granting or withdrawing privileges and rights. These include, for example, metonymic referential strategies such as *prescribed person*, *excluded persons*, etc.

According to some linguists and scholars, one constraint of CMT is the fact that Lakoff and Johnson's original work was 'highly theory-driven' and lacking

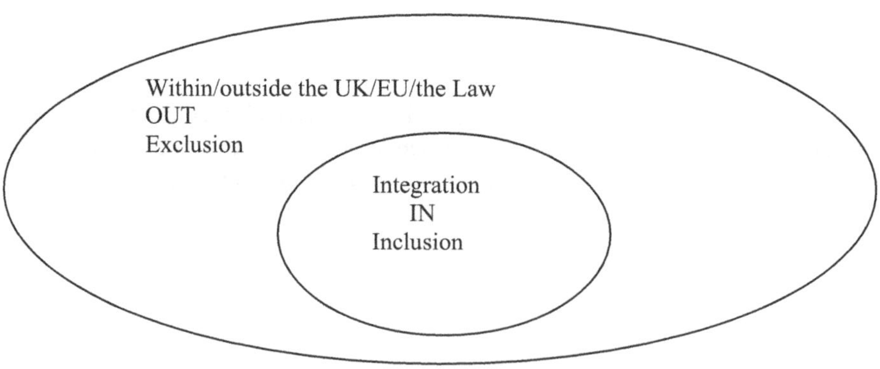

Figure 12.2 CONTAINER/SOCIETY AS BOUNDED SPACE metaphor
Source: Lakoff and Johnson 1980: 26, Koller and Davidson 2008: 312

real empirical data, especially regarding genre (Partington 1998: 107). Therefore, this work tries to draw from more recent 'textually driven' approaches such as Deignan (2005) and Charteris-Black (2006). However, much previous work has focused on pre-selected metaphorical search strings already identified in previous studies in the field, e.g. *flows*, *combat*, *curb*, *smuggle*, etc. (Santa Ana 1999, Gabrielatos and Baker 2008, Incelli 2011). Pre-selected search strings are useful for further metaphor analysis, but such a procedure involves concordancing instances of items already identified in other studies (Deignan 2005). The risk is that of under-representing the metaphors in a corpus by sticking to the familiar ones. In order to secure valid metaphorical representation, I integrated a metaphor identification procedure (Pragglejazz 2007), with a corpus-based framework for metaphor analysis (Hardie et al. 2007).

4. Methodological procedure for identifying metaphors in the texts

In the current state of the art, metaphors and metaphorical mappings cannot be directly associated with parts of word forms, so a fully automatic retrieval of metaphors is impossible, and the problem still remains of how to extract metaphorical expressions from the corpora. The method set out here presents a 'semi-automated' retrieval technique, in which corpus tools are integrated with more traditional manual methods for metaphor identification based on researcher and informed intuition (Hardie et al. 2005).

The procedure for extrapolating and identifying metaphor candidates is encapsulated in the diagram below (Table 12.1). There are two strands to the analysis; one focuses on identifying potential metaphor candidates, while the other involves awareness of the type of legal discourse structure. The continuous

Table 12.1 Methodological procedure for metaphor analysis

1. Identify candidate linguistic metaphors – cut-off point, manual analysis, pre-search items, corpus tools and Pragglejaz MIP (2007)	Discourse topic and genre Immigration laws –manual analysis /keyword analysis
2. Group metaphors according to: – word class: nouns, verbs, adjectives, adverbs, prepositions, phrasal verbs; – technical terminology related to legal discourse.	
3. Find metaphor clusters and semantic groups: – identify large conceptual metaphors and sub-level concepts.	
4. Draw conclusions	

interaction between the two facilitates insight and inference about the context and specialized genre.[10]

We can now proceed to describe various stages in the procedure.

4.1 Locating metaphor candidates

Once the research questions were established, it was necessary to decide a 'cut-off point' for metaphor identification. In fact, it is worth noting here that if an entirely etymological and historical approach to metaphor study were applied, the list would be never-ending as many words in everyday language are experientially based and grounded in bodily experience (Lakoff and Johnson 1980). To avoid the risk of over-interpretation of the data as metaphorical, this chapter does not attempt to extract 'each and every' metaphor, but focuses on identifying as many metaphorical linguistic expressions as possible associated with immigration in legislative texts. This meant dealing to a large extent with: a) standard conventional metaphors in legal English, e.g. *standing arrangements*, *pending judgement*; b) metaphorical expressions peculiar to the specialized fields of security/immigration/crime/terrorism, such as: *freezing orders*, *entry clearance*, *lock-out measures*; c) the identification of the metaphorical linguistic expressions which create the overall dominant conceptual metaphors, e.g. CONTAINER/CATEGORIES, EDIFICE, MIGRANTS AS A THREAT.

Many of the conventional metaphors were retrieved via corpus-assisted retrieval techniques, to which we will now turn.

4.2. Semantic domains

Wmatrix was able to calculate the most frequent semantic domains in a corpus compared to the inbuilt reference corpus of the BNC, sorted on a log-likelihood value, which allows a comparison between the two sub-corpora.[11] Once the semantic domains are identified, the possible candidate 'source' domains can be filtered, followed by the potential metaphoricity of the expressions in the lists under each possible source domain. For example, the source domain WAR (semantic tag G3) in the EU corpus, includes the linguistic expressions *fight*, *strike*, *dismantle*, *target*, *challenge*; and the 'target' domain *immigration* is represented by words such as *alien*, *clandestine immigrants*, *illegal immigration*, *illegal trafficking*, *stateless persons*, *third-country nationals*, *entry ban*, *secure borders*.

A total of 304 semantic domains were identified in the UK corpus, 100 of which were calculated as overused (above average frequency) semantic domains. As the data is a collection of legislative texts, it is not surprising that Law and Order (tag

10 C.f. The Open University Metaphor Analysis Project for a detailed account of possible frameworks for analyzing metaphors in discourse: http://creet.open.ac.uk/projects/metaphor-analysis/index.cfm.

11 See Rayson (2003) for a detailed account of log-likelihood levels.

G2.1) is the top semantic domain in the UK corpus, and fourth in the EU corpus. The top semantic domain in the EU corpus is Government (G1.1), reflecting the EU's priority for governance of the member states. Of relevance to my research were the domains of Inclusion (20th), Exclusion (30th), and Constraint (31st) in the UK corpus. They also appeared in the top 100 overused semantic domains in the EU corpus (out of a total 315 semantic domains), but at lower positions, e.g. Inclusion – 45th, Exclusion – 90th, Constraint – 81st. In addition, other domains, although lower in the frequency list, were important for possible metaphorical candidates, such as tag H – Architecture, buildings, houses and the home; tag O – Substances, materials, objects and equipment; tag B – The body and the individual.

The next stage was to click on the list for each (candidate) source/semantic domain and (manually) investigate the words in that semantic field. The list included both metaphorically used words and non-metaphorically used words. The concordance lines allowed all the instances for each word to be viewed in context, to begin distinguishing the metaphorical candidates (Table 12.2).

Table 12.2 Sample words from semantic field wordlists

Semantic tag	Total frequency	
Freezing (UK) 04.6-	10	Concordance
Domestic (EU) H4	8	Concordance
build/s (EU) H1	15	Concordance
prescribe(UK) B3	166	Concordance

As we can see in Table 12.2, *freezing* belongs to the semantic domain *Temperature* (tag 04.6-). By checking the concordance lines (Table 12.3 below), its metaphorical use emerges as an adjective or present participle in the linguistic expression *freezing orders*.

Table 12.3 Sample concordance lines for *freezing, build, domestic*

1. reason why person is specified in freezing order, make the existing provisions … .
2. Member States set as their objective 'to build up WEU in stages as the defence …'.
3. text of the main provisions of domestic law which they adopt in the field … .

Table 12.3 shows sample concordance lines of how the lexical item appears in its context. The concordance lines can be further expanded to check the whole

text in more detail. The examples *domestic*, *build* and *prescribe* are all used metaphorically in the texts.

This method has the advantage that it is possible to find a wider variety of expressions than simply concordancing a limited set of pre-selected expressions. Nevertheless, this does not solve the problem of deciding whether a linguistic expression is metaphorical or not. This calls for an integrated manual identification procedure, to which I refer below.

4.3 Identifying 'hazy' metaphors

This part of the research is informed by Pragglejaz (2007), a metaphor research group who developed a metaphor identification procedure (MIP) which is particularly useful for identifying the 'hazy' metaphors in discourse, i.e. those that are difficult to decide on. Some metaphors are easy to identify, for example the usual metaphors associated with immigration: *inflow*, *smuggle*, *trafficking*, etc. On the whole, legal terminology is fairly easily distinguishable as metaphor, even though many expressions no longer retain their roots in contemporary use, e.g. *mount a legal challenge*. On the other hand, there are many conventional metaphors that are not so obvious or clear-cut, and therefore require particular decision-making on the part of the analyst.[12] The Pragglejaz group suggests deciding whether a word is metaphorically used or not by 'contrasting its contextual meaning with its basic meaning' (Pragglejaz 2007: 2). For illustrative purposes, we can take the examples in the UK corpus of *fitness*, *unfitness*, *fit*, *unfit*. If we look at the concordance lines below (Table 12.4) and examine the full text, the contextual meaning of *fit/unfit* contrasts with the basic meaning of the adjective *fit*, which refers to physical strength and health, i.e. 'physical embodiment' (Lakoff and Johnson 1999: 5).

Table 12.4 Concordance lines for *fit/fitness* – UK text

1. If in the special circumstances of any particular case the Secretary of State thinks ***fit***, the Secretary of State may for the purposes of paragraph 3 do all or any of the following … .
2. The Criminal Appeal Act 1968 (c. 19) has effect subject to the following amendments. Time limit on grant of certificates of ***fitness*** for appeal.

In the legal context, *fit/unfit* indicates here suitability or unsuitability for *asylum application/appeal/standing trial*, etc. We understand abstract *suitability* in terms of *health* and *strength*, so *fit/fitness* in the context of the corpus is used metaphorically (Pragglejaz 2007: 5).

12 As good practice, Pragglejaz suggests consulting more than one researcher on ambiguous metaphors.

Generally speaking, it is easier to establish the basic meaning for content words than for phrasal verbs or grammatical words such as prepositions and adverbs, especially when they are not attached to a phrasal verb. The same procedure can be carried out for these difficult candidates which, on closer inspection, reveal spatial metaphorical functions and patterns, e.g. *carry forward*, *step back*, *step into.*

Such patterns contribute to the creation of larger conceptual metaphors, for example the EU AS EDIFICE/PATH/PURPOSE/DIRECTION in Table 12.5.

Table 12.5 Concordance lines for *forward/back* – EU text

1. The WEU will contribute to the progressive framing of a common defence policy and carry **forward** its concrete implementation … .
2. The European Council adopted a declaration on terrorism stressing the need to expedite examination of measures in this area and take work **forward** on the proposed Council Directive on the obligation of carriers.
3. Unanimity shall be required for measures under this paragraph which constitute a step **back** in Community law as regards the liberalization of capital to or from third countries.

Another example can be illustrated with the patterns around *outside*, *within*, *falling within/into*. In the concordance lines below in Table 12.6, we can see society (the EU/UK), and the law conceptualized with the same topology as a CONTAINER (*within* or *outside* the *law/framework/directive*) and people or migrants or third-country nationals are conceptualized as CATEGORIES (line 3).

Table 12.6 CONTAINER METAPHOR: *outside*, *within*, *falling within/into the law/categories of people* – EU text

1. Member States may exempt from the visa requirement recognized refugees, all stateless persons, both those under the Convention relating to the Stateless Persons of 28 September 1954 and those **outside of the scope of** that Convention.
2. With respect to the treatment of persons **falling within the scope of** this Directive, Member States are bound by obligations under instruments of international law.
3. Third-country nationals who **fall into** the categories of unremunerated trainees and volunteers who are considered, … as workers under national legislation are not covered by this Directive.

We will now continue to discuss the grouping of metaphorical expressions which create dominant metaphorical concepts.

Table 12.7 Findings grouped according to word class and terminology: EU vs. UK total frequencies

NOUNS	EU	UK	VERBS	EU	UK	ADJECTIVES	EU	UK	LEGAL TERMINOLOGY	EU	UK
annex	80	2	bind	21	*0*	commanding	0	3	burden of proof	3	7
body	40	67	build	17	0	displaced	40	0	closure notice	0	26
breach	15	57	carry forward	5	0	domestic	5	4	closure order	0	65
burden	25	8	combat	37	0	flanking	0	20	binding in its entirety	6	0
campaign	2	0	construe	2	13	flanking	5	0	bring into force	15	1
challenge	14	0	curb	3	0	founded	11	0	come into force	2	82
clearance	1	57	deploy	10	0	freezing	0	5	enter into force	30	0
closure	0	98	enjoy	79	0	frustrated	0	5	entry clearance	0	57
crisis	9	0	entertain	0	6	grooming	0	6	freezing orders	0	5
deployment	52	0	fall	21	36	interlocking	2	2	judicial remedy	6	0
in/flow	11	0	fall within	14	4	neighbouring	2	0	lock-out measures	2	0
framework	53	7	fight	15	0	pending	32	98	miscarriage of justice	0	10
holder	2	11	mount	5	0	open	9	14	mount a legal challenge	5	0
host	199	0	prescribe	11	160	standing	0	12	pending deportation	0	15
house	0	120	recover	2	5	*tighter*	2	0	prescribed by law	6	8
influx	25	1	reflect	4	11				reflection period	7	0
performance	19	*32*	round up	0	1				standing arrangements	0	6
miscarriage	0	10	strike	6	0				Home Office	0	3
remedy	8	*15*	tackle	3	0				open court	0	3
smuggling	3	3	take forward	4	0				sitting adjudicators	0	1
steps	13	*22*	step back	2	0						
strategy	5	*0*									
target	6	*0*									
trafficking	15	*29*									

5. Findings: Systematic grouping of metaphorical expressions and concepts

5.1 Word class

After identifying the linguistic metaphors, to facilitate a systematic ordering of the multi-functionality of the metaphorical expressions, I grouped them according to word class and legal terminology lexical units. In this way, I was able to count the number of metaphorical expressions and emerging metaphor scenarios, and make a contrastive analysis between the two sub-corpora (Table 12.7).

As we can see, the EU tends to have more of the metaphors usually associated with immigration that we see in media and political discourse, e.g. *combat*, *target*, *curb*, *flows*. The UK has a lot of formulaic standard legal English terminology referring to immigration legislation, e.g. *closure notice*, *entry clearance*, *freezing orders*, *frustrated search*, *judicial remedy*, *pending deportation.* However, the list is representative and not an exhaustive account.

5.2 Metaphor clusters and metaphor groups

As long lists of metaphors do not reveal much in themselves, the data needed to be systematically organized with respect to the theoretical and empirical motivations. Thus, the next stage involved grouping the metaphors into semantically connected sets or themes to produce systematic metaphors (Table 12.8).

Table 12.8 Lexical items grouped according to semantic areas

war	e.g. combat, deploy, fight, mount a challenge, strike, strategy, target
architecture/buildings	e.g. annex, build/up/upon, framework, extension, found on, foundations, frame, lay down, ground/s
bounded areas	e.g. clearance stamp, closure, entry ban, fall within, out of, outside
liquid/water	e.g. circulate, curb, flow, inflow, influx, pool
aim/direction/path/purpose	e.g. directive, steps, step back, carry forward, take forward, to this end, with a view to, within the scope of

A close reading of the concordance lines or fuller text around the selected lexical items revealed how the metaphors of the same semantic field occurred in clusters to produce the overall image schema in the discourse (Cameron and Stelma 2004). The sample excerpt below (Figure 12.3) shows how metaphors collocate and

(1.).., the European Council expressed its determination **to tackle** illegal immigration at source, for example **by targeting** those who engage in **trafficking of human beings** and the economic exploitation of migrants ... to concentrate their efforts on detecting and **dismantling** criminal networks while protecting the rights of victims ... as supplemented by Council Directive 2001/51/EC(2), the two types of obligation serving the same objective of **curbing migratory flows and combating illegal immigration.**

Figure 12.3 Metaphor clusters in *Council Directive 2004/82/EC of 29 April 2004 on the obligation of carriers to communicate passenger data*

work in close partnership, creating metaphorical mappings which construct the conceptual schemas.[13]

The above clusters, belonging to different semantic domains – e.g. curbing/flows/WATER, targeting/combat/WAR – contribute to producing the overall conceptual metaphor IMMIGRATION AS ENEMY.

5.3 Conceptual metaphors emerging from key findings: A contrastive analysis

In this way, the recognition and classification of metaphor clusters leads to the identification of the prominent conceptual metaphors and image scenarios, which may be specific to one corpus rather than the other. In view of the above theoretical frameworks, the metaphors found in the two corpora draw on a variety of experiential domains among which the most prominent are those of CONTAINER, PATH, MOTION, OBJECT. These in turn gives rise to further sub-concepts which can be illustrated in the following empirical examples from the data. Figure 12.4 below shows clusters of BUILDING metaphorical lexical units such as *lay down a general framework*, *on the grounds of*, which contribute to the conceptual schema EU AS EDIFICE.

2. The purpose of this Directive is to lay down a general framework for combating discrimination on the grounds of religion …. with a view to putting into effect in the Member States the principle of equal treatment.

Figure 12.4 Metaphor clusters of BUILDING

The excerpt above also provides an example of an additional sub-conceptual schema reflected in the pattern *with a view to putting into effect* which contributes to the image schema the EU AS DIRECTION. Clusters of AIM/DIRECTION

13 The study also revealed minor conceptual metaphors particular to this type of legal genre, e.g. the LAW AS DOCTOR, e.g. *judicial remedy*, *prescribed*, *treatment*, *miscarriage of justice*. The LAW AS EDUCATOR, e.g. *detention centre*, *examination*, *expulsion*, *expel*, *reflection period*.

metaphors (see Table 12.8) reveal the EU's concern with its Director/Leadership role in governing member states and keeping them in line with international requirements. These types of lexical units are far less frequent in the UK corpus, e.g. *framework* = 53 EU vs. 7 UK; *within the framework of* = 22 EU vs. 0 UK; *to this end* = 23 EU vs. 0 UK; *with a view to* = 58 EU vs. 5 UK; *carry forward* = 5 EU vs. 0 UK.

On the other hand, the CONTAINER metaphor is pervasive in both the EU and UK corpus, but to different degrees and in different ways. Drawing on the tenets of BT, the concordance lines in Table 12.9 show how two mental spaces constructed by *flow/influx* and *migration/displaced persons* enter a 'conceptual integration network' (Fauconnier and Turner 2002, Hart 2007: 18).

Table 12.9 Lexico-grammatical metaphorical patterns with *flows/inflow/influx – illegal/immigration/displaced persons* – EU text

1. Council Directive 2001/51/EC(2), the two types of obligation serving the same objective of curbing migratory **flows** and combating illegal immigration.
2. In the event of one or more Member States being confronted with an emergency situation characterised by a sudden **inflow** of nationals of third countries ... the Council may, adopt provisional measures ... .
3. a common European policy on asylum and migration should aim both at fair treatment of third country nationals and better management of migration **flows**.
4. 'temporary protection' means a procedure of exceptional character to provide, in the event of a mass **influx** or imminent mass **influx** of displaced persons from third countries
5. The Asylum system will be unable to process this **influx** without adverse effects for its efficient operation ... .
6. When a Member State is faced with a mass **influx** of third-country nationals attempting to enter its territory illegally ... .
7. When the number of those who are eligible for temporary protection following a sudden and massive **influx** exceeds the reception capacity ... , the Council shall, as a matter of urgency, ... take appropriate action.

The metaphorical mapping is overtly WATER IS UNCONTROLLABLE AND DANGEROUS. This is reflected in the lexical units: *a sudden and massive influx, adverse effects, curbing migratory flows, faced with, emergency situation.* What is particularly interesting is its conjunction with another metaphorical construction in line 7 – '*a sudden and massive influx exceeds the reception capacity*' – conceptualizing the EU as a RECIPIENT with a lid on its *capacity.* The interaction of the metaphors produces a blending network illustrated below in Figure 12.5, in which the EU is conceptualized as a CONTAINER/RECIPIENT and the migration of people as FLOWING WATER INTO A RECIPIENT WITH LIMITED CAPACITY.

The inference (in the blended space in Figure 12.5) is 'overflow'. The entailments define reality and legitimize action, and consequently restrictive immigration

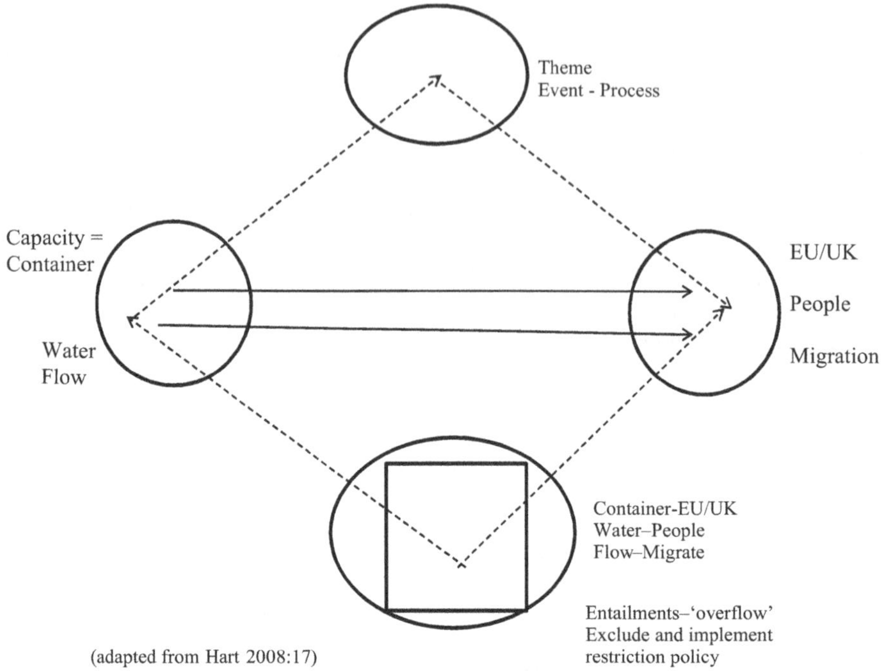

Figure 12.5 Conceptual blending for interaction of *influx/flow–illegal immigrants – exceeds capacity*

policy measures to 'stop the flow'. We see this reflected in the lexis in the above concordance lines in Table 12.9, *better management of, prevent, the need to ensure greater effectiveness, combating illegal immigration.* It is worth noting that these metaphorical expressions are frequent in the EU corpus, with very few instances of the same items in the UK corpus. In fact, each corpus creates different sub-level concepts from the mega-concepts; the EU emphasizes IMMIGRATION AS WAR/THREAT/NATURAL DISASTER, with lexis such as *combat, curb, flows* (there are no instances of these items in the UK corpus). On the other hand, the UK corpus emphasizes depersonalization concepts such as MIGRANT AS OBJECT, e.g. *automatic deportation and removal*, where SECURITY metaphors may also be inferred (Chilton 1996), construed through specialized terminology such as *clearance stamp, closure notice, entry clearance, leave stamp, liable to deportation, leave to enter or remain* (absent in the EU corpus). Nevertheless, in both corpora 'land area' is perceived as BOUNDED SPACE AS PROPERTY (Lakoff and Johnson 1980: 29), like private property, people and houses, which need to be protected from outside threats. Certain terms and metaphors evoke cultural and past historical experience of 'invasion'. The entailments are restriction policies and stronger security measures, leading to EXCLUSION metaphors, i.e. who can enter and who cannot, who is within the law and who is outside it. See for example the concordance lines for *exclude* in relation to *security* and *territory* in Table 12.10.

Table 12.10 Concordance lines for *exclude/excluded*

EU Text
1. the right of Union citizens and their family members who have been **excluded** from the territory of a Member State to submit a fresh application.
2. Member States may **exclude** the individual concerned from their territory pending the redress procedure, but they may not prevent the individual from submitting his/her defence in person.
3. Article 32 Duration of exclusion orders 1. Persons **excluded** on grounds of public policy or public security may submit an application for lifting of the exclusion order.
4. The Member States may **exclude** a person from temporary protection if: (a) there are serious reasons for considering that: (i) he or she has committed a crime against peace,
UK Text
1. A person's exemption from the provisions of this Act as a result of section 8(1), ceases on his becoming an **excluded** person.
2. An **excluded** person must be refused—Kingdom under **excluded** from international (a) leave to enter the United Kingdom;
3. The Secretary of State may make an order ... only if the Secretary of State thinks that it would be conducive to the public good for the person to be **excluded** or removed from the United Kingdom.

In a similar way, the sub-concept of CATEGORIES ARE CONTAINERS entails INCLUSION and EXCLUSION. Table 12.11 below provides an example of the referential legal terminology used in both corpora to distinguish *category* or *class of person*, in order to grant or withdraw eligibility.

Table 12.11 CATEGORIES ARE CONTAINERS: *first/second/third/fourth/fifth/different/prescribed class/relevant category*

UK Text
1. **First class** of ineligible person: refugee status abroad 4 (1) Paragraph 1 applies to a person if he—(a) has refugee status abroad,
2. **Second class** of ineligible person: citizen of other EEA State, Paragraph 1 applies to a person if he—(a) has the nationality of an EEA State,
3. **Third class** of ineligible person: failed asylum-seeker 6 (1) Paragraph 1 applies to a person if—(a) he was (but is no longer) an asylum-seeker, and (b) he fails to cooperate with removal directions.
4. **Fourth class** of ineligible person: person unlawfully in United Kingdom 7 Paragraph 1 applies to a person if—(a) he is in the United Kingdom in breach of the immigration laws within the meaning of section 11, and (b) he is not an asylum-seeker.

Table 12.11 contd.

5."**Fifth class** of ineligible person: failed asylum-seeker with Family 7A (1) Paragraph 1 applies to a person if—(a) he—(i) is treated as an asylum-seeker for the purposes of Part VI of the Immigration and Asylum Act 1999,
6. For the purposes of this Part a person is a 'dependant' of an asylum-seeker if (and only if) that person— (a) is in the United Kingdom, and (b) is within a **prescribed class**.
7. The Secretary of State may by order amend this Schedule so as—a) to provide for paragraph 1 to apply or not to apply to a **class** of person;
EU Text
1. Member States may withdraw or refuse to renew a residence Permit ... wherever it appears that the holder did not meet or no longer meets the conditions for entry and residence laid down in Article 6 and in whichever of Articles 7 to 11 applies to the **relevant category**.

What is more, if we take the conceptual scale *first class* (line 1) as TOP and *fourth/ fifth class* as BOTTOM, following Lakoff and Johnson's UP/DOWN spatial orientation concept, the sub-concept of HIGHER IS STATUS (1980: 14-16) is evoked, denoting referential strategies leading to metonyms of categorization, which carry negative semantic prosody because of the grouping together of negative collocates, making the legal text highly evaluative, e.g. *fourth class of ineligible persons, ... unlawfully in United Kingdom ...* .

As a contrastive analysis, certain conceptual domains are specific to one corpus rather than the other. First of all, it would appear that EU texts contain more of the metaphors commonly associated with immigration discourse in the media than UK texts. The rationale for this is not clear; however, a few observations can be made. It is a known fact that only a small proportion of EU legal drafters are native English speakers (even though most texts are first drafted in English). Considering the complex multilingual and multicultural environment involved in the process of drafting EU legislation, to avoid the risk of a term used in one language leading to a misunderstanding in another (Robinson 2005), the EU *Joint Practical Guidelines* (2003) advises drafters to adopt a clarity principle, to use generic, indeterminate and non-legal terms where possible.[14] This may explain how certain terms and expressions from the media or politics may find their way into EU legal texts, which implies that the terms and concepts are accepted and their meanings are taken for granted.

In the UK, the referential terms *alien* and *immigrant* have disappeared from immigration laws (Incelli 2011). It is difficult to say whether this is a politically inspired avoidance, but such terminology has been widely investigated in discourse studies on how governments, politicians and the media choose terms to suit their wider economic or political purposes (Lakeoff and Ferguson 2006;

14 See points 4, 5, 6 in the *Joint Practical Guidelines* on language quality in drafting EU legislation.

van Dijk 1996). EU drafters have to be aware of this and hence adopt neutral terms in order to avoid legal misinterpretations or accusations of impropriety.

Secondly, the EU is concerned with its Director/Leadership role, overseeing member states with regard to international requirements on immigration. This explains the EU rhetoric on 'building frameworks' and 'laying foundations', even though the EU still has no substantial 'common' European immigration policy. Likewise, the EU mentions the rights of asylum seekers but continues to lay down 'minimum standards' for protection, according to the interests of individual countries. In other words, the popular metaphorical picture of 'Fortress Europe' tends to permeate its legislation. The UK is equally concerned with controlling and keeping people out with a strong emphasis on securing borders. No judgement is being made here, and restriction policies are by all means necessary in certain periods of history, but it is important to be aware of the conceptual metaphors behind the policy. This brings us to the implications discussed in the conclusions.

6. Conclusions: Pedagogical implications and the role of corpus linguistics

First and foremost, the findings were contrary to expectations in that, as stated in the introduction, legal regulative acts tend to use notoriously formulaic language and fixed legal terminology which appears neutral on the surface and not conducive to the metaphorically constructed language frequently found in everyday language, and particularly found in the descriptive evaluative language of genres such as political or media discourse. On the other hand, this study revealed that beneath the surface level of legal reasoning, there are (perhaps unconscious) conceptual metaphorical schemas, and the legal terminology familiar to the legal discourse community appears to have strong etymological roots grounded in experiential theory.

It is apparent from the analysis that both conceptual and lexico-grammatical metaphorical patterns (in particular those related to CONTAINMENT) contribute to the formation of legitimacy, through the lexical realizations of word forms, involving nominalizations, referential strategies and phrasal verbs, which imply spatial metaphorical schemas. This type of exploration is useful for uncovering covert social mappings in discourse, and useful as a tool for Critical Legal Studies (CLS) which work at redefining 'self-perpetuating' metaphors in law and society.

Indeed, heightened awareness of the pervasiveness of metaphors can lead to a whole new methodology in legal education, in that there is a need to look at the metaphorical dimensions of a legal term, not just its 'casebook' definition, and to consider the semantic connotations of lexis as well as the denotative meaning. Corpus studies in this sense are particularly useful for highlighting the phraseological patterns of metaphors and investigating the interaction between metaphor and lexical semantics.

As far as corpus metaphor retrieval techniques are concerned, the basic method in this study has demonstrated the usefulness of applying a semantic field annotation system to extracting metaphor from corpora (within the tenets of CMT). The method has shown how corpus analysis takes the small lexical details to develop the big picture, and makes the leap from linguistic expressions to conceptual metaphors and dominant systematic metaphors. Although this work is by no means an exhaustive account of all the metaphors in the corpus, it is satisfactory in terms of extracting metaphors from a large corpus, which would have been otherwise time-consuming in the traditional way. Quantitatively speaking, the corpus-linguistic tools retrieved more metaphors than expected, together with unexpected metaphorical scenarios.

Finally, as we have seen, metaphors have substantial real world consequences. As pointed out by many scholars in the field, they tend not to tell the whole story, leaving truth as 'relative to our conceptual system' (Lakoff and Johnson 1980: 159-160). In other words, conceptual metaphors are like the tip of the iceberg. Although regulatory texts are only meant to create rules and prescribe what should or should not be done, exploring the 'unseen' metaphors can uncover what lies behind particular language choices and help understand their implications, such as the plight of migrants which is not mentioned. Increased semantic-pragmatic awareness through metaphorical investigation and exploration may help in bringing to the fore the political/ideological component behind seemingly neutral prescriptive texts.

References

Bowker, J. 2009. 'Building out the business': the dynamics of metaphor in the construction of corporate identity in business audio-conferencing. *TEXTUS*, 22 (1), 23-42.

Caballero Rodriguez, M. 2002. The lexicogrammar of metaphor in the discourse of Architects. *Estudios Ingleses de la Universidad Complutense*, 10, 43-66.

Cameron, L. and Stelma, J. 2004. Metaphor clusters in discourse. *Journal of Applied Linguistics*, 1, 7-36.

Charteris-Black, J. 2004. *Corpus Approaches to Critical Metaphor Analysis*. Basingstoke and New York: Palgrave MacMillan.

Charteris-Black, J. 2006. Britain as a container: immigration metaphors in the 2005 election campaign. *Discourse and Society*, 17 (5), 563-581.

Chilton, P. 1996. *Security Metaphors: From Containment to Common House*. New York: Peter Lang.

Deignan, A. 2005. *Metaphor and Corpus Linguistics*. Amsterdam and Philadelphia: John Benjamins.

EUR-Lex European legislation. [Online], Available at: http://eur-lex.europa.eu/en/index.htm [accessed: 2 February 2010].

Fauconnier, G. and Turner, M. 2002. *The Way We Think: Conceptual Blending and the Mind's Hidden Complexities*. New York: Oxford Basic Books.

Fairclough, N. 2001. *Language and Power*. 2nd Edition. London: Longman.

Gabrielatos, C. and Baker, P. 2008. Fleeing, sneaking, flooding: a corpus analysis of discursive constructions of refugees and asylum seekers in the UK Press 1996-2005. *Journal of English Linguistics*, 36 (1), 5-38.

Grady, J.E., Oakley, T. and Coulson, S. 1999. Blending and metaphor, in *Metaphor in cognitive linguistics*, edited by G. Steen and R. Gibbs. Amsterdam and Philadelphia: John Benjamins.

Hardie, A., Koller, V., Rayson, P. and Semino, E. 2007. Exploiting a semantic annotation tool for metaphor analysis, in *Proceedings of the Corpus Linguistics 2007 Conference* edited by M. Davies, P. Rayson, S. Hunston and P. Danielsson. [Online]. Available at: http://www.birmingham.ac.uk/documents/college-artslaw/corpus/conference-archives/2007/49Paper.pdf. [accessed: 5 April 2010].

Hart, C. 2008. Critical discourse analysis and metaphor: toward a theoretical framework. *Critical Discourse Studies*, 5(2), 91-106.

Incelli, E. 2011. A corpus-driven approach to uncovering stance in legislative texts on immigration: an exploratory study, in *Conference Proceedings CLAVIER 2009*, edited by M. Bondi, S. Cacchiani, G. Palumbo, *R.I.L.A.-Rassegna Italiana di Linguistica Applicata* 1-2, Gennaio-Agosto, 117-136.

Johnson, M. 2006. Mind metaphor and law, in *Using Metaphor in Legal Analysis and Communication. A Symposium of the Mercer Law Review*. *Mercer Law Review*, 58, 845-868.

Joint Practical Guide of the European Parliament, the Council and the Commission 2003. [Online]. Available at: http://eur-lex.europa.eu/en/techleg/pdf/en.pdf [accessed: 4 May 2010].

Judge, A. 1995. Social exclusion. A metaphoric trap? [Online]. Available at: http://www.laetusinpraesens.org/docs/socexc.php [accessed: 2 June 2010].

Koller, V. 2004. *Metaphor and Gender in Business Media Discourse: A Critical Cognitive Study*. Hampshire, England: Palgrave Macmillan.

Koller, V. and Davidson, P. 2008. Social exclusion as conceptual and grammatical metaphor: a cross-genre study of British policy-making. *Discourse & Society*, 19(3), 307-331.

Lakoff, G. and Ferguson, S. 2006. *The Framing of Immigration*, The Rockridge Institute. [Online]. Available at: http://www.rockridgeinstitute.org/research/rockridge/immigration [accessed 10 November 2011].

Lakoff, G. and Johnson, M. 1980. *Metaphors We Live By*. Chicago: University of Chicago Press.

Lakoff, G. and Johnson, M. 1999. *Philosophy in the Flesh: The Embodied Mind and its Challenge to Western Thought*. New York: Basic Books.

Open University, *Metaphor Analysis Project*. [Online]. Available at: http://creet.open.ac.uk/projects/metaphor- analysis/index.cfm [accessed: 5 May 2010].

Partington, A. 1998. *Patterns and Meanings: Using Corpora for English Language Research and Teaching*. Amsterdam and Philadelphia: John Benjamins.

Pragglejaz Group. 2007. MIP: a method for identifying metaphorically used words in Discourse. *Metaphor and Symbol*, 22, 1-39.

Rayson, P. 2003. Matrix: A statistical method and software tool for linguistic analysis through corpus comparison. *Ph.D. Thesis*, Lancaster University. [Online]. Available at: http://ucrel.lancs.ac.uk/wmatrix/ [accessed: 4 March 2010].

Robinson, W. 2005. How the European Commission drafts legislation in 20 languages. *Clarity,* 53, 4-10.

Santa Ana, O. 1999. 'Like an animal I was treated': anti-immigrant metaphor in US public discourse. *Discourse & Society*, 10, 191-224.

UK government legislation. [Online]. Available at: http://www.legislation.gov.uk/all?title=immigration [accessed: 2 September 2011].

van Dijk, T. 1996. 'Illegal aliens'. *Discourse & Society*, 7, 291-292.

PART III
Applications

Chapter 13

Legal linguistics as a line of study and an academic discipline

Tarja Salmi-Tolonen

1. Introduction

In the present-day accelerated globalization process where our lives are regulated by national legislators, international and supranational legislative bodies with their coercive control devices and also by a number of other institutions and organizations that draw up regulations, research in law and language and legal linguistics curricula based on the findings are of vital importance in legal education and training. Legal linguistics is a fairly new concept to many, even if some of us have been conducting research in order to compile a body of knowledge for the basis of education and made efforts to have it recognized and established for decades. Therefore the term legal linguistics, now that it has become more commonly used, is given many meanings and interpretations – some broader, some narrower. Apparently it is the novelty of the term itself that has attracted many writers to adopt this designation and therefore the variety of meanings given to it is perplexing. The large variety of meanings also gives rise to the impression that legal linguistics is sometimes treated as the trash bin containing all spill-over that does not fit within the boundaries of legal dogmatics and legal positivism and only on the surface related to language.

In this chapter, I will present a view that legal linguistics goes far beyond mere comparative law and cultural studies, teaching foreign languages to law students or studying multilingual legal terminology, comparing legal terms, or translating legal texts. The purpose of this chapter is to present my agenda of legal linguistics as part of legal science. It is based on academic research I have conducted, theses supervised and experiences collected over the years as a student of legal language, planning and setting up a curriculum of legal linguistics and as holder of a chair in legal linguistics.[1]

Until recently, legal science has examined language either through jurisprudence, legal theories, or legal philosophy or studied them with the help of the language philosophical framework. Even if it is acknowledged that law in modern societies

1 Thoughts summarized in this chapter are discussed more extensively in Salmi-Tolonen (2008).

could not exist without language, no legal methodology introduces any kind of linguistic approach or linguistic method for studying or interpreting law.

The role of language has basically been seen as instrumental among legal practitioners and scientists, a necessary tool for the legislator and legal professionals for carrying out their duties. Linguistics, again, does not accept such a reductionist view of language merely as a tool or instrument; language is inherently connected with human cognitive processes and law is constituted in language – not just with or through language. Since law is a consequence of continued human cooperation and interaction, law must be a communicative system (Searle 1995: 27). Today, these issues are combined in questions of linguistic knowledge and legal knowledge and how they are intertwined in legal discourse.

Whoever studies law, be it for applying, translating or in search of information, is first of all confronted with language. It should therefore be acknowledged that because of the way in which language and law are intertwined, the study of legal language and its methods should be more evident in the legal science and consequently in legal education and training. If this were the case, it would constitute legal linguistics.

2. Defining legal linguistics

Law and linguistics have thus far been understood as separate fields of expertise.[2] Therefore the connection between law and language has been treated at a rather superficial level.[3] As Goodrich (1987: ix) remarks, the conjunction 'and' has marked a constant separation of distinctive areas of expertise. Consequently an important opportunity has been missed and a considerable body of knowledge ignored.

The field therefore deserves the designation *legal linguistics*, instead of mere language and law, as a field of study which integrates linguistic and legal theories and approaches. The field of study examines language in all domains concerning law. In this view, legal linguistics is an independent, developing interdisciplinary field of study within legal science.[4] The term is often mistakenly understood to mean narrowly either teaching law students foreign legal languages, translating juridical texts, revising statutory texts or terminology work or even forensic

2 In Nordic legal scholarship, it is customary to distinguish internal and external contributions to law. This distinction implies that the contributions of formally trained legal professionals are considered internal and having a direct impact on law whereas the contributions of researchers from other disciplines, such as social sciences and linguistics, can only have an indirect impact by being quoted and referred to by legal scholars (cf. Tuori 1997: 318).

3 Already noted by Hartmann in the 1970s (1970: 47).

4 See also Busse's characterization of *Rechtslinguistik* (1992: 14).

linguistics or making word lists.[5] Although the term 'legal linguistics' has been coined in a way that it appears to be a translation loan, a calque, from French-speaking Canada – *linguistique juridique* – the conceptual and cognitive content it represents is different.[6]

Below, I shall give an overview of legal linguistics as I see it as an academic subject and a field of study especially in legal science and legal education. Compared with the notion of law and language, legal linguistics embodies the synergy and synthesis which I have called for. In the English-speaking world, the field I have described has so far been more commonly known as 'law and language' or 'law and communication', as mentioned above. However, there are signs that the term legal linguistics might be catching on. The reason for this is presumably the fact that the concept which the term represents brings together research generated from diverse disciplinary perspectives. Although the disciplines can have different points of departure and/or goals, they can be said to occupy the same paradigmatic space while studying legal language phenomena. These views focus on all aspects and functions of judicial life, such as specialized forensic applications used during pre-trial investigations. In general, legal linguistics can comprise all approaches categorized, for instance, by Stygall (1994: 6) as involving legal language-as-object, legal language-as-process, and legal language-as-instrument.

It is necessary to integrate the methods of legal science and linguistics before one can truly speak of legal linguistics. In that sense, discussing the surface structures or linguistic symbols is hardly sufficient. What is new from the point of view of legal science is the introduction of linguistic explanation as a method of explaining legal phenomena in legal science. From the linguistic point of view, what is new is bringing legal theory and thinking into the study of language in context. These approaches should enable scholars to extract new and interesting research results to gain a better understanding of the interaction between language and legal reality and phenomena. Moreover, useful applications for legal practice can only be found using linguistic methods.

Linguists see language as a social entity which cannot be reduced merely to mental processes or neurophysiological functions (Karlsson 1998: 32) but, by the same token, they do not believe that the capacity for language exists in isolation from other things the mind does.[7] The fact that language research cannot be reduced to the study apart from other aspects of the mind means that the methods and concepts used are characteristic of linguistic research. The most important of the methods is observing language in use and analyzing it using

5 It should be noted here that *language* and *linguistics* have been given many meanings and sometimes they are treated even as synonyms among those who write under the rubric of legal linguistics. See e.g. the sources of the numerous quotes in Goddard (this volume).

6 See Mattila (1997) for the term creation and usage in Finnish.

7 Chafe (1992: 80) notes the need for acceptance and integrating into our work the realization that language cannot be separated from the mind as a whole, that 'understanding language and understanding the mind are at bottom the same endeavor'.

linguistic methods and concepts typical of linguistic research (Karlsson 1998: 32). Therefore, linguistics offers the methods for approaching and studying law and legal language or language use in the legal domain in all its forms.[8]

The analysis of language in use has developed from the linguistic analysis of texts towards incorporating different sources of information.[9] Linguistic methods are also needed for studying real-world problems such as the complex relationship between language functions and their representations in legal reality.[10] These issues are centred on communication and are essentially discursive.

Over time, the meanings attributed to concepts such as justice and law change, even if their linguistic symbols remain unchanged. As is well known, different paradigms provide different perspectives for examining the world, and conceptual systems can be changed. The trend today is towards a more decentralized view of law that includes not only rules made by state legislatures but also a new body of rules, practices and processes by private actors, firms, NGOs, and independent experts such as technical standard setters and epistemic communities, either exercising autonomous regulatory power or implementing delegated power conferred by international law or national legislation.[11] This development accentuates the enabling and empowering quality of law, thus also emphasizing its future-orientation and pre-emptiveness. This reflects of course the reallocation of regulatory power and changes in the world. These changes and the shift of interest in legal thinking and studies of law reflect an elaboration and broadening of the traditional paradigms in law and legal education – along with them, legal linguistics. As language is not powerful *per se* and only gains power in the use of those who have been given institutional power, studying this use is more important than ever before. By the same token, some might argue that one can mean by

8 It should be emphasized here that when we talk of linguistics in connection with an academic discipline and part of a curriculum, we refer to academic-scientific study of language conducted with scientifically contested methods (see e.g. Häkkinen 1998: 12). According to the principles of lexicography and terminology work, it is better to define concepts in terms of what they are rather than what they are not. Despite this principle, it is necessary to point out that linguistics and consequently legal linguistics are not hard sciences although some of the characteristics of legal language are measurable. The categorization, descriptions and explanations can always be challenged and this perhaps is the reason why legal linguistics has become an umbrella under which everyone can play their own games as long as they have something to do with words and law.

9 Candlin categorized these as the upbeat phenomena in the development of discourse analysis in his plenary address in 'Speculating Futures Drawing on Current Accounts' at the ABC European Convention on Business Communication across Contexts, Cultures and Continents, May 23, 2002 in Aarhus, Denmark.

10 Hatz (1963: 66) points out that the matter of the fact is that law is not just expressed with the help of or through language but law is within the language. This is in keeping with Speech Act theory and the thought that law is constituted in language. See Austin (1962) and Searle (1975), discussed also in Salmi-Tolonen (2008) from this point of view.

11 See specifically Cafaggi (2011: 20-21) and Cafaggi (2009).

legal linguistics or language or linguistics whatever one wishes; however, the truth remains that it requires a wider consensus.

In keeping with Wittgenstein (1958), language is part of social activity and is related to rules; language use equals obeying a rule. The prerequisite for the existence of a rule constituting language is that a number of people obey the rule on several occasions. 'It is not possible that there should have been only one occasion, on which someone obeyed the rule ... To obey a rule, to give a report, to give an order, to play a game of chess, are *customs*.' A rule and the social system of interaction constitute the semantic meaning of language. In this sense 'to mean' and 'to obey a rule' are equivalent.[12]

Along with the development towards a more pluralistic view of legislation and the reallocation of legislative powers, judicial practice has diversified: alternative and private mechanisms of dispute resolution have been established. International commercial arbitration is an alternative to national jurisdiction in which the states, their coercive judicial measures and public judicial practices are considered the default. From this point of view, alternative dispute resolution mechanisms and arbitration practice entail the privatization of public practices and transferring legal practice – conflict resolution – to private commercial actors (Salmi-Tolonen 2011: 1-13).

The growing number of international trade disputes has prompted the development of alternative instruments for settling such disputes. In Europe, as in the rest of the world, arbitration has become more and more common as a mechanism for the settling of commercial disputes. In conflicts concerning cross-border exchanges, arbitration is regarded as an economical and effective alternative to litigation. However, the question has been raised as to whether there is a gap between the ideal and the real. What has been observed in recent discourse-analysis-oriented research[13] is the increasing colonization of arbitration practices by litigation – a development that seems to be contrary to the spirit of arbitration, which aims to resolve disputes outside of the courts (Nariman 2000: 261-78) – and the tensions due to involvement in the arbitration process of actors from different nations and jurisdictions (Bhatia et al. 2003). Thus, the discourse of international commercial arbitration is influenced by a range of factors at the level of national culture, legal culture and professional culture (Hafner 2011: 117-28).

The natural consequence from the above described developments is that the work of a legal linguist has also diversified. The material studied can no longer be limited to the discourse in national courts but also the discourse of private jurisdiction such as arbitration discourse, and not only public legislation but also

12 Wittgenstein (1958: § 85, 86, 197, and § 199). Compare also Stegmüller (1975: 600) and Günther (1988: 121).

13 'The generic integrity of legal discourse in international commercial arbitration in multilingual and multicultural contexts' and 'International arbitration practices: a discourse analytical study', both led by Professor Vijay K. Bhatia of the City University of Hong Kong.

private regulation.[14] Furthermore, legal studies and curricula should not only focus on conflict situations *ex post* but also on how to enable success *ex ante*.

3. Methods and approaches

The following paragraphs explain what the new and developing line of study – or academic discipline – of legal linguistics encompasses, as I see it. Legal linguistics is one of those new fields of study that have emerged between disciplines. It is typical of a new discipline to start out as a marginal school or an approach of a group of researchers focusing on a certain aspect of study within two already well-established fields. Social sciences, legal science among them, experienced linguistic and narrative turns at the end of the twentieth century. This accentuated the need of shifting interest also to the methods of studying the relationship of language and the functions of law. As language and its use are knowledge-based as are law and its praxis, a need to focus on those two knowledge bases became obvious. Ways of thinking, making decisions and exercising power vary over time. Law is no longer understood only within the confines of the positivist tradition which has dominated legal thinking in the western world for the better part of a century and which saw law as a body of rules made by the national legislator.[15] Legal theory today sees legal thinking as less formal than before and more dialectical, such as the polycentric theories of law, more ethical as with the neo-naturalist theories, or more ideological, such as critical legal studies and more multidisciplinary and proactive, such as proactive law. These new approaches are accompanied by what are known as the *law and …* fields, such as law and economics, which studies legal systems using methods provided by economics, law and sociology, law and informatics, and law and language. The shift of interest in the studies of law and language reflects an elaboration and broadening of the traditional paradigm in both legal studies and linguistics. One should note, however, that legal linguistics is by no means 'disciplinarily challenged'; it is a field of study in its own right and the eclectic approach it espouses is one of its merits.

It would be detrimental for the further development of these disciplines to force legal linguistics into a rigidly defined framework. On the contrary, it is new because it brings together studies which have been carried out in various other fields. Furthermore, it has started to develop theories devoted exclusively to it. To my mind, there is no set framework or methodology unique to legal linguistics

14 Private regulation refers to a body of rules, practices, and processes, created primarily by private actors, such as firms, non-governmental organizations, independent experts or epistemic communities, either exercising autonomous regulatory power or implementing delegated power conferred by international law or by national legislation (see e.g. Cafaggi 2011: 20-49).

15 Legal positivism is based on the belief that society is and must be governed and changed by legislation or case law (cf. Green 2003).

any more than there is in legal science[16] or linguistics. In the same way as many other new fields of investigation, legal linguistics started to develop as schools of thought within the disciplines and then between the disciplines of legal science and linguistics. It is nevertheless imperative that the body of knowledge that it is based on is not collected merely for anecdotal purposes but compiled through academic research conducted on contested methods. One should recognize that the lack of conventions in the field presents a problem. No doubt, then, there are various views on the definitions, some open-ended, some more rigid. The lack of conventions has its drawbacks and advantages – drawbacks in that such a lack entails uncertainty, advantages in that the researcher has more freedom as regards choice of methods and approaches.

In order to give legal linguistics a structure as a discipline, I have proposed two components: *the general* and *the particular* or *special*. In the same way as in many other attempts to structure a field of study, the general and the particular are not completely separable. Rather, they are both always present, but the point of view or approach adopted determines whether a study, or a part of it, is general or particular. In the following paragraphs, I will discuss this structure after situating the field of study in a scientific theoretical framework.

As I view it and define it as a discipline, legal linguistics is *multidisciplinary*, *cross-disciplinary*, and *interdisciplinary*. These three terms are sometimes used and understood as synonyms but I would like to join those who see the need to give all three a specific meaning. In this perspective, *multidisciplinary* refers to approaches where the same research topic or area is approached from the point of view of several different disciplines by researchers in each of those fields. This approach has successfully been put to use in Women's Studies. In the studies of law and language, multidisciplinarity is found in studies conducted in applied linguistics and languages for special purposes or LSP studies. Such studies might, for instance, focus on deconstructing or analyzing the complex syntax of legal texts for translation purposes. Legal scientists, on their part, engage in a similar deconstruction process but for the purpose of extracting the meaning in order to see how a legal norm should be interpreted.

To my mind, *cross-disciplinary* refers to approaches that successfully integrate views, approaches, and the methodologies of two or more disciplines. By the third concept – *interdisciplinary* – I mean approaches that also successfully integrate methods and approaches from various disciplines but do so in a way that enables them to claim a position between the disciplines involved. Figure 13.1 below illustrates these three approaches. The research topic (X) remains the same but the approaches are different (Salmi-Tolonen 2008: 8-10).

16 *Minun metodini* (My method) (edited by Häyhä 1997) proves my point at least as far as Finnish legal science and profession are concerned. The word *method* is given as many senses both research and professional methods as there are writers in the volume, namely 17.

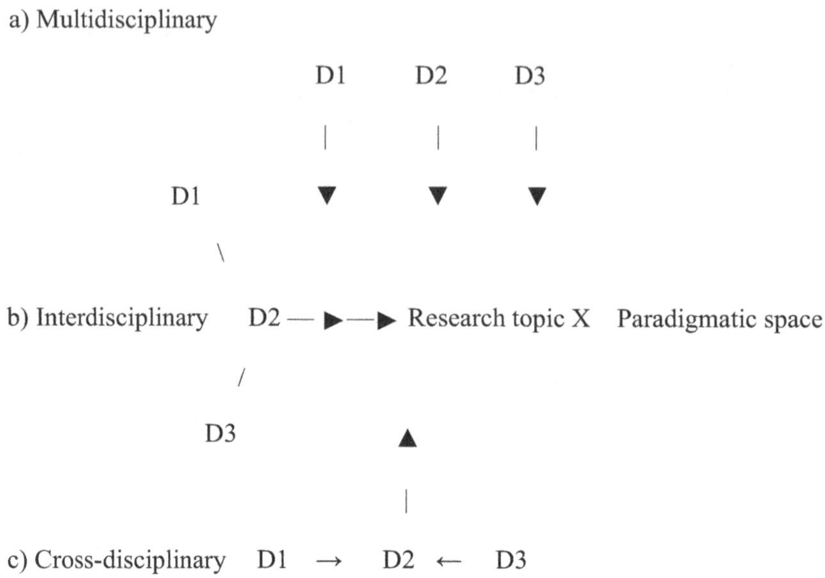

Figure 13.1 Different approaches to a research topic X
Source: Salmi-Tolonen 2008: 8

In Figure 13.1, D1, D2, and D3 refer to disciplines 1, 2, and 3. There could be only two disciplines involved or there could be more than three.

Figures 13.2, 13.3, and 13.4 below specify the three approaches in more detail. The basic point of departure is that legal linguistic study is based on real-life data.

In Figure 13.2, it is assumed that there are three or more disciplines (D1, D2, Dn) investigating the same research object in the legal domain. The disciplines are represented by researchers in each discipline. They all move in the same paradigmatic space and may study the same data collected on the research object, albeit from the point of view and methods of their own areas of expertise.

The research object and the aims and objectives determine what kind of data will be collected – written, spoken or both. The previous academic research on the subject is naturally also reviewed. If the methodology so requires, data can be collected from a wide variety of sources – oral data (e.g. recorded court discourse, interviews etc.), written documents (e.g. Acts of Parliament, wills, contracts etc.) or previous academic research. These are then analyzed and juxtaposed to ascertain their validity and reliability and to delineate the object of study. In social sciences, especially in qualitative research, this methodology is known as triangulation (see e.g. Seale 1999 on qualitative research methods).

It is only by approaching the research topic using the methods and perspectives of different disciplines that new knowledge on the topic can be generated. Multidisciplinary research can be compared to constructing a building where a

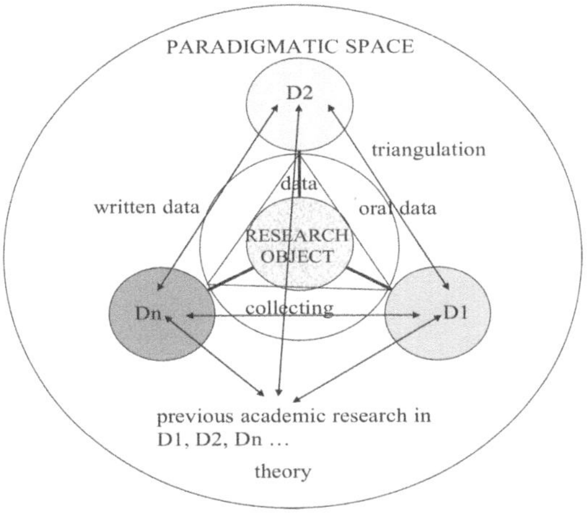

Figure 13.2 A multidisciplinary approach design
Source: Salmi-Tolonen 2008: 8

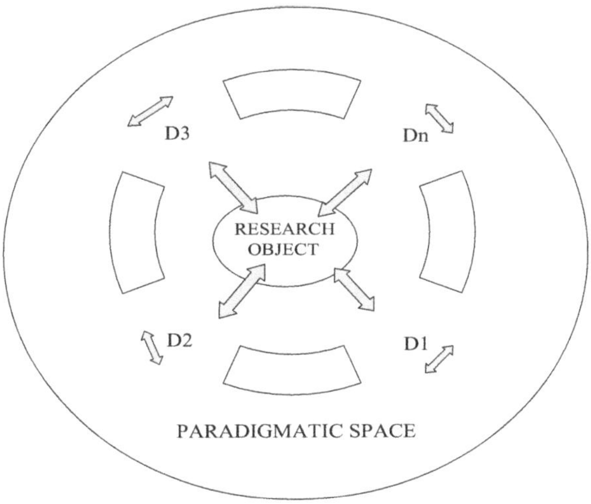

Figure 13.3 An interdisciplinary approach design
Source: Salmi-Tolonen 2008: 9

number of professionals in different fields of expertise are needed. Without their collaboration, no building could be safely erected.

As explained above, I consider the interdisciplinary approach to be the one that best represents the core of the new field of study, legal linguistics. The other two – the multidisciplinary and the cross-disciplinary approaches – are nevertheless equally valid and necessary for enriching legal linguistic research.

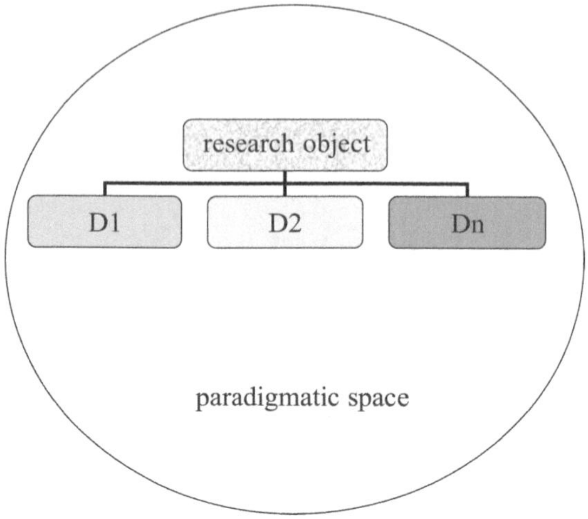

Figure 13.4 A cross-disciplinary approach design
Source: Salmi-Tolonen 2008: 10

Cross-disciplinary refers to approaches that successfully integrate views, approaches, and the methodologies of two or more disciplines.

A fourth notion – 'transdisciplinary' research – should be added, although it would be hard to present graphically. Researchers today are increasingly stepping beyond their disciplinary boundaries to provide accounts of social life and discourses in terms of the new issues of change, globalism and pluralism (Iedema and Wodak 1999: 6). These investigators are essentially engaged in what Martin (1992) refers to as 'transdisciplinary' research, by which he means the fine-tuning of linguistic, discursive and semiotic perspectives to investigate specialized social, institutional, and organizational issues, to which legal and legal language issues also belong.

To sum up, legal linguistics is a multi-, cross-, inter-, and transdisciplinary field at the same time. In the following paragraph, the structure and research questions that may be posed in the domain of legal linguistics will be discussed.

4. The structure of legal linguistics and research questions

In general terms, legal linguistics studies the characteristics, development, and use of legal languages. Legal linguistics focuses on language being used for legal purposes or in the legal domain: 'legal' is the only variable that separates it from linguistic study as such and implies a function, in other words, use. Therefore the development and characteristics of the discipline can only be studied from the language-in-use aspect.

The field is far too wide to be handled as such and it needs to be structured in order to be of use either as part of the curriculum or research. Legal linguistic research can approach legal language at the macro level by studying the society surrounding a linguistic event. This approach has been favoured in social studies. The linguistic turn in social studies has meant that even in social studies the trend is from macro-level to micro-level analysis. Social studies have adopted conversation analysis from ethnomethodology and applied it to institutional discourse in particular. In linguistics, it is acknowledged that it is only through investigating the micro-level that the macro-level can be reached. In legal linguistics, micro-level approaches involve analyzing legal texts and their linguistic features, which was long the type of analysis used in linguistics. Today macro-level analysis has caught the interest of linguists as well. In this respect, social studies and linguistics have moved in opposite directions but closer to each other. The two kinds of analysis can be combined and complemented by the study of interaction between society and legal texts. The current trend in research favours the latter, with micro-level analysis typically complementing macro-level analysis. Cicourel (1976) has pointed out that one cannot understand the macro without the micro.

Research in legal linguistics can focus on various levels of language in judicial texts:[17] semantics at the utterance or lexical level, or syntax at the sentence or clause level. Larger units such as texts and their characteristics as speech acts are also of interest. The focus can also be placed on either intratextual or intertextual characteristics of legal texts or the function of judicial utterances or texts. In other words, their pragmatic meaning, an aspect that reaches beyond boundaries of traditional semantic studies. Cognitive approaches investigate the relationship between specialist legal knowledge and text or specialist legal knowledge in relation to lay knowledge and text (see Lundquist 2000, 2004).

Legal linguistics can focus on a particular language or investigate what are known as universals; that is, features that are unique to most judicial languages. The research approach can be either synchronic or diachronic. One can focus on the changes in judicial language/s within a shorter or longer period of time or look at the same phenomena at a given moment or time in history.

The study of legal linguistic universals I call *general legal linguistics*. General legal linguistics is not bound to any particular legal language (legal English, legal French, legal Finnish etc.) but rather studies phenomena unique to legal language that are shared by all – or at least most – western legal systems and languages.

Particular legal linguistics[18] investigates the juridical language of a single legal culture or legal order that is dependent on a single given language: Finnish, English, French and so on. Comparing two or more juridical languages and cultures constitutes *Contrastive legal linguistics*. The necessary prerequisite for particular

17 Text can be either a written or a spoken or even a signed language event.

18 I chose to call this part *particular* rather than *special* basically to avoid aligning the term with research in linguistics within the so-called *LSP* studies, where *special* refers to language variation for professional purposes rather than a particular language or culture.

legal linguistics, and thus also contrastive legal linguistics,[19] is the study of general legal linguistics. In a manner of speaking, comparative law uses the same methods as contrastive legal linguistics as it is always necessary to compare the contents of conceptual systems in two or more jurisdictions first but legal linguistics takes the study a step further to the language level. What are the linguistic means these conceptual systems are constituted and expressed by? Where comparative law and studies in legal culture describe and explain the circumstances of the linguistic event, legal linguistics does that but, in addition, it also conducts a linguistic analysis.

An additional branch of particular legal linguistics is what I call applications of legal linguistics, by which I mean the investigation of juridical translation or interpretation, the study of courtroom discourses, or various forensic applications which comprise forensic phonetics and forensic linguistics, for instance speaker or writer identification. Terminology work and legal lexicography also fall under the applications of legal linguistics.

A legal scientist poses research questions such as: What are the means in this legal system to regulate this situation? A legal linguist would ask: What are the linguistic means for expressing the propositional content of this legal rule? What are the linguistic means the legal order employs in order to regulate this particular situation? How are the functions of the judiciary accomplished linguistically? How does language constitute and represent legal reality?

Variation in legal discourse is one possible area of study in contrastive legal linguistics. Variation is a concept in sociolinguistics and refers to extralinguistic variables. A typical sociolinguist investigates the changes in language and its categories in relation to socio-economic changes. The variables used for examining change in language use are extralinguistic, e.g. time or geography. In legal linguistics or legal discourse, analogous variables could be a) geographical, b) temporal, or c) institutional (related to a legal system or legal order).

When geography is chosen as the main variable of an investigation, some writers talk about legal dialects.[20] A case in point is legal English as it is used

19 I use *contrastive* in order to emphasize the fact that the purpose of the contrastive study is more than simply describing two or more legal languages by describing them one after another or even by setting them side by side. It is necessary to explain and evaluate the similarities and differences found. The comparatists in law more often than not are content with setting legal systems side by side, or describing them one after another, as in David and Jauffret-Spinosi (1982, 1986). The same method is seen in studies that are referred to as comparative legal linguistics. It is difficult to see why linguistics has been added since they stop at what clearly is comparative law and leave out linguistic explanation.

20 'Legal dialect' is perhaps not the best possible designation even if the language-external criterion is geography for the simple reason that dialect in sociolinguistics is almost invariably related to socially inferior variants of language. It is not possible today to think that, for instance, American English or British English is a dialect and one of them is the 'correct' or default variant setting the norm. No more is Swedish – the second official language in Finland spoken in Finland and used in Finnish national legislation – a dialect. It

in various common law countries (see e.g. Tiersma 1999: 133-135). Although a number of countries are characterized as common law countries, their legal systems have undergone changes over time. They have diverged and developed in a way peculiar to each country. Along with the changes in the legal systems, the legal languages used have diverged and therefore we cannot speak of one legal English any more than we can talk about one English with reference to the general language.

Legal language develops concurrently with the social institutions of law and maintains and is maintained by them. Legal language does not develop independently of a powerful institutional setting but in close interaction with it; this is one of the basic assumptions in this chapter. Each system has its distinctive linguistic as well as institutional features. Therefore it is self-evident and perhaps even unnecessary to mention to a linguistic audience that the study of legal culture is incorporated in the study of legal linguistics. Linguistics and therefore also legal linguistics borrows methods from other disciplines such as ethnomethodology which studies organization and practical actions (see Garfinkel 1967) and anthropology. Ethnomethodology – which conversation analysts have borrowed – can also be applied to courtroom discourse studies. Although scholars disagree on the definition of legal anthropology, the gist of it is that law is an important component of culture and seeks to describe the ordering of human society. Ethnomethodology, anthropology and linguistics have all drawn on the work of such scholars as Sir Henry Maine (1860s) and Joseph Malinowski (1920s).

Language itself is a cultural phenomenon that is tied to the community where it is used: language is characteristically a social practice. Persistence and change in the social system are both reflected in texts and brought about by means of texts.[21] Research in legal linguistics encompasses culture. One can ignore language while studying legal culture, as seems to be the case in general, but one cannot study legal language using linguistic methods without at the same time studying culture, because the two are inseparable. If time is taken as the main variable, the study is diachronic or synchronic. In the former case, the research examines changes in legal language over time, in the latter variations in either legal genres or legal languages in different legal orders. As mentioned above, changes over time are intertwined with socio-economic changes and changes in the legal systems. The four factors that give legal languages their essential characteristics are social, political, historical and linguistic. Using Braudel's (1982) framework,[22] we can

should be noted, however, that there is only one variant of EU Swedish for which the Prime Minister's Office in Stockholm is responsible.

21 See, generally, e.g. Halliday (1978).

22 Braudel suggests three kinds of duration with respect to time and society. The first is long duration (*la longue durée*), which is associated with slowly developing things such as climate, nature, trade routes and cultivation methods; Braudel's followers have concluded that language, mentalities, world views, and people's everyday habits and customs belong to this category. The second level is *les conjunctures*, a time that is more rapid than the first

deduce that from the viewpoint of legal language and legal culture, all three durations of time are interdependent, but culture in general – comprising language, mentalities and customs, and belonging to the long duration – is primary to legal language and culture, which would belong to the *conjunctures*; but only the third – short-term duration – gives us history and the power elite which, in our knowledge society today, would also refer to the expert elite. It is the third, then, which is the most subject to change, but simultaneously and in interaction with the other two.[23]

Linguistic legal research started from an interest in language use rather than in language as an autonomous system in general linguistics. In the Nordic countries, the study of legal language was at first widely based on social criticism that focused on institutional languages, the language of administration and the language of the law (see e.g. Gunnarsson 1970). In multilingual countries or countries with more than one official language, statutory texts and other legal documents have been translated for a long period of time, but surprisingly the history of research on legal language is not nearly as long as the history of legal translation. Today, it would not be natural to embark on such a difficult task without systematic research. Even after the research in translation studies began, the work being done focused for a very long time on the results of the translation process rather than on the process itself. Unfortunately, even today, equivalence questions are often discussed in law, totally forgetting the conceptual issues – or worse still, mistaking the two for equivalents.

It was in fact Bible translators such as Nida and Taber (1969) and others who started systematic translation research and outlined the first translation theories. To some extent, the problems faced by Bible translators coincide with those encountered by legal translators: the texts they translate are normative and therefore source-text focused. It should be noted here, however, that legal translation varies according to its communicative situation. When, for instance, a Finnish parliamentary act is translated into English, the translation is unofficial and accordingly does not carry the force of law. Its function is not normative, but informative. Therefore it may take the readership into consideration and be more reader and target text-oriented than translations that are considered authentic. In contrast, when a parliamentary act drafted in Finnish is translated into Swedish, the second official language in Finland, the target text must retain the normative

---

category, yet slower than time experienced by an individual in everyday life; this category includes phenomena such as economic systems, societies, and civilization. Only at the third level do we encounter what is traditionally called history: Braudel calls it short-term duration (*les évenéments*). This last concept is governed by the elite in power of each age (see also Salmi-Tolonen 2011).

23 Understanding the concept of time has ramifications in judicial translation. Considerations of time are particularly critical in juridical translation since tradition and conventions are prominent. For possible approaches and strategies, see Salmi-Tolonen (1995).

function of the source text: they are equally authentic.[24] The same applies, of course, in supranational organizations such as the European Communities, where all official language texts are deemed to be as authentic as the 'original'.[25]

In common law countries, the investigation of legal English has produced an impressive body of research. In the British adversarial system, resolving conflicts can be said to depend entirely on the linguistic skills of those involved on the day in question. The study of spoken legal English is therefore extremely important. Courtrooms in the UK are very highly institutionalized and dependent on special rules of language use: elaborate forms of address and forms of politeness and rules restricting what may be said, such as the rules about hearsay evidence. Furthermore, in a court of law it becomes most evident that language has the utmost social significance.

In Finland, a reform of judicial procedure in the 1990s introduced features from the adversarial system which were not there before. The most conspicuous change is the introduction of oral hearings also at the appellate courts. Given these developments, it is extremely important to get the study of courtroom discourses started also in Finland.

Videoconferencing in criminal proceedings is now widely used to speed up cross-border cooperation, reduce costs and increase security.[26] At present, the training for legal practitioners and interpreters on VCI/RI is, as far as I know, non-existent.[27] Quite recently, a Finnish district court had to try a case of genocide and some of the hearings were held in Rwanda. The hearings were transmitted to Finland, where the defendant stayed on his own request for safety reasons, by video. It soon turned out to be clear that many of the legal professionals were inexperienced in this method. The method without doubt added to the complexity of this already difficult case. One of the consequences was that one of the advocates was fined for breaching the professional code of conduct.[28] No doubt these kinds of situations are increasingly common in our global world. In Europe, *Directive 2010/64/EU of the European Parliament and the Council on the right to interpretation and translation in criminal proceedings* is aimed at advancing

> the implementation of the principle of mutual recognition of decisions in criminal matters presupposes that Member States have trust in each other's criminal justice systems. The extent of mutual recognition is very much dependent on a number of parameters, which include mechanisms for safeguarding the rights

---

24 For a comprehensive discussion on legal translation, see Šarčević (1997).

25 The original here referring to the document in the language it was first drafted.

26 A 2008 survey by the European working group of E-Justice.

27 Presently an ongoing EU-funded AVIDICUS project at the University of Surrey, the UK has as one of its aims to produce course modules for training purposes.

28 This incident is also interesting in that the Finnish Bar Association exercised judicial power which is private and delegated by the Finnish government.

> of suspected or accused persons and common minimum standards necessary to facilitate the application of the principle of mutual recognition.

This directive is to be transposed by October 2013 and will pose demands on translator and interpreter training and also to the training of judges and other legal professionals; in other words, the users of translation and interpretation.

To my mind, legal linguistics plays a key role in producing the kind of knowledge that is needed in these new situations where it is not only the questions of multicultural legal situations that cause contingencies but also the challenges that electronic transmitting poses.

5. Implications

What then are the implications of the above-said? Curricular aims and objectives in today's Europe are defined in terms of the European Qualifications Framework of Lifelong Learning (EQF 2008). In a broad sense, we can think of legal linguistic competences in terms of attitudes, knowledge and skills. In other words, what are the competences a legal professional needs and how does one develop those competences further in working life in relation to legal linguistics? It is the mission of legal linguists first of all to conduct relevant studies with contested methods to add to the body of knowledge that can facilitate understanding the complex relationship between law and language. Next, it is necessary to develop curricula based on that knowledge. A legal professional does not need to be able to conduct a phonetic analysis of a speech sample but it is necessary for every legal professional to know enough to be able to find an expert to do it and judge how an expert could help a client. In legal education, students acquire their professional attitudes – what one needs to believe and feel, along with knowledge and what one must be able to do – in other words, skills to perform successfully. A competence may have various skills associated with it but here the focus is on those that best represent or identify with the competence characteristics we intend to emphasize in legal linguistics.

At present, there is still a lot of work to be done with attitudes because they shape one's decisions and actions. They are very difficult to define as they consist of qualities and beliefs that are non-tangible but nevertheless learned tendencies. Knowledge refers to the body of knowledge compiled by studies on legal (broadly understood) language. One needs this knowledge to be able to perform optimally: law is both theory and praxis and skills. Skills are defined as expertness, practised ability, a facility in doing something, dexterity. The acquisition of skill leads to unconscious and automatic actions. Skills associated with the competence are observable behaviours which serve as indicators when measuring competence acquisition (see e.g. Fishbein and Ajzen 1975).

A paradigm shift is needed in legal education to accommodate it to our world today which requires attitudes, skills and knowledge not only in solving problems but also in looking ahead. Systemic innovation is needed to change law curricula – legal linguistics curriculum offers such a systemic innovation.

6. Conclusion

In this short analysis, I have presented some of my views of legal linguistics as an integral part of legal science. It is a field of study which is crucially important to the legal profession. Legal linguistics studies law with linguistic methods and the outcome of the studies can help legal scientists and legal practitioners do and understand their work better through an increased understanding of how language works in general and in legal domains in particular. The mission of legal linguistics is to compile, conduct and develop research relevant to legal scientists and practitioners and make it accessible to them. It would also benefit the general public as law touches everyone and therefore some legal astuteness and legal literacy is needed in our everyday lives to form transaction and labour contracts, to claim benefits, to fill in income tax return forms, to name only a few. The history of legal linguistics in this sense has hardly begun.

It is clear that research for producing the body of knowledge needed in teaching legal linguistics is conducted not only by legal linguists, but by legal scientists, linguists, translation scientists and so on, as is required by a discipline which is at the same time multi-, cross-, inter-, and transdisciplinary. Interaction between the different traits and disciplines is a necessary condition. However, it is the task of legal linguists to compile the relevant studies into the body of knowledge that can then be expressed in terms of competences such as knowledge, skills and attitudes, and be operationalized in teaching and in the various law-related tasks that legislators, law appliers and legal subjects perform. This important work must go on.

References

Austin, J.L. 1962. *How to Do Things with Words.* Cambridge: Cambridge University Press.

Avidicus 2009. Assessment of videoconference interpreting in the Criminal Justice Service, EU Criminal Justice Programme, Project JLS/2008/JPEN/037, 2008-2011. [Online]. Available at: http://www.eulita.eu/avidicus [accessed: 19 December 2012].

Bhatia, V.K., Candlin, C., Engberg, J. and Trosborg, A. (eds.) 2003. *Multilingual and Multicultural Contexts of Legislation. An International Perspective.* Frankfurt am Main: Peter Lang.

Braudel, F. 1982. *On History.* Translated from the French original *Écrits sur l'histoire* by Sarah Matthews. London: University of Chicago Press.

Busse, D. 1989. Was ist die bedeutung eines gesetztextes? Sprachwissenschaftliche argumente im methodenstreit der juristischen auslegungslehre – linguistisch gesehen, in *Untersuchungen zur Rechtslinguistik. Interdisziplinäre Studien zu praktischer Semantik und Strukturierender Rechtslehre in Grundfragen der juristische Methodik*, Schriften zur Rechtstheorie, Heft 133, edited by F. Müller. Berlin: Duncker & Humblot, 93-149.

Cafaggi, F. 2009. Private regulation in European private law, *EUI Working Papers*, RSCAS 2009/31. Available at: http://hdl.handle.net/1814/12054 [accessed: 18 December 2012].

Cafaggi, F. 2011. New foundations of transnational private regulation. *Journal of Law and Society*, 38(1), 20-49 at 20-21. Available at: http://cadmus.eui.eu/bitstream/handle/1814/15284/RSCAS_2010_53.pdf?sequence=1 [accessed: 18 December 2012].

Candlin, C. 2002. Speculating futures drawing on current accounts. Paper to the ABC European Convention on *Business Communication across Contexts, Cultures and Continents*, Aarhus, Denmark, 23 May 2002.

Chafe, W.L. 1982. Integration and involvement in speaking, writing, and oral literature, in *Spoken and Written Language: Exploring Orality and Literacy*, edited by D. Tannen. Norwood: Ablex.

Cicourel, A.V. 1973. *Cognitive Sociology: Language Meaning in Social Interaction*. Harmonsworth: Penguin.

Commission Communication May 2008 on a European e-Justice Strategy (COM(2008)329 final), e-Justice Action Plan. Available at: http://eur-lex.europa.eu/LexUriServ/LexUriServ.do?uri=OJ:C:2009:075:0001:0012:EN:PDF [accessed: 19 December 2012].

Council Conclusions on a European Case Law Identifier (ECLI). Available at: http://eurlex.europa.eu/LexUriServ/LexUriServ.do?uri=OJ:C:2011:127:0001:0007:EN:PDF [accessed: 19 December 2012].

Directive 2010/64/EU of the Euriopean Parliament and of the Council of 20 October 2010 on the right to interpretation and translation in criminal proceedings. 26.10.2010 *Official Journal of the European Union*, L 280/1. [Online] Available at: http://eur-lex.europa.eu/LexUriServ/LexUriServ.do?uri=OJ:L:2010:280:0001:0007:en:PDF [accessed: 19 December 2012].

David, R. 1982. *Les grands systemes de droit contemporains*. Huitième édition. Paris: Dalloz.

Fishbein, M. and Ajzen, I. 1975. *Belief, Attitude, Intention and Behavior: An Introduction to Theory and Research*. Reading, MA: Addison-Wesley.

Goodrich, P. 1987. *Legal Discourse. Studies in Linguistics, Rhetoric and Legal Analysis*. New York: St. Martin's Press.

Garfinkel, H. 1967. *Studies in Ethnomethodology*. Englewood Cliffs, NJ: Prentice-Hall.

Green, L. 2003. Legal Positivism. Stanford Encyclopedia of Philosophy. Available at: http://plato.stanford.edu/entries/legal-positivism/ [accessed: 18 December 2012].

Günther, K. 1988. *Der Sinn für Angemessenheit*. Frankfurt am Main: Suhrkamp.

Hafner, C.A. 2011. Professional reasoning, legal cultures, and arbitral awards. *World Englishes*, 30(1), 117-28. Available at: http://onlinelibrary.wiley.com/doi/10.1111/j.1467-971X.2010.01691.x/abstract [accessed: 19 December 2012].

Halliday, M.A.K. 1978. *Language as Social Semiotic*. London: Arnold.

Hartmann, P. 1970. Sprachwissenschaft und rechtswissenschaft eine vergleichende konfrontation. *Rechtstheorie* 1, 45-68.

Hatz, H. 1963. *Rechtssprache und juristischer Begriff. Vom richtigen Verstehen des Rechtssatzes*. Stuttgart: Kohlhammer.

Häkkinen, K. 1998. Kielitieteen Perusteet. (The Foundations of Linguistics). 4th Edition. Tietolipas 133. Helsinki: SKS.

Häyhä, J. (ed.) 1997. *Minun Metodini*. (My Method), Helsinki: Werner Söderström Lakitieto OY.

Iedema, R. and Wodak, R. 1999. Introduction: organizational discourses and practices. *Discourse and Society*, 10(1), 5-19.

Karlsson, F. 1998. *Yleinen Kielitiede*. (General Linguistics). Helsinki: Helsinki University Press.

Lundquist, L. and Jarvella, R.J. (eds.) 2000. *Language, Text, and Knowledge*. Berlin: Mouton de Gruyter.

Lundquist, L. 2004. From legal knowledge to legal discourse – and back again. In *Approaches to Cognition through Text and Discourse*, edited by T. Virtanen. Berlin: Mouton de Gruyter, 123-147.

Maine, H.S. 1861, 1960. *Ancient Laws*. New York: Dutton.

Malinowski, B. 1926. *Crime and Savage Society*. London: Routledge & Kegan Paul.

Martin, J.R. 1992. *English Text; System and Structure*. Amsterdam and Philadelphia: John Benjamins.

Mattila, H.E.S. 1997. Oikeuslingvistiikka oppiaineena. *Oikeustiede-Jurisprudentia XXX*. 198-216.

Nariman, F.S. 2000. The spirit of arbitration: the tenth annual Goff lecture. *Arbitration International*, 16(3), 261-278.

Nida, E.A. and Taber, C.R. 1969. *The Theory and Practice of Translation*. Leiden: Brill.

Salmi-Tolonen, T. 1995. Time and translation, in *Aspectus varii translationis*, edited by R. Oittinen and J-P. Varonen Studia translatologica. Ser. B, vol. 1. Tampere, Tampere University Press, 47-58.

Salmi-Tolonen, T. 2008. *Language and the Functions of Law: A Legal Linguistic Study*. Rovaniemi: Painosalama Turku.

Salmi-Tolonen, T. 2011. Introduction. In *Law and Language in Partnership and Conflict. A Special Issue of the Lapland Law Review*, edited by T. Salmi-Tolonen, I. Tukiainen and R. Foley vol. 1: Issue 1. 1-13. Available at: http://www.ulapland.fi/LaplandLawReview [accessed: 18 December 2012].

Šarčević, S. 1997. *New Approach to Legal Translation*. The Hague: Kluwer.

Seale, C. 1999. *The Quality of Qualitative Research. Introducing Qualitative Methods Series*. London: Sage.

Searle, J. 1995. *The Construction of Social Reality*. New York: The Free Press.

Stegmüller, W. 1975. *Hauptströmungen der Gegenwartsphilosophie*. Stuttgart: Kröner.

Stygall, G. 1994. *Trial Language. Differential Discourse Processing and Discursive Formation.* Amsterdam and Philadelphia: John Benjamins.

Tiersma, P.M. 1999. *Legal Language*. Chicago: University of Chicago Press.

Tuori, K. 1997. Law, power and critique, in *Law and Power. Critical and Socio-Legal Essays*, edited by K. Tuori, Z. Bankowski and J. Uusitalo. Liverpool: Deborah Charles Publications, 7-29.

Wittgenstein, L. 1958. *Philosophical Investigations*. Oxford: Blackwell.

Chapter 14

Learning to fly: The prospects for legal linguistics in the academic curriculum ... and beyond

Christopher Goddard

In the field of legal communication, the fledgling discipline of legal linguistics offers vital knowledge and skills required by, for example, lawyers and legal translators operating in two or more legal languages. This is especially so in the context of globalization and transnationalization of the law, where English is the *de facto* global legal language, with attendant linguistic challenges. However, legal linguistics currently occupies a precarious foothold in the academic curriculum. The analysis in this chapter attempts to establish core and peripheral legal linguistic skills with a view to completing both the spectrum and content of course and programme components. To balance the academic aspect, the chapter also explores practical applications of legal linguistics. The aim is to affirm the relevance of legal linguistics in the curriculum for future law professionals with a view to examining how to nurture the fledgling discipline until it takes wing and soars as an established component of the academic curriculum linked to its use in professional life. References to the literature complemented by focus group survey data form the basis of analysis and discussion.

1. Introduction

Legal linguistics as an academic discipline is in its infancy. This chapter aims to clarify the focus that legal linguistics courses or programmes require so as to be seen by educational institutions, potential applicants, employers, and stakeholders as having clear practical professional relevance. The context, examined briefly, is linguistic challenges to legal communication against a background of globalization and transnationalization of the law with English as the *de facto* global legal language and law professionals operating in two or more legal languages. In addition to contextual references to the literature, a survey questionnaire is addressed to a focus group consisting of academics in the legal linguistics field to establish their views on what they identify as core and peripheral legal linguistic skills and practical applications of legal linguistics.

2. Legal linguistics as an emerging discipline

According to Marcus Galdia, legal linguistics is in a 'state of emergence' (Galdia 2009: 35), in that 'until recently ... Legal Linguistics did not exist as an autonomous branch of legal science or linguistics, and its status as an interdisciplinary field of research has not been particularly strong either' (Galdia 2009: 65; see also Mattila 2006: 8-10). Salmi-Tolonen (this volume)[1] asserts that 'legal linguistics is an independent, developing interdisciplinary field of study within legal science' and goes on to explain (this volume):

> What is new from the point of view of legal science is the introduction of linguistic explanation as a method of explaining legal phenomena in legal science. From the linguistic point of view, what is new is bringing legal theory and thinking into the study of language in context.

However, this is not to say that interest in legal language is new (Mattila 2006: 6-7). While examples of other emerging disciplines are many,[2] one concrete example will suffice for this paper: knowledge management (Wiig 2000).

Moreover, if new and emerging branches of law, such as medical and bio-law, communications law, information law, and pharmalaw, must jostle for position, recognition, and space in the curriculum (Tuori 2011: 159-160), this suggests an analogy with emerging disciplines such as legal linguistics. Tuori notes (2011: 160):

> In the early phases of the campaign, a central claim would be over a chair at the law faculty and acknowledged status in the legal curriculum. When a chair has been obtained, it is turned into a bridgehead, allowing consolidation of victories achieved and the prospect of new conquests.

More specifically in the field of legal linguistics, Salmi-Tolonen (this volume) notes:

> Legal linguistics is one of those new fields of study that have emerged between disciplines. It is typical of a new discipline to start out as a marginal school or an approach of a group of researchers focusing on a certain aspect of study within two already well-established fields.

---

1 Interestingly, while this chapter and that of Salmi-Tolonen (this volume) seem to cover similar ground, a glance through the respective reference lists shows that the two chapters share only one source.

2 See generally http://www.emergingdisciplines.org/http://www.krii.com/downloads/km_emerg_discipl.pdf.

Again, if proponents of an emerging field of law have their 'external patrons' such as trade unions, non-governmental organizations and employers' organizations for labour law (Tuori 2011: 160), this, too, may suggest that a similar need applies to emerging disciplines. Legal linguistics as an emerging discipline appears to have no such patronage, a matter worth exploring elsewhere.

Before briefly examining the role of legal linguistics in the field of legal communication, the paper sets the context, in the shape of globalization and transnationalization of the law, with English as the *de facto* global legal language.

3. Globalization and transnationalization of the law: Legal linguistic challenges

In legal terms, globalization could be said to comprise, firstly, the legal consequences of activities that go beyond the borders of the nation-state, therefore beyond nation-state control and thus requiring 'corresponding cross-boundary reactions' (Tuori 2011: 296), and secondly, denationalization of law coupled with the growth of non-state transnational legal systems (Tuori 2011: 291-304) including EU law or Europeanization of law (Tuori 2011: 244-247, 300-301). According to Husa (2011: 255):

> [p]resent challenges set forth by globalisation and Europeanisation have stirred the former tranquillity of the nationally oriented doctrinal study of law throughout Europe ... nation-States and their systems of positive law are on the decline.

These developments in turn lead to legal pluralism, which Husa defines as the simultaneous existence of 'multiple legal systems (or normative orders) in one geographical area' (Husa 2011: 255). Here we should distinguish between the 'legal order' as mainly the sum of lawmaking, the 'totality of valid legal norms', 'the law in force'; 'legal system' as an analytical breakdown of normative material by legal science into discrete areas of law; and 'legal practices such as lawmaking, adjudication and legal scholarship' as themselves social practices involved in producing and reproducing the legal order (Tuori 2011: ix, 6).

Examples of transnational legal systems based on functional grounds include the European Union and the World Trade Organization (Husa 2011: 259), the *lex mercatoria* of international trade, the *lex sportiva* of international sports, and the *lex digitalis* of the Internet. In none of these transnational legal systems have either municipal legal orders or international law subsumed the applicable norms. Moreover, designated transnational bodies settle disputes and impose sanctions in those same fields.[3] While international arbitration bodies apply *lex mercatoria*,

3 For presentation of transnational legal systems, see B. Zangl, M. Zürn (2004: 12-45), *Make law, not war*: Internationale und transnationale Verrechtlichung als Baustein für Global Governance, in B. Zangl, M. Zürn (eds), Dietz, Bonn.

lex sportiva largely combats doping. Transnational *lex digitalis* is most developed in its regulation of disputes over domain names. Additionally, with or without nation-state consent, transnational law in the shape of European Union law or human rights law affects private individuals. Moreover, specific courts or other monitoring bodies are established to implement them, again with or without nation-state consent (Tuori 2011: 302-305; see also Salmi-Tolonen, this volume).

What does this mean in legal linguistic terms? De Groot (1996: 155) observes:

> An international legal technical language is almost wholly lacking. It only exists to the extent that certain legal areas have become 'internationalized': this is particularly true for international law and European Community law. An international (multilingual) terminology is gradually developing in these fields. But for legal areas such as constitutional law, administrative law, criminal law or civil law, an international terminology is fundamentally absent.

One of the challenges facing a potential single legal language remains absence of equivalence and mismatch between terms and concepts (see e.g. discussion in Goddard 2009: 178-181). Galdia asserts that '[l]egal concepts can be expressed by ordinary language ... legal language does not consist of concepts alone' (2009: 95) while acknowledging the '[s]ystemic incompatibility of legal concepts' (2009: 119).

However, even unified or harmonized concepts do not necessarily lead to unified legal language: as Heutger notes (2005: 205) it is '[t]he use of different languages [that] is one of the obstacles to the EU-integration process.'

Indeed, as Twining rightly asserts (2002: 4), a 'cosmopolitan' discipline of law needs a vocabulary and conceptual apparatus that can be used confidently across jurisdictions and cultures: 'If jurisprudence is to be general, its vocabulary and concepts need to travel well.' For example, in the field of corporate law, Kraakman (2004: 4) argues 'the need to develop an appropriate language in which issues of comparative (corporate) law could be addressed without confusion and misinterpretation.' At the same time, others in specific fields such as contracts warn against the unsuitability, or pitfalls, of English as an international legal language (Beveridge 2002, Triebel 2009), of which more in the following section.

An additional complication is that, even where two legal systems and the corresponding languages are very similar, actual day-to-day practice of the law may differ between those two systems. Moreover, de Groot (1996: 159) points to the challenge posed to translators of legal texts 'between two legal systems which differ from one another in their systems and contents, while the legal languages used are closely related to one another', citing as an example German-Dutch translation of legal texts (1996: 159):

> [p]recisely because these two languages are so closely related linguistically, it is widely believed to be relatively easy to translate even legal texts from one into the other. However, this view frequently overlooks differences of system and

> detail. As a result of these differences, dangerous mistakes can easily find their way into translations, since there are extraordinarily many legal 'false friends' between Dutch and German.

According to de Groot (1996: 159), 'the main difficulty in translating terms … does not lie in linguistic problems, but … is due to the fact that the concepts have different meanings in the Dutch and German legal systems.'

Further comparison between The Netherlands and Germany, in the shape of the role of courts, yields another interesting result. According to Blankenberg and Bruinsma (1996: 345), 'even though on paper the various legal systems are very much alike, the law in action may differ considerably.' Citing low litigation rates and numbers of judicial personnel in Holland compared with neighbouring Germany, they drily note: 'the Dutch manage to settle cases out of court.'

But what if different societies and their legal systems address social (and other) institutions and issues differently, or even not at all? (Goddard 2011: 129-132). Indeed, as Galdia relevantly notes (2009: 53), '[l]egal language … is value-laden and transports convictions and views about the social practice … fundamental for the society in which it had emerged … values manifest themselves in legal language as an inherent part of it.' Also to be borne in mind are external factors influencing legal systems (Goddard 2011: 132-137) as well as internal influences (Goddard 2011: 123, 132, 139).

To add zest to the discussion, Husa (2012: 173) notes that '… *what the text says* and *what the text means* cannot always be separated which indicates that the roles of a translator and lawyer cannot always be separated …', thus explaining the existence of the jurist-linguist.[4]

In short, the literature discussed above suggests that to some extent – that is, in certain legal fields – an international technical legal language is developing, but not so in others. At the same time, it also highlights significant challenges in this respect, some purely legal linguistic, others with comparative legal linguistic and other issues as symptomatic of deeper challenges to further development. This would suggest the need for a nuanced (comparative) legal linguistic response.

So what does this mean in terms of responses in legal education? As an example, Bussani and Mattei (1997) present the Common Core Project. The project, aimed at scholars, seeks to 'unearth the common core of … European private law' in the 'general categories of contracts, torts, and property',[5] with a view to 'building a common European legal culture … through the creation of a model "European law school" capable of shaping a truly common legal education' (see also Cooper 2011: 13). Presumably, the project is a considerable legal linguistic exercise in itself.

---

4 Footnote 55 citing J. F. Morgan, Multilingual legal drafting in the EEC and the work of Jurist/Linguists, *Multilingua* 1 (1982: 109-118).

5 Though omitting 'procedure and legal institutions where the diversity of legal tradition may be even more important.'

The Common Core Project is matched by the European Casebooks.[6] This is another scholarly project with practical outcomes in the shape of publication of comparative law casebooks in several areas of law, with work in progress on other areas. As the project website states: 'The aim of the Project is to enable students across Europe and beyond to discuss the same leading cases and materials. … [The Casebooks] intend to uncover common principles already underlying existing laws.' The ultimate goal is to produce a common European lawyer (Cooper 2011: 13).

As Cooper (ibid.) points out, 'a common European law … cannot be formed without common European *concepts*. The theme that keeps recurring … is that common European concepts are necessary for the foundation of a common European legal language.' Infantino also notes the need for a '… common vocabulary and a standard terminology capable of summarizing the different notions arising from the European linguistic and legal plurality' (2009: 9).

According to Gessner et al. (1996: xv-xvi), 'legal education in a period of rapid globalization, must enable future practitioners to deal with foreign legal systems,' especially in the context of a growing legal community with a focus 'which goes far beyond the EU.' Galdia (2009: 73) suggests legal linguistics as a major driver of work in this field: '[o]ne task for future Legal Linguistics is to form a conceptual characterization of the research. This would help overcome geographic boundaries and help develop a unified Legal Linguistics.' Salmi-Tolonen (this volume) asserts that '[i]n the present-day accelerated globalization process, research in law and language – legal linguistics – and curricula based on the findings are of vital importance', adding that '[t]he changes in the world and shift of interest in legal thinking and studies of law reflect an elaboration and broadening of the traditional paradigms in law and legal education – along with them legal linguistics.' Focus on the role of legal linguistics in legal communication and in legal education follows after a brief review of the role of English as the lawyers' global *lingua franca*.

4. English as *de facto* global legal language

Although focus on a particular language may at first sight seem inappropriate in a study on legal linguistics in the academic curriculum, nevertheless the practical reality of English as the global lawyers' legal *lingua franca* cannot be ignored. This reality implicitly intensifies the need for translation of legal texts into (or from) English, and – as a corollary – production of legal texts in English, often by non-native speakers of English. Moreover, warnings noted earlier from Triebel and Beveridge as to the unsuitability or pitfalls of English, at least in the field of international contracts, should not go unheeded.

6 Officially known as *'Ius Commune Casebooks for the Common Law of Europe'*. See: http://www.casebooks.eu/welcome/ [accessed: 8 October 2012].

For if Latin was once the *lingua franca* of law professionals (Mattila 2006: 22-23, 128-131, Husa 2012: 168-169),[7] today English could arguably be said to occupy the same role (Mattila 2006: 24, 27, 240-254, 259). However, as Husa notes, the two are not comparable. In particular, today's Euro-English lacks an 'interwoven legal grammar ... English is situated on the surface level of law enabling technical and practical legal communication, but it does not contain a common European legal-language grammar.' (Husa 2012: 169).

Yet according to the European Commission (2010: 89), 'English as a drafting language of EU texts is ... a neutral English, distinct from the common law systems and from the cultural constraints of countries using English as a national language.' Additionally, English is seen as 'more capable of expressing creativity than other EU languages, and to be practical and flexible enough to be the *lingua franca* for the drafting (of) EU texts.' This seems to reflect an earlier view (Jenkins 2003: 42) of a 'nativised hybrid variety of English, in effect, a European version of English which contains a number of grammatical, lexical, phonological, and discoursal features found in individual mainland European languages along with some items common to many of these languages but not to standard British (or American) English.'

The same view is supported by Galdia (2009: 274-275), who proposes a legal language developed by comparative legal linguistics for use in establishing and supporting global law and concurs with Jenkins and the European Commission in noting that '[w]ithin the European Union considerable progress has been achieved to develop a more neutral legal English.' Moreover, while Husa also notes serious challenges to English as a legal lingua franca, ultimately he endorses Mattila's solution of a comparative legal linguistic approach, 'a genuine amalgamation of skills in law *and* skills in ... linguistics and translation' (Husa 2012: 180 [my italics]).

To investigate the extent that English may, or may not, be adaptable to use as Galdia's above-noted globally applicable 'legal language developed by comparative legal linguistics', we should examine what 'legal language' means and what it does.

5. Legal language

Legal language can be seen in a variety of ways. According to Mattila (2006: 3-4), legal language operates as a 'functional variant of natural language with its own domain of use and particular linguistic norms ... a language for special purposes.' Galdia (2009: 52) asserts that '[l]aw is predominantly a linguistic phenomenon because it is created and applied in linguistic operations' and that '[l]egal language

7 Though as Husa points out (2012: 169) 'the actual key-factor was not Latin itself; [Latin] was merely the *linguistic vessel of legal grammar*' (italics in original).

means "legally relevant aspects of language use"' but that 'legal language is much more than terminology' (Galdia 2009: 138).[8]

Husa (2012: 168) gives a dynamic definition of legal language: 'a *form of communication* allowing legal discourse between ... legal actors' (italics in original).[9] Galdia (2009: 177) proposes that '[w]e rather should speak about linguistic aspects of law than about legal language'. Salmi-Tolonen (2004: 1167) sees 'law and all legal activity as communication.'

Leaving aside problems with definition of 'discourse', a simplified and somewhat broad synthesis of the above might be that legal language defines as *communication in legal contexts*, thus also embracing e.g. legal semiotics, at the same time neatly fitting with approaches to legal linguistics in the following section.

6. Legal linguistics and legal communication

According to Mattila, '[l]egal linguistics examines the development, characteristics, and usage of legal language.' According to Salmi-Tolonen (2004: 1169), '[t]he purpose of legal linguistics is to study the language of the law ... and its development and usage in order to create new knowledge of the interplay between language, law and society'. While Galdia (2009: 37) asserts that 'Legal Linguistics deals with ... language use in law', he goes on to develop concrete expressions of legal linguistic tasks and activities:

- 'Legal Linguistics deals with the most essential linguistic phenomena and linguistic operations in law' (2009: 84)
- 'discourse, text type, speech acts, narrative, style, prototype-stereotype, form of life, equivalence in legal translation' (2009: 85)
- '[l]inguistic operations in law, e.g. creating law with the help of language, legal argumentation, legal interpretation, legal translation, justifying legal decisions, providing legal advice, stating and commenting on the law' (2009: 142)
- '[l]egal Linguistics deals primarily with the language in which propositions about law are expressed' (2009: 329).

Before examining the role of legal linguistics in legal communication, first we need to define legal communication. To find clues in this respect, we need only revisit the quotes above from Salmi-Tolonen who sees 'law and all legal activity

8 Though recognizing the relevance of legal linguistics 'in modernising legal terminology' (2009: 126).

9 Citing Anne Lise Kjær, A Common Legal Language in Europe, in *Epistemology and Methodology of Comparative Law*, ed. M. Van Hoecke (Oxford/Portland: Hart, 2004: 377-398, 387-388).

as communication' perhaps because (as she notes in this volume) '[s]ince law is a consequence of continued human cooperation and interaction, law must be a communicative system'; and from Galdia, who gives examples of 'linguistic operations in law' in the shape of 'creating law with the help of language, legal argumentation, legal interpretation, legal translation, justifying legal decisions, providing legal advice, stating and commenting on the law.' Further concrete examples appear in the section on core and peripheral legal linguistic skills.

Having at least partly clarified the role of legal linguistics in legal communication, this chapter raises the corresponding need for legal linguistics in the academic curriculum for law professionals. This will complete the academic section of the chapter, which then goes on to present replies from a focus group of academics in the legal linguistics field to a questionnaire (see Appendix) aimed at establishing the views of focus group members on what are core and peripheral legal linguistic skills and what are the real-world tasks that practical application of legal linguistics can help resolve. These replies are seen in the light of the theoretical part now concluding. The aim is to establish the relevance of legal linguistics in the curriculum and link it to the world of work, with a view to promoting legal linguistics as an academic discipline.

7. Legal linguistics in the academic curriculum for law professionals

Salmi-Tolonen suggests that legal linguistics requires application of systematic academically approved methods in order to become a basis in legal training (2004: 1169-1170). Specifically, as noted above, she sees the aim as examining the interaction between 'language, law and society' by studying 'the language of the law' along with 'its development and usage' (Salmi-Tolonen 2004: 1169). However, she cautions (this volume) that '[t]he field is far too wide to be handled as such and it needs to be structured in order to be of use either as part of the curriculum or research.' Heutger (2005: 213) proposes that law schools should incorporate 'law and language' courses into their curricula, so that students could learn how to work with law and legal languages, rather than expecting them to memorize a legal dictionary (Cooper 2011: 13). For his part, Galdia sees legal linguistics as:

- an introduction to the law especially in legal education (2009: 75)
- [f]rom the perspective of legal theory, [as] a linguistic view on law and legal theory (2009: 86)
- including 'legal logic, such as analysis of legal reasoning and argumentation, interpretation and justification – for these reasons close to a theory of law' (2009: 84, 86).[10]

10 Contrary to the general use of the terms as synonyms in legal theory, for Bengoetxea (1993: 144) legal reasoning includes both argumentation, which takes place in the process

Earlier research by the author (Goddard 2010) has revealed a notable absence of comparable academic programmes in legal linguistics from which to extract what the content should be, in the shape of specific legal linguistic skills for specific courses. Nonetheless, some help is available from the literature, as we shall see in the following section.

8. Core and peripheral legal linguistic skills

To obtain perceptions of legal linguistic skills and how these might be deployed in practice, the author framed a survey questionnaire sent by email to a focus group of academics in the field of legal linguistics. The questions were arranged to test the consistency of replies. Replies were received from five academics. The full questionnaire is reproduced in the Appendix, while replies to selected questions relevant for this chapter[11] appear below in this and the following section. Replies are discussed in the light, and with the help, of the earlier theoretical section of this chapter.

Question 1.1 elicited the following replies:

How would you define:
1.1 Core legal linguistic skills: legal research, statutory interpretation, legal translation, legal drafting, revising, editing; theoretical knowledge of legal linguistics; legal terminology; characteristics of legal discourse
Core legal linguistic skills
In my mind, core legal linguistic skills are skills that enable the student to get an insight into the relationship between language as a communicative system for creation of meaning and the legal meanings that emerge from communication in the legal field. A legal linguist must be able to perform systematic analyses of a text in order to follow the process of creating specialized legal meaning. Concrete, I think that insight into the distinctions between lexicon (especially terminology), sentential syntax (especially complexity) and textual features is relevant. Furthermore a legal linguist needs insight into the legal basics of interpretation, argumentation and meaning creation. Knowledge about principles of statutory interpretation in different legal systems I would also see as core legal linguistic skills.
1.1 Core legal linguistic skills/The essential legal words and phrases, concepts and institutions

of arguing the case, and justification, which refers to the reasoning the deciding court has accepted as justification for the judgment.

11 Replies to other questions will be dealt with elsewhere.

1.1 Core legal linguistic skills: To master legal linguistics means being able to use language efficiently in all social contexts relevant to law. These social contexts (situations in which language is used) are mostly institutional (language use in courts, in administrative proceedings, attorney's advice etc). The legal linguistic skills are therefore closely linked to institutions because legal language does not exist outside contexts that are defined by social institutions such as courts of law. Incidentally, institutions also define these skills; there is no private legal language. Therefore, at least theoretically, the most salient legal linguistic skill is to use language efficiently under conditions defined by others, i.e. by institutions that impose the rules for its use. Practically, when the improvement of such skills should be reached, some methodical steps must be taken. First, the circumstances of language use must be identified; second, the relevant legal linguistic skills must be defined and trained. For instance, (1.) cross-examination is identified as a relevant linguistic operation in law, (2.) language use strategies that are most appropriate and efficient in such a context of use are identified and trained with students. Legal linguistic skills are acquired in numerous such language games. As a matter of fact, in common law countries some of these skills are already trained, yet at random and unsystematically, e.g. in moot courts. In the civil law countries this practical training is even more reduced or does not exist at all. Disappointingly, today, this professional training in legal linguistic skills takes place only in practical life, haphazardly and superficially; academic institutions that should provide legal education offer sterile legal doctrine instead of professional training in legal linguistic skills. Consequently, law as a teaching subject is deficient because it does not teach the most essential skills for the practice of law, i.e. the efficient use of the legal language. The legal linguistics addresses this deficiency and provides remedies for these shortcomings that are viewed by many law students rather critically.
1.1 Core legal linguistic skills
The legal text must be: functional (not rhetorical), objective, clear, formal, precise, concise. The language of law is an important element for bettering the image and prestige of public institutions. People who work in the field of law have to learn: legislation on documents, terminology, the key aspects of grammar and the principles of modern law writing style
1.1 Core legal linguistic skills: legal and linguistic reasoning and to have the capacity to combine both. Contact with more than one legal culture and more than one language.

In discussing replies, some help is available from the theoretical section of the chapter, in particular Galdia, who proposes specific skills in the shape of:

> linguistic operations in law, e.g. creating law with the help of language, legal argumentation, legal interpretation, legal translation, justifying legal decisions, providing legal advice, stating and commenting on the law. (2009: 142)

and

> legal logic, such as analysis of legal reasoning and argumentation, interpretation and justification. (2009: 84, 86)

These skills all seem to fit within Galdia's 'linguistic operations in law' (2009: 84) referred to above.

Comparing concrete items on Galdia's list with the replies, only three are a precise match:

- legal argumentation
- legal translation
- legal reasoning.

This is followed by two near matches from the replies: statutory interpretation (x2) and 'legal basics of interpretation'(x1) (compared with Galdia's 'legal interpretation') and 'legal drafting' (x1) compared with Galdia's 'creating law with the help of language'.

Although 'analysis' appears both in the replies and in Galdia's list, on closer inspection Galdia's 'analysis of legal reasoning and argumentation' may to some extent match 'perform systematic analyses of a text in order to follow the process of creating specialised legal meaning' from the replies.
Items from replies that do not appear on Galdia's list include:

- theoretical knowledge of legal linguistics
- legal terminology
- characteristics of legal discourse
- lexicon (especially terminology)
- sentential syntax (especially complexity)
- textual features
- concepts and institutions.

However, Galdia's 'linguistic operations in law' could cover other items from the replies, such as:

- legal research
- revising
- editing.

Additionally, 'linguistic operations in law' could cover many items not given in the replies, such as client letters, legislative drafting, interlingual or intralingual translation of, for example, a piece of legislation into a public information leaflet or a court report into a newsletter item on a law firm's website, drafting a court judgment, preparing memorials in litigation, advocacy before courts and tribunals, negotiations in legal contexts, conference interpreting, legal lexicography, writing and presenting legal scholarly works. These are merely examples that spring to mind but the list is far from exhaustive. If all are legal linguistic activities, then the relevance of legal linguistics in legal education seems clear, unless we want to separate education from training, a matter which deserves discussion but for which space is unavailable in this chapter.[12]

One reply that stood out from the others was the comment that 'professional training in legal linguistic skills takes place only in practical life, haphazardly and superficially; academic institutions that should provide legal education offer sterile legal doctrine instead of professional training in legal linguistic skills' with the result that 'law as a teaching subject is deficient because it does not teach the most essential skills for the practice of law, i.e. the efficient use of the legal language … legal linguistics addresses this deficiency and provides remedies for these shortcomings.'

While this comment bears further investigation, at the same time it explicitly raises the issue, implicit at the end of the preceding paragraph, as to what differences exist between (legal) education and training and, assuming that such differences do exist, the further issue of allocation of responsibility for delivery of suitable programmes.

Turning now to replies to question 1.2, these were as follows:

1.2 Peripheral legal linguistic skills: presentation skills: meetings, negotiations; intercultural communication
Peripheral legal linguistic skills
Peripheral legal linguistic skills could include insights into the linguistic fields of genre, of pragmatic functions and of the sociology of knowledge as expressed in textual representations. From the legal field studies into legal cultures and deeper insights into philosophical backings of different approaches to statutory interpretation as well as deeper insights into the legal background of legal drafting are relevant.
1.2 Peripheral legal linguistic skills/Applying these to writing, constructing and revising legal texts

12 However, a Google search elicits a course in Legal Communication and Research at the University of Miami School of Law at http://www.law.miami.edu/about_us/legal_communication_and_research_skills.php in which 'Students develop and master advocacy skills in the context of a client's simulated problem, evolving through initial case assessment, pretrial motion practice, oral argument, and appeal. By employing diverse written and oral communication strategies, students practice and hone important professional skills' [accessed: 8 October 2012]. This seems to confirm some of the items listed as legal linguistic operations.

1.2 Peripheral legal linguistic skills: These skills mostly include qualities cherished by administrative bodies: 'good' grammar, correct spelling, using language that sounds formally and is perceived as presentable, editing skills and quick drafting. In all, being a perfect secretary. Legal linguistics includes also these skills as an incidental part of all legal linguistic operations.
1.2 Peripheral legal linguistic skills
Is always useful to get a good knowledge on history of the language of law of the own language in each case, about recent international trends in this field and on comparative matters, to understand better how it works in different languages
1.2 Peripheral legal linguistic skills: previous specialization in the legal or linguistic field.

Apart from presentation skills, meetings, negotiations, intercultural communication, which are clearly skills though not necessarily purely legal linguistic skills, replies yielded studies of legal culture and legal (linguistic) history, in addition to 'previous specialization in the legal or linguistic field.'

To sum up, replies to question 1.1, read in the light of parts of the theoretical section, do seem to help establish the spectrum and content of course and programme components, though perhaps unsurprisingly the same seems not to be the case for replies to question 1.2. Perhaps most importantly, this section has already begun to bring out some of the practical applications of legal linguistics.

9. Practical applications of legal linguistics

Only one reply was received to question 3:

3. What real-world tasks can the practical application of legal linguistics help to resolve?
• Tasks involving the interaction of more than one legal system and more than one legal language. It may be the interpretation or drafting of multilingual contracts, counselling clients in such cases, investigating background knowledge for lawyers involved in multilingual and multilegal cases.

In terms of legal education, this reply suggests the need for comparative law studies in education of law professionals. Moreover, as Galdia notes (2009: 272), '[i]n its core, seen from the perspective of … Legal Linguistics, comparative law is about comparing legal languages.' This evokes earlier comments we have noted above from Husa, who endorses Mattila's solution of a comparative legal linguistic approach in legal education, resulting in 'a genuine amalgamation of skills in law and skills in … linguistics and translation' (Husa 2012: 180). This leads us to the final section.

10. Relevance of legal linguistics in the curriculum for future law professionals

4. Please state the practical benefit of legal linguistic knowledge and skills to the following:
4.1 Lawyers: better understanding of language, translation strategies, improved legal writing, contract drafting, editing 4.1 Lawyers: - Insights into the actual role that language plays in the emergence and development of legal meanings in intra- as well as interlingual cases - Analytical skills to be used when solving problems of interpretation of legal texts 4.1 Lawyers/Writing and interpreting legal texts better 4.1 Lawyers: When legal linguistics is perceived as a theory of law, the benefits for lawyers are obvious. First of all, a lawyer who reflects upon legal linguistic issues begins to understand the essence of the activities he/she performs, i.e. using language efficiently in legally relevant social contexts. Basically, all activities exercised by lawyers are covered by this broad description. Therefore, a lawyer who deals with legal linguistics understands the rules that govern his/her profession. 4.1 Lawyers For lawyers to improve their legal linguistic skills helps them to feel surer in expressing themselves when they write or speak in a formal legal context. If they use language in a more efficacious and convincing way, they become better and more respected and admired lawyers. For lawyers language is the second skill (the first is obviously law) they need to know well to be successful in their job.
4.1 Lawyers: For scholars: To allow a more open-minded approach to legal theory. For practitioners: to better communicate with an everyday more multicultural and multilingual clientele. For both: to improve their capacity to understand, create and interpret legal notions.
4.2 Legal translators: better understanding of legal concepts and terminology; using specific translation tools 4.2 Legal translators - Insights into the actual role that language plays in the emergence and development of legal meanings in intra- as well as interlingual cases - Analytical skills to be used when solving problems of interpretation of legal texts 4.2 Legal translators/Better comparatists and translators

4.2 Legal translators: Legal translation without legal linguistics is blind; it is unsystematic and nebulous. Legal linguistics is able to describe the problems of legal translation and it shows why this profession is and will remain challenging. It prevents mechanistic approaches to legal translation and prepares the translator for creative work. Legal translators become professionals through legal linguistic education. Neither languages courses alone, nor separate legal education, nor both tracks completed one after the other can replace legal linguistic education. 4.2 Legal translators Often translators have a lot of difficulties in translating legal documents, because of terminology problems and misapprehension of legal concepts and documents. 4.2 Legal translators: be protagonists of the creation, understanding and interpretation of legal notions. It enhances the profession opening more job possibilities.
4.3 Others: e.g. teachers of foreign languages for lawyers can benefit from legal linguistics by learning more about law, legal terminology and specific characteristics of legal texts 4.3 Others 4.3 Others/Judges: writing reasons more clearly and simply (and shorter judgments). Legislators: writing better (i.e., clearer, simpler and shorter) laws, & better construction of statutes. 4.3 Others: Legal linguistics allows linguists, sociologists, philosophers and other representatives of arts and social sciences to approach law from a perspective that is understandable for them. It makes plain for them how law is created and how it is applied. When described in terms of legal linguistics law as a social phenomenon can be integrated into methodological approaches that dominate these branches of knowledge. This is a great progress because the methodology of the traditional subject 'law' is much too particular and hermetical to become accessible to other professions. Therefore, legal linguistics functions also as a bridge between law as an academic discipline and other social disciplines. This shows again how central this branch of knowledge actually is.
4.3 Others As lawyers, civil servants as a general rule need to use in a fit way legal language to succeed in their job. 4.3 Others

These replies, taken in synthesis and with earlier evidence noted above, combine to suggest both the need for and the relevance of legal linguistics in the curriculum for future law professionals. Again, one reply stood out from the others:

> When legal linguistics is perceived as a theory of law, the benefits for lawyers are obvious. First of all, a lawyer who reflects upon legal linguistic issues begins to understand the essence of the activities he/she performs, i.e. using language

> efficiently in legally relevant social contexts. *Basically, all activities exercised by lawyers are covered by this broad description.* (my italics)

In closing this section, the views of two legal linguistics specialists seem appropriate. The first is from Salmi-Tolonen, who avers that '[t]he first and foremost purpose of legal linguistics is to look forward and see how linguistic methods can help legal professionals at the various stages of their careers' (2004: 1168). The second is from Galdia: 'Legal Linguistics has also a practical dimension ... to contribute to the emergence of ... global law' (2009: 271). However, the last word here goes to Salmi-Tolonen (this volume) who affirms that 'it is the task of legal linguists to compile ... a body of knowledge that can then be expressed in terms of competences such as knowledge, skills and attitudes, and be operationalized in teaching and in the various law-related tasks that legislators, law appliers and legal subjects perform.'

11. Conclusion

This chapter has made a case for inclusion of legal linguistics in the academic curriculum and has also to some extent clarified the spectrum, content and components of programmes and courses, although much further work remains to be done in this respect. Clearly, too, allocation of institutional responsibility as between education and training is a matter that requires attention. This could be key in attracting patronage as one aspect of nurturing legal linguistics as an emerging discipline. Here, the practical applications of legal linguistics as embracing many, if not all, activities by lawyers (not to mention, other law professionals) would be crucial, as would evidence of the growing need for legal linguistics alongside globalization and transnationalization of the law. At the same time, research would be desirable to establish the extent to which law professionals do in fact operate between two or more legal systems and languages. In the same context, the feasibility of English as a global legal language remains to be seen. However, there is no suggestion that English should necessarily be the language of legal linguistic education. Again in the same context, further research is required into the extent to which an international technical legal language is developing, as well as the (comparative) legal linguistic and other challenges to that development as noted above. Among other areas for further research in this respect, institutional and procedural differences between different legal orders would seem to be a fruitful area for legal linguistic research.

References

Baaij, C.J.W. (ed.). 2012. *The Role of Legal Translation in Legal Harmonization*. The Netherlands: Kluwer Law International BV.

Bengoetxea, J. 1993. *The Legal Reasoning of the European Court of Justice: Towards a European Jurisprudence*. Oxford/New York: Oxford University Press.

Beveridge, B. 2002. Legal English. How it developed and why it is not appropriate for international commercial contracts, in *The Development of Legal Language*, edited by H. Mattila. Helsinki: Talentum Media, 55-79.

Blankenberg, E. and Bruinsma, F. 1994. *Dutch Legal Culture Compared in Dutch Legal Culture*. 2nd Edition. Deventer (Netherlands): Kluwer Law and Taxation Publishers, 3-13, reprinted in *European Legal Cultures*, 1996, edited by V. Gessner et al. Dartmouth: Aldershot, 345-352.

Bussani, M. and Mattei, U. 1997. The common core approach to European private law. *Columbia Journal of European law* 12. Available at: http://works.bepress.com/ugo_mattei/18 [accessed: 8 October 2012].

Chauvel, D. and Despres, C. (eds). 2000. *Knowledge Horizons: The Present and the Promise of Knowledge Management*. Boston: Butterworth-Heinemann.

Cooper, C. 2011. Legal languages: European legal English: an evolving legal language. A Paper presented to the 20th International Annual Meeting of Geselleschaft für Sprache und Sprachen (GeSuS) Emerging disciplines http://www.emergingdisciplines.org/http://www.krii.com/downloads/km_emerg_discipl.pdf [accessed: 8 October 2012].

De Groot, G-R. 1991. Law, legal language and the legal system: reflections of the problems of translating legal texts – Recht, rechtsprache und rechtsystem: betrachtungen über die problematik der Übersetzung juristischer texte', in *Terminologie et Traduction* 3, 279-312, reprinted in Gessner *et al.* (eds), 1996, 155-160. Translation by John Blazek Brussels.

European Commission 2010. *Study on Lawmaking in the EU multilingual environment*.

Galdia, M. 2009. *Legal Linguistics*. Frankfurt am Main: Peter Lang.

Gessner, V., Hoeland, A. and Varga, C. 1996. Series foreword in *European Legal Cultures*, edited by V. Gessner et al. Dartmouth: Aldershot, xv-xviii.

Goddard, C. 2008. Where legal cultures meet: translating confrontation into coexistence, in *Investigationes Linguisticae* Vol XVII, 2009 Adam Mickiewicz University, 168-205.

Goddard, C. 2010. Legal linguistics as an academic and professional discipline: identifying clients, customers, stakeholders, in *Reconceptualizing LSP. Online proceedings of the XVII European LSP Symposium 2009*, Aarhus 2010, edited by C. Heine and J. Engberg. Available at: http://www.asb.dk/fileadmin/www.asb.dk/isek/goddard.pdf [accessed: 8 October 2012].

Goddard, C. 2011. Fishing with new nets in familiar waters: a legal linguistic foray into comparative law, legal culture, and legal ideology. *Lapland Law Review*, 1. *Law and Language in Partnership and Conflict*, edited by T. Salmi-Tolonen, I. Tukiainen and R. Foley, 122-144.

Heutger, V. 2005. Towards a common European legal understanding. *London Law Review*. Vol 1, October 2005, 2, 205-213.

Husa, J. 2011. The method is dead, long live the methods! European polynomia and pluralist methodology. *Legisprudence*, 5(3), 249-271.

Husa, J. 2012. Understanding legal languages: linguistic concerns of the comparative lawyer, in *The Role of Legal Translation in Legal Harmonization*, edited by C.J.W. Baaij. The Netherlands: Kluwer Law International BV, 161-181.

Infantino, M. 2010 Making European tort law: the game and its players. *Cardozo Journal of International & Comparative Law*, 20, 45-87.

Ius Commune Casebooks for the Common Law of Europe. See: http://www.casebooks.eu/welcome/ [accessed: 8 October 2012].

Jenkins, J. 2003. *World Englishes: A Resource Book for Students*. London and New York: Routledge.

Kjær, A.L. 2004. A common legal language in Europe, in *Epistemology and Methodology of Comparative Law*, edited by M. Van Hoecke. Oxford/Portland: Hart, 377-398.

Kraakman, R. et al. 2004. *The Anatomy of Corporate Law: A Comparative and Functional Approach*. New York: Oxford University Press.

Leib, V. 2004: Verrechtlichung im internet. Macht und recht bei der regulierung durch ICANN, in Verrechtlichung – Baustein für Global Governance?, edited by B. Zangl and M. Zürn. Bonn: Dietz, 198-219.

Likosky, M. (ed.). 2002. *Transnational Legal Processes: Globalisation and Power Disparities*. Boston: Butterworth-Heinemann.

La Porta, R. Lopez-de-Silanes, F. and Shleifer, A. 2008. The economic consequences of legal origins. *Journal of Economic Literature*, 46:2, 285-332. Available at: http://dare.uva.nl/document/130386 [accessed: 16 May 2013].

Mattila, H.E.S. 2006. *Comparative Legal Linguistics*. Aldershot: Ashgate.

Salmi-Tolonen, T. 2004. Legal linguistic knowledge and creating and interpreting law in multilingual environments, *Brooklyn Journal of International Law*, 29(3), 1167-1191.

Triebel, V. 2009. Pitfalls of English as a contract language, in *Translation Issues in Language and Law*, edited by F. Olsen et al., 147-168.

Tuori, K. 2011. *Ratio and Voluntas: The Tension Between Reason and Will in Law*. Farnham: Ashgate.

Twining, W. 2002. Reviving general jurisprudence, in *Transnational Legal Processes: Globalisation and Power Disparities*, edited by M. Likosky. Boston: Butterworth-Heinemann, 3-22.

University of Miami School of Law at http://www.law.miami.edu/about_us/legal_communication_and_research_skills.php [accessed: 8 October 2012].

Wiig, K.M. 2000. Knowledge management: an emerging discipline rooted in a long history, in *Knowledge Horizons: The Present and the Promise of Knowledge Management*, edited by D. Chauvel and C. Despres. Boston: Butterworth-Heinemann, 3-26.

Zangl, B., Zürn, M. 2004. Make law, not war: internationale und transnationale verrechtlichung als baustein für global governance, in *Verrechtlichung –*

Baustein für Global Governance?, edited by B. Zangl, M. Zürn. Bonn: Dietz, 12-45.

Zangl, B., Zürn, M. (eds). 2004. *Verrechtlichung – Baustein für Global Governance?* Bonn: Dietz.

Appendix

Invitation to participate in a Research Paper focus group survey

I am currently writing a research paper addressing practical issues related to **legal linguistics** in academic programmes and in practical application in professional life. The questions below supplement the main part of the paper delivered on 19 June 2010 at the conference 'The Language of Law: pulling together different strands and disciplines' held at Second University of Naples. The title of the paper is 'Learning to fly: the prospects for legal linguistics in the academic curriculum … and beyond'.

The aim of the paper is to clarify the focus that legal linguistics courses or programmes require so as to be seen by potential applicants, employers, and stakeholders as having clear practical professional relevance. This survey questionnaire is addressed to a focus group consisting of academics in the legal linguistics field. The survey is performed as partial fulfilment of the requirements for a doctoral degree in legal linguistics at the University of Lapland, where my supervisor is Professor Heikki Mattila.

Your participation in this survey will provide useful information on the topic. You have been selected to participate because of your involvement in legal linguistics. The total time required to fill out the survey should be no more than 60 minutes. All data from this survey are confidential and will be used for research purposes only. Data are anonymous. Names of participants will not be connected to information.

If you have any questions about the survey, I shall be happy to deal with them.

If you would like to receive a summary of the results of this research, please let me know.

Christopher Goddard. Christopher.Goddard@rgsl.edu.lv + 371-28376208
Riga Graduate School of Law, Strelnieku iela 4 k-2, Riga LV- 1010, Latvia.

---

1. How would you define:
1.1 Core legal linguistic skills
1.2 Peripheral legal linguistic skills
1.3 [Space for additional comment]

2. The optimum means of delivering legal linguistic knowledge and skills is:
[On a band from strongly agree 10 to strongly disagree 0]
2.1 Courses integrated with programmes at bachelor level
2.2 Courses integrated with programmes at master level
2.3 Dedicated programmes at bachelor level
2.4 Dedicated programmes at master level
2.5 Other (please specify)
2.6 Single institution
2.7 Two or more institutions
2.8 Involving a distance learning component
2.9 [Space for additional comment]

3. What real-world tasks can the practical application of legal linguistics help to resolve?

4. Please state the practical benefit of legal linguistic knowledge and skills to the following:
4.1 Lawyers
4.2 Legal translators
4.3 Others

5. Please briefly describe your own language and law programme or link to home page

Index

For Product Safety Concerns and Information please contact our EU representative GPSR@taylorandfrancis.com Taylor & Francis Verlag GmbH, Kaufingerstraße 24, 80331 München, Germany